REFORMING THE CONSTITUTION
Debates in Twentieth-Century Britain

CASS SERIES: BRITISH POLITICS AND SOCIETY
Series Editor: Peter Catterall
ISSN: 1467-1441

Social change impacts not just upon voting behaviour and party identity but also the formulation of policy. But how do social changes and political developments interact? Which shapes which? Reflecting a belief that social and political structures cannot be understood either in isolation from each other or from the historical processes which form them, this series will examine the forces that have shaped British society. Cross-disciplinary approaches will be encouraged. In the process, the series will aim to make a contribution to existing fields, such as politics, sociology and media studies, as well as opening out new and hitherto neglected fields such as management history.

Peter Catterall (ed.), *The Making of Channel 4*
Brock Millman, *Managing Domestic Dissent in First World War Britain*
Peter Catterall, Wolfram Kaiser and Ulrike Walton-Jordan (eds), *Reforming the Constitution: Debates in Twentieth-Century Britain*
Brock Millman, *Pessimism and British War Policy, 1916–1918*
Adrian Smith and Dilwyn Porter (eds), *Amateurs and Professionals in Postwar British Sport*

CASS SERIES: THE COLONIAL LEGACY IN BRITAIN
Series Editor: Peter Catterall
ISSN: 1467-0518

The British Empire was a significant historical phenomenon which had a major effect on both the territories it colonised and the colonisers themselves. What, however, of the experience of imperial subjects who came to the metropole? How did this shape perceptions of empire and of Britain? And what impact did they have upon Britain, both during the heyday of empire and in its aftermath? In seeking to explore these questions, this series will contribute to an understanding both of empire and of the impact and legacy of race relations in Britain.

Shompa Lahiri, *Indians in Britain: Anglo-Indian Encounters, Race and Identity, 1880–1930*

 Institute of Contemporary British History

ICBH

The Institute of Contemporary British History was founded in September 1986 to stimulate research into and analysis of recent history, through conferences, publications, and archives and other research tools, which will be of value to decision-makers, students and the wider public. It aims to be both a centre of excellence for research into recent British history and a source for advice and information for researchers and those with a general interest in the field.

REFORMING THE CONSTITUTION

Debates in Twentieth-Century Britain

Edited by

Peter Catterall, Wolfram Kaiser
and Ulrike Walton-Jordan

FRANK CASS
LONDON • PORTLAND, OR

First published in 2000 in Great Britain by
FRANK CASS PUBLISHERS
Newbury House, 900 Eastern Avenue
London, IG2 7HH

and in the United States of America by
FRANK CASS PUBLISHERS
c/o ISBS, 5824 N.E. Hassalo Street
Potland, Oregon, 97213-3644

Website: www.frankcass.com

British Library Cataloguing in Publication Data

Reforming the constitution: debates in twentieth-century
  Britain. – (Cass series. British politics and society; no.
  3)
  1. Constitutional law – Great Britain 2. Great Britain –
  Politics and government – 20th century
  I. Catterall, Peter, 1961 – II. Kaiser, Wolfram, 1966 –
  III. Walton-Jordan, Ulrike 342 . 4'1'02

ISBN 0-7146-5056 0 (cloth)
ISBN 0-7146-8107 5 (paper)
ISSN 1467-1441

Library of Congress Cataloging-in-Publication Data

Reforming the constitution: debates in twentieth-century Britain /
edited by Peter Catterall, Wolfram Kaiser, and Ulrike Walton-Jordan.
  p. cm. – (Cass series – British politics and society, ISSN 1467-1441)
  Includes bibliographical references and index.
  ISBN 0-7146-5056-0 (cloth) – ISBN 0-7146-8107-5 (paper)
  1. Constitutional history – Great Britain. I. Catterall, Peter, 1961 – II.
  Kaiser, Wolfram, 1966 – III. Walton- Jordan, Ulrike, 1962 –IV. Series.

KD3966 .R44 2000
342.41'029–dc21   00-031541

Printed in Great Britain by
Creative Print and Design (Wales), Ebbw Vale

Contents

Notes on Contributors

Peter Catterall lectures in history at Queen Mary and Westfield College, London and was Fullbright-Robertson visiting professor of British history at Westminster College, Fulton, Missouri 1999–2000.

Brian Girvin is senior lecturer in the Department of Politics at the University of Glasgow.

Joe Jacob lectures in the Law Department at the London School of Economics.

André Kaiser is Wissenschaftlicher Assistent (lecturer) in the Department of Political Science at the University of Mannheim.

Wolfram Kaiser is Professor of European Studies at the University of Portsmouth and visiting professor at the College of Europe, Bruges.

Eugenia Low is currently completing a doctoral thesis at St John's College, Oxford.

James Mitchell is Professor of Government at the University of Strathclyde.

Elfie Rembold is a Research Fellow at the University of Hanover.

Jutta Schwarzkopf is Wissenschaftliche Assistentin (lecturer) in the Department of History at the University of Hanover.

Ulrike Walton-Jordan is Manja Leigh Research Fellow at the Centre for German-Jewish Studies at the University of Sussex.

Introduction

When the Blair government was elected in May 1997, it immediately set in motion a programme for a far-reaching reform of the British system of government. Its centrepiece was devolution to a Scottish parliament and a Welsh assembly. The subsequent Scottish referendum produced a large majority in favour, though the government's proposal for a Welsh assembly with more limited rights was only just accepted. Subsequently, elections were held in May 1999 using proportional representation (PR) systems. Other reform measures included the reintroduction of government for London and, in accordance with a previous promise to the Liberal Democrats, the setting up of a special commission to consider electoral reform for Westminster. In November 1998, the Jenkins Commission submitted its report advocating the alternative vote with a number of top-up members. Finally, the automatic right of hereditary peers to sit in the House of Lords was abolished in 1999.

The reform process has been portrayed by Labour as the attempt to modernise Britain's system of government and to transform its political culture. In an increasingly fragmented United Kingdom, the reforms are billed as providing government nearer to the people, and thus a re-invention of British democracy at the turn of the twenty-first century. As his opponents have pointed out, they might also facilitate Blair's declared strategic task of securing a stable centre-left majority for the foreseeable future. After all, the origins of the reforms are all essentially Liberal, and they seem designed to help create an informal progressive alliance which could be turned into a more formalised coalition at a later stage. In any case, the reforms clearly relativise the uniqueness of some of Britain's constitutional traditions and could be seen by reformers as complementing a Europeanisation of Britain's economic interests and political orientation.

A substantial reform of the British system of government could be interpreted as marking the end of a British constitutional *Sonderweg* – a unique path separate from the norm of economic, social and political development elsewhere in Europe or among western democracies. European historiography is in fact full of such *Sonderweg* theses. They have often served as political instruments for fostering national identities, as well as for justifying particular domestic political causes or foreign-policy goals. This is true, for example, of the geopolitical *Sonderweg* thesis of German history at the time of the late *Kaiserreich* and the Weimar Republic which emphasised, among other aspects, the alleged foreign-policy effects of the so-called *Mittellage* of the German Reich at the centre of Europe.[1] Similarly, the nineteenth-century Whig interpretation of English history as a steady progression of moderate and peaceful reforms helped to contain more far-reaching demands for the democratisation of the British system of government. The allegedly unique and superior path taken by the English since the Glorious Revolution of 1688 seemed to compare favourably with the at times extreme violence of political change in continental Europe, culminating in the revolutions of 1789, 1830 and 1848.[2] The Whig *Sonderweg* thesis at the same time reflected and was designed to enhance a particular national image of the British as moderate, rational and flexible, but, if necessary, capable of decisive action.

In the age of nationalism and imperialism, *Sonderweg* theses fulfilled a culturally and politically affirmative and integrative function in several European countries. In the post-nationalist age in western Europe since 1945, such theses have continued to flourish. However, they have usually reflected a preoccupation with the search for a parting of the ways in a particular national history, at which the country in question took a less than ideal or even dangerous path deviating from the alleged norms of economic and political development elsewhere in western Europe. Such theses ascertain a delay in the modernisation process within a particular country. This delay can be in respect to its economic development, societal change or reform of its constitutional framework, although these aspects are mostly seen as closely linked. It is either argued explicitly or is implied that the lack of timely reform is a key to understanding a particular national *Sonderweg*. Reform, especially reform of the constitutional framework and political structure and culture, thus becomes an important analytical tool for the comparative explanation of modern European history.

In Britain, the 'decline' debate, which started in the 1960s, saw the growth of often implicit *Sonderweg* theses about modern British history with negative connotations. British historiography was temporarily obsessed with the phenomenon of relative economic decline in comparison to other west European states after 1945. One such *Sonderweg* thesis concerned Britain's late conversion to the allegedly normal, virtuous and economically successful path of European integration. This interpretation of British and European postwar history was based on a selective and superficial comparison, essentially with France and the Federal Republic of Germany. It completely ignored, for example, the pronounced reluctance of other mature democracies, such as the Scandinavian states, to embark on an open-ended process of economic and, ultimately, political integration with supranational features.[3]

The more explicitly economic historical explanations of Britain's meagre performance in terms of gross domestic product (GDP) and productivity growth were highly controversial, not least because they were closely linked to the domestic political debate about economic policy during the 1970s and 1980s. The conflicting explanations of Britain's relative economic failure had one common feature. They were based on mostly implicit comparisons between some kind of British *Sonderweg* and the more virtuous paths taken by other countries. Depending on the respective political viewpoint, they included the United States and other west European countries, such as Germany and Scandinavia. From the mid-1980s, the British economy saw a partial recovery in comparison to some other west European economies. As a result, the obsession with finding a convincing historical explanation for Britain's economic decline subsided, but only to be replaced by a new preoccupation with the historical reasons for the allegedly peculiar lack of modernity of Britain's society and its political system.

The Whig interpretation of nineteenth-century British history implicitly dominated the British elite's perception of the British system of government until at least the 1960s. It continues to influence historians, albeit mostly outside Britain. This interpretation asserted more or less explicitly that special factors guaranteed the progressive adjustment of Britain's political system to the changing economic and social conditions in the Victorian era. These factors included the positive class-consciousness of the British and their deferential attitude to political authority, as well as the inertia of Britain's institutions combined with the relative political flexibility of British conservatism.

For some time now, the analysis of nineteenth-century British history has seen a serious debate about how adaptable the British political system really was before 1914, and how it might have accommodated continued political and national frictions in the absence of war or in case Britain had lost the war. Moreover, it has been argued with increasing force that such peculiarities of Britain's historical development as can be defined, like the pronounced class-consciousness and the deferential attitude of the British to political authority, have actually impeded the modernisation of the British political system during the twentieth century.

The political-reform debate is again a key feature of British politics since the 1960s. It progressively shifted 'from problems of the constitution to the constitution as a problem of British politics'.[4] The new *Sonderweg* debate in Britain was concerned with why the British system of government, Europe's *ancien régime*,[5] was so much less modern and possibly less democratic than those of other west European countries and former dominions, and definitely ill-prepared for integration into the new constitutional framework of the European Union.

Whether with positive or negative connotations, the debate about the development of Britain's political system is clearly a key theme of modern British history and historiography, and of British politics at the turn of the twenty-first century. This book aims to improve our understanding of the driving forces behind the political-reform debate and the economic, social and political preconditions for actual reforms in Britain in the twentieth century, wherever possible in a comparative European perspective. In this book, political reform is not defined narrowly as constitutional reform. The inquiry is not limited to the institutional structures of the British political system. Important as they are, institutional issues often seem to have distracted attention from more intangible issues, such as participation in the political process by disadvantaged social groups, or the fragmented nature of the United Kingdom.

Accordingly, this book concentrates on three issues which played an important role during the period until 1918, and again during the period from the 1960s to the present. These issues are, firstly, the debate about reform of Britain's law and institutions; second, the role of women and the transformation from a position of constitutionally enforced discrimination to socially based disadvantage in the political process; and, finally, the nationality conflicts and the question of reform of territorial politics. The first two chapters analyse the broader background to the more detailed chapters which follow by looking at the most important themes of the constitutional-reform debate as well as the role of the political parties and their influence on the reform process.

As yet, it is still much too early to foresee the long-term structural effects that the recent reforms could have on Britain's system of government or its political culture. These are potentially far-reaching. For example, the introduction of PR, first in Scotland and Wales and perhaps for Westminster later, could change the patterns of party conflict and co-operation and is likely to result in coalition government. Substantial reform of the House of Lords might tend to undermine the hereditary principle as such, and thus also the monarchy. Devolution to a Scottish parliament, finally, might result in pressure for more systematic decentralisation in England, or it might lead to independence for Scotland and the break-up of the United Kingdom. Whether the reforms and their potential structural effects reflect the overdue modernisation of the British system of government or the adoption of practices which some believe have failed to produce convincing results elsewhere, is clearly a matter for political debate. What is certain, however, is that the reform process and the ongoing party-political and public debate about it make Britain by far the most interesting case study in the increasingly international debate about the best means to secure and enhance the legitimacy of modern democracies in the age of globalisation.

NOTES

1. See Bernd Faulenbach, *Ideologie des deutschen Weges. Die deutsche Geschichte in der Historiographie zwischen Kaiserreich und Nationalsozialismus* (Munich: Beck, 1980).
2. See, in particular, Thomas B. Macaulay, *The History of England from the Accession of James the Second: Vol. II* (London: Longman, 1861 [first published 1848]); Walter Bagehot, *The English Constitution* (London: Fontana Press, 1993 [first published 1867]).
3. For a critical assessment of this *Sonderweg* thesis see Wolfram Kaiser, *Using Europe, Abusing the Europeans: Britain and European Integration, 1945–63* (London: Macmillan, 1996), especially pp. v–vii and 204–27.
4. Hans Kastendiek and Richard Stinshoff (eds), *Changing Conceptions of Constitutional Government: Developments in British Politics and the Constitutional Debate since the 1960s* (Bochum: Universitätsverlag Dr N. Brockmeyer, 1994), p. ix.
5. Andrew Gamble, 'The British Ancien Regime' in Kastendiek and Stinshoff, *Changing Conceptions of Constitutional Government*, pp. 3–20.

'Efficiency with Freedom'? Debates about the British Constitution in the Twentieth Century

PETER CATTERALL

In 1950 the Labour Lord Chancellor, Lord Jowitt, sought to reassure peers that, since the time of Marlborough, 'The genius of the British race has shown that it is possible to combine efficiency with freedom.'[1] The merit of the British constitution for its supporters has always been the apparent achievement of this balancing trick between strong government and respect for liberty, which, it is argued, has both history and flexibility on its side.[2] For them a historically well-established political culture predicated upon the defence of liberty against arbitrary government is a key facet of this balance, more important and reliable than any legislative or constitutional safeguards.[3] As Baroness Gaitskell argued in 1969, 'my experience at the United Nations does not make me feel that a Bill of Rights by itself is any substitute for the spirit of liberty'.[4]

Jowitt's reference in the debate cited above to Dunning's famous motion in 1780 reflected his awareness of Britain's long history of suspicions of an overbearing Crown needing the reciprocating checks of Parliament and law. The result of these suspicions was a lengthy process of constitutional evolution, the smoothness of which was emphasised if not exaggerated by the Whiggishly inclined (most of them) of all parties, whereby power leached from the Crown to ministers, hastened by the Reform Acts of the nineteenth century. This powerful myth in turn had a number of influential effects. Even though these effects were also substantially mythic in quality, as critics of Dicey have pointed out in recent years,[5] and were indeed already so by the time Dicey and Anson produced their magisterial works in the 1880s and 1890s, they nevertheless played an important role in shaping the cognitive realities and therefore the practice of the constitution for much of the British political elite for much of the twentieth century.[6]

FLEXIBILITY AND EFFICIENCY

First, these beliefs reinforced ideas of the value of a flexible constitution. Asquith in 1909 commented:

> the great bulk of our constitutional liberties … rest upon usage, upon custom, upon convention – often of slow growth in their early stages, not always uniform, but which in the course of time have received universal observance and respect.[7]

At the same time, he pointed out, outdated aspects have fallen gradually into desuetude without, by implication, the violence often detected in constitutional adjustments elsewhere. In this view the constitution is thus a matter of generally respected adaptable usage rather than entrenched documents. Indeed, flexibility at the apex of the British state was seen as much preferable to hard and fast rules. It both facilitated adaptability and provided a studied ambiguity which could maximise consent.[8]

Second, this flexibility was held to derive in large part from the relationship developed between Crown, Parliament and the law in the settlement following 1688. Besides an anxiety, understandable in the circumstances, to secure the Protestant succession in the face of the Jacobite threat, this settlement, as interpreted by nineteenth-century authorities such as Dicey, established parliamentary supremacy over the courts. The judiciary, after the unhappy experiences of the reign of James II, were not to interpret what was and what was not constitutional or set a limit on Parliament's actions.[9] Statute was supposed to provide them with clear evidence of the mind of Parliament on specific issues. Parliament, meanwhile, was seen as bound neither by the law nor by its predecessors. Instead, for the enthusiasts for parliamentary sovereignty, it was a representative assembly able to respond flexibly to the changing needs of the society it governed. Condemning in 1969 proposals for a Bill of Rights, Labour MP Alex Lyon vehemently denied the implied criticism that Parliament 'does not have the foresight to preserve liberty in a changing economic and social climate'.[10]

Third, in practice, Parliament continually operated as if it were indeed bound by its predecessors. There was no question, for instance, at the start of the century, of repealing the Reform Act of 1884, only of when further enfranchisement would be enacted. This did not mean that it could not be done. It was certainly judged expedient temporarily to set aside constitutional legislation such as the quinquennial provisions of the Parliament Act of 1911 (section 7) during the emergency of war twice in the first half of the century. Such prolongations were always liable to conjure up visions of the abuse of power by the seventeenth-century Rump Parliament, until forcibly ejected by Cromwell, but the risk of a reoccurrence was seen in practice as slight, 'with public opinion maintaining sufficient influence and control over parliamentary events and sufficient authority over the House of Commons to prevent that body from an undue departure from the general will'.[11] Indeed, these limitations were repeatedly seen as, if anything, too effective for the military needs of the Empire. The century began with Balfour lamenting, in the light of the early defeats in the South African War that, 'when the opinion of the community lags behind the necessities of the case, there may be occasions when sufficient rapidity of action is denied to the executive Government'; a refrain to be reprised during the war-threatened 1930s.[12]

The constitutional boundaries of parliamentary action may not have been established by entrenched legislation, but they nevertheless existed in the minds of legislators, in generally accepted usages and principles.[13] Parliament, in other words, was not limited by the courts but was in effect limited by what was deemed to be the view of the people, by what was consistent with the shibboleth of liberty, and by the rule of law.

The common-law concept of the rule of law was enshrined, not in a fundamental document as such, but in the quasi-religious contract known as the Coronation Oath.[14] As C. T. te Water, the South African High Commissioner, argued in 1936, 'The oath which the King takes to govern according to law reveals the formulation upon which the structure of democratic government has been reared throughout the Commonwealth.'[15] This is that government is, in theory, in accordance with, but not controlled by law. One corollary was the entrenched system of Crown immunities encapsulated in the misleading doctrine 'the Crown can do no wrong', or rather was not seen as justiciable by law.

THE ROLE OF THE CROWN

In what is still a dynastic state all institutions ultimately derive from, and government remains in, the name of the Crown. George V indeed attached great importance to his being consulted on the publication or disclosure of Cabinet documents; 'a principle which is inherent in the constitutional relations of the Crown and Ministers'.[16] The distinction between Crown and ministers was, however, increasingly meaningless. Nevertheless, the monarch herself retains some residual powers to ensure the Queen's government is carried on should the electorate fail to deliver a clear verdict.[17] But it is to this electorate that responsibility for choosing the government passed during the nineteenth century. Ministers, even on the still restricted franchise of the Edwardian years, saw themselves as both democratically elected and accountable.

Government was thus legitimated by both the Crown and the people. As Churchill emphasised in 1910:

> The great prerogatives of the Crown, peace and war, making treaties, dissolutions, prorogations of Parliament, and the creation of peers, are and have long been exercised upon the advice of responsible Ministers ... who, as long as the House of Commons retains its control over finance, will be responsible to this House and this House alone.[18]

This combination of Crown and representation – Bagehot's efficient secret of the near fusion of legislative and executive functions in the Cabinet – was the recipe for strong government in Britain.[19] And the carrying on of this representative government in the name of the King was central to the objectives of both major parties, something which Leo Amery, writing during the Second World War, contrasted favourably with the apparent weakness of factional parties in Third Republic France.[20] Britain, accordingly, does not have the pillarisation of continental politics, with a range of social partners forging a consensus between them. Instead, the Crown not only acts as an integrating symbol and a guarantor of continuity and stability, but also ensures that, whatever party is in power, government remains in the name of the Crown. Legitimacy in a parliamentary democracy may, as Tony Blair's repeated invocation of the people bears witness, flow upwards. But it is the centrality of the Crown which facilitated the smoothness of the transition of power, despite 18 years of Tory rule – a smoothness which Blair was publicly to praise.

The centrality of the Crown has two important consequences as far as the ruling assumptions of the constitution were concerned. First, as Balfour put it in 1927:

> our whole political machinery pre-supposes a people so fundamentally at one that they can safely afford to bicker; and so sure of their own moderation that they are not dangerously disturbed by the never-ending din of political conflict.[21]

He might have added that such assumptions also rested on the idea of an essential unity of purpose of all parts of the kingdom, ensured by both political and fiscal integration, rather than a pork-barrel quarrel over the division of the spoils, whatever the implications of the establishment the previous year of a Secretaryship of State for Scotland.

Second, the monarchy's gradual withdrawal from politics after the eighteenth century meant that the powers of the Crown also gradually transferred to the party politicians who ruled in its name. The result was, as Amery put it, that 'In no other country is there such a concentration of power and such a capacity for decisive action as that possessed by a British Cabinet, provided always that it enjoys the support of a majority in the House of Commons.'[22] This is, however, a significant caveat. The loss of that support could prove fatal to a government, as Chamberlain found in 1940. So could the withdrawal of popular consent, as reflected, for instance, in the public hostility to the poll tax at the end of the 1980s. Popular consent is the ultimate arbitrator, but the political parties have long sought to be its interpreters in their electoral contests. By the 1880s the doctrine of the mandate to rule had already developed. This view of popular legitimation for government was taken furthest by Radicals of that era such as Joseph Chamberlain, who desired strong, reforming government,[23] and it was inherited in the twentieth century by the newly formed Labour Party.

SOCIALISM AND THE CONSTITUTION

There were some on the left who nevertheless felt radical constitutional surgery would be necessary in order to build a socialist political economy.[24] Even Clement Attlee flirted after the First World War with guild socialist ideas[25] which, in their most developed form, would have replaced a territorially based Parliament with negotiating assemblies representing producers and consumers. By the early 1930s, however, such ideas had all but disappeared with the advent of prolonged unemployment and economic depression.[26] Instead, the Labour Party had been founded to win representation to the existing House of Commons, and the vast bulk of its membership favoured using this to build popular support for an inevitably gradual transition to socialism.[27] Indeed, in the face of the slump which engulfed the second Labour administration and the perceived need for decisive planning to deal with the crisis, there was a widespread feeling that parliamentary government, far from being replaced, needed to be strengthened. New Party defectors from Labour called for government by Orders in Council with Parliament reduced to a debating chamber, whilst, for Cripps, the myth of the bankers' ramp of 1931 meant that the first act of a future incoming Labour government should be to pass emergency powers legislation to give ministers authority to take necessary actions.[28]

Nothing quite so drastic was attempted by the first majority Labour government of 1945–51. At the end of a long war it in any case inherited well-developed planning controls which could be used, in association with private enterprise, to direct production and address the problems of postwar reconstruction. In the process, largely unsuccessful attempts were made to increase public consultation or control in fields such as housing and industry.[29] The exigencies of reconstruction, however, militated against this. But to criticise an apparent failure to do more is to mistake Labour's diagnosis. This was that the rise of industrial combines in the late nineteenth century had produced private monopolies inimical to the interests of the public. Labour in the interwar years saw itself as seeking to secure, in addition to the civil liberties won by their Radical forebears, economic liberties by directing production in the interests of the whole.[30] As Morrison made clear, the emphasis was therefore not on individual liberties but on general economic rights achieved through the planning of a popularly elected government.[31] From such a perspective it was certainly possible to see the Attlee government as combining efficiency with freedom.

Jowitt's comment on this subject was, however, made in reply to an opposition motion the subject of which – the power of the Cabinet – demonstrated that not all shared his confidence that a satisfactory balance had been struck. The opposition view that the radical reforming government of which Jowitt was a member placed more emphasis on socialised efficiency than on individual liberty was underlined a few weeks later when the Minister of Town and Country Planning's distaste for 'experiments in freedom' in the form of public inquiries was quoted at the Lord Chancellor.[32]

Even in the late nineteenth century, concern, shared by Dicey, was growing that the threat to liberty now came not from the Crown but from its ministers. The rise of disciplined parties from the 1860s,[33] adjusting rapidly to democracy, meant Cabinets could control Parliament's legislative programme, whilst the rise of the press, the platform and photography increased the pre-eminence of party leaders. Dicey complained in 1890 that 'Sham Parliamentary government' was really 'a very vicious form of government by party'.[34] Party government elected by a plurality system meant the risk of dominance by a caucus. As Quintin Hogg put it in 1947, 'It seems intolerable that this country … should be at the mercy of a single body of men … who are led and closely disciplined by the party system, and who, during the lifetime of a Parliament, can do anything they desire.'[35]

Such, as another Conservative pointed out in the same debate, was the price of a constitution centred upon:

> the statutory omnicompetence of Parliament. That gives us here an immense responsibility. In every other country, when you want to make constitutional changes, you have to have longer notice, larger majorities, discussions with your constituents … In this country there is nothing of that sort at all.[36]

The resulting need for safeguards against party government was already encouraging debate about possible constitutional rearrangements by the end of the nineteenth century. As Vernon Bogdanor shows, there was considerable interest in both proportional representation (PR) and the referendum in the period between 1860 and 1931. The former was designed to limit party government by ensuring the representation of minorities, whilst the latter promised a means of balancing its excesses. However, their advocates were largely those marginalised by the intense party conflict of the late Victorian or Edwardian years; they were Liberal Unionists disaffected over Irish home rule, or Tory free traders opposed to tariff reform. For them these devices were the means of resolving the problems of minorities within parties, and, unless managing their problems became important for the party leadership as well, as was the case in

Labour's support for referendums in 1975 and 1979, they had limited prospects of making progress.[37]

The situation was more complicated in the case of electoral reform. Whilst referendums were seen as means of resolving major issues, electoral reform involved a whole series of considerations, the merits of which were contentious between the parties (such as plural voting), or within the parties (such as redistribution, women's suffrage, the alternative vote or PR). Though electoral realignments were prompting consideration of the merits and consequences of reform before 1914, these issues came to the fore as a result of political manoeuvring over the extension of Parliament during the First World War. The subsequent innovation of the Speaker's Conference in 1916–17 provided a measure of agreement which made redistribution and a measure of women's suffrage possible.

Despite considerable debate, however, little progress was made either in the introduction of referendums, or of electoral reform. By the Second World War, indeed, the latter had, for the main parties, become largely a matter of technicalities, such as the use of motor cars. Both, at the same time, favoured the maintenance of a system felt to ensure strong party government. As the Irish Nationalist MP T. M. Kettle observed in 1910, 'You both support the Crown as long as you are able to advise it what to do.'[38] The centrality of party was also apparent in the only real, as opposed to proposed, constitutional innovations of the late nineteenth century. One of these was the assumption, after the interparty conferences to resolve differences over Parliamentary reform in 1884–85, that:

> matters affecting the interests of rival parties should not be settled by the imposition of the will of one side over the other, but by an agreement reached either between the leaders of the main parties or by conferences under the impartial guidance of Mr Speaker.[39]

The fact that Churchill made this point when complaining that this had not occurred with the Representation of the People Bill 1948, however, showed that even this constitutional convention was not always observed.

The other constitutional innovation was the streamlining of Commons procedure in response to Irish filibustering and the doctrine of the mandate from the 1880s which, by the end of Balfour's ministry in 1905, had placed further powers in the hands of party government in the form of the guillotine and other timetable resolutions.

THE SECOND CHAMBER

In these circumstances the only readily available safeguard against party government was an existing device – the House of Lords. This, however, could only be used by the Conservatives. It meant, as Liberals complained, that the veto on party government, was only used against them. Conservatives were aware of this weakness, and from the 1880s a number of proposals for reconstitution of the second chamber were made, given greater impetus by the prolonged crisis of 1909–11. Typically, these would have reduced and changed the membership to representative hereditary peers, peers qualified by offices held and life peers. As Lord Loreburn pointed out, these schemes would still leave an in-built Tory majority whilst the Crown prerogative to create peers would disappear; 'The House of Commons would thereby be held as in a vice.'[40] It is not suprising that instead the Liberals concentrated on reducing the powers of the Lords. Although the case for placing the composition of the Lords 'on a popular basis' was recognised in the preamble to the Parliament Act of 1911, it was realised that such a reform might increase not only the legitimacy but also the powers of the Lords. In practice, few governments were prepared to risk this eventuality.

Indeed, whilst Asquith respected the value of a revising chamber, for Labour the House of Lords was an unnecessary encumbrance to democratic rule. Labour moved the deletion of the preamble, arguing that the powers of the second chamber were now such that it was not worth getting elected to. Furthermore, as Ramsay MacDonald recognised, 'if you set up an elective Second Chamber ... It is going to develop on its own lines ... and sooner or later you are going to have precisely the same difficulties in reference to the present hereditary House of Lords.'[41] A change in its composition which did not involve elections, however, remained open to his charge against Conservative proposals for reform in the late 1920s; the Tories, he claimed, were 'gerrymandering the Constitution'.[42] In its 1935 manifesto, Labour remained unicameral.

Ironically, there was little disagreement between the parties as to the predominance of the Commons, as the inter-party conference of 1948 made clear. Nor was there great disagreement on the problems of an elected second chamber that, far from helping to check party government, might actually compound it.[43] The Conservatives, however, felt the need for reconstitution which, whilst preserving the character and expertise of the Lords, would increase its legitimacy and redress somewhat the balance between the two Houses. Otherwise, they claimed, Parliament was, in practice, unicameral. Indeed, one Tory MP argued in 1910 that the safeguard of the Lords was so threatened that a supreme court on the American model was needed to limit party government.[44]

Conservative-led attempts to reform the composition of the Lords during the interwar years made little progress, however, not least because of the suspicion that they remained skewed in favour of the Tories, as if, according to one Labour MP, when they were in power the Trades Union Congress (TUC) should constitute the second chamber.[45] Attitudes changed by the late 1940s, aided by the positive approach of the peers to the Attlee government and their strict observance of the doctrine of the mandate. Although left-wingers remained substantially unicameral, most Labour MPs now accepted the value of a revising chamber; indeed, the government was to make heavy use of it as such to remedy badly drafted legislation. As a result Labour showed a greater willingness than hitherto to accept the Conservatives' reconstitution proposals. This, however, was only as the price for a further reduction in the delaying powers of the Lords in order to facilitate the passage of iron and steel nationalisation. With the breakdown of the party negotiations, changes in composition were never referred to or agreed by the Parliamentary Labour Party (PLP). And for the PLP such changes remained deeply problematic. Whilst they were unwilling to give a new lease of life to the hereditary principle, concern about the risks of conflict with a second chamber whose authority had been strengthened by elections remained strong. In the circumstances it was best to leave well alone.

The difficulties were illustrated by Labour's experience in the late 1960s. By then the Conservatives, in 1958 and 1963, had finally achieved some of their reconstitution proposals by a more piecemeal route. There remained, however, the Conservative majority in the upper house. The chief merit of the Wilson government's proposals, from Labour's point of view, was that they would tackle this by removing voting rights from hereditary peers and ensure a working majority for the existing government by the creation of life peers. This would have retained a revising chamber whose special character had been augmented by the independence and expertise added by the life peers, whilst actually strengthening party government. Such an arrangement had merits for both front benches, if not for a miscellany of back-benchers – Tory traditionalists and Labour abolitionists – concerned at the increase in prime ministerial patronage powers that would result, whose tactics effectly killed the bill.[46]

By the 1970s Labour had reverted to unicameralism, which was overwhelmingly endorsed at the 1977 party conference, and also by the Liberals in the same year. The risks inherent in reconstituting and thus strengthening the Lords were apparent from the constitutional crisis sparked by a conflict between the two houses in Australia in 1975. Labour's abolition proposals, however, provoked the Conservative Commission, set up under Lord Home, to recommend a second chamber two-thirds elected by PR. This was seen as a means of strengthening the constitutional safeguard of the second chamber.[47] After their return to power in 1979, however, Margaret Thatcher showed more interest in reducing the Lords' ability to frustrate her purposes.[48] At the same time Labour moved towards the idea of an elected second chamber, though this commitment was to be dropped after Blair became party leader. Instead, the 1997 Labour manifesto simply referred to removing the right of hereditary peers to sit and vote, though what he proposed to install in their place was unclear, probably even to him. Although the Liberals have argued for an elected second chamber since at least the 1950s and both the major parties have occasionally favoured this solution since the 1970s, what the current government proposes remained unclear, even after the report of the Royal Commission established in January 1999.

THE RISE OF OFFICIALDOM

The House of Lords question thus remains a cockpit of the debate between the opposed ideals of strong representative government and the need to limit government by party. For those of the latter tendency the problem was exacerbated by the steady growth of the state during and since the nineteenth century. One writer in 1930 lamented 'that the Mother of Parliaments had come down to being the charwoman of Whitehall'.[49] Public legislation, administration and expenditure expanded steadily, all with implications for the intrusive powers of the state. By 1884 that committed individualist, Herbert Spencer, was already complaining: 'Regulations have been made in yearly growing numbers, restraining the citizen in directions where his actions were previously unchecked and compelling actions which previously he might perform or not as he liked',[50] trespassing upon the protection of the public presumed hitherto to have been provided by the common law.

This can also be illustrated by changing attitudes to the right to privacy. This was not even discussed in Anglo-American juris-prudence until the 1890s; instead privacy was a socially assumed

corollary of property rights.[51] That such common-law presumptions
no longer fully protected the citizen, if they ever adequately did, was
clear from the 1977 Megarry judgment that telephone tapping, for
instance, did not conflict with the common law because it had no
general provision for privacy.[52]

For Edwardian Liberal distributivists like Hilaire Belloc the wide
holding of property rights remained the best guarantor of liberty.
Belloc denounced the paternalistic Liberal collectivism of the
Edwardian era – though predicated on T. H. Green's ideas that liberty
should not just be conceived of in the negative terms of Spencer, but
can be advanced by positive actions – as the consolidation of 'a Servile
State'.[53] For Belloc, collectivisation might ostensibly advance, for
instance, the provision of welfare, but it did so by placing power in
the hands of the state and undermining the independence of the
individual citizen.[54] Welfarism, far from being a means to the end of
creating an independent and active citizenry, is thus seen as
undermining this objective, both for Belloc and the dependency
theorists who developed such views in the postwar years.[55]

There was certainly concern, not least because of increasing social
and industrial legislation, at the growing powers of officials. The
MacDonnell Commission in 1914, for instance, drew attention to the
development of administrative boards 'outside effective Ministerial
control and Parliamentary criticism'.[56] Such trends were greatly
furthered by the massive expansion of the state and its legal powers
during the First World War. The Cabinet Secretariat, for instance,
which grew up after 1916 to tackle the deficiencies in the field of
defence identified by Balfour in 1900, was strongly denounced in 1922
in the press and the Commons as fostering the personal rule of a
mercurial and increasingly unpopular premier and undermining the
accountability of the executive to Parliament,[57] an attack which,
however, it was eventually to survive.

Even before the war internal and external threats were being used
to furnish reasons to bolster these powers. At the time of the Agadir
crisis in 1911 the Official Secrets Act (OSA) was rushed through both
Houses; the most cogent reason given for the replacement of the more
tightly drafted 1889 legislation with these much broader provisions
being the difficulty of prosecuting someone found in the fortifications
at Dover who claimed he was merely listening to birdsong.[58] Whilst
section 1 of the OSA dealt with espionage, however, section 2 was a
catch-all for unauthorised disclosures of official information. This was
extended by section 6 of the Official Secrets Act of 1920 which, as the
Lord Chancellor noted in a 1939 debate, was the only example in

English law where an individual could be penalised for refusing to disclose information.[59] However, after Duncan Sandys, an MP and Churchill's son-in-law, had been prosecuted under section 6 in 1938 for refusing to divulge his source for what might later have been described as a whistleblowing article in the public interest on the state of air defences, this provision was tightened in a 1939 statute to refer only to suspected espionage.[60]

Wide potential powers for the state to deal with perceived threats were also enacted with the passage of the Defence of the Realm Act of 1914 (DORA) on the outbreak of war and, in the face of a gathering Cold War abroad and industrial disputes at home, the Emergency Powers Act of 1920. The state, for good political reasons nevertheless, even in the emergency of total war proved reluctant overtly to use all the powers vested within it by DORA, although the preparedness to use coercion steadily gathered during the war.[61] With such broadly drafted legislation, however, restraint could only be exercised voluntarily by the authorities according to what they saw as the liberal principles of the British polity, for there was little safeguard against the use of such powers in the courts. By the end of the war this restraint was becoming distinctly frayed.

Restraint, accordingly, was essentially political. Therefore, the means to strengthen this restraint was Parliament. Contending that state collectivism was unlikely to produce positive results unless officialdom was restrained, the Labour MP F. W. Jowett argued in 1909 that Parliament should be reconstructed. He advocated the creation of a committee system that would control the executive in the manner of British local government – an idea which was to be briefly revived by the Tory MP Bob Boothby in 1960 as a means of restraining a seemingly increasingly presidential Prime Minister.[62] Executive committees, however, do not seem to have subsequently found general favour; indeed, the committee system in local government is now under attack in some quarters as 'time-consuming and cumbersome'.[63]

However, some kind of parliamentary committee system to scrutinise the executive was put forward by the Haldane Committee on the Machinery of Government in 1918 and was thereafter a recurring theme of proposals for parliamentary reform. Haldane argued that such committees would not only secure 'fuller knowledge of the work of Departments and of the objects which Ministers had in view', but would also encourage officials:

to lay more stress upon constructive work in administering the service entrusted to them for the benefit of the community than upon anticipating criticism which may, in present conditions, often be based upon imperfect knowledge of the facts or the principles at issue.[64]

Secrecy, in another enduring theme of reformers, was thus not only against the interests of the citizen, but was also administratively bad. For reformers this was the major blemish amongst the many admitted merits of Britain's non-political civil service. It was, as the Webbs recognised, 'an able and honest but secretive bureaucracy'.[65] Nevertheless, successful attempts to cast more light on the inner workings of government were limited in the first half of the century to the ineffective Estimates Committee established in 1912. In 1919 the Cabinet Finance Committee discussed the idea of a parliamentary budget committee:

> It would go far to remove the present criticisms, inside and outside of Parliament, of government expenditure if a statement could be made, during the forthcoming financial debate in Parliament, to the effect that, without committing themselves to the establishment of the French system of Parliamentary Committees as an institution the Government were considering whether some system could not be arranged for obtaining the co-operation of Parliament in framing the Budget.[66]

After the detrimental effects of such committees on the French navy had been pointed to, however, the idea was dropped. Although the committee system idea continued to be advocated by distinguished parliamentarians of all parties,[67] it continued to be resisted by officials. Not the least of several criticisms by Cabinet Secretary Sir Edward Bridges in 1942 was that it would constrain the frankness with which a non-political civil service could advise ministers.[68]

Parliament, however, was not the only means of restraining these officials. In 1921 the Treasury Solicitor, Sir John Mellor, drew attention to the fact that wartime contact with officialdom 'has greatly accentuated the feeling that it ought to rest with the law and not with the official to protect the interests of the individual'.[69] The law, however, remained substantially constrained by the legal immunities enjoyed by most departments of state. Meanwhile there seemed to be more and more of it around, not least in the form of delegated legislation. Attention to this problem was powerfully drawn by Lord Chief Justice Hewart's brilliant polemic *The New Despotism* in 1929, which conveniently ignored his own role in several of the statutes criticised therein in his earlier incarnation as Attorney General.[70] This raised three issues – the justiciability of the Crown, the growth in ministers' powers and the problem of administrative and legislative overload – all of which were felt to make government more remote and less accountable.

DEVOLUTION AND OVERLOAD

The problem of administrative and legislative overload interwove with the existing issue of devolution. This had returned to the fore in Ireland from 1870 onwards. Ireland had always, since the Act of Union of 1800, retained a degree of administrative devolution. It had, however, never been politically integrated into a UK system, and the electoral success of the Home Rule Party by the 1880s meant it was never likely to be. It had also been subject to repeated exercises in crisis management. Schemes for Irish home rule from 1885 onwards could be seen as continuing this theme; attempts at crisis management to deal with this particular problem, rather than the general constitutional architecture of the United Kingdom.

The rise of the Irish issue, nevertheless, prompted a wider interest in home rule amongst Scottish and Welsh Liberals, whilst raising the idea of 'home rule all round' as a means of settling Ireland, including the Ulster issue that immediately arose in 1885, and binding it into a UK-wide solution. The Scottish Liberal MP Murray Macdonald argued in 1911 that home rule would promote local efficiency and relieve the congestion of business in Westminster.[71] He also shared the views of Liberal Unionist peers like Grey and Selborne, informed by their experiences of federalism in Canada and South Africa, and Liberal Imperialists like Herbert Samuel, that devolution would facilitate more general federal unity within the Empire.[72] Macdonald's view of the benefits devolution offered the imperial government as well as Scotland, Wales and Ireland was widely shared in the Cabinet committee on home rule established in 1911, for whom it also offered a way of resolving difficulties such as Ireland's continuing representation at Westminster (in an early version of the West Lothian question). However, Churchill's attempt to tackle the problem of how to fit England into home rule all round, by suggesting seven regional assemblies, foundered on the obvious lack of any public sentiment for this. Asquith commented: 'we could not go back to the Heptarchy'. The Irish were hostile, seeing such schemes as a way of further delaying their own home rule project. And the Unionist leadership, whatever the success of federalism elsewhere in the Empire, did not favour it at home.[73] Whilst the merits of administrative devolution continued to appeal to the Speaker's Conference of 1919–20, these political difficulties remained insuperable. Nor could the conference agree on the form of the bodies to be devolved.[74] The founding of Welsh and Scottish nationalist parties in the 1920s reflected the lack of progress towards their ends in the main political parties.[75] Ironically, the only people to get devolution were those who had most fervently opposed it before 1914 – the Unionists of Ulster.

By 1931, arguing the continuing case for devolution to relieve an overloaded Parliament, Sir Herbert Samuel regretted the lack of enthusiasm for home rule in Wales and Scotland.[76] In fact, he was mistaken. In 1938, for instance, an all-party Welsh delegation pressed for some measure of devolution citing, amongst other matters, the fact that Wales had only been specifically debated twice in the last 17 years. Neville Chamberlain, however, rejected such calls on grounds of expense,[77] and it was not until the late 1940s and 1950s that the process of administrative devolution culminating in the creation of the Welsh Office in 1964 began.

The interwar economic depression meanwhile stimulated calls for greater self-government across the political spectrum in Scotland.[78] Furthermore, there was a much stronger home rule tradition in the Labour Party in Scotland than in Wales, where the cultural bases of nationalism limited its appeal amongst party activists.[79] Discontent in Scotland was met by the administrative devolution undertaken by the National government in the 1930s and consolidated by the former Home Ruler, Tom Johnston, as Scottish Secretary during the Second World War.[80] The collection of over 1 million signatures by the Scottish Covenant movement in the 1940s nevertheless prompted considerable anxiety in the Scottish Office at a time when a majority of supporters of all the parties, at least according to opinion polls, supported some form of devolution.[81] The solution adopted was further administrative change implemented by the Tories in the early 1950s. This perhaps helped to undermine home rule sentiment in Labour; by the late 1960s interest in devolution seems to have all but disappeared in the party,[82] if not in Scotland as a whole as Scottish National Party by-election successes after 1967 bore witness.

Administrative devolution should not be confused with legislative devolution. There was a case for the latter, as Samuel's concern about parliamentary overload and Hewart's about delegated legislation shows. Beatrice Webb in 1931 revived the Webbs' 1920 scheme to tackle both by devolving consideration of delegated legislation to a different assembly. And Churchill, in the face of the economic difficulties of the decade, suggested an economic sub-parliament.[83] Neither idea made progress. Legislative devolution on a territorial basis was meanwhile off the agenda until the 1970s. Nor, despite the various reforms suggested in the Donoughmore Committee on Ministers' Powers, set up in response to Hewart's claims, was much progress made on other fronts. For Samuel in the late 1940s, by then Liberal leader in the Lords, the situation remained unsatisfactory.

LIBERTIES AND RIGHTS

Jowitt claimed in 1950 that the Attlee government had made a greater contribution to liberty than any previous administration through the reductions to Crown immunity in the Crown Proceedings Act of 1947.[84] This did not stop the Liberals from introducing Liberties of the Subject Bills in 1947, 1950 and 1954, similar in tone to the Charter of Liberties agreed at the 1947 Conservative Party conference. Concern focused not just on delegated legislation, but on the twentieth-century growth of administrative tribunals and the lack of response to public inquiries. Despite Donoughmore's recommendations, both Liberals and Tories complained, tribunals were still being established without any right of appeal, giving ministers quasi-judicial powers.[85] A minister, claimed the Inns of Court Conservative and Unionist Society in its influential 1954 pamphlet, *Rule of Law*:

> may pronounce his will, like an oriental despot, without reason, without justification, without appeal, without redress. Where such a system flourishes, we may truly say that the rights of the subject depend no longer on Law, but on the indulgences of his rulers.[86]

Both Liberals and the group responsible for this publication showed growing interest in imitating the French *droit administratif* and in importing ideas on administrative procedures from the USA, to sceptical responses from officials. There was strong support for a French-style *Conseil d'Etat* from academic witnesses such as W. A. Robson and C. J. Hansom to the subsequent Franks Committee inquiry established in 1955.[87] The eventual report, however, rejected this on the grounds that 'it would constitute an appeal from a body expert in a particular subject to a relatively inexpert body'.[88]

Demands for an administrative division of the High Court, however, continued. Concerns that Diceyan formulae would no longer suffice to protect citizens against an ever more powerful state meanwhile showed no signs of ebbing. New technology fed this concern.[89] It both furnished new means of communication and new challenges to the state to extend its surveillance of possible subversive activity to such forms of communication.

Nor was the state the only potential threat to liberties. Wartime service by colonial subjects had led to Colonial Office concern about race relations.[90] In the late 1940s back-bench Labour MPs began to prepare private legislation on the subject.[91] However, a Cabinet committee chaired by the then Cabinet Secretary, Sir Norman Brook, concluded in 1950 that 'there was no reason to believe that either legislation or administrative action could profitably be undertaken for this purpose'.[92] The common-law tradition of liberties militated against conceiving of positive protection for minorities against the ignorance and prejudice of landladies or private employers. It was not until 1965 that the first, limited, race-relations legislation was introduced by the new Labour government.

Anxieties about the implications of surveillance technology and computers had led, by then, to a shift in emphasis amongst reformers from the common-law concept of liberties of the subject to the entrenching of rights. This shift was also influenced by the treatment of the European Convention on Human Rights. When this was introduced in the late 1940s the then Labour government treated it with scepticism. It was felt that it conflicted with colonial responsibilities and the objective of a planned economy, and Jowitt was horrified at the ambit the vagueness of the convention would leave to the courts.[93] However, after Labour's return to power, Harold Wilson in 1965 decided to allow individual petition to the European Court of Human Rights. Claiming that there was still insufficient provision for litigation against the Crown, the Liberal MP Emlyn Hooson attempted to introduce a Bill of Rights drafted by John Macdonald in 1969.[94] A similar attempt, based on the Canadian legislation of 1960, had been introduced earlier in the year by the Conservative MP, Lord Lambton.[95] Indeed pamphlets on the subject appeared from members of all three parties in the late 1960s.[96] However, the leadership of both major parties showed little interest when in government. For Labour in 1969 not only was such a proposal impossibly general; there was also the risk that it would be interpreted by a politicised judiciary in a conservative manner, as had been the case with the US Supreme Court down to the 1954 Brown case. The flexibility of Parliament continued to seem a better way of 'tackling the fundamental injustices in our society'.[97]

THE IMPACT OF ECONOMIC AND POLITICAL CHANGE

For reformers, however, the flexibility of the British system, for instance in passing the Commonwealth Immigrants Act of 1968 thanks to agreement between the two front benches, showed, Lord Wade argued, how rapidly important rights can be taken away.[98] Nor was strong majoritarian government seen as such an unalloyed virtue in an era of relative economic decline and the renewed decay of staple industries during the 1960s. Government was instead portrayed as both more remote and more ineffective. For instance, in 1968 the Conservatives set up an inquiry, aware of 'a widespread feeling that Parliament was too remote from Scottish problems', which recommended limited legislative devolution to Scotland (a commitment dropped after 1976).[99]

These economic problems have had a number of important effects. Party identification was weakened. Instead of the straight fights characteristic of 1950s electoral politics, nationalist parties began to command more support in an increasingly volatile political landscape, which sapped the legitimacy both of the Union and of the existing electoral system. Traditional arrangements were seen as unequal to the task of tackling the problems. Unlike in the 1930s, they were indeed believed by reformers to be part of the problem. The concern about adversarial politics, which reached its height in the 1970s, reflected the view that the antagonism between the parties compounded Britain's economic difficulties. It was this anxiety, and the problems that it might lead to if it went unchecked, which then animated Lord Hailsham's influential constitutional analyses.[100] However, although this gave a new basis to the diagnosis of the dangers of party government – and the phrase he coined, 'elective dictatorship', provided an arresting image for the threat he sought to describe – there was in fact nothing novel in the idea of those dangers.

The problem, if exacerbated by economic troubles, remained that which had long been diagnosed by would-be reformers; an over-mighty (and apparently increasingly ineffective) state with insufficient legitimacy and freedoms. The debate, however, has become qualitatively different, held against a background of political change wrought by economic travails. As a result of these, attitudes to government have become more sceptical. Both major parties initially responded in the 1960s by exploring changes to the machinery of government, moving the Whitehall furniture and attempting to reshape the civil service.[101] The Conservatives, in particular, also began to consider the range of activities of government, and its relationship with society. Sir Geoffrey Howe, for instance, argued in 1977 that government needs to do less better, though he was to find the reality under Margaret Thatcher rather different.[102]

Although Margaret Thatcher came to power with a rhetoric of removing quangocracy and the remoteness of government, the underlying emphasis was managerial. Power was to be devolved under her and her successor to, for instance, tenants or parents, to improve the accountability, in the absence of market disciplines, and thus the management of public services. But, at the same time, managerial considerations drove the creation of a resurgent and seemingly unaccountable quangocracy; an enormous increase in often badly drafted legislation; equally enormous delegated powers, including the so-called Henry VIII clauses allowing ministers to amend statutes without requiring parliamentary approval; bullying of the media; and a dramatic reduction in local government autonomy which, if anything, increased the sense of governmental remoteness and centralisation. At the same time managerial imperatives and a stress on improving economic performance at the expense of other criteria acted as a solvent on respect for existing institutions. Meanwhile, party competition to be 'tough on crime' and the concern of Michael Howard as Home Secretary in the 1990s to restore public confidence in the criminal justice system, led him to interfere with the freedom of action of judges and the liberties of the individual;[103] a process continued under Blair by, for instance, the changes to the law of evidence and the right to silence in the Criminal Justice (Terrorism and Conspiracy) Act of 1998. However, the Conservative governments of the time were not the only factor in constitutional change. Judicial decisions, over education and transport policy for instance, have also eroded local government's freedom of action.[104] This reduction in local autonomy has also been driven by European directives, particularly since the Single European Act was passed in 1987.

Hitherto, the Tories had always portrayed these evils as most likely to come from a Labour government; indeed charges of badly drafted legislation being amended during its parliamentary passage and the reduction of local authorities to 'mere branch offices, with no real authority'[105] were made by Conservatives during the Attlee years. It was Labour which seemed to have a dirigist, 'man-in-Whitehall-knows-best' culture; and left-wing Poplarist objections to the differential financial means (and therefore local service provision) of local authorities in the interwar years[106] had been a factor in this process of centralisation. However, as the stripping of financial responsibilities from local government reached new heights, by the 1990s Labour politicians came to use these same taunts once aimed at them against the Tories and adopted the language of bringing government closer to communities.[107]

In government after 1997, however, this seemed more rhetoric than reality as managerial and political considerations led the Blair administration to, if anything, tighten the financial straitjacket on local authorities and intervene intensively in schools. This tendency held true even for apparently decentralising measures, such as the creation of an executive mayor for London. The idea of executive mayors, floated by the Tories in 1991, was widely applauded as a way of increasing democratic accountability in local government. However, the ring-fencing of budgets will apply to the new mayor as much as elsewhere in local government; 'In other words, Whitehall officials, rather than the mayor and assembly, will decide how much Londoners spend ... the mayor will be a Whitehall agency' with responsibility but little power.[108] Accordingly, by 1999 it was the Conservatives, seeking to dissociate themselves from the over-mighty Whitehall of Major and Blair, who were again using the language of local government and community as a stick to beat a Labour government.[109]

DEVOLUTION, WESTMINSTER AND WHITEHALL

Although the diagnosis of the constitutional problem may be substantially the same, against this background of economic and political change there has been some development in the range of remedies adopted or proposed in recent years. These broadly fall into three categories.

First, there is the territorial issue which re-emerged in the 1970s and again in the 1990s. The differences were the extent to which legislative, as opposed to administrative, devolution was taken seriously – even though the nature and powers of devolved bodies remained important bones of contention – and the apparent strength of feeling for independence, especially in Scotland. Political concern emerged rapidly; the Kilbrandon Royal Commission on the Constitution, having started in 1969 with the assumption that it would reject devolution,[110] ended with recommendations for both

Scottish and Welsh devolution in 1973. It continued to reject the idea
of regionalising England as a necessary precursor to home rule all
round; federalisation was seen as unsuitable for a heavily traded
economy dominated economically as well as politically by south-east
England[111] – though others might have argued that this domination
was why federalism should be attempted. Nevertheless, the Scottish
Liberal Party, in the 1980s, was envisaging some kind of federal
structure;[112] whilst the Scottish Nationalist Party, building on the
various British–Irish bodies instituted since the 1973 Sunningdale
talks as a means of delegitimising terrorism in Northern Ireland,
outlined plans for a Council of the Isles as a vehicle for tackling all
inter-territorial relations in the archipelago – a concept which was also
to appear in the Anglo-Irish *Propositions on Heads of Agreement* of
January 1998.

Devolution, however, was largely to be driven by distinctively
Scottish or Welsh, rather than wider UK considerations. Nevertheless,
there were also signs by the 1990s that, partly because of European
funding considerations and partly because of growing sentiment
in favour of regional devolution amongst at least north-east Labour
MPs, some tentative moves towards regionalising England were
contemplated. The ten regional-development agencies introduced
by the Blair government were, however, a long way from representing
home rule all round and, with no control even over inward
investment, 'risk being one more agency in an over crowded field'.[113]

Second, according to Liberal Democrats, 'Without PR, the cancer at
the heart of Britain's body politic – single-party governments with
minority support lording it over a docile Parliament – will remain
untreated.'[114] As Jo Grimond argued in the 1950s, an electoral system
established to represent communities manifestly no longer did so
with the rise of party.[115] PR then, even for the Liberals, was perhaps
more of a shibboleth than a programme; according to Richard Holme
in his first election address in 1964, it had an importance roughly level
with site-value rating.[116] It was the adversarial politics of the 1960s and
1970s and the spectre of ungovernability which alarmed a wide cross-
section of the political classes in the early 1970s which brought it back
onto the agenda. For instance, Conservative Action for Electoral
Reform (CAER) was set up shortly after the Tory defeat (despite
winning more votes than Labour) in the 'Who Governs?' election of
February 1974.[117] Like Hailsham, they were very concerned about the
risk of left-wing extremism, which the industrial troubles of the 1970s
seemed to hint at. This view played a major part in persuading the
Hansard Commission in 1975–76 under the chairmanship of the

Conservative historian Lord Blake to support the adoption of a variant on the German electoral model,[118] and was further championed in 1977 by Holme in his *A Democracy Which Works*.[119]

Holme, who had in 1974 returned from four years in the United States where he was very active in and influenced by Common Cause, in 1976 became founding Director of the cross-party umbrella group, the National Committee for Electoral Reform (which included CAER), deliberately established on the model of the European Movement. He had not previously been interested in constitutional reform, but hereafter Holme was a central figure in a number of single-issue organisations on a variety of constitutional matters; from PR to the rights campaign with Lord Scarman in the early 1980s, culminating in the setting up of the Constitutional Reform Centre in 1985 and Charter 88 three years later.[120]

Conservative interest in PR, however, waned after they returned to government in 1979. Labour, meanwhile, remained lukewarm. Three successive general election defeats brought a greater willingness to contemplate alternative arrangements, as exemplified by the setting up of the Plant Commission in 1990. But the split in the commission over its eventual recommendation of a supplementary vote arrangement for elections to the Commons in 1993, and the reaction in the party, demonstrated how far Labour was from possessing an internal consensus for change,[121] as remained clear from the Cabinet divisions over the 1998 Jenkins Report.[122]

Third, there were changes affecting Parliament. Parliamentary reform proposals have two main objectives. One is to streamline procedures, allow consideration of long-term issues and provide better scrutiny of legislation in passage. The other is to shift the imbalance between the executive and Parliament, for instance, by restraining the use of prerogative powers. Sir William Armstrong in the 1960s even suggested that there should be a Department of the Opposition which would place the resources of the civil service at its disposal and help it both scrutinise the government and prepare to replace it; an idea which was revived by Labour suggestions, before the 1997 election, that there should be civil servants for the opposition in handling foreign and defence policy.[123]

Some developments have meanwhile occurred. The idea of a Parliamentary Ombudsman, inspired by the Swedish example, was first conceived in response to the 1957 Franks Report, and was introduced by the ensuing Labour government ten years later.[124] Subsequently the ambit of the Ombudsman has been increased – though efficacy remains limited by lack of public awareness of his existence – whilst since the 1960s parallel or similar offices have been introduced to police other areas of public life. And though parliamentary control of finance remains limited, the Commons did reassert control of the National Audit Office in 1983.

To some extent, proposed remedies address both of the objectives outlined; for instance, the idea of pre-legislative committee scrutiny of bills. The Commons Select Committee on Procedure advocated greater use of committees in this way in 1967,[125] but this was not to be introduced, even in a limited form, until the late 1990s. Significant though it was as an improvement to Westminster's scrutiny of Whitehall, the introduction at last of departmental select committees in 1979 did not include this activity amongst their functions. Meanwhile, lack of expertise has hamstrung the effectiveness of select committees, which is why some reformers have suggested that pre-legislative scrutiny might best be carried out by a reformed second chamber with co-opted committee members.[126] The committees have also been weakened by the difficulties of acquiring the information necessary to carry out their inquiries, which is why this innovation has been seen as insufficient in itself; what is also needed, reformers argue, is change in the civil-service culture which Bridges was so keen to defend.

In the 1950s Bridges, as head of the Treasury, objected to the American political scientist Samuel Beer's book on his department on the grounds that if people knew how policy making occurred it would be easier to criticise.[127] The idea that greater accountability, if inconvenient for civil servants, might help to make government better was then already established as a principal reason for setting up select committees.

Since then civil servants have certainly become more visible and more regulated. As one senior official recently put it, 'When I joined the Civil Service in 1974 we were anonymous. That is going going, gone … [and now] I find myself very much under control' from the judiciary, the Ombudsman and the National Audit Office in the balkanised world of the new public management.[128] Although the Crown Proceedings Act of 1947 established new liabilities much remained at the discretion of departments, not least the power to determine where the public interest lies in the disclosure of documents. A plea to allow the courts to decide instead was made by one of the authors of *Rule of Law*, J. E. S. Simon:

> I cannot believe that this would impede the work of administration any more in this country than it would in America

or the Dominions where, as you will have seen from the Bar Council memorandum, the Executive has no rights of determination – to say nothing of Scotland.[129]

The last had recently been established by *Glasgow Corporation* v. *Central Land Board*. Although incorporated into English law through *Conway* v. *Rimmer* in 1968, leaving the matter to the courts to decide could still pose problems, as became apparent in the arms-to-Iraq affair and the Scott inquiry into the use of what had come to be known as public-interest immunity certificates in the *Matrix Churchill* case.

The issue was not just the perversion of the course of justice in the courts. It also raised, as Scott put it, the problem that 'A failure by Ministers to meet the obligations of Ministerial accountability by providing information about the activities of their departments undermines … the democratic process.'[130] In other words, the boundaries of the managerial state should not just be tested by ad hoc legal action, but established by democratic scrutiny. For, as the 1978 White Paper on the OSA had noted, without information people 'cannot call their representatives to account and make informed use of their rights as citizens and electors'.[131]

The OSA was, however, one of the means of controlling access to that information. Nevertheless, it was not until the failure of a prosecution of the *Sunday Telegraph* that a committee under Sir Oliver Franks was set up in 1971 to reconsider this legislation. In 1947 a Cabinet committee had taken the complacent view that 'the record of this country in these matters is extremely good'.[132] Franks, however, concluded that 'any law which impinges on the freedom of information in a democracy should be much more tightly drawn'.[133] Tightening, however, meant moving away from the studied ambiguity of the 1911 legislation, drawn up in an age when such catch-all statutes, like the wartime DORA, were there to support a system of control of information which was largely informal rather than enforced in the courts. Instead, the Thatcher government's replacement in 1989 was designed to be more readily enforceable, not least in removing the public-interest defence which had led to Clive Ponting's acquittal in the celebrated trial which led to the decision to change the law. The establishment of a statutory basis for the security services which followed, accordingly, did not necessarily involve any shift in the boundary between state and citizen.[134] In particular, it did not broaden the ambit of access to official information.

Nevertheless, rights of access to particular information have been extended piecemeal in the 1980s and 1990s, partly as a result of

European initiatives.[135] And MPs of all parties have since 1979 attempted to introduce freedom-of-information legislation or have been involved in the Campaign for Freedom of Information established in 1984. They have argued that the supposed incompatibility of such legislation with ministerial accountability in Westminster systems is demonstrably false, as the introduction of freedom of information in Australia, Canada and New Zealand in the 1980s bears witness.[136]

Governments have, however, moved cautiously in this area. The Conservatives launched an open-government initiative in 1993, involving codes subject to investigation by the Ombudsman, which William Waldegrave claimed 'will be cheaper for the citizen because there is no need to employ lawyers and others, who tend to waste a lot of money'.[137] Labour, in contrast, promised freedom-of-information legislation, but when introduced in 1999 it met with a wave of criticism. It did, however, introduce public-interest-disclosure legislation in 1998, though whether this will provide the promised protection for whistleblowers, not least given concern about its possible incompatibility with the OSA, remains to be tested in the courts.

LEGAL REMEDIES?

The rules governing the operation of the state are increasingly laid down by statute or regulation and are testable in the courts. This process, however, has been driven as much by the state's requirement to clarify those rules for its own benefit as to enhance the liberties of the individual. This is partly because the rules of engagement remain unclear. The state and the judiciary have danced a gavotte, in which the rising tide of administrative action has fuelled the growth of judicial review since the 1960s, which in turn has prompted a juridification of the administrative process. Nevertheless, the ways in which they interact have continued to be subject to the vagaries of litigation and judicial discretion, creating an unpredictability which is arguably inimical both to good administration and good law. Indeed, this unpredictability may also have encouraged ministers to run the risk of judicial review, aware that they have comparatively easy access to legislation if the decision goes against them.[138] None of this suggests that the courts provide the ideal, let alone the cheapest, means of regulating executive action.

Nevertheless, for reformers, none of the alternatives were any more effective. As the Conservative back-bencher, Richard Shepherd, complained in 1993, 'Much of our freedom and liberty is no longer dispensed by this House; it is secured for us by the courts.'[139] The felt need amongst many reformers has been to increase the courts' ability to act as a key restraint on elective dictatorship. In 1974 Lord Scarman called for 'a new constitutional settlement that makes use of judicial power to keep within constitutional bounds the legislative sovereignty of Parliament'.[140] More trenchantly, the Liberal Democrats argued in 1993: 'We need to get rid of the doctrine of Parliamentary Sovereignty and start again.'[141] To do this would be to overturn the centrepiece of the existing constitution. But by the 1990s an increasing number of reformers had decided that this was necessary. After the Thatcher years the only way to restrain the executive, for some reformers, was to replace the rule of law with entrenched rule by law.

There is a paradox to be explained here. The British have, in the process of losing an Empire, been responsible for more Bills of Rights than any other people in history.[142] There was a recognition, as one Labour policy document put it, that 'The British system ... is only one of many ways of finding a true expression of the will of the people', and was not necessarily the most appropriate one in the circumstances of racial tension which often accompanied decolonisation.[143]

Such devices, however, have not been for the British themselves (though see Chapter 3). Safeguards did not need to be written into a political culture founded on Pym and Hampden and a constitution forged in the face of the Jacobites. And their introduction could trammel its flexibility, as Attlee wrote in 1942: 'Have we not found in dealing with the Dominions that the more we avoid precise definitions, the better.'[144] In 1909 Asquith praised Britain's unwritten constitution, 'although some signs in the sky would seem to portend that this happy state is not long to last'.[145]

Despite the growth of the state, in 1969 Lord Wade still regarded a written constitution as superfluous.[146] Lord Hailsham in the 1970s was the first major figure to advocate this innovation, though it was not until 1990 that draft proposals began to appear with the Liberal Democrats' *We, The People*. This was followed in 1992 by Tony Benn's Commonwealth of Britain Bill, the only major constitutional proposal thus far to envisage the replacement of the monarchy, either in Britain as a whole or in a future independent Scotland. Benn's bill, however, was more traditional in its approach to parliamentary supremacy. In contrast, the Institute for Public Policy Research (IPPR) justified its version on 'the belief that restraints on the Executive and on the centralisation of power must be given constitutional rather than political force'.[147]

They shared Shepherd's pessimism about Parliament as the safeguard of liberties. Liberals have meanwhile come some way from their last experience of government, when one Liberal minister commented: 'Let us conceive a House of Commons misrepresenting the people. I think they must be almost imbeciles who can imagine such a situation.'[148] Instead, for reformers, the failure, in their view, of Parliament to be as responsive and effective as J. A. Pease made it out to be, is the central problem. For them, Jowitt's balancing trick between efficiency and freedom has been tilted steadily in the direction of an often far from effective executive for too long. Whether the law, given the suspicions of the judiciary, especially on the left, can achieve greater legitimacy is, however, open to doubt.[149] Furthermore its elevation, to the British mind, involves the cardinal sin of inflexibility, hence Lord Nolan's preferences for codes of practice governing public life to the more cumbersome, and not necessarily more effective, use of legislation.[150]

The drafting of written constitutions is a symptom of the coming together of the various threads of the movements for constitutional reform by the late 1980s. However, it remains, perhaps because of the caveats given above, very much a minority pastime. Even the enthusiasts of the Constitutional Reform Centre concluded at a 1986 conference that there was 'a general reluctance to contemplate the drafting of a written constitution as being feasible or desirable'.[151] Instead, there were a number of back-bench attempts in both the Commons and Lords during the 1980s to provide entrenched legislation by incorporating the European Convention on Human Rights into UK law. These attempts continued to be opposed on the grounds that it might encourage litigiousness, whilst judges feared the politicisation of the judiciary. There also remained the view that it is better to base the law on 'firm remedies rather than vague and resounding rights',[152] as the latter may increase arbitrariness in the operation of the law and establishment of the boundaries of the state, rather than vice versa.

The main elements of the convention were nevertheless incorporated in the Human Rights Act of 1998. This was probably enacted largely to reduce the embarrassment and expense of taking cases to the European Court of Human Rights at Strasbourg. Unlike European legislation, however, it will only be able to undermine subordinate legislation, not statute law. For legislation such as the Financial Services and Markets Bill of 1998 which, in establishing the regulator as investigator, judge, jury and executioner, arguably conflicts with the right to a fair trial under article 6 of the European

Convention on Human Rights,[153] all the courts will be able to do is issue a declaration of incompatibility.

However, the question might arise whether, if legislators in the twentieth century had not chosen increasingly to hedge about common-law concepts of reasonableness and good faith with ever more complex rules, a process which has not been necessary in the field of financial services nor in many other areas of public life,[154] such safeguards would have come to be regarded as expedient. After all, rules in themselves do not create morality, they are the fail-safes when that morality is transgressed. The more complex they are the more likely they are, firstly, to be applied arbitrarily; and, secondly, to replace the presumption that 'we have a liberty in this country to do anything which is not specifically prohibited'[155] with the notion that the risk of abuse is such that the ambit of prohibitions must be steadily widened. In other words, specific statutes, instead of building on the common law, have tended to its dissolution.[156] The result has been calls for its substitution by importing a convention which ironically was largely drawn up by British lawyers for the rather different circumstances of late 1940s Europe. However, given that the rights the government has chosen to incorporate are, rather negatively, primarily rights against the state, whether importing the convention will achieve a revival of public morality, rather than aiding the descent into a litigious and amoral victimhood which some fear is already occurring,[157] seems open to doubt.

A BLAIR REVOLUTION?

Reformers have talked of the objective of 'restoring faith in politics'.[158] How this objective coheres with shifting accountability from Parliament towards the courts and the vagaries of litigation remains to be seen. Supporters nevertheless argue: 'The political process affords the citizen no equivalent effective access to the Minister and decision-making.'[159] Whether the legal process will instead is another matter. In any case, this misses the point. If the political process and Parliament is flawed as a check upon the executive then surely it needs reform, if not instead of then as well as the law. The fundamental concern of reformers from all points of the political spectrum in the twentieth century has been that the political process has been rendered increasingly ineffective in this role by the rise of party government, professional politicians and the payroll vote. Meanwhile, checks on this development have if anything become more attenuated; for instance the by-elections that used to be required at new appointments of ministers to provide popular endorsement for the office were discontinued after the First World War.

Whatever its activities in other areas of the constitution, nothing the Blair government has so far done in office gives much ground for comfort that the balance is being redressed on this point. In contrast to the interparty conferences of the late nineteenth and early twentieth centuries, major constitutional legislation has been guillotined through. Far from strengthening Parliament, there has been a willingness to use prerogative power, which cannot be readily controlled either by Westminster or the courts, even on such constitutional matters as the powers of the Welsh Assembly. The power of the party in the electoral system has been strengthened by introducing a party-list method for European elections; when this was repeatedly rejected by the House of Lords on the grounds that in denying the electorate a choice between candidates it was undemocratic, the government forced the legislation through by invoking the Parliament Act – hardly a reassuring sight for those who suspect that the reform of the Lords is intended to gerrymander the constitution in favour of further examples of over-mighty government.

Referendums have been used to secure blank cheques from the people of Scotland, Northern Ireland, Wales and London – endorsing proposals the detail of which at the time remained a mystery. The suspicion that referendums can become exercises not in public consultation but in plebiscitary dictatorship, with the right result secured both by the careful wording of the ballot and the expenditure of large amounts of public money – a concern which clouded Britain's only national referendum on membership of the European Economic Community in 1975[160] – prompted the Neill Committee on Standards in Public Life in 1998 to recommend that the government should remain neutral in future referendums. And the Blair government has introduced legislative devolution without more than strictly limited financial competence (and only in the case of Scotland); an exercise in accountability without power which, by obscuring rather than tackling the widespread and erroneous perception that Scotland is badly treated by the Exchequer,[161] may sow the seeds of future conflict.

Government ministers may be right in claiming that Britain since 1997 has embarked on its 'most intensive programme of constitutional change since 1689'.[162] To some extent they have bought into the agenda of Charter 88 and its associated organisations. But what has emerged is a shopping list of changes which is more intensive than it is programmatic. When Robert Hazell was asked[163] in 1995 if the Constitution Unit he was just setting up to map a series of constitutional changes was also going to address the purpose of these reforms and their interconnectedness, he replied that he did not have time. Similarly, despite the number and range of constitutional issues addressed by the Blair government, the approach has been piecemeal, prompting the Scottish Affairs Select Committee to conclude: 'If there is an overall blueprint showing how all the pieces fit together, none of our interviewees were aware of it.'[164] Instead, it might be seen as an unusually extensive, but still essentially pragmatic and therefore essentially British, programme of change. The fact that changes such as devolution, as Blair's preference for the term decentralisation bears witness, or the Human Rights Act seem to be seen as having but limited effects on Westminster and Whitehall furthermore suggests that, despite the potentially great and unpriced consequences of these developments, the intention of the Blair government is essentially conservative.

CONCLUSIONS

Continuity rather than change has, indeed, been the hallmark of Britain's constitutional arrangements throughout the twentieth century. Such major shifts as have occurred have tended to have an extra-territorial dimension to them; such as the 1921 Anglo-Irish Treaty and the Ireland Act of 1949, the Statute of Westminster of 1931 or the entry to the European Community in 1973. In internal arrangements there has been less dramatic change. In 1905 Balfour told Randall Davidson 'his resignation may be hereafter looked back to in history as the ending of the present Parliamentary and Constitutional position'.[165] Balfour was, however, too melodramatic. Admittedly he and Davidson were both shortly engulfed in the major political contest which culminated in the Parliament Act of 1911, but the significance of that act was arguably as much for its social as its constitutional effects. Certainly it did not effect a major adjustment of the balance of power between the two Houses, rather it merely clarified the nature of that balance.

Another of Davidson's correspondents predicted disestablishment by the end of his tenure as Archbishop of Canterbury.[166] This has not occurred, but no one could deny that there has been substantial change to the relationship between church and state in the twentieth century. The principal constitutional arrangements have remained in place, but their nature and relationships have been altered incrementally.

More substantial changes were discussed towards the end of and immediately after the Great War. These ideas, however, foundered on party-political differences, postwar austerity and the success of *Sinn Féin*, which helped to undermine the movement towards legislative devolution.

The Second World War was to have less effect on constitutional thinking. The radicalism of 1940–41 was concerned more with the failings of an appeasing and incompetent Tory elite and with inequality of sacrifice. The calls for revolution therefore from, for instance, Orwell's Searchlight series, focused more upon property and nationalisation than new constitutional forms.[167] And, despite its title, the only book in the wartime Democratic Order series (from a more orthodox position on the left), edited by Francis Williams, which looked at constitutional arrangements was Ivor Jennings' *Parliament Must Be Reformed*.[168]

This is not a sign of the ludicrous complacency of Mr Podsnap,[169] but of the primacy of property and planning in thinking on the left in the aftermath of the 1930s. However, Jennings' work or the advocacy of PR by figures on the right like Leo Amery[170] show constitutional reform continued to be discussed. Nevertheless, it has to be accepted that most constitutional thinking in Britain in the first half of the twentieth century was self-referential; though given events elsewhere it is not surprising that external models, with the exception of the United States, did not really commend themselves in these years. However, with the advent of the Attlee government, interest in constitutional reform grew again, not least in the French system of *droit administratif*. If the temperature of the constitutional-reform debate increased in the 1970s that did not mean that the issue had been entirely dormant before, though it did come to be expressed in different ways.

There also continued to be reference to overseas examples. These, however, seem to have cropped up very much on a case-by-case basis. Nor does entry to the European Community, initially at least, seem to have had much impact upon this. The interest taken in the German electoral system or in German lessons for devolution in the 1970s, for instance, would probably have occurred whether or not Britain was in the European Community, whilst other facets of the period, such as Scottish nationalism, reflected considerable hostility towards Europe.

There were, in any case, some difficulties in borrowing from European practice. Apart from in Scotland, the basis of the legal system in Britain is different. Comparators, during debates on freedom of information or Bills of Rights since the 1960s, have therefore always been, and continue to be, Commonwealth countries or the United States, rather than continental partners.[171]

Nevertheless, the growing impact of Europe upon Britain, especially since the Single European Act, has meant that there is an increasing awareness that Parliament and constitutional arrangements have to be seen in a European context. The result has been seen particularly at the regional and local level, where the tightness of Whitehall spending controls in contrast to the bidding process for European programmes has led to an increasing focus on the European pork-barrel, despite the fact that the vast majority of funds continue to come from London rather than Brussels.

Parliament has been much slower to try to establish its role in the new situation in which it finds itself. But its competence, and that of British ministers, has certainly been trammelled by European membership. This has affected both sides of the balance which Jowitt referred to. The efficiency of the British government has been reduced; in effect Britain has acquired entrenched law in the form of European law and a supreme court in the European Court of Justice. So has democratic freedom. Change in Britain's relations with Europe since 1975 has occurred without democratic sanction, and in spite of the specific promises given in the referendum of that year. And, in any case, European decision making is not directly accountable, but intergovernmental. Implementation is also by the member states. This can lead to the infamous 'gold-plating' of European directives in, for instance, the Ministry of Agriculture, Fisheries and Food. But it can also mean that there is no direct redress, either political or legal, against the source of the law. Nor is the boundary between the competences of the European Union (EU) and either the competences of the member state or the liberties of the individual citizen clear. It is on such grounds that Donald Sassoon has argued that the problem is not so much that Britain does not have a written constitution, but that the EU does not.[172]

Even if the Blair government's apparent assumption proves correct – that statute will provide a sufficient regulator of relations in a polity with the assymetrical devolution it has introduced – statute, in the form of the European Communities Act of 1972, does not seem to have succeeded in clarifying the ambit of sovereignty as far as relations between Britain and Europe are concerned. Nor do treaty arrangements.[173] The result has been the frequently sterile intraparty debate about parliamentary sovereignty, although some commentators have called for the importation of the German concept of *Kompetenz-Kompetenz* as a means of tackling such matters.[174]

To do so would mean moving towards a written constitution. Arguably a written constitution is, in any case, likely to be needed to manage devolution. It need not mark a major departure; Australia's written constitution, for instance, is essentially just a codification of Westminster principles. Whether this would restore balance to a constitution undermined by a tide of officialdom and the rise of party government, still less secure efficiency with freedom, however, is another matter. Anything which shifts competence from politics to the law is unlikely to further the latter objective. Reformers might not mind, taking the view that constitutional efficiency has rendered the British state over-mighty, but not conspicuously effective. On the other hand, the ability of Britain to effect structural reforms which have eluded, for instance, post-unification Germany, has been used to argue in the 1990s for the continuing virtue of the efficiency of the constitution.

Efficiency with freedom essentially involves a political trade-off, though one which in twentieth-century Britain has often been set by governments for their own benefits. This tendency, however, has not been corrected by political remedies and can only be unevenly tackled by legal ones. That did not matter so much at the start of the century when constitutional understandings were underpinned by widely held if partly mythic views and a generally accepted political culture founded both on Balfour's dictum and the assumption of the coincidence between liberty and Britishness,[175] comically contrasted with German petty officialdom in Jerome K. Jerome's *Three Men on the Bummel*.[176] The first was to be undermined by a proliferation of rules which commodified and relativised these understandings, whilst the latter is increasingly threatened by European and territorial developments. Efficiency with freedom rests, in contrast, upon the studied ambiguity that has been steadily if not completely squeezed out of the British constitution, although the result has not necessarily ensured greater clarity in where power resides.

NOTES

I am grateful to the Economic and Social Research Council, award number L124251002. Research on this project contributed greatly to the drafting of this piece. I am also grateful to Joe Jacob for his comments on an earlier draft.

1.   *House of Lords Debates*, 5th ser., vol. 167, col. 336, 17 May 1950.
2.   See, for instance, John Patten, *Political Culture, Conservatism and Rolling*

Constitutional Change, (London: Conservative Political Centre, 1991), p. 9.

3. See, for instance, *The Times*, 9 March 1956.

4. *House of Lords Debates*, 5th ser., vol. 302, col. 1053, 18 June 1969.

5. See, for instance, Ian Harden and Norman Lewis, *The Noble Lie: The British Constitution and the Rule of Law* (London: Hutchinson Education, 1986).

6. Reference, for instance, might be made to the habitual culling of constitutional principles from authorities like Anson and Dicey for guidance on contemporary problems by officers such as the Treasury Solicitor.

7. Quoted in *The House of Lords: A Handbook for Liberal Speakers, Writers and Workers* (London: Liberal Publications Department, 1910), p. 86.

8. See Peter Catterall and Chris Brady, 'Cabinet Committees in British Governance', *Public Policy and Administration*, 13, 4 (1998), pp. 67–84; Peter Catterall, 'How Imperial was the Committee of Imperial Defence?', paper given at the 'Dominion Concept' conference, University of Warwick, July 1998.

9. For a twentieth-century expression of this, see Lord Morris in *Pickin* v. *British Railways Board* [1974] AC765, at 789.

10. *House of Commons Debates*, 5th ser., vol. 782, col. 478, 23 April 1969.

11. C. S. Denman, *House of Commons Debates*, 5th ser., vol. 374, col. 884, 7 October 1941.

12. F. A. Johnson, *Defence by Committee: The British Committee of Imperial Defence 1885–1959* (London: Oxford University Press, 1960), p. 44; Public Record Office, London (henceforward PRO): CAB 21/472, Notes for the Lord President of the Council in connection with his speech in the Commons debate on 22 May 1935.

13. See the discussion in Ian Harden, 'The Constitution and its Discontents', *British Journal of Political Science*, 21, 4 (1991), pp. 502 ff; P. McAuslan and J. F. McEldowney (eds), *Law, Legitimacy and the Constitution*, (London: Sweet & Maxwell, 1985), p. 8.

14. Though this is itself based on statute, the Coronation Oath Act 1688.

15. PRO: PREM 1/208, The Coronation of King George VI and Queen Elizabeth, 12th May 1937: Memoranda and Correspondence 1936–1937, p. 27.

16. PRO: PREM 1/171, H. G. Vincent to J. Ramsay MacDonald, 23 January 1935.

17. See Peter Hennessy, *The Hidden Wiring: Unearthing the British Constitution* (London: Victor Gollancz, 1995), pp. 49–72.

18. *House of Commons Debates*, 5th ser., vol. 16, col. 1429, 14 April 1910.

19. Walter Bagehot, *The English Constitution* (London: Fontana, 1963 [first published 1867]), p. 68.

20. Leo Amery, *The Future of Parliament* (no place or publisher given, c. 1944), pp. 4–5.

21. Quoted in John D. Fair, *British Interparty Conferences: A Study of the Procedure of Conciliation in British Politics 1867–1921* (Oxford: Clarendon, 1980), p. 275.

22. Leo Amery, *Thoughts on the Constitution* (London: Oxford University Press, 1947), p. 70.

23. Writing to Balfour he argued: 'I think a democratic government should be the strongest government from a military and imperial point of view in the world, for it has the people behind it. Our misfortune is that we live under a system originally contrived to check the excesses of Kings and Ministers, and which meddles far too much in the Executive of the country', cited in *Liberty in the Modern State* (London: Conservative Political Centre, 1957), p. 34. See also C. S. Emden, 'The Mandate in the Nineteenth Century', *Parliamentary Affairs*, 11 (1958), pp. 260–72.

24. See in particular, Logie Barrow and Ian Bullock, *Democracy and the British Labour Movement 1880–1914* (Cambridge: Cambridge University Press, 1996).

25. Clement Attlee, 'Guild v. Municipal Socialism', *Socialist Review*, 21 (1923), pp. 213–8.

26. However, J. A. Hobson was still advocating a House of Industry in the early 1930s.

27. See Philip Williamson, *National Crisis and National Government: British Politics, the Economy and Empire 1926–32* (Cambridge: Cambridge University Press, 1992), pp. 37ff.

28. John Strachey and C. E. M. Joad, 'Parliamentary Reform: The New Party's Proposals', *Political Quarterly*, 2 (1931), pp. 319–36; *Problems of a Socialist Government* (London, Socialist League, 1933).

29. See Jim Tomlinson, 'The Labour Government and the Trade Unions 1945–51', in Nick Tiratsoo (ed.), *The Attlee Years* (London: Pinter, 1991), p. 98.

30. See Peter Catterall, 'The Free Churches and the Labour Party in England and Wales 1918–1939', unpublished London PhD thesis, 1989, pp. 93ff.

31. Herbert Morrison, 'The State and Industry' in *Can Planning Be Democratic?* (London: Routledge, 1944), pp. 1–23. See also Viscount Hall, 'We can have adequate safeguards for the liberty of the individual if they coincide with the safeguarding of the standards of the people', *House of Lords Debates*, 5th ser., vol. 167, col. 1104, 27 June 1950.

32. Lord Winster, *House of Lords Debates*, 5th ser., vol. 167, col. 1094, 27 June 1950.

33. As W. S. Gilbert put it in *Iolanthe:*
    When in that House MPs divide
    If they've a brain and cerebellum too
    They have to leave that brain outside
    And vote just as their leaders tell 'em to.

34. Quoted in Vernon Bogdanor, *The People and the Party System: The Referendum and Electoral Reform in British Politics* (Cambridge: Cambridge University Press, 1981), p. 15.

35. *House of Commons Debates*, 5th ser., vol. 444, col. 89, 10 November 1947.

36. Sir Kenneth Pickthorn, ibid., cols 152–3.

37. Bogdanor, *The People and the Party System, passim.*

38. *House of Commons Debates*, 5th ser., vol. 16, col. 1448, 14 April 1910.

39. Ibid., 5th ser., vol. 447, cols 859–60, 16 February 1948.

40. *House of Lords Debates*, 5th ser., vol. 8, col. 442, 16 May 1911.

41. *House of Commons Debates*, 5th ser., vol. 25, cols 466–9, 3 May 1911.

42. Quoted in *The House of Lords: A Survey of its History and Powers* (London: Conservative Political Centre, 1947), p. 22.

43. Amery, *The Future of Parliament*, p. 6.

44. Sir Frederick Banbury, *House of Commons Debates*, 5th ser., vol. 16, col. 1275, 14 April 1910.

45. Eric Fletcher, *House of Commons Debates*, 5th ser., vol. 444, col. 120, 10 November 1947.

46. See Jeremy Mitchell and Anne Davies, *Reforming the Lords* (London: Institute for Public Policy Research, 1993), pp. 11, 68ff; Donald Shell, *The House of Lords* (Deddington: Philip Allan, 1988), pp. 18–19.

47. Mitchell and Davies, *Reforming the Lords*, pp. 20–27.

48. Lord Denham, *House of Lords Debates*, 6th ser., vol. 597, col. 863, 22 February 1999.

49. Quoted in H. Sidebotham, 'The Inefficiency of Parliament', *Political Quarterly*, 1 (1931), p. 353.

50. Quoted in *House of Commons Debates*, 5th ser., vol. 782, col. 474, 23 April 1969.
51. See Maurice Cranston, *The Right to Privacy*, Unservile State Papers 21 (London: Liberal Publications Department, c. 1975).
52. In *Malone* v. *Metropolitan Police Commissioner*, 1979.
53. Hilaire Belloc, *The Servile State* (Edinburgh: T. N. Foulis, 1912); see also Peter Wiles, 'Property and Equality' in George Watson (ed.), *The Unservile State: Essays in Liberty and Welfare* (London: Allen & Unwin, 1957), p. 100.
54. Hilaire Belloc and Ramsay MacDonald, *Socialism and the Servile State* (London: SW London Federation of the ILP, 1911), pp. 5–7.
55. See also A. V. Dicey, *Lectures on the Relation between Law and Public Opinion in England during the Nineteenth Century* (London: Macmillan, 1914), p. 258.
56. Quoted in Joseph M. Jacob, *The Republican Crown: Lawyers and the Making of the State in Twentieth Century Britain* (Aldershot: Dartmouth, 1996), p. 91.
57. See PRO: CAB 21/221.
58. Lord Haldane, *House of Lords Debates*, 5th ser., vol. 9, col. 641, 25 July 1911. See also Oonagh McDonald, *The Future of Whitehall* (London: Weidenfeld & Nicolson, 1992), p. 161.
59. *House of Lords Debates*, 5th ser., vol. 111, col. 918, 23 February 1939.
60. See PRO: CAB 21/4705; J. P. Harris, 'The "Sandys Storm" of 1938: The Politics of British Air Defence in 1938', *Historical Research*, 62 (1989), pp. 318–36.
61. Brock Millman, *Managing Domestic Dissent in First World War Britain* (London: Cass, 2000).
62. F. W. Jowett, *What is the Use of Parliament?* (London, Pass On Pamphlets 11, 1909); Letter to *Daily Telegraph*, 4 August 1960.
63. *The Internal Management of Local Authorities in England* (London: Department of the Environment, July 1991), p. 10ff. Instead, the idea of US-style directly elected mayors to provide executive leadership and accountability has increasingly appealed to both left and right; see Tony Blair, John Smith Memorial Lecture, 7 February 1996, p. 7; *Daily Telegraph* leader, 2 May 1996.
64. *Report of the Machinery of Government Committee*, Cd 9230, 1918, p. 15.
65. Sidney and Beatrice Webb, *A Constitution for the Socialist Commonwealth of Great Britain* (Cambridge: Cambridge University Press, 1975 [first published 1920]), p. 69.
66. PRO: CAB 27/72, Conference notes, 29 October 1919.
67. See Hansard Society, *Parliamentary Reform 1933–1960: A Survey of Suggested Reforms* (London: Cassell, 1961), pp. 43ff.
68. PRO: PREM 4/63/2, Sir Edward Bridges to Martin, 24 April 1942. The other reasons given were the impact on consistency in policy and on collective responsibility, the stress on the time of ministers and officials, and the risk of dividing civil servants' loyalties between ministers and committees. See also Herbert Morrison's objections given in Hansard Society, *Parliamentary Reform*, pp. 47–8.
69. Quoted in Jacob, *The Republican Crown*, p. 89.
70. Ibid., p. 140.
71. Murray Macdonald, 'The Constitutional Controversy and Federal Home Rule', *Nineteenth Century* 70, (1911), pp. 33–43.
72. Patricia Jalland, 'United Kingdom Devolution 1910–14: Political Panacea or Tactical Diversion', *English Historical Review*, 94 (1979), p. 761; D. George Boyce (ed.), *The Crisis of British Unionism: The Domestic Political Papers of the Second Earl of Selborne 1885–1922* (London: The Historians' Press, 1987), pp. 106–7; Bernard Wasserstein, *Herbert Samuel: A Political Life* (Oxford: Clarendon, 1992), p. 149.

73. Jalland, 'United Kingdom Devolution', pp. 764–85.
74. *Conference on Devolution*, Cmd 692, 1920, p. 6.
75. Vernon Bogdanor, *Devolution* (Oxford: Oxford University Press, 1979), p. 39.
76. Sir Herbert Samuel, 'Defects and Reform of Parliament', *Political Quarterly*, 2 (1931), pp. 309–12.
77. PRO: PREM 1/292.
78. Richard J. Finlay, 'National Identity in Crisis: Politicians, Intellectuals and the "End of Scotland" 1920–1939', *History*, 79, 256 (1994), pp. 242–59.
79. See W. Knox (ed.), *Scottish Labour Leaders: A Biographical Dictionary* (Edinburgh: Mainstream, 1984); H. J. Hanham, *Scottish Nationalism* (Cambridge, MA: Harvard University Press, 1969), p. 108; Kenneth O. Morgan, *Rebirth of a Nation: Wales 1880–1980* (Oxford: Oxford University Press, 1982), p. 256.
80. After the Balfour Commission in 1954 there was further administrative devolution. And the Scottish Office has proved consistently successful in bargaining for public expenditure; Peter Hennessy, *Whitehall* (London: Secker & Warburg, 1989), pp. 464–5.
81. See PRO: CAB 21/3329.
82. According to Donald Dewar, he and John Mackintosh were the only Scottish Labour MPs who supported devolution in the late 1960s; witness seminar on Devolution in Scotland in the 1970s, University of Glasgow, 10 May 1996.
83. Beatrice Webb, 'A Reform Bill for 1932', *Political Quarterly*, 2 (1931), pp. 1–22; Philip Norton, *The Constitution in Flux* (Oxford: Martin Robertson, 1982) p. 100; Hansard Society, *Parliamentary Reform*, pp. 31–2. The latter idea was again broached by Amery in the 1940s, see Amery, *The Future of Parliament*, p. 8.
84. *House of Lords Debates*, 5th ser., vol. 167, col. 1068, 27 June 1950.
85. See Philip M. Shelby, 'Civil Liberties' in Watson, *The Unservile State*, p. 62.
86. Quoted in Jacob *The Republican Crown*, p. 176.
87. Shelby 'Civil Liberties', pp. 65–6; Jacob *The Republican Crown*, pp. 181–3; Frank Stacey, *The British Ombudsman* (London: Oxford University Press, 1971), pp. 4–6.
88. Quoted in Jacob *The Republican Crown*, p. 204.
89. As was already apparent at Conservative Party conferences in the 1950s; see Jacob, *The Republican Crown*, p. 210.
90. Kate Morris, 'Race, Propaganda and Empire during the Second World War', paper presented at the Institute of Historical Research, London, 13 November 1996.
91. National Museum of Labour History, Manchester: Labour Party Archives, Commonwealth Committee minutes 1953–54.
92. PRO: CAB 21/1734, minutes, 22 March 1950. See also ibid.: draft memorandum by Colonial Secretary, 29 March 1950.
93. Anthony Lester, 'Fundamental Rights: The United Kingdom Isolated?', *Public Law*, Spring (1984), pp. 49–54.
94. *House of Commons Debates*, 5th ser., vol. 787, cols 1519–20, 22 July 1969.
95. *House of Commons Debates*, 5th ser., vol. 782, cols 474–82, 23 April 1969. The Tory peer, Lord Mancroft, drafted, but did not introduce, a Bill of Rights in 1950; see *House of Lords Debates*, 5th ser., vol. 167, cols 1083–4, 27 June 1950.
96. Anthony Lester, *Democracy and Individual Rights* (London: Fabian Society, 1968); John Macdonald, *A Bill of Rights* (London: Liberal Publications Department, 1969); Quintin Hogg, *New Charter* (London: Conservative Political Centre, 1969).

97. Baroness Gaitskell, *House of Lords Debates*, 5th ser., vol. 302, col. 1054, 18 June 1969. For similar Labour attitudes at the time of the 1987 Gardner Human Rights Bill, see Cosmo Graham and Tony Prosser (eds), *Waiving the Rules: The Constitution under Thatcherism* (Milton Keynes: Open University Press, 1988), pp. 184–5.
98. *House of Lords Debates*, 5th ser., vol. 302, col. 1027, 18 June 1969.
99. Sir Alec Douglas-Home (Chairman), *Scotland's Government* (Edinburgh: Scottish Constitutional Committee, 1970), p. 10. See also Martin Burch and Ian Holliday, 'The Conservative Party and Constitutional Reform: The Case of Devolution', *Parliamentary Affairs*, 45, 3 (1992), pp. 386–98.
100. Lord Hailsham, *The Dilemma of Democracy: Diagnosis and Prescription* (London: Collins, 1978).
101. See, for instance, PRO: CAB 128/36, CC(62) 73rd Conclusions, minute 8, 6 December 1962; Richard Wilding, 'The Fulton Report in Retrospect', *Contemporary Record*, 9, 2 (1995), pp. 394–408.
102. Geoffrey Howe, *Conflict of Loyalty* (London: Macmillan, 1994), pp. 622–3.
103. For a critique of Howard, see Robert Alexander, *The Voice of the People: A Constitution for Tomorrow* (London: Weidenfeld & Nicolson, 1997).
104. See, for instance, *Bromley LB* v. *GLC* [1982] All ER 129; *R* v. *Greenwich LB ex parte Governors of the John Ball Primary School* [1990] Family Law Reports at 469; *R* v. *South Glamorgan Appeal Committee ex parte Evans*, 10 May 1984.
105. Lord Salisbury, *House of Lords Debates*, 5th ser., vol. 167, col. 366, 17 May 1950.
106. See Noreen Branson, *Poplarism 1919–1925: George Lansbury and the Councillors' Revolt* (London: Lawrence & Wishart, 1979).
107. See, for instance, Blair, 'John Smith Memorial Lecture', pp. 2, 4–5, 7.
108. Simon Jenkins, 'Two Cheers for the New Mayor', *Evening Standard*, 26 March 1998.
109. William Hague, speech to Conservative local government conference, 20 February 1999.
110. Devolution in Scotland in the 1970s witness seminar.
111. *Royal Commission on the Constitution 1969–1973*, Vol. I, Cmnd 5460, 1973, pp. 159–60.
112. Margo von Romberg and Jenny Robinson (eds), *Scottish Self-Government* (Edinburgh: Scottish Liberal Party, 1982), p. 6.
113. *Monitor: The Constitution Unit Bulletin*, 1 (September 1997), p. 4.
114. *Here We Stand: Proposals for Modernising Britain's Democracy*, Federal White Paper 6, Liberal Democrats, September 1993, p. 11.
115. Jo Grimond, 'The Reform of Parliament' in Watson, *The Unservile State*, p. 31.
116. Interview with Lord Holme of Cheltenham, 1 July 1996.
117. Conservative Action for Electoral Reform pamphlets and papers, papers of the 2nd Viscount Caldecote, Box 35 (privately held), by kind permission of Lord Caldecote.
118. Holme interview.
119. Richard Holme, *A Democracy Which Works* (London: Parliamentary Democracy Trust, 1977).
120. Holme interview.
121. See Simon Burgess, 'The Political Parties' in Peter Catterall (ed.), *Contemporary Britain: An Annual Review 1994* (London: ICBH, 1994), pp. 41–2.
122. Lord Jenkins of Hillhead (Chairman), *Report of the Independent Commission in the Voting System*, Cm 4090, 1998.
123. Interview with Peter Jay, 29 October 1994; Ann Taylor MP at Charter 88 seminar, 14 May 1996. See also Douglas Wass's Harry Street Memorial

Lecture, 'Checks and Balances in Public Policy-Making', April 1987, British Library of Political and Economic Science, London (henceforward BLPES): CRC 3/3.

124. Stacey, *The British Ombudsman*, pp. 7ff.

125. John Garrett, *Westminster: Does Parliament Work?* (London: Victor Gollancz, 1992), pp. 71–2, 131–47.

126. See Mitchell and Davies, *Reforming the Lords*, p. 2.

127. Samuel H. Beer, 'Reform of the British Constitution: An American View', *Political Quarterly*, 64 (1993), p. 205. See also James E. Cronin, 'Power, Secrecy and the British Constitution: Vetting Samuel Beer's *Treasury Control*', *Twentieth Century British History*, 3, 1 (1992), pp. 59–75; William Waldegrave, *House of Commons Debates*, 6th ser., vol. 219, col. 603, 19 February 1993.

128. David Wilkinson in Terence Daintith (ed.) *Constitutional Implications of Executive Self-Regulation: The New Administrative Law* (London: Institute of Advanced Legal Studies, 1997), pp. 61–2.

129. PRO: CAB 21/3004, Simon to Butler, 1 June 1956.

130. Quoted in Jacob, *The Republican Crown*, p. 363.

131. Quoted in *House of Commons Debates*, 5th ser., vol. 998, col. 514, 6 February 1981.

132. PRO: CAB 134/422, Steering Committee on International Organisations, working party on freedom of information, note by secretaries, 26 April 1947, p. 4.

133. Quoted in *House of Commons Debates*, 6th ser., vol. 55, col. 739, 6 March 1984.

134. Ann Rogers, *Secrecy and Power in the British State: A History of the Official Secrets Act* (London: Pluto Press, 1997), p. 108.

135. See Graham and Prosser, *Waiving the Rules*, pp. 176–7; McDonald, *The Future of Whitehall*, p. 168. These measures include the Data Protection Act 1984, the Local Government (Access to Information) Act 1985, the Access to Personal Files Act 1987, the Access to Medical Records Act 1988, the Education Reform Act 1988, the Access to Health Records Act 1990, the Environmental Protection Act 1990 and the Environmental Regulations 1992.

136. McDonald, *The Future of Whitehall*, pp. 168–9; Mark Fisher, *House of Commons Debates*, 6th ser., vol. 219, col. 585, 19 February 1993.

137. *House of Commons Debates*, 6th ser., vol. 228, col. 1125, 15 July 1993.

138. Terence Daintith, 'Legal Control of Administrative Action: Constraints on Performance' in Daintith, pp. 8, 14–15.

139. *House of Commons Debates*, 6th ser., vol. 219, col. 620, 19 February 1993.

140. Quoted in Norton, *The Constitution in Flux*, p. 145.

141. *Here We Stand*, p. 41.

142. Not that the Colonial Office experience has been used to good effect in Britain's own constitutional arrangements. For instance, no old Colonial Office hands were used in Harold Wilson's Constitution Unit set up in 1974. One former CO official apparently later said he could have wept when he saw the inadequacies of the devolution legislation of the 1970s; interview with Robert Hazell, 5 July 1996.

143. *Labour's Colonial Policy: I The Plural Society* (London: Labour Party, 1956), pp. 33ff.

144. PRO: CAB 104/180, C. R. Attlee to W. S. Churchill, 22 July 1942.

145. Quoted in *The House of Lords* (1910), p. 86.

146. *House of Lords Debates*, 5th ser., vol. 302, cols 1031–2, 18 June 1969.

147. Institute for Public Policy Research, *A Written Constitution for the United Kingdom* (London: Mansell, 1993), p. 7.

148. J. A. Pease, *House of Commons Debates*, 5th ser., vol. 16, col. 1454, 14 April 1910.

149. Norton, *The Constitution in Flux*, pp. 253–8; Garrett, *Westminster*, p. 40. After all, part of the background to the founding of the Labour Party was the need to seek parliamentary redress from the judge-made trade union case law of the 1890s. Lord Gardiner's concern that a Bill of Rights 'either contains something which is already law, or is in such general terms that it is impossible to say what effect it would have' (*House of Lords Debates*, 5th ser., vol. 302, col. 1046, 18 June 1969) meanwhile remains a source of criticism (see Beer, 'Reform of the British Constitution', pp. 203–4). Norton, indeed, argues that such general provisions would, amongst other things, undermine existing safeguards against racial abuse provided by, for instance, the Public Order Act 1936 or the Race Relations Acts; see Philip Norton, *The Constitution: The Conservative Way Forward*, (London: Conservative Political Centre, 1992), p. 8.

150. Hennessy, *The Hidden Wiring*, p. 183.

151. BLPES: CRC 1/1.

152. Lord Lloyd of Hampstead, *House of Lords Debates*, 5th ser., vol. 469, col. 179, 10 December 1985.

153. David Mayhew, 'City Bill Lacks a Sense of Fair Play', *Daily Telegraph*, 28 October 1998.

154. See Reyiza Harrison, *Good Faith in Sales* (London: Sweet & Maxwell, 1998).

155. See above, note 152.

156. Jacob, *The Republican Crown*, p. 340.

157. See Leo McKinstry, *Turning the Tide* (London: Penguin, 1997).

158. *Central Lobby*, December/January 1999, p. 1.

159. Michael Zander, *A Bill of Rights?*, 4th edn (London: Sweet & Maxwell, 1996), p. 79.

160. Roger Broad and Tim Geiger (eds), 'The 1975 British Referendum on Europe', *Contemporary British History*, 10, 3 (1996), pp. 82–105.

161. See Treasury Select Committee report, 22 December 1998.

162. Peter Riddell and Philip Webster, 'Citizen Straw Has His Eye on Reform', *The Times*, 29 December 1998.

163. By the author.

164. *The Operation of Multi-Layered Democracy*, HC 460–I, 1998.

165. Lambeth Palace Library, London: Archbishop Randall Davidson Papers, vol. 5, fol. 45, notes on a conversation with A. J. Balfour, 1 October 1905.

166. Ibid., fol. 16ff, Lord Halifax to Archbishop Davidson, 20 January 1903.

167. See John Newsinger, 'George Orwell and Searchlight: A Radical Initiative on the Home Front', *Socialist History*, 9 (1996), pp. 55–81.

168. W. Ivor Jennings, *Parliament Must Be Reformed* (London: Kegan Paul, Trench, Trubner & Co., 1941), Democratic Order series No. 8.

169. See Charles Dickens, *Our Mutual Friend* (London: Oxford University Press, 1952 [first published 1864–65]), chapter XI, especially p. 133.

170. Amery, *The Future of Parliament*, p. 7.

171. See, for example, the letter of Francesca Klug, policy adviser to Charter 88 to the *Daily Telegraph*, 3 July 1996.

172. Donald Sassoon, *Social Democracy at the Heart of Europe* (London: Institute for Public Policy Research, 1996).

173. Kenneth Baker, *The Turbulent Years: My Life in Politics* (London: Faber, 1993), pp. 439ff; Nigel Lawson, *The View from No 11: Memoirs of a Tory Radical* (London: Bantam Press, 1992), p. 894.

174. The concept of *Kompetenz-Kompetenz* deals with the respective responsibilities

of the tiers of government in the Federal Republic of Germany; Ian Harden, 'The European Union and its Influence on Constitutional Reform in the UK', paper presented to an LSE Public Service Seminar, 5 July 1996, p. 7.
175. See Paul Ward, 'Socialists and "True" Patriotism in Britain in the Late Nineteenth and Early Twentieth Centuries', *National Identities*, 1, 2 (1999), pp. 179–94.
176. Jerome K. Jerome, *Three Men on the Bummel* (Harmondsworth: Penguin, 1983 [first published 1900]), pp. 127ff.

2

The Decline and Rise of Radicalism: Political Parties and Reform in the Twentieth Century

WOLFRAM KAISER

When the sweeping victory of the Labour Party in the 1945 general election had made him redundant as a politician, the Conservative Imperialist Leo S. Amery wrote a series of lectures on the evolution of the British constitution. In the first of these he reminded his students at Oxford University of the 'sheer influence of chance and … of the momentous consequences of some trivial detail' for the political development of Britain since the French Revolution. 'Suppose', Amery suggested, 'that the murder of an Austrian archduke had not come just in time to avert civil war over Ireland?'[1]

In Amery's lecture, this intriguing question was not followed by what, from a historical perspective, could have proved a fascinating comparative analysis of the relative internal cohesion of the United Kingdom and Austria–Hungary as nation states before 1914. The reference to the murder of the Habsburg heir Franz Ferdinand in Sarajevo on 28 June 1914 was not intended to lead to a critical enquiry into the ability of the British political system before the First World War to absorb national economic and social stresses. Instead, the question was a playful, intellectual and rhetorical device that was followed by a Conservative variant of the Whig interpretation of British history, as a progression of moderate reforms 'always tending to follow the direction of its [the constitution's] inherent instincts and traditions'.[2] Amery insisted that the managerial reforms suggested in his lectures were merely intended to improve the efficiency of Cabinet government as it existed.[3]

Amery's casual mention of how explosive the Irish question was in British politics in the years before the First World War is nonetheless a useful reminder to present-day British historians of the danger in taking a too deterministic view of political reform since the late nineteenth century. Instead, it is necessary to analyse the driving forces behind the reform process in order to understand why, overall, the British political system was indeed relatively successful in adjusting to rapidly changing economic and social conditions and external circumstances until after the First World War. It is also necessary in order to explain why so few substantial reforms were implemented in the interwar period and after 1945 at a time of accelerated economic and societal change and far-reaching political and constitutional reforms in several other west European countries and in some former dominions.

Of the driving forces behind the reform process, the political parties have played a very important role in formulating and articulating reform proposals and in mediating societal pressure for change. To a large extent, the approach of the political parties to reform has been formed by public pressure and party interest, or lack thereof, in particular reform proposals. However, some of the peculiarities of the reform debate and of the reform process in Britain since the late nineteenth century are also the result of other factors. These include, in a comparative European perspective, the indirect influence of Britain's external environment on the self-perception of the British and the evolution of the reform debate, as well as the specific development of the British political parties and their party ideologies.

PUBLIC PRESSURE AND PARTY INTEREST

Extra-parliamentary pressure has often led reluctant politicians to adopt particular reform options. Such pressure was especially pronounced during the process of democratisation of the British parliamentary system until after the First World War. In this period, organised reform movements repeatedly challenged the closed and exclusive character of Westminster politics. New interests, such as those advanced by the nonconformists, the nationalist movements and the women's movements, were appeased, when they seemed to become irresistible, and were co-opted within the liberal order.[4]

Pressure for reform from without Parliament usually became linked with tactical considerations in the competition between political parties for electoral and parliamentary support. This linkage between public pressure from organised reform movements and party interest was especially important for the reform initiatives of the Asquith governments before 1914. At this time, the Liberal Party was to a large extent a coalition of reform movements, and it depended on the parliamentary support of the Irish Nationalists. Equally, the lack of public pressure or party interest in particular reforms helps to explain the absence of far-reaching reforms of the British political system after 1945. This is especially true of the conflict over a possible switch of the electoral system from simple-majority voting to some form of proportional representation (PR), which has played a significant role in the reform debate ever since the 1860s, without leading to actual reforms.

Viewed over the entire period from the 1880s to the 1990s, it is arguably the nationality conflicts within the United Kingdom as a mixed nation state and nationality state – and dynastic state – which have combined the greatest extra-parliamentary pressure for reform with the most vociferous party conflict over particular reform proposals. At the same time, the debates about territorial reform since 1885–86 also illustrate well how even very strong extra-parliamentary pressure for reform does not necessarily lead to the formation of clear-cut party interest in particular reforms. Public pressure for territorial reform on the periphery has never resulted in an obvious party advantage for any party in the country as a whole, thus complicating and delaying the reform process. This is true both for the debate about Irish home rule before 1914 and for the debate about devolution to Scotland and Wales since the 1970s.

The Irish question had of course played a major role in British politics during the nineteenth century, but mostly as an economic, social and religious issue, most importantly over the potato famine of 1845–49 and the repeal of the Corn Laws of 1846 as well as over disestablishment. As a national question, it only became the dominant and politically most divisive domestic issue within the United Kingdom from 1885 onwards after William Gladstone's decision to support Irish home rule. At this time, Irish home rule was of course still treated in traditional terms of reform designed to accommodate popular demands for change in the status quo within the existing constitutional framework in order to avert any serious disruption to the United Kingdom as a whole.

The ensuing debate and the defeat of Irish home rule in the House of Commons in 1886 had two significant consequences for the British party system. The first was the split in Gladstonian Liberalism with the defection of many traditional Whigs as well as some Radicals like Joseph Chamberlain – a split that allowed the Tories and Unionists to become the dominant political force for nearly 20 years. The second consequence was to link the fate of the subsequent Liberal governments until the First World War to the home rule issue and parliamentary support from Irish Nationalists. With the exception of the Parliament of 1906–10, the Liberal Party could never again muster a majority of its own in the Commons after 1886.

The domestic reform debate about Irish home rule between 1886 and 1914 illustrates very well the mixed blessing its advocacy was for the Liberals solely in terms of party competition. Even after the split of 1886, Irish home rule initially continued to be a divisive intraparty issue. Its advocacy by Gladstone created serious frictions with nonconformity which exerted a growing influence on party policy towards the end of the nineteenth century. Nonconformists supported disestablishment, including for Ireland, where it was implemented in 1869. However, many nonconformists feared that home rule would lead to the highly undesirable, increased influence of the Vatican on Irish society and politics, with adverse repercussions for Ulster Protestants; or, in the words of the Radical and Quaker, John Bright, that 'Home Rule Means Rome Rule'.[5] In addition, support for Irish home rule was also most likely, on balance, a vote loser for the Liberal Party within Britain before 1914. The evidence on the electoral impact of the home rule issue is not entirely conclusive. Yet it has been estimated that the Liberal vote from Irish immigrants in Britain was more than cancelled out by voters who switched their allegiance to the Tories because they were opposed to home rule.[6]

Thus, in terms of its electoral prospects, pressure for territorial reform from the Irish periphery of the United Kingdom provided no party advantage for the Liberals. However, the Liberal government after 1910 was dependent on the parliamentary support of the Irish Nationalists. This gave the Nationalists considerable leverage over Liberal policy on Irish home rule and all issues linked to it, such as reform of the House of Lords. The Asquith government finally pushed the Government of Ireland Bill through the Commons in 1912. This bill provided for the setting up of a bicameral Irish parliament, with Westminster remaining responsible mainly for defence, foreign and trade policy. It was rejected by the Lords and passed once more by the Commons. Its implementation was then suspended until after the end of the war.[7]

The Liberals' confrontational strategy over Irish home rule in this period was not least motivated by a desire to avoid at all costs a blockade of their wider government programme which, too, was potentially electorally damaging. By 1910, this strategic interest overrode all other possible tactical considerations, including the long-term disadvantage of a reduction of Irish seats in Westminster as a result of home rule which would make it even more difficult for the Liberals to muster a parliamentary majority. The strategic impasse reached in 1910 was thus that the Asquith government went ahead with Irish home rule in the face of stiff opposition from Conservative Unionists and despite the very real danger that its policy would not avoid civil war in Ireland and could have potentially grave consequences for the British state and parliamentary system.

Neither did the issue of 'home rule all round' provide the Liberals with a clear party advantage. It was thought at the time that devolution to Scotland and Wales could perhaps make Irish home rule more palatable for Unionists. Moreover, the Scottish Liberal Association, formed in 1881, supported Scottish home rule. There was thus an intraparty incentive for adopting this reform proposal. Yet the espousal of Scottish home rule remained a contentious issue throughout, not only in the British party, but also within Scotland. Lord Rosebery, for example, reminded his colleagues in the party leadership of the extreme tactical difficulty of reconciling the party interest in Scotland and in Britain as a whole, arguing that it was 'difficult to go far in the direction of Scottish HR without doing an infinity of harm in England, where we shall hear the cry of the "Heptarchy" again'.[8]

The Conservatives and Labour have faced similar strategic dilemmas in their policies on devolution ever since the revival of Scottish nationalism since the 1960s. The decline of unionism and the perceived danger of long-term decline of electoral support for the Conservatives in Scotland first led the Tories to adopt devolution in the Declaration of Perth of May 1968. This declaration involved a vague commitment to an elected Scottish assembly which Edward Heath hoped could bridge the widening gulf between growing support for devolution in Scotland and the unionist sentiment which was still deeply engrained in the English party.[9] As a result of the accelerated electoral decline of Scottish Conservatism in the 1980s, the Tories later came to see the defence of the constitutional status quo as the best means of retaining what minority support they still had in Scotland. They combined this strategy with the symbolic appeasement of nationalist sentiment, as in November 1996 over the transfer to Edinburgh of the Scottish coronation stone – the Stone of Scone – a potent symbol of Scottish identity.

Unlike in the years before 1914, however, Conservative support for the constitutional status quo in territorial politics was largely a tactical device used in the run-up to the 1997 general election to sustain its minority support in Scotland and Wales and to shore up English nationalism. The staunchest defenders of constitutional conservatism within the Conservative Party mostly believe that the imperial doctrines are exhausted, and that the component nations of Britain, including the English, need to reassert themselves.[10] Moreover, after the Conservatives failed to win a single seat in Scotland in 1997, an increasing number of English Tories began to reckon that – as with Irish home rule in 1912 – devolution to a Scottish parliament will result in a distinct party advantage for themselves as a result of the likely reduction in the number of Scottish seats in Westminster.

At the same time, the Labour Party as the dominant political force in Scotland since the 1970s was placed in a strategic dilemma over devolution until the 1997 referendum, broadly comparable to that faced by the Liberals over Irish home rule before 1914. By comparison with the 1970s, support for a substantial form of devolution or for independence was much more solid in Scotland. From a purely tactical point of view, it would have been very difficult for the Blair government to dishonour Labour's long-standing commitment to set up a Scottish parliament in Edinburgh without risking the party's dominant political position there and thus undermining both its ability to implement its wider government programme and its prospects of winning another absolute majority in Westminster.

On the other hand, some in the Labour Party feared that strong support for systematic devolution in accordance with the proposals of the Scottish Constitutional Convention[11] could alienate voters in England, would lead to reduced Labour representation in Westminster as a result of a reduction in the number of Scottish seats, and could still prove insufficient to stop the advance of the Scottish Nationalists. As a result, the Labour leadership began to consider the best tactical means to avoid a strategic impasse where an incoming Labour government would almost inevitably suffer electorally, either in Scotland or in England and Britain as a whole, whatever the course it followed over devolution. The decision the Labour leadership finally took in 1996 to ask two questions in the devolution referendum – one on the principle and one on the question of whether a Scottish parliament should have tax-raising powers – was seen as an attempt to reconcile the diverging interests within Scotland and to defuse the Tory 'tartan tax' argument that devolution leads inevitably to increased taxation.[12]

In contrast to reform of territorial politics, other reform issues have often involved a more clear-cut party interest. The abolition of the absolute veto of the House of Lords in 1910–11 is a case in point. By 1909, the veto power of the unelected second chamber had long since been a contentious issue, especially after the House of Lords, with its inbuilt Tory majority, rejected Irish home rule in 1893 after it had already passed the Commons. There was increased agitation in the first decade of the twentieth century for the abolition of the veto or even of the chamber itself as part of the process of democratisation of the British parliamentary system. In 1907, for example, a parliamentary motion of Labour MPs for the abolition of the House of Lords, which was not supported by the Campbell-Bannerman government, received 40 votes from Liberals, 26 from Labour and 36 from Irish Nationalists.[13]

The House of Lords eventually provided a suitable occasion for an all-out attack on its veto power, if not its continued existence, when it rejected the Finance Bill of 1909 by 350 votes to 75 on 30 November 1909, thus breaking a constitutional convention of nearly 200 years' standing that the unelected chamber would not veto budgetary measures. Moreover, the House of Lords did so over a budget which the Chancellor, David Lloyd George, had carefully styled in successive powerful public speeches as a 'People's Budget' that would create new financial scope for social reform through increased taxation for the wealthy, particularly through new land taxes.[14] Even before the actual veto, Lloyd George succeeded in transforming the budget issue into one of 'peers versus people', for example in his Limehouse speech to working-class citizens in the East End of London in July 1909.[15] He subsequently likened the Lords to 'five hundred men chosen at random from among the unemployed' in another speech at Newcastle in October 1909.[16]

The Lords' veto was followed by the general election of January 1910 which saw the Asquith government returned, albeit with the support of Labour and the Irish Nationalists. The death of King Edward VII in May 1910 then provided a sufficient incentive to attempt the reform of the House of Lords through an interparty constitutional conference, in order to avoid a destabilising polarisation over the issue.[17] Leading Conservatives like Arthur Balfour and Austen Chamberlain were now prepared to sacrifice the Lords' veto power, although they initially hoped that it could be retained for constitutional measures, particularly Irish home rule. Such a compromise, however, was inconceivable for the Asquith government, if only because it was now dependent on the parliamentary support of the Irish Nationalists. After the breakdown of the constitutional conference and another general election in

December 1910, the Lords' absolute veto was finally transformed into a suspensive veto in the Parliament Act, which came into force in August 1911. Since then, the composition and the powers of the House of Lords have been adjusted further, most importantly with the reduction of the suspensive veto from two years to one year in 1949 and the introduction of life peerages and the admission of women in 1958.[18] However, the abolition of the absolute veto sharply reduced the measure of party advantage that the Liberals and Labour could hope to obtain from further democratic reform of the House of Lords.

The issue of electoral reform, too, has traditionally been dominated by considerations of party advantage. Since the Reform Act of 1832, party support for electoral reform has largely, although not exclusively, depended on the concrete benefits and disadvantages which a particular system will provide for the party or cause it favours.[19] This includes leading Conservatives who, instead of defending the threatened constitutional status quo, have not hesitated to demand even very far-reaching electoral reform when they expected their party to benefit from it. The most striking example of sharp calculation of party advantage remains Benjamin Disraeli's successful attempt to steal a march on the Liberals with the 1867 extension of the franchise – a decision designed both to outdo his Liberal rivals in the competition for the newly-to-be-enfranchised electorate and to consolidate his leadership position within the Tory Party as a social outsider.[20]

Since the introduction of a fully democratic franchise, including women, in 1918–28, leading Conservatives have occasionally also advocated a switch from simple-majority voting to PR. Throughout the twentieth century, the main motivation for their support, which was never consistent, has been to avert what they have temporarily regarded as the spectre of long-term political dominance of the Labour Party. Balfour saw this danger in the early 1920s.[21] This fear had already been behind the proposal made during the debate about the Representation of the People Bill during 1916–17 to introduce PR for large cities only.[22] Leading Conservatives later came back to the idea of limited PR to hurt Labour. After the Conservatives had narrowly lost a by-election in the autumn of 1950, for example, Harold Macmillan thought that it was necessary for purely tactical reasons to reconsider the question of electoral reform. He argued:

> We ought to get a Liberal alliance, and to offer proportional representation in the big cities in exchange. There is a great deal

to be said, in principle, for an experiment in P.R. limited to the big cities. It could do no harm and might do good. How else are the great Socialist 'blocs' to be eaten into? It seems absurd that an immense and dangerous change like Steel nationalisation should be made effective by a majority of six … Ought we not to reconsider the old arguments against P.R. Do we want a 'strong' government, if this means a strong Socialist Government, doing things which can never be undone.[23]

Lord Hailsham later took up the argument against strong socialist government as a result of simple-majority voting in the 1970s, when the growing influence of the left within the Labour Party appeared set to turn the British parliamentary system into an 'elective dictatorship'. In essence, Hailsham was arguing that a government elected on a minority of votes lacked the legitimacy to pursue radical policies that might be irreversible. To him, this was a distinct possibility which spoke for the introduction of PR.[24] Approximately 50 Conservative MPs, who organised themselves in the Conservative Action for Electoral Reform, also advocated a switch to PR.[25] However, their agitation for PR subsided soon after the Tories had won the 1979 general election, illustrating how much it had been motivated by purely tactical considerations.

The Labour Party, too, has largely treated electoral reform under the imperative of party advantage during the twentieth century. Labour supported PR until it began to do better electorally than the Liberals in the early 1920s and was able to form its first government in 1923–24. Its landslide victory in the general election of 1945 reconciled the Labour Party fully to simple-majority voting which now appeared to work to its advantage. However, it soon became clear in the general election of 1951 that the effects of simple-majority voting were unpredictable and that it was not necessarily advantageous for Labour. The Tories won more seats in this election and formed the government despite polling approximately 500,000 fewer votes than Labour.[26]

The 1970s then saw considerable interparty debate on electoral reform. In its report submitted in June 1976, the Hansard Society for Parliamentary Government, under the chairmanship of the historian Lord Blake, recommended the introduction of a variant of the German additional-member system. Three months earlier, Labour supporters of PR had founded the Labour Campaign for Electoral Reform.[27] Yet the Labour Party only began to take electoral reform more seriously in the 1980s. The creation of the Social Democratic

Party and the formation of the Alliance in 1981, the slump of the
Labour vote in the general election of 1983 and the party's slow
recovery thereafter all seemed to suggest that the system of simple-
majority voting might well allow the Conservatives to rule
permanently with minority support of around 42 per cent or even
less. However, Labour's interest in electoral reform has weakened
considerably since the revival of its electoral fortunes. After its
landslide victory in the 1997 election the Labour government formed
an electoral reform commission headed by Lord Jenkins in November
1997 and it remained committed to its promise to hold a referendum
on a concrete reform proposal. However, Blair stressed on several
occasions that he was not convinced of the advantages of PR for
Westminster elections, and it remains to be seen whether his
government will endorse electoral reform and campaign for it in a
referendum.

Of all parties, the Liberals have supported PR most consistently,
but only since they themselves became the main electoral victims of
simple-majority voting in the early 1920s. The Speaker's Conference
of 1916–17 in fact had unanimously recommended the introduction of
the single transferable vote for multi-member constituences with
more than three MPs and the alternative vote for other constituencies.
The Commons, however, rejected the proposed change by a narrow
margin in 1917, not least because Prime Minister Lloyd George
refused to endorse PR. The Asquithian Liberals officially supported
PR for the first time in their 1922 election manifesto.[28] The united
Liberal Party subsequently endorsed PR in 1924, but it failed to extract
electoral reform from Labour in the Lib–Lab pacts of 1930–31 and
1977–78.

Due to the party's evident strategic interest in PR, Liberal support
for electoral reform was never taken very seriously by the two larger
parties until the advent of the adversary-politics thesis in the 'decline'
debate in the early 1970s. According to one version of this thesis,
which Hailsham supported, the electoral system of simple-majority
voting resulted in party-political polarisation which could lead to
significant and frequent reversals in economic policy. A second
version argued that the electoral system favoured a two-party system
which contributed to the phenomenon of competitive bidding of
parties for votes. This bidding created excessive expectations among
the electorate which had to be met by manipulating the economic
cycle. The indirect consequence of simple-majority voting thus
seemed to be economic failure. The remedy advocated was the
introduction of PR to produce coalition government. This in turn

would guarantee, or so it seemed, an open and rational debate about policies and provide the necessary policy continuity.[29]

The dominant concern in the 1970s with improving macroeconomic management meant that electoral reform was temporarily treated as a substantive political issue rather than merely a partisan question of party advantage. The progressive erosion of the two-party system of the postwar period during the 1970s and 1980s strengthened this trend. The long-standing argument that the British constitution overemphasised the elective function – to produce governments with clear majorities – at the expense of the representative gained in credibility when in the general election of October 1974 the Liberal Party gained 18 per cent of the votes, but only 13 seats. Lord Avebury, the former Liberal MP Eric Lubbock, now claimed with evident satisfaction that supporters of PR were no longer treated 'as harmless and rather amusing cranks, like nudists or the eaters of nut-cutlets'.[30] The argument that the system was unfair was strengthened further when in the general election of 1983 the Alliance polled just 2 per cent fewer votes than Labour, but – due to the even regional distribution of its support – gained only 23 seats by comparison with Labour's 209.[31] Ever since, opinion polls have registered broad sympathy among the electorate with the idea of greater fairness in the operation of the electoral system. There is, however, little public pressure for reform.[32] As a result, the actual implementation of electoral reform essentially continued to depend on the short-term calculation of party advantage.

Short-term party interest has also dominated the reform debate about the use of referendums. Balfour offered in November 1910 that his party would accept a referendum on tariff reform, if the Liberals in turn agreed to a referendum on Irish home rule. However, his tactical proposal to prevent Irish home rule backfired. It merely heated up the internal strife within the Conservative Party over tariff reform versus free trade.[33] The Wilson government's use of referendums on continued European Economic Community (EEC) membership in 1975 and on devolution in 1979 were exclusively motivated by a desire to delegate responsibility for difficult political decisions which could have split an already deeply divided party even further. A possible referendum on British participation in European monetary union would also be the result of tactical considerations. Of course, it could be argued that a referendum would lend such a momentous decision greater democratic legitimacy. On this basis, the Liberal Democrats, who support British participation in monetary union, advocated the use of a referendum early on. In contrast, the late decisions of the

Conservative and Labour leaderships in favour of a referendum were evidently the result of political manoeuvring before the 1997 election.

Thus, even the selective analysis of only some of the most important reform issues shows very clearly the importance of public pressure and party interest for the reform process. As the unorthodox Conservative Ferdinand Mount has argued in his penetrating study of the British constitution:

> It is the political struggle rather than the pursuit of good Government which ultimately decides rulers and ruling classes whether or not to drive through or give in to proposals for reform; and it is the balance of forces rather than the balance of arguments which dictates which side is to prevail.[34]

Yet the pressure of reform movements and the struggle between the political parties does not suffice for an explanation of how the reform process has developed in Britain since the late nineteenth century.

THE AGE OF REFORM UNTIL 1918

In his essay *On Liberty*, published in 1859, John Stuart Mill first asserted the need for 'a party of order or stability and a party of progress or reform'. Such a combination would guarantee the progressive and peaceful adjustment of a political system to changing economic and social conditions.[35] Broadly speaking, the Liberals and the Conservatives conformed to a large extent to this idealised conception of constitutional progression during the age of reform between 1886 and 1918, which helps to explain the relative success of the process of democratisation of the British parliamentary system in this period. As Vernon Bogdanor has put it:

> The nineteenth-century constitution survived because it was able to accommodate itself to the pressures of reform. The Victorians decided to make a 'leap in the dark' and found that democracy, contrary to the fears of its critics, made both for stability and progress.[36]

In particular, the Liberals were a more internally cohesive reform party after 1885–86. Within the old coalition of Gladstonian Liberalism, the Radicals had long since formed the advance guard of political reform with their agitation against what Richard Cobden called 'feudalism': the dominant political influence of the landed aristocracy, curtailed as a result of the repeal of the Corn Laws of 1846, and their privileged role in the army and the foreign service.[37] The defection of many Whigs to the Conservatives and Unionists over Irish home rule enabled the Radicals more clearly to set the political agenda within the Liberal Party and in the country as a whole.

Towards the end of the nineteenth century the National Liberal Federation acted more and more as an umbrella group for most of the active and assertive protest and reform movements in late Victorian Britain.[38] These movements stood for clearly defined interests, and their concern with the electoral performance of the Liberals was often indirect insofar as a Liberal government helped them to advance their particular cause. It has been argued that their interests were so diverse that they gave the impression that the Liberal Party was disunited and ineffective, thus accelerating its decline and replacement by Labour as the second major party in British politics alongside the Conservatives.[39] Whatever the effects on its long-term electoral fortunes, the coalition of reform movements made the Liberals a vibrant party of ideas and productive internal debate and conflict.

This is true, for example, of Scottish home rule which was taken up with mounting clamour after 1902, especially by the Young Scots Society. In 1909, they committed themselves 'to further the National Interests of Scotland to secure for Scotland the right of self-government', and, in 1910, they organised a conference on Scottish home rule, followed by the publication of a political pamphlet, *60 Points for Home Rule*.[40] Their agitation did not bring about home rule. However, it provided an additional incentive for Labour leaders such as Keir Hardie and Ramsay MacDonald also to advocate home rule in order to avoid being outdone by the Liberals.

More generally, to reduce an explanation of Liberal policies over political reform to a question of party advantage would be highly misleading. It was not at all clear, for example, whether to advocate Irish home rule would be in the best interest of the party in terms of its electoral success and parliamentary support. Instead, through linking the national grievances of the Irish with the question of economic and social reform, this issue quickly developed a moral dimension for Gladstone and many other supporters of Irish home rule. Even electoral reform, where party advantage has undoubtedly played an important role, has always also been a matter of serious constitutional debate among members and supporters of the Liberal Party. This debate goes back at least to the publications of Thomas Hare[41] and John Stuart Mill who believed that PR would be a cure against bribery and corruption and would improve the general quality of the ruling class in Britain.

At least as important as the progressive contribution of the Liberals to reform politics was the generally constructive attitude of the Tories to reform. Unlike most of its continental counterparts before the First World War, English Conservatism, as John Barnes has put it, 'did not set its face against the possibilities of change. Rather it held with Burke that a society without the possibility of change is without the means of its conservation.'[42] British Conservatives, too, tended to subscribe to values of hierarchy, tradition and deference. They mostly shared a continued suspicion of democratic politics, and their party ideology had strong authoritarian elements in it.[43] Yet they mostly accepted constitutional change to accommodate extra-parliamentary pressures, for example over the Reform Act of 1832.[44] One reason for the generally pragmatic attitude of the Tories was their managerial orientation with its priority for retaining power and influence over supporting lost causes. According to Francis Pym, 'the party has survived by combining a strong motive for unity with a firm refusal to let ideology threaten it ... The Conservative Party has a strong instinct for power.'[45]

Of course, party behaviour until 1918 did not always conform to Mill's idealised conception of two complementary political parties. Until the 1880s, for example, there was still considerable resistance within Gladstonian Liberalism from Whigs against the extension of the franchise. Many Whigs were opposed to Disraeli's reform of 1867. Walter Bagehot, for example, in *The English Constitution*, published in 1867, freely expressed his continued distrust of 'the lower orders, the middle orders [of people], [who] are still, when tried by what is the standard of the educated "ten thousand", narrow-minded, unintelligent, incurious'.[46] Later on, the Liberals also remained divided over one key reform issue – women's suffrage. Many Liberals, including Asquith, remained opposed to women's suffrage and delayed its parliamentary progress before 1914. Their reserved attitude led the National Union of Women's Suffrage Societies to establish closer contacts with Labour leaders in 1912 who, however, were also reluctant to associate themselves too closely with the more militant sections of the women's movement.[47]

At the same time, the Conservatives could not always be relied upon to the same extent to accept political reform, especially not during the decade before 1914. This period was one of crisis of legitimacy of the political system characterised by rising political tensions, increased popular agitation and greater militancy of reform movements. Many Conservatives, including Balfour, were afraid of what they saw as the possible revolutionary consequences of the popular politics of Lloyd George and others on the political left.[48] Increased pressure for a more thorough and rapid democratisation strengthened sentiment on the political right for a Conservative counter-revolution.[49] The limits of accommodation became particularly clear over the reform of the House of Lords and Irish home rule. Some peers continued their violent protest against the abolition of their absolute veto in 1910–11 despite the threatened mass creation of Liberal peers and against the advice of their leadership.[50] More importantly, there was considerable doubt before 1914 as to the loyalty of the Conservatives to the British state and to the elected Liberal government over Irish home rule amid the possibility of an armed uprising of Ulster Protestants.

In the event, the First World War presented Britain with an external challenge which concealed these serious internal frictions. By the end of the war, the economic, social and political circumstances had changed so fundamentally that most of the reform issues, which had been so explosive before 1914, were hardly controversial any longer.

THE DECLINE OF RADICALISM, 1918–61

In the second volume of his study, *The History of England*, first published in 1848, Thomas B. Macaulay asserted in his Whig interpretation of British history that after 1688 there was 'a conviction, daily strengthened by experience, that the [means] of effecting every improvement which the constitution requires may be found within the constitution itself'.[51] After 1918, and especially after 1945, there was a conviction, strengthened by experience and shared widely among the political elite as well as the electorate, that the state of the British constitution was broadly satisfactory and that it needed only minor improvements, if any. The satisfaction with Britain's system of government reflected a decline of constitutional Radicalism until the 1950s which mainly resulted from three factors: a preoccupation with questions of economic management and social reform, the progressive marginalisation of the Radical tradition within Labour as the new main reform party, and the mental de-Europeanisation of Britain since 1914.

The political necessity of prioritising questions of economic reconstruction after 1918 and after 1945, as well as in the wake of the economic slump after 1929, created a permanent preoccupation of the British political elite with questions of economic management and social reform which to a large extent transcended party divisions. Political reform was of secondary importance only and was usually subjected to a managerial approach; that is, it was discussed in terms of improving the efficiency of macroeconomic management. The preoccupation with economic efficiency and social reform is reflected, for example, in the election manifestos of Labour and the Conservatives in the interwar and immediate postwar period. In its 1918 manifesto, Labour mentioned the Irish right to self-determination. The clear priority, however, was economic reconstruction, including the nationalisation of mines, railways, shipping, armaments and electric power, as well as the introduction of a minimum wage.[52] Subsequently, political reform was conspicuously absent from Labour's manifestos of the interwar period. In the general election of 1945 the issue of economic reconstruction once more completely dominated the manifestos and the campaign. Among the promises made by the two parties were an 'all-out housing policy' (a Conservative priority) and 'jobs for all' (Labour's clarion call).[53]

Yet it is Liberal Party policy which illustrates best the relative lack of importance of political reform issues in British politics after 1918. Having propagated the democratisation of Britain before 1914, the Liberals continued to advance particular political reforms, such as electoral reform and devolution. Nonetheless, their main contribution to the political debate in the interwar period and during the war was also in the field of economic and social policy. With the link between social reform and liberal democracy firmly established in the New Liberalism of the writings of L. T. Hobhouse, the sociologist, and J. A. Hobson, the economist, 'liberty without equality', as Hobhouse called it, now seemed to most Liberals 'a name of noble sound and squalid result'.[54] Property rights became linked ideologically to social responsibility, and the state had to help secure, in modern language, not only equality of rights, but also of opportunities. It was the Liberals' changing attitude to the role of the state that made possible the *Yellow Book* of 1928, written by John Maynard Keynes and Hubert Henderson, which advocated, among other policies, deficit spending to 'conquer unemployment', as the Liberal election manifesto of 1929 promised.[55]

The preoccupation with economic management and social reform in Britain was accentuated by the decline, even before 1914, of Radicalism and the 'strong view' of democracy in the British Labour movement.[56] According to this view, which descended from a long-held British and European tradition of radical democracy, political reform had to go beyond universal suffrage and representative government to include, for example, the substitution of the House of Lords with referendums. This was a reform proposal that outside the Labour movement was also supported by Hobhouse after 1907 and by many other Liberal Radicals.

However, the managerial approach to socialism increasingly dominated Labour thinking on the state and further political reform. The state and its institutions came to be seen as a useful tool in the hands of an enlightened avant-garde of experts, such as professional politicians, civil servants and other specialists, to whom the active and initiatory role in politics was essentially confined. The acceptance by Labour of the political system as it existed after 1918 'tended gradually to turn into identification of that system as "representative government" and of representative government as democracy'.[57] Labour aspirations to 'popular government' became ever more muted.[58]

The decline of constitutional Radicalism within Labour is also reflected in the ideological preoccupation with what Herbert Morrison called 'centralised management in private hands' which he blamed, for example, for the rise of National Socialism in Germany. According to Morrison, 'the peril to-day' was 'the over-Mighty Subject'. It was the dangerous subjects that had to be controlled by a patriarchical state through economic and social reform.[59] The experience of coalition government during the war, followed by the election victory of 1945, finally reconciled the Labour Party completely with the strong state of Britain's traditional constitutional arrangements, as it discovered just how much they facilitated the implementation of the party's far-reaching programme of economic and social reform, including nationalisation.

The third factor behind the decline of constitutional Radicalism was the almost complete absence of external stimuli for political reform. Before 1914, the political-reform debate in Britain had been influenced by a strong comparative European perspective which had its roots in the intellectual and political argument over the French Revolution. Towards the end of the nineteenth century, reforms in continental European countries increasingly served as a mirror for the analysis of the state of political reform in Britain. For example, comparisons were sometimes drawn in the debate about Irish home rule with the Austro-Hungarian *Ausgleich* of 1867 which placated Hungarian nationalism. European comparisons also influenced the electoral-reform debate. Germany, for example, had no parliamentary government, but, unlike Britain, it did have universal manhood suffrage after 1871. In a more general sense, the united Germany with its thriving industrial economy was increasingly taken as a model in the late nineteenth and early twentieth centuries, for example over the reform of the British university system and over the question of social reform. The debate about the vote for women, too, was highly internationalised, as became clear, for example, at the Chicago Columbian world exhibition of 1893 where women from all over Europe and North America debated their future role in rapidly changing societies.[60]

Once the most important political reforms had been implemented by 1918, however, it became clear that the experience of the First World War was not conducive to the continued comparative debate of the British political system, and most certainly not to comparisons with the former enemy states. Such comparisons now seemed either defeatist or outright absurd. In a debate about electoral reform in the House of Commons in 1923, for example, the Conservative MP R. W. Barnett ridiculed the drawing of European comparisons when he asked ironically, if there was 'no lesson to be learnt from Lithuania? How do they elect their borough councils in Yugoslavia and alderman in Lapland?'[61] The effect of the First World War to de-Europeanise the reform debate was strengthened by the experience of the pronounced instability of the political systems of the other large European countries, particularly of Germany in the 1920s and of France in the 1930s, and by the rise of communism and fascism on the continent. As a result, the ideology of British singularism once more developed into a major theme of British politics, a theme that is crucial, for example, to understanding the mental reserve of the British elite towards the integration efforts in western Europe after 1945.

In essence, the idea of British singularism was equally typical of Conservative and Labour thinking on political reform. For the Tories, the idea of British singularism was instrumental in the political struggle against Labour which they accused, in the words of Stanley Baldwin, of adhering to un-British 'imported ideologies'.[62] The political left, Baldwin argued, were 'filling their bellies with the east wind of German Socialism and Russian Communism and French Syndicalism' when it should be clear that 'the power of managing our own affairs in our own way is the greatest gift of Englishmen'.[63] At a more sophisticated level of analysis, Amery argued after 1945 against a political system with horizontal and vertical divisions of power and with detailed constitutional checks and balances which to him was incompatible with British traditions. It also seemed obvious that:

Such a system of government, not in and with Parliament, but by Parliament, is bound, by its very nature, to be weak and unstable, subject to the continual shifting and reshuffling of coalition ministries and to the influence of personal ambitions. Face to face with the growing need of the age for more governmental action and more definite leadership, it has almost everywhere broken down. The rise of dictatorships and of one-party Governments has been the almost inevitable consequence of the ineffectiveness of constitutions which reproduced the outward form of the British constitution without that spirit of strong and stable government.[64]

In view of the rise of totalitarian government on the continent, the Labour Party, too, increasingly distanced itself from 'imported ideologies'. Marxism became stigmatised by the majority of the Labour Party as an alien ideology which George Orwell dubbed in his book, *The Lion and the Unicorn*, published in 1941, 'a German theory interpreted by Russians and unsuccessfully transplanted to England', and in which 'there was nothing that really touched the heart of the English people'.[65] Instead, Orwell recommended that the Labour Party should continue to develop a specifically English socialism. When it came to political reform, Orwell suggested that a future postwar Labour government would 'not be doctrinaire, nor even logical … It will leave anachronisms and loose-ends everywhere, the judge in his ridiculous horsehair wig and the lion and the unicorn on the soldier's cap-buttons.'[66] Three years later, Morrison, in his Fabian thesis on economic planning, similarly advised the Labour leadership to 'keep close to the hard-headed, practical common-sense of the average British man and woman, who may not be good at political ideology in the continental manner but who know very well when a shoe pinches'.[67]

After the Second World War, it was almost taken for granted that the British political system with its centralised government and strong executive had provided the ideal institutional setting for surviving the Nazi threat. Britain's constitutional arrangements were now generally 'regarded by the British as a glorious example, to be envied by less fortunate nations, of a flexible and adaptable method of governing a modern democracy with the consent of the governed and with freedom under the law'.[68]

The British political system appeared even more superior when compared only with west European democracies after the war. During the first decade after 1945 the strength of communist parties, particularly in France and Italy, did not inspire confidence in continental political systems. In the 1950s, domestic political developments in France once more seemed to confirm the view that, among the larger west European states, Britain was the only stronghold of democratic stability. Initially, the internal crisis of the Fourth Republic, which experienced frequent changes of government, made a military *coup d'état* over the Algerian issue seem a distinct possibility. Later on, the extensive executive powers of the Fifth Republic constitution of 1958 seemed to many, not just in Britain, to transfer semi-dictatorial powers to the new French President Charles de Gaulle.

The development of the Federal Republic of Germany was also followed in Britain with pronounced scepticism after its creation in 1949. The domestic situation initially seemed stable, so long as Chancellor Konrad Adenauer was in political control. In the 1950s, however, the dominant view among the British political elite was that a return to some form of authoritarian rule could certainly not be ruled out for the post-Adenauer period – an expectation that was being reinforced by frequent reports in the British press of neo-Nazi activities in the Federal Republic.[69] The British occupation power had influenced and approved the Federal Republic's Basic Law constitution. Whatever the merits of the institutional arrangements, however, they could not be relied upon when the democratic credibility of the Germans themselves was still much in doubt so soon after the end of Nazi rule.

The generally positive view of the British system of government corresponded to a self-assured cultural self-perception, strengthened by the war experience, of the British as moderate, rational and flexible, but, if necessary, capable of decisive action.[70] This British view of themselves was strongly reinforced after the war by the widespread admiration on the European continent for Britain's role during the war and for its resilient system of government. After the humiliating experience of fascism or collaboration with the German occupation power, Britain was widely regarded in western Europe, and not only in France, as 'the classic land of democracy, the homeland of parliamentary government … of reasonable and gradual reforms, of a civilised and tolerant political life'.[71]

As a result of the mental de-Europeanisation of Britain in the interwar and the early postwar period, Britain received no significant external stimuli for a more critical inquiry into the possible need for more substantial adjustments in the British system of government to the rapidly changing economic and social conditions after the war.

This was at a time when other major west European countries experienced far-reaching changes to how they operated their political systems, including, for example, the introduction of the German Basic Law in 1949 and of the Fifth Republic constitution in France in 1958.

THE RISE OF RADICALISM SINCE 1961

Since the 1960s, British politics has seen the progressive renewed rise of constitutional Radicalism. Various key features of the British system of government, from the electoral system to its high degree of centralisation, have been questioned with increasing force. The renewed rise of Radicalism has transformed the reform debate significantly. Despite the continued importance of party advantage, which has tended to impede major reforms, it has also enhanced the prospects for further political reform at the turn of the twenty-first century. This change has taken place slowly over more than three decades. It is nonetheless possible to identify the debate within and between the political parties about British policy towards the EEC in 1960–61 as a major turning-point in the political-reform debate.[72]

At this juncture, large sections of the British political elite, not just the Liberals, became prepared to embark upon an open-ended process; not only of economic modernisation, as it was seen at the time, but also of potentially far-reaching societal and political change in a new European context beyond the immediate consequences of membership, such as the partial delegation of sovereignty and the acceptance of majority voting in certain policy areas. The issue of EEC membership implicitly raised questions about the future of the British political system, for example about its unitary nature, which was the main reason why the European debate was so heated then and why it has been so controversial ever since.

The European debate of 1960–61 also reflected the extent to which the comparative dimension was beginning to re-enter British politics, first through the comparative European discussion of the reasons for Britain's relatively disappointing economic performance since the war, with repercussions for the debates about administrative and parliamentary reform.[73] Subsequently, the European dimension also influenced the electoral-reform debate during the 1970s. In the general election of 1950 the Liberals had thought it prudent to base their case for PR on a comparison with Sweden and Switzerland which allegedly proved that PR led to political stability.[74] By the 1970s, protagonists of electoral reform would often refer to the German case where coalition government due to PR appeared to have assisted the Germans in the postwar period to establish a low-inflation, high-growth economy. On the other hand, opponents of electoral reform often drew upon the Italian case which seemed to prove that PR could easily lead to political instability with frequent changes in government – hardly an ideal framework for economic policy making.

The comparative dimension of the reform debate has been strengthened since 1973 as a result of EEC membership. Community membership has sharply accelerated the shift in the intellectual focus of the British economic and political elites towards Europe through a dramatic increase in transnational contacts within western Europe. This phenomenon also encompasses the political parties. Community membership has also had far-reaching legal and political consequences for the British constitution. It has indirectly influenced the reform debate, for example over the controversies about citizenship, sovereignty, allegiance and territorial reform, all of which have played an important role in British politics in the 1990s.

The territorial-reform debate is perhaps the most significant example of the indirect effect of EEC membership. For example, it has allowed the important change in the policy of the Scottish Nationalists from the regressive, anti-European nationalism of the 1970s to the more outward-looking and inclusive 'independence in Europe' nationalism which envisages a Scotland independent from England, but fully integrated in what is the European Union (EU) since 1993.[75] Institutionally, the concept of subsidiarity in a Europe of the Regions, which aims at decision making at the most appropriate and usually the lowest possible level, was a serious challenge to the unitary nature of the British state.[76] At the same time, the EU provides an ideal economic and constitutional framework for territorial reform. Within this framework, it is even possible to envisage that a break-up of Britain, if devolution proves economically or politically ineffective, could be managed, as in Czechoslovakia, under conditions acceptable to all sides.

Thus, the rapidly changing external environment, into which Britain is now integrated, has exerted considerable pressure for change and has provided manifold stimuli for the political-reform debate. These external stimuli have encouraged the rise of Radicalism since the 1960s, which is reflected in the changing attitudes of the political parties to more substantial reforms in the British system of government.

The Liberals, after 1945, continued their support for further political reform. They remained committed to devolution and electoral reform, and they also began to advocate the transformation of the House of Lords into an elected second chamber. Since the 1960s they have broadened their reform agenda to include, for example, the demand for a Bill of Rights. Viewed over the entire twentieth century, the Liberals have made a unique contribution to the political debate in Britain with their consistent insistence on constitutional reform in the widest sense as a necessary precondition for the modernisation of British society.[77] It is only since their electoral recovery in the late 1950s and early 1960s, however, that their reform agenda has been taken more seriously by the two larger parties. This is exemplified by the determination of the Conservative leadership, after de Gaulle's veto against British EEC entry in January 1963, not to allow the Liberals to monopolise the theme of Europe, seen at the time as representing modernity. Iain Macleod, the then Conservative Party Chairman, advised Macmillan:

> The building of a united and outward-looking Europe is felt by many of the best elements in our society, and by centre opinion generally, as the great task and adventure that faces us. To shrug it off, turn our backs on what we have been trying to do … would be politically damaging and would involve the hazard of leaving the Liberals as the only 'European' party in Britain.[78]

Similarly, the Labour Party's transformation during the 1980s as well as Tony Blair's complimentary remarks, made during 1995–96, about the Liberal Democrats' contribution to the political-reform debate, have illustrated Labour's increased responsiveness to the Liberal reform agenda. Labour has also been forced to be more responsive to the Nationalists' agenda.

In addition to these political pressures from third parties, Labour's attitude to political reform has also changed significantly since the mid-1980s as a result of the decline within the party of socialist centralism which had required a strong state and centralised economic management for a programme of nationalisation and interventionist economic and social policies. By the time of Labour's progressive social democratisation since the mid-1980s, most of its sister parties in western Europe had long since reformed themselves and their party programmes. After the experience of totalitarian rule, they had traditionally been more suspicious of a strong, centralised state. In contrast, Labour thinking on the state and political reform had been influenced for a long time by the myth of the Attlee years during which it was the strong state that had apparently made exemplary, progressive economic and social reforms possible. Only the experience of the strong state under Thatcher during the 1980s made the Labour Party more responsive to arguments about horizontal and vertical divisions of power, about checks and balances in the constitution, and about citizens' rights. Another factor behind the much greater openness of the Labour Party to the political-reform agenda is, of course, the progressive democratisation of its internal party structures.

'New Labour' appears to have discovered political reform almost in the same way that New Liberalism assimilated social reform in the decade before 1914. It is true that Blair downplayed the reform agenda before the 1997 election, in order not to deter conservative middle-class voters. However, the quick holding of the successful devolution referendums, the introduction of a version of PR for the Scottish Parliament and the Welsh Assembly and the formation of the electoral reform commission are sufficient proof that Labour attitudes to political reform have changed significantly. As Tom Nairn observed in a newspaper article as early as 1991, 'once upon a time it was believed that Chartism might bring Socialism. In fact the terminal stage of British socialism has brought the return of Chartism.'[79]

The political-reform debate has also been transformed by the Tory Radicalism of the 1980s, as reflected in Margaret Thatcher's exclamation at the 1979 Conservative Party conference that 'those who voted Conservative know the principles we stand for. We have every right to carry them out and we shall.'[80] The Tory Radicalism of Disraeli in the nineteenth century partly resulted from calculations of party advantage, particularly over the 1867 extension of the franchise. Moreover, Disraeli remained committed to preserving the image of the Conservatives as the conserving party, according to Mill's idealised conception of British politics.

In contrast, the Tory Radicalism of Thatcher and the supporters of a neo-liberal economic counter-revolution deliberately broke with this long-established tradition. Thatcher vehemently rejected the principle of moderation and gradual reform which in her view was behind Britain's relative decline and the stagnation of its society.[81] Instead, the evolving neo-liberal agenda of what came to be known as Thatcherism was supposed to have revolutionary effects on the British economy and society. The main theme of Thatcherism was the freeing of the economy, but the reforms of the 1980s also affected Britain's system of government: in the form of institutional changes at the sub-national level, for example through the abolition of the metropolitan councils, and in the form of the organisation of institutions and their administrative culture and political objectives at the national level.[82] Thatcher continued to defend key features of the British political system, such as the unitary nature of the state and the House of Lords. However, her radical rhetoric has contributed significantly to the development of a political climate in which anything can be called into question.

CONCLUSION

Political reform has been a major theme of British history since the late nineteenth century. It was the dominant political issue before 1918, and it has again played a major role in British politics since the 1960s. Domestic and external influences on the evolution of the reform debate and on the implementation of actual reforms have been mediated by the political parties who have also followed their own changing agendas.

As has been shown here, questions of party interest and party advantage have greatly influenced the attitudes of the political parties to particular reform proposals. Such considerations have tended to impede major reforms in Britain's system of government. Other significant factors include the effectiveness of interest groups in advancing a particular cause as well as the scale of external stimuli for reform, or lack thereof, as during the interwar and early postwar period. Finally, party ideology is also important for understanding the relative success of political reform until 1918 as well as the absence of more substantial reform in the interwar period and after 1945, despite rapidly changing economic and social circumstances. In particular, the specific development of 'English socialism', as Orwell called it in 1941, combined with the effect of the simple-majority voting system of marginalising the Liberals as the main party of political reform, have contributed to the inertia of the British political system during much of the twentieth century.

The 1997 election result has paved the way for a substantial reform of the British system of government, and one very important reform – devolution – was implemented shortly afterwards. At the end of the twentieth century it certainly appeared to be much more widely accepted, as Bernard Crick argued in his book, *The Reform of Parliament*, first published in 1964: 'No longer is it so easy to take for granted that somehow tradition will always … spontaneously adapt old institutions to new circumstances.' [83]

NOTES

1. Leo S. Amery, *Thoughts on the Constitution* (Oxford: Oxford University Press, 1947), p. xv.
2. Ibid., p. viii.
3. Ibid., p. x.
4. See also Andrew Gamble and Stuart Walkland, *The British Party System and Economic Policy 1945–83: Studies in Adversary Politics* (Oxford: Clarendon Press, 1984), p. 9.
5. Quoted in G. R. Searle, *The Liberal Party: Triumph and Disintegration 1886–1929* (London: Macmillan, 1992), p. 31.
6. Ibid., p. 34.
7. Roy Douglas, *The History of the Liberal Party 1895–1970* (London: Sidgwick & Jackson, 1971), p. 58.
8. Quoted in I. G. C. Hutchison, *A Political History of Scotland 1832–1924: Parties, Elections and Issues* (Edinburgh: John Donald, 1986), p. 173. See also Keith Robbins, *Nineteenth Century Britain: Integration and Diversity* (Oxford: Oxford University Press, 1995), pp. 106–8.
9. See Jim Bulpitt, *Territory and Power in the United Kingdom: An Interpretation* (Manchester: Manchester University Press, 1983), p. 174.
10. For this tendency, see J. C. D. Clark, 'The History of Britain: A Composite State in "Europe des Patries"?' in J. C. D. Clark (ed.), *Ideas and Politics in Modern Britain* (London: Macmillan, 1990), pp. 32–49. For the historical significance of the foreign economic and territorial expansion of Britain for the emergence of a British national identity, see Linda Colley, *Britons: Forging a Nation 1707–1837* (New Haven, CT: Yale University Press, 1992).
11. *Scotland Parliament: Scotland's Right. Presented to the People of Scotland by the Scottish Constitutional Convention on 30 November 1995 in the General Assembly Hall, Edinburgh,* (Edinburgh: Scottish Constitutional Convention, 1995).
12. 'Referendum Backlash for Labour', *Scotsman*, 27 June 1996.
13. Douglas, *The History of the Liberal Party*, p. 39.
14. See Bruce K. Murray, *The People's Budget 1909–10* (Oxford: Clarendon Press, 1980).
15. Douglas, *The History of the Liberal Party*, p. 44.
16. Quoted in Kenneth O. Morgan, *The Age of Lloyd George* (London: Allen & Unwin, 1971), p. 46. As a result, they were not only influential in bringing about democratic reform until 1918, but also in formulating and debating long-term reform options.
17. On the 1910 constitutional conference, see John D. Fair, *British Interparty Conferences: A Study of the Procedure of Conciliation in British Politics 1867–1921* (Oxford: Clarendon Press, 1980).
18. See Donald Shell, *The House of Lords*, 2nd edn (Hemel Hempstead: Harvester Wheatsheaf, 1992).
19. Vernon Bogdanor, 'Electoral Reform and British Politics', *Electoral Studies*, 6, 2 (1987), pp. 115–21.
20. David Judge, 'Why Reform? Parliamentary Reform since 1832: An Interpretation' in *idem* (ed.), *The Politics of Parliamentary Reform* (London: Heinemann, 1983), p. 17. See also Philip Norton and Arthur Aughey, *Conservatives and Conservatism* (London: Temple Smith, 1981).
21. Jenifer Hart, *Proportional Representation: Critics of the British Electoral System 1820–1945* (Oxford: Clarendon Press, 1992), p. 273.
22. John Ramsden, *The Age of Balfour and Baldwin 1902–1940* (London: Longman,

1978), p. 121.

23. Department of Western Manuscripts, Bodleian Library, Oxford: Harold Macmillan Diaries, 5 October 1950. On the question of a Conservative/ Liberal Pact in the early 1950s, see also Michael Kandiah 'Lord Woolton's Chairmanship of the Conservative Party 1946–1955', unpublished PhD thesis, University of Exeter, 1992.

24. Lord Hailsham, *Elective Dictatorship* (London: BBC, 1976); Lord Hailsham, *The Dilemma of Democracy: Diagnosis and Prescription* (London: Collins, 1978).

25. Hart, *Proportional Representation*, p. 280.

26. Ibid., p. 277.

27. Ibid., p. 283.

28. Michael Steed, 'The Evolution of the British Electoral System' in Samuel E. Finer (ed.), *Adversary Politics and Electoral Reform* (London: Anthony Wigram, 1975), p. 48.

29. Stuart Walkland, 'Parliamentary Reform, Party Realignment and Electoral Reform' in Judge, *The Politics of Parliamentary Reform*, pp. 37–53. For a more differentiated analysis and assessment of the impact of the voting system on economic performance, see Andrew Gamble's contribution to Gamble and Walkland, *The British Party System*.

30. *House of Lords Debates*, 5th ser., vol. 359, col. 903, 23 April 1975.

31. See also John Curtice and Michael Steed, 'Electoral Choice and the Production of Government: The Changing Operation of the Electoral System in the United Kingdom since 1955', *British Journal of Political Science*, 12 (1982), pp. 249–98.

32. John Curtice and Wolfgang Rüdig, 'Do Attitudes towards Constitutional Reform Matter?' in Hans Kastendiek and Richard Stinshoff (eds), *Changing Conceptions of Constitutional Government: Developments in British Politics and the Constitutional Debate since the 1960s*' (Bochum: Universitätsverlag Dr N. Brockmeyer, 1994), p. 175.

33. Ramsden, *The Age of Balfour and Baldwin*, p. 36.

34. Ferdinand Mount, *The British Constitution Now: Recovery or Decline?* (London: Heinemann, 1992), p. 2.

35. John Stuart Mill, *On Liberty* (Harmondsworth: Penguin, 1974 [first published 1859]), p. 110.

36. Vernon Bogdanor, *The People and the Party System: The Referendum and Electoral Reform in British Politics* (Cambridge: Cambridge University Press, 1981), p. 260.

37. Searle, *The Liberal Party*, pp. 13–15.

38. Morgan, *The Age of Lloyd George*, p. 24.

39. Searle, *The Liberal Party*, pp. 13–15.

40. Hutchison, *A Political History of Scotland*, pp. 241–2.

41. Thomas Hare, *Treatise on the Election of Representatives. Parliamentary and Municipal* (London: Longman, 1859).

42. John Barnes, 'Ideology and Faction' in Anthony Seldon and Stuart Ball (eds), *Conservative Century: The Conservative Party since 1900* (Oxford: Oxford University Press, 1994), p. 321.

43. Brian Girvin, 'The Party in Comparative and International Context' in Seldon and Ball, *Conservative Century*, p. 696. See also Brian Girvin, *The Right in the Twentieth Century: Conservatism and Democracy* (London: Pinter, 1994).

44. Girvin, 'The Party', p. 695.

45. Francis Pym, *The Politics of Consent* (London: Hamish Hamilton, 1985), p. 192.

46. Walter Bagehot, *The English Constitution* (London: Fontana Press, 1993 [first

published 1867]), p. 65.

47. Sandra Stanley Holton, *Feminism and Democracy: Women's Suffrage and Reform Politics in Britain 1900–1918* (Cambridge: Cambridge University Press, 1986), pp. 69–79.

48. Ruddock F. Mackay, *Balfour: Intellectual Statesman* (Oxford: Oxford University Press, 1985), pp. 227–39.

49. G. R. Searle, 'The "Revolt from the Right" in Edwardian England' in Paul Kennedy and Anthony Nicholls (eds), *Nationalist and Racist Movements in Britain and Germany before 1914* (Basingstoke: Macmillan, 1981), pp. 21–39. See also Frans Coetzee, *For Party or Country: Nationalism and the Dilemmas of Popular Conservatism in Edwardian England* (Oxford: Oxford University Press, 1990).

50. Peter Rowland, *The Last Liberal Governments: Vol II, Unfinished Business 1911–1914* (London: Macmillan, 1971), pp. 50–1.

51. Thomas B. Macaulay, *The History of England from the Accession of James the Second: Vol II* (London: Longman, 1861 [first published 1848]), p. 669.

52. F. W. S. Craig (ed.), *British General Election Manifestos 1918–1966* (Chichester: Political Reference Publications, 1970), pp. 5–6.

53. Ibid., pp. 87–105.

54. Leonard T. Hobhouse, *Liberalism* (London: Williams & Norgate, 1909), p. 48.

55. Searle, *The Liberal Party*, p. 158. Another major contribution was the 1942 Beveridge Report. Beveridge became a Liberal MP in 1944 and played a major part in the 1945 election campaign, although he himself lost his seat to a Conservative.

56. Logie Barrow and Ian Bullock, *Democratic Ideas and the British Labour Movement 1880–1914* (Cambridge: Cambridge University Press, 1996).

57. Ibid., p. 292.

58. Ibid., p. 301.

59. Herbert Morrison, 'Can Planning be Democratic? The State and Industry' in Herbert Morrison *et al.* (eds), *Can Planning be Democratic?* (London: Routledge, 1944), p. 12.

60. Paul Greenhalgh, *Ephemeral Vistas: The Expositions Universells, Great Exhibitions and World's Fairs 1851–1939* (Manchester: Manchester University Press, 1988), pp. 179–82.

61. *House of Commons Debates*, 5th ser., vol. 160, col. 1475, 23 February 1923.

62. Stanley Baldwin, *On England and Other Addresses* (London: Allen & Co, 1926), p. 39.

63. Ibid.

64. Amery, *Thoughts on the Constitution*, p. 18.

65. George Orwell, *The Lion and the Unicorn* (London: Penguin, 1982 [first published 1941]), pp. 102–4, 112–13.

66. Ibid.

67. Morrison, 'Can Planning be Democratic?', p. 2.

68. Anthony Lester, 'The Constitution: Decline and Renewal' in Jeffrey Jowell and Dawn Oliver (eds), *The Changing Constitution* (Oxford: Clarendon, 1985), p. 274.

69. Sabine Lee, 'Anglo-German Relations 1958–59: The Postwar Turning Point?', *Diplomacy and Statecraft*, 6, 3 (1995), pp. 787–808.

70. See Kenneth O. Morgan, 'The Second World and British Culture' in Brian Brivati and Harriet Jones (eds), *From Reconstruction to Integration: Britain and Europe since 1945* (Leicester: Leicester University Press, 1993).

71. François Crouzet, 'Problems of Communication between Britain and France

in the Nineteenth and Twentieth Centuries' in *idem* (ed.), *Britain Ascendant: Comparative Studies in Franco-British Economic History* (Cambridge: Cambridge University Press, 1990), p. 490. For perceptions of the British system of government in France, see also Clemens Wurm, 'Westminster als Modell: Parlament, Parteien und "Staatsreform" im Frankreich der Dritten und Vierten Republik' in Jürgen Kocka *et al.* (eds), *Von der Arbeiterbewegung zum modernen Sozialstaat: Festschrift für Gerhard A. Ritter* (Munich: K. G. Saur, 1994), pp. 409–28.

72. Wolfram Kaiser, *Using Europe, Abusing the Europeans: Britain and European Integration 1945–1963* (Basingstoke: Macmillan, 1996), chapter 5.

73. Wolfram Kaiser, 'The Political Reform Debate in Britain since 1945: The European Dimension', *Contemporary British History*, 12, 1 (1998), pp. 48–76.

74. 1950 Liberal manifesto in Craig, *British General Election Manifestos*.

75. See Andrew Marr, *The Battle for Scotland* (London: Penguin, 1992), pp. 191–4.

76. Andrew Scott, John Peterson and David Millar, 'Subsidiarity: A "Europe of the Regions" v. the British Constitution?', *Journal of Common Market Studies*, 32, 1 (1994), pp. 47–67.

77. Cosmo Graham and Tony Prosser, *Waiving the Rules: The Constitution under Thatcherism* (Milton Keynes: Open University Press, 1988), p. 186.

78. Quoted in John Ramsden, *The Winds of Change: Macmillan to Heath 1957–1975* (London: Longman, 1996), p. 175. Incidentally, Macleod also advised Macmillan to 'firmly discourage … the latent xenophobia and jingoism of the Parliamentary Party and in the constituencies'.

79. *Scotsman*, 4 November 1991.

80. On the intellectual roots of this development, see Richard Cockett, *Thinking the Unthinkable: Think-Tanks and the Economic Counter-Revolution 1931–1983* (London: HarperCollins, 1994).

81. See Andrew Gamble, *The Free Economy and the Strong State* (London: Macmillan, 1988).

82. See also Vernon Bogdanor, *Politics and the Constitution: Essays on British Government* (Aldershot: Ashgate, 1996), part I.

83. Bernard Crick, *The Reform of Parliament* (London: Weidenfeld & Nicolson, 1968 [first published 1964]), p. 258.

3

Constitutional Law Reform:
Inside the Motor

JOE JACOB

This chapter does two things. First, with an unusual perspective and, at least for a contemporary lawyer, over an unusually long period, it sketches the fault lines of the constitution which, under the impact of modernity, have caused it to change. Second, in the light of this discussion, it offers a brief assessment of some of the more legal aspects of the current spate of reforms: the mutation of the judiciary; the reform of civil justice; and the introduction of the Human Rights Act of 1998.

SOURCES OF CONSTITUTIONAL LAW

The apparent dominant characteristic of the British constitution is that it is unwritten. Before going further it is necessary to inject a word of caution. It is customary to talk about this British constitution or sometimes even the English constitution as if the adjective were unproblematic. Elsewhere, however, I have argued, in effect, that what exists is something of an ideological competition between a tradition-based but rather vacuous set of English arrangements and a somewhat hidden but more committed Scottish system.[1] Whatever the strength of that argument, for simplicity, here I have adopted the more common account that there is one constitution, and I have not distinguished whether it is British or English. The terms are used interchangeably.

The unwritten nature of the constitution leads some to say that it does not exist. More commonly, commentators, worrying about what it might contain, go in search of what other nations put in their written constitutions. Finer is one these. Falling into this habit of looking abroad to find out what is here, he says that there is no special device to signal 'the redundancy of "ordinary" laws to those we choose to regard as laws forming part of the constitution'. He says that the constitution[2] 'is marked by three striking features: it is indeterminate, indistinct, and unentrenched'. By 'indeterminate' he means that what is or is not part of the constitution is a matter for scholars' individual judgements. By 'unentrenched', he rightly tells us that there are no special formal requirements for enacting or amending constitutional norms. Nor, indeed, could there be when there is no official definition of what they are or how they may be found. It is this absence which leads him to describe the constitution as 'indistinct'.

The constitution, Finer tells us, 'is a rag-bag of statutes and judicial interpretations thereof, of conventions, of the Law and Custom of Parliament, of common law principle, and jurisprudence'.[3] The truth is none of this. To begin with, one may express alarm at this elevation of common-law principle and jurisprudence. The view has little resonance with the pragmatic way the law goes about its business. The common law arguably has principles, but, characteristically, their articulation is highly plastic. The role played by jurisprudence presumably depends on what the word means. Certainly, in our courts there is no correspondence with the jurisprudence of continental Europe. There, at least, the term has a technical meaning, although it is more commonly called doctrine. For reasons we shall come to, the English are not much interested in theory, legal or otherwise.[4] It is not much less odd to find statutes and their interpretation placed alongside each other. The one is logically dependent on the other – they cannot be equals. The more interesting issue is the extent to which only the judges (whom this passage assumes to be independent of something) may give authoritative interpretations. Further, having gone to the trouble of including Parliament, despite our secular age, it is strange to find the law and custom of the church wholly omitted.[5]

ROOTS OF THE CONSTITUTION

There is a more fundamental reason to doubt Finer's description. The constitution is at once more simple and more complex. Finer is too elementary as he begins by telling us:

> Constitutions are of codes of norms which aspire to regulate the allocation of powers, functions, and duties among the various agencies and officers of government and to define the relationship between these and the public.[6]

This is correct but only up to a point. We must also be told, if not what are and what are not agencies and officers of government, at least the procedures or mechanisms by which we can find out. Nor, it will be noted, does this description of a constitution say anything about relations between individual members of the public among themselves. Not all British lawyers would be happy to confine ideas of civil liberty to relations between the individual and the state. It is contrary to Dicey's notion that our liberty is part of the ordinary law.

The British constitution is simple because it works in the sense that it is not noticed. If something needs to be done differently, it gets done differently, and an academic may say that the constitution has been amended. The favoured method of change is silently, secretly and even surreptitiously. Hitherto, the British have not been impressed by the idea that they have to explain what they are doing. Hitherto, they have used the maxim 'if it works, don't fix it'. The constitution is simple because all that is required to understand it (but it is a big 'all') is a conception of the historical processes by which it has developed. This understanding may be intuitive (as it is most of the time) in which case it retains its simplicity or it may be explicit in which case the understanding is complex. In this, it is an application of the truth that good laws are not enforced. They exist when people comply rather than obey. Law in this sense is only required to deal with delinquent behaviour. For example, we know what the law of contract is, not by studying its application, but by reviewing the cases where it is alleged to have been breached. The idea creates difficulties in the field of constitutional law. By definition, because they make it, the actors in the constitution are not delinquent. As far as lawyers are concerned, finding the constitution is largely a matter of searching for the inarticulate.

Beyond this, the constitution is complex for two reasons. The first is that it pre-dates the Enlightenment; and the modern mind has the greatest difficulty in understanding anything earlier than that critical revolution in western intellectual thought. It justified Sir Maurice Amos in saying:

> To anyone familiar with the legislative apparatus of France, Germany and Italy the body of English substantive law [and the Constitution] must inevitably present, by comparison, an aspect which can best be compared to that of the Chinese language; picturesque, replete with historical and logical interest, an engaging subject for scholarship, no doubt, but profuse, intricate, frequently lacking in order and rational discipline, inconveni-

ently unbusinesslike, and not infrequently unjust, to a degree which seems barely credible.[7]

The second reason why the constitution is complex lies in its dependency on descriptions of British social history over a very long time. Associated with this, is the fact that British institutions tend to remain in place even when their utility is past. This led Bagehot to the distinction between the dignified parts of the constitution which 'excite and preserve the reverence of the population' and the efficient parts by which 'it, in fact, works and rules'.[8] There are those who say that the dignified parts are useless but they bring a force which the efficient parts can use: 'They raise the army, though they do not win the battle.'[9] In his hands, the most important of these was the monarchy.

In order then to understand the British constitution, even at the end of the second millennium, it is essential to be aware of the residues of its past. Pre-Renaissance and pre-Enlightenment ideas still direct constitutional forms as they still direct British law and indeed British culture. This is not to say the British have not moved on. It is to say that it is not possible to know where the British are without knowing where they came from. Van Caenegem, the Belgian legal historian, has tried to answer the question why, at least in matters concerning the law, there is a contrast between English pragmatism and continental principle; why, that is, the English have prided themselves on having no theory. His starting point is that, the 'explanation for differences lies in political history, rather than in the national character or something inherent in the legal system'.[10] He points out: 'In the early middle ages up to the mid-twelfth century English and continental law were recognisably Germanic and feudal in substance and in procedure.'[11] Nevertheless, he argues:

> England is the oldest unified nation-state or national monarchy in Europe, going back if not to the days of Alfred the Great, then certainly to the kings of the first half of the tenth century who reconquered the Danelaw. This Old-English state was the best administered in its time. When the national monarchies on the Continent were suffering in various degrees from the break-up of administration, which started at the end of the Carolingian period, the English monarchy built up a solid system of local government. It invented the Royal writ, imitated on the Continent, and this writ ran throughout the country. The Normans took over this solid monarchy with its nationwide

impact. They added the military element of continental feudalism.[12]

He goes on:

> Henry II, the first Plantagenet King, was the founder of a corps of royal judges, who were competent in first instance for the whole country for a limited but expanding number of actions or writs. Their substantive law was feudal custom, their procedure was based on the writs and jury.

Crucially, this happened before the re-discovery of the full text of Justinian's *Digest* in Italy at the end of the twelfth century. The basis of our law and constitutional law was formed before the reception of Justinian elsewhere in Europe and before the Renaissance and Enlightenment took hold. Making a pardonably simplified comparison with the continent, Van Caenegem says:

> Church courts … began to apply the new law from the Bolognese textbooks around 1200. Around the middle of the 13th century the kingdoms followed suit … Gradually, under the influence of the universities and following the example of the ecclesiastical courts, Roman law was transforming continental … law, with the active help of governments. But it was the universities that created the new and modern, as opposed to the archaic and feudal law; they provided the books and the men who alone could bring about this new departure on the Continent.[13]

His assessment is that:

> Roman public law was useful to the rising monarchies of the later Middle Ages … It was … anti-feudal … because its basic idea that all power derives from one central source was the antithesis of the dispersion of power over numerous centres, which was a conspicuous element of feudal society as it developed in Europe after the fall of the Frankish Empire.[14]

But of England Van Caenegem says she 'was prosperous enough to afford a relatively large body of professional central judges'.[15] He argues that although English law is in contrast to the rest of Europe, it has followed the more usual path.[16] It is based, as was Roman law itself, on judicial answers to specific problems.

Continental civilian law is curious because it bases itself on ancient text.

THE ORGANIC CONSTITUTION

Both Dicey and Hayek emphasise the organic nature of English constitutional law. Hayek argued:

> The efforts of the judge are ... part of that process of adaptation of society to circumstances by which the spontaneous order grows ... the outcome of whose efforts will be a characteristic instance of those 'products of human action but not of human design' in which the experience gained by the experimentation of generations embodies more knowledge than was possessed by anyone.[17]

And Dicey said:

> the dogma that the form of a government is a sort of spontaneous growth so closely bound up with the life of a people that we can hardly treat it as a product of human will and energy, does, though in a loose and inaccurate fashion bring into view that fact that some polities, and among them the English constitution, have not been created at one stroke, and, far from being the result of legislation, in the ordinary sense of that term, are the fruit of contests carried on in the Courts on behalf of the rights of individuals. Our constitution, in short, is a judge-made constitution, and it bears on its face all the features, good and bad, of judge-made law.[18]

In a well-known passage he suggested:[19]

> the constitution is pervaded by the rule of law on the ground that the general principles of the constitution (as for example the right to personal liberty or the right of public meeting) are with us the result of judicial decisions determining the rights of private persons in particular cases brought before the Courts.[20]

As I discuss the Human Rights Act of 1998 I shall return to this organic notion of the rule of law. For the moment, we shall stay with this method of development. It led Coke to his famous, and misunderstood, early seventeenth-century aphorism that the common law, and we can add therefore, since it is founded in law – the English constitution – is the perfection of human wisdom. And, because there has been no lasting rift in British constitutional arrangements what now exists is even more 'perfect' than in Coke's day. Against this background, this chapter assesses the contemporary endeavour to make reason of British perfection. First, however, it is necessary to note some of the larger landmarks on the road of British development.

Before, say, 1500 England was a feudal state. Nevertheless, government was a matter of estate management. People were not yet individuals. They felt themselves part of and embodied in their lord and ultimately in their King, who himself ruled by divine providence. It was the Renaissance that created individuals with differing hopes and aspirations, and which broke the feudal state throughout Europe. For whatever reason, England became a Protestant country. With only partial attention to facts, the new wealth of the late sixteenth and seventeenth centuries was attributed to the absence of Catholic priests. At the end of the seventeenth century, the King appeared to be threatening to become a Roman Catholic. There was undoubtedly revolution.[21] The new King appeared to adopt the powers of the old. But, the old could not be reinstated. The new King came to the throne by way of a contract, and with that took Britain into the modern world.[22]

From his Catholic perspective, Alexander Pope put it like this:

> But we, brave Britons, foreign laws despis'd,
> And kept unconquered, and unciviliz'd;
> Fierce for the liberties of wit, and bold,
> We still defy'd the Romans, as of old.
> Yet some there were, among the sounder few
> Of those who less presum'd, and better knew,
> Who durst assert the juster ancient cause,
> And here restor'd Wit's fundamental laws.[23]

The British had a monarchy that was limited and a parliament which represented 2 per cent of all the people. The whole business was called the Glorious Revolution.[24] Soon the judges were given a security of tenure and began to create a British notion of the separation of powers. The succession to the throne was fixed by statute. Then, when that succession failed, again in the endeavour to avoid having a Catholic monarch, the British took on a German prince who, together with his son, spoke no English. For 50 years, the English developed the machinery of government largely without reference to any monarch. What was created was corrupt and inefficient. Its inefficiency was shown in the loss of the American colonies. The corruption was blamed.[25]

INFLUENCE OF THE ENLIGHTENMENT

These constitutional developments were taking place at the same time as the Enlightenment was sweeping Europe. This is not the place to embark on a general criticism of that movement. It suffices to indicate three dominant characteristics. Only the knowable is worth knowing, and if something cannot be measured it does not exist; reasoning is to be by deduction from general principles to a particular – inductive, analogical methods being disallowed; and, individual human beings must be considered as if they are alone – the merging of one's self in others is an illegitimate metaphor.

In the sphere of constitutional law, these ideas have come to mean that constitutional practices ought to be described within the bounds set by a written text. Thus, since there is no such text, following reasoning of the Enlightenment, some reach the conclusion that the British or the English do not have a constitution. Because reasoning should be from the general to the particular, ideally the constitution should be brief but in any event it should be set in broad terms. Because of the Enlightenment's recognition of the individual self, a constitution should define the relation of individuals to the state. It is obvious that such a written text, and such a constitution, stands in contrast to the organic basis of the English method. This is not say that British practices could not be reduced to writing. Indeed, that is exactly what the American revolutionaries tried to do as they formed their constitution, with the necessary adaptations of the English ways to deal with the abolition of the monarchy and a few other perceived injustices.[26] Later developments even established that the judges would determine its meaning.[27] What such a text could not do was to recreate the spontaneous order of which Dicey and Hayek spoke, and to which the English were devoted until the election of 1997.

The beginning of the nineteenth century saw the gradual reformation of government. The Enlightenment, the growth of industry, the increase in population all played their part. What is notable about this is that these factors are all non-legal. Once more, we see that the law follows and does not lead. This is one of the less noticed characteristics of constitutional law. In other countries, the constitution tries to define political relationships: in Britain, such relationships unambiguously define the constitution. In this country, for the past several centuries fundamental questions have not had to be asked. The British just got on with changing this or that and then changing it again. Despite Bentham's Enlightenment in the early nineteenth century, the British never asked, because there was no purpose in asking, what it was all about. The British never got, because they never wanted, a rational, defined constitution, a constitution of the Enlightenment.[28]

There seems no doubt that the election of 1997 marked a turning point. It is special because for the first time a new government has proposed an extensive programme of constitutional reform in its manifesto before the election. The New Labour government is raising, if not asking, the fundamental questions, which hitherto had been dormant. Perhaps it has to. Certainly, the authority of Parliament and its members is under question. People in Britain, as elsewhere, have become cynical of politicians. British membership of the European Union probably requires the adoption of rational forms: it has rules that bind organs of the state, a proposition that is meaningless unless there is a state.[29] Accordingly, the government has embarked on an 'integrated programme for constitutional change'.[30] It is not possible here to discuss it all. I shall discuss just three interlinked issues: the mutation of the judiciary; the transformation of the role of civil litigation; and, the enactment of the Human Rights Act of 1998. It suffices here to mention the more significant of the other measures. So far, they have included a series of measures devolving power to Scotland, Wales and London. Local government in England will follow later. There is to be some sort of legislation giving access to official information, known under the very American, and un-English, name of 'freedom of information'. The procedures of the House of Commons are being reformed so that it becomes a chamber more fitted for rational debate but at the cost of the destruction of the weapons of Her Majesty's Opposition, itself another very English institution.[31] The absurdity not so much of having a second legislative chamber, but having one like our House of Lords is to be ended.[32] And there is promised reform both of the electoral system and the political parties.

MUTATION OF THE JUDICIARY[33]

In political theory, the doctrine of the separation of powers has an ancient origin. Its practical importance was recognised during the Enlightenment. As Lord Oliver (a law lord) put it in a debate in the House of Lords:

> We have no written constitution, but the concept of judicial independence, which goes back to the Act of Settlement [1701], is one with which we have all grown up. It is a concept of no very certain content and there is concern both in the judiciary and in the legal profession now that in recent years, under pressure from government, from civil servants and particularly from the Treasury, it is being more and more narrowly construed with an eye more to what is boasted to be 'value for money' than to fairness and impartiality in our system of justice.[34]

This assumes a threefold structure consisting of: the legislature, the executive and the judiciary. If we accept an analysis which accepts only two powers in the state, we can more clearly see that judges and administrators share the common purpose of ensuring that the work of the legislature is executed accurately.[35] They can differ as financial and audit sections of a large organisation are separated from its line management. They share an overall purpose and seek its achievement by playing different roles. The result is twofold. First, even if in substantive matters judges do not yet substitute their view for that of an administrator, they certainly do, on some occasions, insist that decisions shall be made using particular procedures which are not always reconcilable with the intended administrative scheme. Second, the new generation of our judges has moved from Lord Oliver's worries. This current generation has joined the Treasury in also being concerned that the courts are giving value for money.

The Lord Chancellor (who now hardly ever sits as a judge in any court) is appointed by the Prime Minister. He is the administrative head of the judiciary and a member of the Cabinet. His department is also responsible for the framework documents which govern the Next Steps Agency and the Court Service, which provides the court buildings.[36] In the present day, the confusion of his roles is at its most acute, not as is usually supposed in the matter of appointments, where recent Lord Chancellors have been exemplary. It is in the matter of the granting of resources to enable the judges to carry out their task. As an Australian judge argued:

A court in which those responsible to the Executive decide the way in which the operations of the court will be managed, the way cases will progress towards hearing, and which cases will be heard by which judge at which time, is not likely to produce the impartial strength and independence of mind which the community requires of its judges. The relationship between administrators and judges will tend to develop to one where the judges are well cared for and even prized, but are treated as senior staff who do specialised public work in the courts which the administrators run on behalf of the Executive.[37]

Lord Mackay, as Lord Chancellor, acknowledged as much. In discussing the function of the judges, he said:

[it] is to decide cases and in so doing they must be given full independence of action, free from any influence. But in order to preserve their independence the judges must have some control or influence over the administrative penumbra immediately surrounding the judicial process. If judges were not, for example, in control of the listing of cases to be heard in the courts, it might be open to an unscrupulous executive to seek to influence the outcome of cases (including those to which public authorities were a party) by ensuring that they were listed before judges thought to be sympathetic to a particular point of view, or simply by delaying the hearing of the case if that seemed to advantage the public authority concerned.[38]

As we shall see, the importance of the mythology of the independent judiciary is accentuated as the judges become more involved in what is called case management.[39] Beyond this, senior judges hold office during 'good behaviour' and can be removed only by the Queen on an address from both Houses of Parliament. The other judges may be removed for 'incapacity or misbehaviour', a far more precarious form of tenure. One difference between the two forms, is what should happen if a criminal offence is committed. Minor offences do not lead to dismissal. More serious offences such as drunken driving, in two cases separated by a couple of decades, did not lead to the dismissal of Lords Justice, where it would probably have done so as constituting misbehaviour in relation to the lesser judiciary. There is no formal control over judges who are 'rude, slow, lazy, discourteous or insensitive'[40] but, no doubt as a sign of the times, one judge resigned in 1998 after the Court of Appeal described the gap between a hearing and judgment as 'intolerable'.[41]

It is a general truth that the smaller the group, the better each of its members know each other: in particular, the better is their understanding of how and why they have acted or spoken as they have. So long as the judges were a small, tightly knit group it was likely that each of them would seek to face the outside world demonstrating a loyalty to each of the others. It was a loyalty which can usefully be called comity. There was an ethos of brotherhood. It can be argued that the common-law method itself was largely predicated on this comity. The converse of the causes of this comity is also true. In respect of the judges, although each of them will almost certainly have some acquaintance with each of the others, the large and rapid increase in their numbers has meant a weakening of their familiarity with each other. The consequent question is whether the basis of the common law is being undermined. On this basis it is useful to look at the growth in numbers of the senior judiciary. See Table 1.

TABLE 1:
GROWTH OF THE JUDICIARY[42]

	House of Lords	*Court of Appeal*	Puisne *Judges*	*Total*
1900	4	6	21	31
1910	5	6	22	33
1920	7	5	24	36
1930	6	6	26	38
1940	6	9	30	45
1950	9	9	34	52
1960	9	9	44	62
1970	10	14	67	91
1980	10	19	78	107
1990	10	27	84	121
1998	12	38	97	147

If the common law itself were largely predicated on the comity of this small, powerful group, it is unlikely the method can work in the same way without it. On this basis, comity is gradually undermined by the expansion in the judiciary. So far the dilution of comity as regards its effect on common-law method has been partly masked by the rule within the doctrine of precedent which gives priority to decisions of the House of Lords and Court of Appeal. Here, the increase is from ten in 1900 to 50 in 1998. These 50 judges continue to work almost exclusively in London and do not quite constitute a group too large to act together. Nevertheless, if they are dispersed (for example, to regional centres)[43] or their numbers increase still further, their unity will be destroyed. Then something will have to take the place of the older common-law method. Most likely, in place of the tacit understandings which until recently underpinned the legal system, this will be an inchoate understanding of 'objective' enforceable rules reinforced by a new managerial hierarchy. There seems little doubt that many of the old certainties have been cast aside in favour of the pursuit of 'justice'.

For the last hundred years, in rough terms, the proportion of judges in the Court of Appeal and House of Lords compared with those in the High Court has remained constant. Nevertheless, the overall rise in every court has tended to introduce a feeling that promotion is a desired goal. One doubts whether this was true at the beginning of the century. At that time, the Court of Appeal itself and the rank of Lord of Appeal in Ordinary[44] were relatively new (1876). Judges considered themselves (and were largely considered to be) apart and above the normal mobilities of social and career hierarchies. If promotion is now such a goal, we have not only a hierarchy of courts but also a hierarchical career judiciary. And it has been acquired with none of the formal safeguards which might maintain the independence of the judiciary. This new hierarchical career judiciary is at its most visible in the creation, without statutory authority, of designated judges of the Court of Appeal to supervise lower courts and of other designated judges in the county courts to run the trial centres which stand mid-way between the High Court and ordinary county courts.

Judicial method itself is moving from an emphasis on technique to substance, from its organic, spontaneous form to rationality, from denial of responsibility for the consequences of decisions to assertions of policy. The maxim *fiat justicia ruat coelum* (let justice be done though heaven falls)[45] is falling into disuse. When judges were grand public figures, they did nobody's bidding.[46] Now they are public servants, and have corresponding duties to what they perceive as the public. A question, not yet answered, is how far this new role is compatible with the kind of assertion of independence that hitherto has underpinned the status of the courts.

CIVIL JUSTICE

Here I must explain why consideration of the administration of justice has to be thought of as part of constitutional arrangements. It is necessary to digress because the classification offends that which is almost universally adopted – that is, the constitution is concerned with big issues; the legal system is too technical to be big. The converse analysis is simple. The legal system is the mechanism by which meaning is given to the rule of law. Without access to the courts there is no constitutional right or indeed access to any other right.[47] Most particularly, in a legal system which regards the functions of the court as including the policing of state power, the student of the constitution cannot (sensibly) avoid also being a student of the legal system. Such a student must know which rights the courts will encourage and which they will seek to avoid, and why.[48]

We are beginning to live, I have argued, in ahistorical times; that is, under a Whiggish hegemony.[49] It is a child of the Enlightenment, a world which believes it has no relevant past and no tradition. Its learning is not of experience but only of measurement. The shift is characteristic of our age, and England and its legal system are not immune. The problem of the change in judicial method is that it opens the courts to bear assertion dressed, at best, as reason: general conclusions are pronounced without examination of underlying assumptions. And these assumptions cannot be examined because the intellectual and even physical tools available to the courts lag behind the general tools of our age. As we shall see, the courts now adopt the slogans of modern management despite having technology that is half a decade out of date. Their conception of information technology is based on its capacity for information storage, retrieval communications and display, rather than its role in analysis.[50] In the pursuit of the new justice, the courts do not even try to use the disciplines of sociology, psychology or economics.

In line with this ahistorical and undisciplined approach, the civil justice reforms, now encapsulated in the Woolf Reports and the Civil Procedure Rules,[51] contain a range of contradictory themes. The system is to be reformed so that it is less concerned with the settlement of private disputes and more concerned with the legal control of government and serious wrong-doers. Private parties, particularly to small or medium-sized disputes, are encouraged to find some alternative means of settling their affairs.[52] If there is principle in this, it most closely evokes the apparent naivety of the revolutionary France of which Van Caenegem remarked, 'Many …

wanted to do away with Law altogether: all conflicts between citizens were the result of misunderstandings, and there was nothing that conciliation could not put right.'[53]

The new rules are based, so it would seem, on a similar belief in the simple goodness of citizens[54] and also on a Whiggish predilection against state power being invoked where any means can be found to avoid it. The modern, kindly creed of universal goodness is no more in accord with experience than the harsh seventeenth-century Puritan, Calvinist view of pleasure and sin. In relation to the pursuit of justice, the predilection against state power permits nothing of the cathartic effect of judicially imposed solutions, itself more likely to be of importance to private individuals than to corporations.

The court procedure is now drafted as a single code written in language fit for the layperson.[55] Old words such as 'plaintiff' are replaced with 'claimant', and 'pleadings' with 'statements of case'. Once more it is helpful to find Van Caenegem placing such attempts in their historical setting: 'It was the Cromwellian revolutionaries who wanted the law to be codified in a pocket-size book, well within the grasp of the ordinary citizen.'[56] To him, codification failed to make headway in England for several reasons: 'Codes are associated with the Puritan interlude and the regime of a minority of military and religious fanatics. They are also associated with the "enlightened despots" of the eighteenth century.'[57] They were also thought of as part of the French Revolution and as something to do with Napoleon. Since our times deny any relevant past, none of these terms – 'the Puritan interlude', 'enlightened despots of the eighteenth century' (or any other time except perhaps 1930–50, and, to the English, codes were not the problem then), 'the French Revolution', nor even 'Napoleon' – have any special meaning. Their effect on English thought can now be forgotten. The British are becoming ready to relearn the limits of legal codification.[58]

The new code of civil procedure supplemented by judicially approved Practice Directions is equipped with a non-binding glossary,[59] for all the world giving the impression that its covers contain all that is to be said. The problem the Woolf Report does not face is that the litigation that it would leave to the courts – cases involving large sums and group litigation – is, of its nature, complex. At times in Rome, only the praetors knew the law. Their lawyer heirs in modern England will still be the only ones with access to the elite knowledge of the law – how can it be otherwise in our age of specialisation? – but the pretence will be that it is democratically universal. Previously, for all their intricacy the rules of civil procedure were subject to annulment, if not by Parliament, at least by each of its Houses.[60] There was a real democratic shroud. Henceforth, the democracy will be a sham.

Probably the biggest change is the introduction of case management. The time was, and not long ago, when party control of litigation could be asserted as one of the foundational principles of the English common law.[61] Within the last ten years, however, twin problems have been discerned. First, it is said that there is too much delay in litigation and this is attributed to the parties' lawyers; and second, it is said that they fight too hard, using the complexity of the rules for their clients', and their own, advantage. The cure to these ills is that the control of litigation should be moved from these allegedly grasping lawyers into the hands of judges. It goes beyond the purpose of this chapter to complain about the destruction of independent systems of professional power.[62] It suffices here to say it is characteristic of our times.

Much has already been implemented towards a full system of judicial case management, and it is not necessary here to explain it all. Briefly, at the lower end, small claims are decided in a forum where the winner must pay for the costs of his or her own lawyer, if one is used. Many of the procedural rules, designed to achieve a fair trial, are abrogated and the procedure is in the hands of the court. The upper limit on this procedure is set at £5,000, as if, for most of the population and most disputes, that is a small figure. Above that, and up to £15,000, a fast track will be introduced. Here, the fees payable, and hence the amount of work that can be recompensed, will be fixed by rule in advance. Beyond this figure there will be a multi-track. Here, litigation will be individualised but the steps to be taken will be supervised by the court. At the appeal level, judges will monitor what is happening below, and in the guise of co-ordinating cases, give directions as to what lower courts should be doing: the Court of Appeal is to gain an additional and managerial mechanism for controlling the development of the law.

In all this, there is little historical antecedent. It amounts to a revolution to be accomplished in the space of a decade, and most of it in 1999. It is a new system of civil justice, and one, moreover, that apart from using the same personnel and some of the same words has very little to do with the old. The reforms that ended in 1876 were begun in 1834. They established a single Supreme Court, with its High Court and Court of Appeal, in place of the galaxy of superior courts of record. The county court was left alone. A new set of rules was established for the new court. These rules were intended to streamline procedure. In the context of what is now proposed three features are important. First, those new rules were a rationalisation of the measures that had been developed over the previous 40 years. Second, the law reports indicate that it took the best part of the next 30 years for the litigation determining their meaning to subside. Third, all this happened at a time when certainty in the law was considered a necessity. The current reformers seek to achieve in ten years what their predecessors did in 40 and to do it at a time when certainty and consistency are no longer highly prized. If any prediction is appropriate, it is that we are entering a period of continual change, and that those in authority will regard this as virtue not hardship.[63]

THE HUMAN RIGHTS ACT OF 1998[64]

The scheme of the Human Rights Act of 1998 seeks in effect to give legislative form to the description of the constitution proposed by A. V. Dicey. He ended his *Law of the Constitution* saying: 'the English constitution is still marked … by peculiar features [which] may be summed up in the combination of Parliamentary Sovereignty with the Rule of Law'.[65] The open-textured and flexible nature of the substantive rights the bill grants leaves them in the same hands as Dicey applauded when he spoke of our liberties being the 'result of judicial decisions determining the rights of private persons in particular cases brought before the Courts'.

By intent or otherwise, there are however two major differences between Dicey and the current legislation. The act introduces a complex system whereby the courts must strain the interpretation of legislation to bring it in line with the European Convention.[66] Where, however, that proves impossible, instead of striking down the offending statute, it proposes that the court may issue a certificate of incompatibility.[67] Thus far, Dicey is largely intact. The act then goes on to provide that, on the proposal of a minister, Parliament may by order amend primary legislation so as to avoid the incompatibility. This offends Dicey's analysis. He insisted:

> The sovereignty of Parliament is (from a legal point of view) the dominant characteristic of our political institutions … [It] means … that Parliament … has, under the English constitution, the right to make or unmake any law whatever; and further, that no person or body is recognised by the law of England as having a right to override or set aside the legislation of Parliament.[68]

Giving Parliament the power to amend legislation by order does not maintain that same sovereignty. Dicey also told us that the only way Parliament can talk is by its acts. He was quite clear that a resolution even where passed by both Houses is not an act of Parliament.[69] Not merely does it miss the royal assent, but it is not subjected to the same type and extent of debate. In particular, Members of Parliament are effectively deprived of the (theoretical) right to introduce the legislation and of the (still realistic) right to amend proposals of the executive.

The second departure from Dicey relates to the content of the rights that the act grants. To Dicey, the rule of law operated on everyone – government and subject alike. Under the act, only public authorities (whatever they might be) are bound. There are a series of interesting questions. Is there any change in substantive rules when they are written in an international instrument and are then reimported? The spontaneous order that was the British constitution is replaced by a text whose meaning is not intended to be developed as years pass. On the contrary, the meaning is intended to vary over time. The continual refining of human wisdom is replaced by pragmatic rationalism.

In terms of its content, there are four issues. First, the Human Rights Act of 1998 is often called a Bill of Rights, as if previously the British did not have one. There is of course the obvious fact that the English invented the term and put such a bill in place 100 years before the Americans. What, then, is the difference in philosophy between the seventeenth-century bill and this twentieth-century instrument? Second, why does the bill not follow Dicey and indeed the European Convention on Human Rights which it purports to 'bring home', and grant the rights it speaks about generally but instead limits them so that they are only enforceable against organs of the state?[70] Third, having answered that much, what meaning is attached to the idea that the courts are public authorities so that the possibility is created that they will be bound to use the act in interpreting the common law.[71] Why is it that, for example, the act cannot say in terms whether the judges have the power or the duty to develop a right to privacy?[72] One notes *en passant* that it is Lord Chancellor Irvine's view that:

> the courts may not act as legislators and grant new remedies for infringement of Convention rights unless the common law itself enables them to develop new rights or remedies … the true view is that the courts will be able to adapt and develop the common law by relying on existing domestic principles in the laws of trespass, nuisance, copyright, confidence and the like, to fashion a common law right to privacy.[73]

Fourth, what is the rationale of the 'human' rights movement in giving rights to corporate bodies, including commercial companies?[74]

The resolution of these issues lies in understanding the peculiar philosophy that underpins the Human Rights Act. Both the seventeenth and twentieth-century bills, like the Magna Carta before them, give statutory force to the things which were important when they were drafted. The Magna Carta, including the prohibition on the sale of justice, was concerned to limit the power of the Crown. But that charter was concerned with the rights of what it called free men, and its authors could not have conceived a world where even a majority of the population was free, or even freedom in its contemporary meaning. They wrote for a feudal society, whose economy and law was based on serfdom. Whatever we may now think of the use of the word 'men', in 1215 there was no anxiety to include women.

The seventeenth-century bill was mainly concerned with Parliament. It asserted restrictions on the royal prerogative and sought to advance the liberties of Parliament. It dealt, too, with some other rights of which the most notable are the prohibition on excessive bail and of cruel and unusual punishments. In terms which have been deformed by the Americans, it asserted the right of Protestants to bear weapons.[75] Whether there is still a need for a free parliament, is not the question. From the seventeenth to the twentieth centuries, the original Bill of Rights protected it. Now the issue does not seem to matter.[76] Parliament is no longer free and is no longer the grand inquest of the nation. Its freedom has been undermined by the growth of the disciplined mass political party (itself related to the expansions of the franchise) and the significance of its debates by the ever greater sophistication and reach of the mass media and those who brief it.[77]

The twentieth-century act deals in matters which the middle classes now find important. It is not concerned, as are several international instruments, with positive rights that might protect the underprivileged.[78] It says nothing about rights to education, to work, to social security and the rest. These matters are still to be settled by individuals making individual choices. Further, even where statute makes provision for these other things, they can be cut down by judicial interpretation of this twentieth-century act.

Despite the rhetoric of rights in the plural and despite granting the legal form, this philosophy conceives power as being of only two sorts. On the one hand, there is repressive state power controlling, regulating and sometimes menacing. On the other hand, there is economic power. Conceived in this way, human rights are intended to give economic actors the liberty to pursue wealth to the maximum of their capacity and without fear of unnecessary control by the state. This materialistic conception and limited view of power is why, under the guise of protecting human rights, the act extends them to corporations, which cannot ever be more than institutions of the legal imagination. Ultimately, then, the act is not about humanity, but about limiting state power. Its talk of human rights is more of a Whiggish smoke screen than mitigation for a harsh political philosophy which permits and requires:

> Nature in the raw,
> Red in tooth and claw.[79]

CONCLUSION

The Human Rights Act of 1998 is at one with the contemporary Whig hegemony. Some see it as a transfer of power from the legislature to the judges. It is not or, at least, not in any way that matters. The legislature itself has in a sense been depoliticised. What matters there is the application of the common sense of our age. In politics that is now determined by 'focus groups' sensing and gauging public opinion. Under the Human Rights Act, the judges will have no more to do than apply the same common sense. As Fifoot said of the previous time when they held sway, the eighteenth century, the Whigs 'offered, above all, the stability without which trade must languish … political interest was centred in personalities rather than principles'.[80]

The reforms to the system of civil justice ought to be considered as part of the same movement. The pursuit of justice between private parties is no longer considered to be an essential part of what the state is for. Indeed, even where private parties insist on using the courts, one of the new rules[81] provides that they, and the court, must have regard to ways of dealing with the case that is proportionate to the amount of money involved, its importance (to whom is not stated), its complexity and the parties' financial position. They and the court must allocate only an appropriate share of the court's resources. This language is of course meaningless, unless reinforced by the common sense of our times.

Given the existence of this common sense, the Human Rights Act and the civil-justice reforms are attempts at the creation of rational forms. At the beginning of the century the judges were grand public figures worthy of carrying the royal standard in an age when royalty, even if not popular, was at least awesome, and when royalty was indeed real majesty. Today, although the judges are important and respected public servants, the awe has gone. There are many more of them and they go about their work, doubtless, even more conscientiously but with less drama. They are still a team, but it is a team that is differently and more formally knit than in the days of old.[82] Unlike the other changes we have discussed, there is less reason to attribute all this directly to the Enlightenment. Indirectly, however, the growth in the judiciary is a consequence of the increase in litigation – both criminal and civil – which itself is to be attributed to the increasing emphasis on self, self-determination and self-reliance. These themselves are consequences of Enlightenment rationalism embedded in the Whig hegemony.

The British have a constitution in Finer's sense of a set of rules allocating the powers of the institutions of government. But they are malleable. In the days when change was slow, almost between generations, the strength of the unwritten and flexible constitution was that it preserved nothing that was transient. Its weakness is that, in the face of the Whig hegemony and modern fashion to reject anything that is remotely old, it guarantees nothing that is of lasting value.

NOTES

1. J. Jacob, *The Republican Crown: Lawyers and the Making of the State in Twentieth Century Britain* (Aldershot: Dartmouth, 1996), especially pp. 305ff. The argument is based on C. F. Arrowood (ed.), *The Powers of the Crown in Scotland, being a translation, with notes, of George Buchanan's 'De jure regni apud Scotos'* (Austin TX: University of Texas Press, 1949). My argument there adds this to an assessment of the influence of Presbyterian forms of government and their secularisation, and a judgement of the continuing influence of the origins of the Whig and Tory factions.
2. S. E. Finer, V. Bogdanor and B. Rudden, *Comparing Constitutions* (Oxford: Clarendon, 1995), p. 40.
3. Ibid., pp. 42–3.
4. Jacob, *The Republican Crown*, pp. 29, 32, 305.
5. Halsbury divides English law into two classes, common law and ecclesiastical, *Halsbury's Laws of England*, 4th edn, vol. 14 (London: Butterworths, 1993), pp. 138ff., para. 303ff.
6. Finer, *Comparing Constitutions*, p.1.
7. Sir M. Amos, 'Should We Codify the Law?', *Political Quarterly*, 4 (1933), pp. 358–9. Tastes vary. G. Williams, *The Reform of the Law* (London: Gollancz, 1951) quotes Sir James Fitzjames Stephen as saying the shape of English law is 'studiously repulsive'.

8. Walter Bagehot, *The English Constitution*, (London: Fontana, 1963 [first published 1867]), p. 61.
9. Ibid., p. 62.
10. R. C. Van Caenegem, *Judges, Legislators and Professors: Chapters in European Legal History* (Cambridge: Cambridge University Press, 1997), p. 84.
11. Ibid., pp. 114–15.
12. Ibid., pp. 93–4.
13. Ibid., p. 117. Its simplicity is pardonable despite the reception of Roman law in the ecclesiastical courts and some courts of civil jurisdiction, of which the main one was Admiralty and despite the Roman references in Glanvill and Bracton.
13. Ibid., p. 82.
14. Ibid., p. 116.
15. Ibid., p. 124.
17. F. A. Hayek, *Law, Legislation and Liberty: A New Statement of the Liberal Principles of Justice and Political Economy: Vol.1, Rules and Order* (London: University of Chicago Press, 1973), p. 119.
18. A. V. Dicey, *Lectures Introductory to the Study of the Law of the Constitution* (London: Macmillan, 1885), p. 191.
19. Ibid., p. 192.
20. A note adds 'Compare *Calvin's Case*; *Campbell* v. *Hall*; *Wilkes* v. *Wood*; *Mostyn* v. *Fabregas*.' And goes on, with more endeavour to sustain the point than accuracy, 'Parliamentary declarations of the law such as the Petition of Right and the Bill of Rights have a certain affinity to judicial decisions.'
21. F. Maitland, *The Constitutional History of England* (Cambridge: Cambridge University Press, 1908), pp. 283–4.
22. See e.g. Jacob, *The Republican Crown*, p. 313.
23. A. Pope, 'An Essay on Criticism', J. Butt (ed.), *The Poems of Alexander Pope* (London: Routledge, 1996), lines 715–22.
24. 'Glorious', because very little Protestant blood was lost.
25. Emmeline W. Cohen, *The Growth of the British Civil Service, 1780–1939* (London: Allen & Unwin, 1941).
26. K. Bradshaw and D. Pring, *Parliament and Congress* (London: Quartet Books, 1981), pp. 1–4.
27. *Marbury* v. *Maddison* (1803) 1 Cranch 103.
28. In relation to the general law, J. H. Baker, *An Introduction to English Legal History*, 2nd edn (London: Butterworths, 1979), pp. 79–82, attributes what he calls the 'End of the Common Law System' to changes in the system of pleading and the abolition of the jury and creation of the modern style of judgment.
29. In Jacob, *The Republican Crown*, pp. 252ff., I argue that the judges first recognised the state as a juridical body in order that it could be limited.
30. Lord Irvine of Lairg, The Lord Chancellor, *House of Lords Debates*, 5th ser., vol. 582, col. 1228, 3 November 1997.
31. See T. A. Hockin, 'The Roles of the Loyal Opposition in Britain's House of Commons: Three Historical Paradigms', *Parliamentary Affairs*, 25 (1971–72), pp. 50–68; W. I. Jennings, 'Technique of Opposition', *Political Quarterly*, 6 (1935), pp. 208–21. See also A. Milman, 'The House of Commons and the Obstructive Party', *Quarterly Review*, 145 (1878), pp. 231–57.
32. See the White Paper, *Modernising Parliament: Reforming the House of Lords*, Cm 4183, December 1998 and the House of Lords Bill 1999.
33. What follows is taken from J. Jacob, 'I giudici inglesi' in R. Romanelli (ed.),

Magistrati e Potere Nella Storia Europea (Bologna: il Mutino, 1997).

34. *House of Lords Debates*, 5th ser., vol. 554, col. 779, 27 April 1994.

35. T. Paine, *Rights of Man*, ed. H. Collins (Harmondsworth: Penguin, 1971), pp. 220–1.

36. The Lord Chancellor also provides the support services for the courts.

37. Quoted in Sir Francis Purchas, 'The Constitution in the Market Place', *New Law Journal*, 143, 6624 (1993), p. 1604.

38. Lord Mackay of Clashfern, 'The Lord Chancellor in the 1990s', *Current Legal Problems*, 44 (1991), p. 247.

39. See J. Jacob, 'The Bowman Report', *Modern Law Review*, 61 (1998), pp. 396–8.

40. *Guardian*, 28 September 1992. It is otherwise in, for example, Australia; see *Daily Telegraph* (Australia), 26 May 1998. And for highlights of the later proceedings, see *Daily Telegraph* (Australia), 16 June 1998; The *Australian*, 16 June 1998; *Sydney Morning Herald*, 25 June 1998; and, *Daily Telegraph* (Australia), 26 June 1998.

41. *The Times*, 14 February 1998.

42. The table is adapted from J. Jacob, 'From Privileged Crown to Interested Public', *Public Law* (1993), p. 121. The figures to 1990 are derived from the annual *Whitaker's Almanac*. 1998 is taken from the Lord Chancellor's website. They omit serving Lord Chancellors and peers who could and sometimes did sit *ex officio* in the Judicial Committee (former Lord Chancellors who were appointed as Lords of Appeal in Ordinary are however included). Other judges have been included in the court in which they usually sat. Judges on secondment are not included for that period. The number can be varied by Order in Council, Administration of Justice Act 1968, s.1(2).

43. *The Times*, 3 August 1998, p. 6 reported on plans to devolve Court of Appeal work to the regions and to Wales. And see *Sunday Times*, 9 August 1998 discussing the current cost of judges' lodgings.

44. See R. B. Stevens, *Law and Politics: The House of Lords as a Judicial Body, 1800–1976* (London: Weidenfeld & Nicolson, 1979), especially pp. 40–44.

45. In *R. v. Wilkes* (1770) 4 Burr 2527, 2561–2, 98 E.R. 327, 347, Lord Mansfield CJ said:
    > The constitution does not allow reasons of State to influence our judgments: God forbid it should! We must not regard political consequences; how formidable soever they might be: if rebellion were the certain consequence, we are bound to say '*fiat justicia ruat coelum*'.

46. See R. B. Stevens, *The Independence of the Judiciary: The View from the Lord Chancellor's Office* (Oxford: Clarendon Press, 1993), p. 4.

47. See Laws J, *R. v. Lord Chancellor, Ex parte Witham*, *The Times*, 13 March 1997.

48. Stephen Sedley, 'Improving Civil Justice', *Civil Justice Quarterly*, 9 (1990), pp. 348–52.

49. See Jacob, *The Republican Crown*, pp. 316ff. And see J. Jacob, *Doctors and Rules: A Sociology of Professional Values*, 2nd edn (New Brunswick NJ: Transaction, 1999), afterword, discussing Giambattista Vico's more complex ways of knowing.

50. Lord Justice Brooke, keynote speech to the 13th BILETA Conference, The Changing Jurisdiction, 'IT and the English and Welsh Courts: The Next Ten Years', Dublin, 28 March 1998, http://www.open.gov.uk/lcd/lcdseafr.htm. But see now *Resolving and Avoiding Disputes in the Information Age*, A Lord Chancellor's Department Consultation Paper, September 1998.

51. Lord Chancellor's Department, *General Issues Paper*, 1987; The Review Body on Civil Justice, *Final Report*, Cm. 394, 1988; The Heilbron and Hodge Report,

Civil Justice on Trial – The Case for Change, Law Society and Bar Council, 1993; Woolf, *Access to Justice – Interim Report* <Resources\ACCESSTOJUSTICE–INTERIMREPORT.doc>, 1995 Woolf, Access to Justice – final Report <Resources\Access–FinalReport.doc>, 1996; Middleton Review of Civil Justice and Legal Aid, 1997; and the Bowman Review of the Court of Appeal (Civil Division), 1998. In addition to the consultation on the *Interim Report*, there were ten or so consultation documents on various aspects of the final proposals and draft rules. The first stage of the reform was implemented in April 1999. Other parts, including changes to the Court of Appeal, changes to the legal-aid system and other methods of payments to lawyers, and changes in the rights of audience, came into operation with the commencement of the Access to Justice Bill 1999. See the Lord Chancellor's speech to the Law Society, 18 October 1997 and the White Paper, *Modernising Justice, The Government's Plans for Reforming Legal Aid and the Courts*, Cm. 4155, December 1998. On the changes generally, see J. Jacobs, *Shifting Cultures and the Resolution of Civil Disputes* (CLT, forthcoming, 2000). Further changes will follow the Bowman inquiry into the Crown Office which reported in April 2000. These will streamline the procedures for obtaining the judicial review of administrative acts and consideration of Human Rights Act cases.

The seeds of the current spate of changes were in place before the 1990s. See e.g. Sir John Donaldson, *The Litigation Letter*, April 1983.

52. Lord Justice Woolf, *Access to Justice* (1996), Interim Report, chapter 4, para. 4; Final Report, chapter 10, para. 2.
53. Van Caenegem, *Judges, Legislators and Professors*, p. 11.
54. Not subjects, Jacob, *The Republican Crown*, p. 20.
55. Woolf, Interim Report, chapter 26; Final Report, chapter 20.
56. Van Caenegem, *Judges, Legislators and Professors*, pp. 45–6.
57. Ibid., p. 49.
58. See, for example, Lord Scarman, *A Code of English Law* (Hull: University of Hull, 1966); Csaba Varga, *Codification as a Socio-Historical Phenomenon* (Budapest: Akademiai Kiado, 1991); A. S. Hartkamp (ed.), *Towards a European Civil Code* (Dordrecht: M. Nijhoff, 1994).
59. Civil Procedure Rules, Part 2.2.
60. Supreme Court Act 1981, s. 84(8).
61. Sir Jack Jacob, *The Fabric of Civil Justice* (London: Stevens & Sons, 1987), pp. 9–19.
62. See Jacob, *Doctors and Rules*.
63. See Jacob, *The Republican Crown*, especially pp. 331ff.
64. The summer 1998 issue of *Public Law* contains a series of articles on the bill by Lord Irvine, Lord Lester, Sir John Laws and M. Taggart.
65. Dicey, *The Law of the Constitution*, pp. 472–3.
66. Human Rights Act 1998, s. 3.
67. Human Rights Act 1998, s. 4.
68. Dicey, *The Law of the Constitution*, pp. 37–8.
69. Ibid., pp. 407–9.
70. Human Rights Act 1998, s. 6.
71. Human Rights Act 1998, s. 6(3).
72. The act says that, subject to some additional procedural safeguards, the court 'must have particular regard to the importance of the Convention right to freedom of expression', s. 12(4).
73. Lord Irvine of Lairg, The Lord Chancellor, Address to the Third Clifford Chance Conference on the Impact of A Bill of Rights on English Law, Friday,

28 November 1997.

74. The proposition is not exceptional. For an example of one such case see *Tinnelly & Sons Ltd* v. *The United Kingdom*, European Court of Human Rights, 10 July 1998 (62/1997/846/1052–3).

75. A society which permits the possession of weapons for self-defence, or allows private security guards, rejects the monopoly use of state power.

76. See Defamation Act 1996, amending the Bill of Rights 1689.

77. N. Jones, *Soundbites and Spin Doctors: How Politicians Manipulate the Media – and Vice Versa* (London: Cassell, 1998); Leon H. Mayhew, *The New Public: Professional Communication and the Means of Social Influence* (Cambridge: Cambridge University Press, 1997).

78. See e.g. Louis Henkin (ed.), *The International Bill of Rights: the Covenant on Civil and Political Rights* (New York: Columbia University Press, 1981); Leandro Despouy, *Human Rights and Disabled Persons* (Geneva: Centre for Human Rights, 1993).

79. See Jacob, *The Republican Crown*, pp. 319–20.

80. C. H. S. Fifoot, *Lord Mansfield* (Oxford: Clarendon Press, 1936), p. 5.

81. Civil Procedure Rules, Part 1.1, the 'Overriding Objective'.

82. In days of old the judges met on a regular and informal basis. As their numbers increased a formal Council of the Judges was established. Now, with so many, it is only a representative body.

4

House of Lords and Monarchy: British Majoritarian Democracy and the Current Reform Debate about its Pre-Democratic Institutions

ANDRÉ KAISER

In his classic analysis of stable democracies after the Second World War Arend Lijphart characterises the institutional structure of the British political system as a near-complete majoritarian democracy.[1] This type of political system concentrates as much decision-making power as possible upon a democratically elected government. All institutional structures and procedures are designed to assist majority rule: single-party cabinets; a legislature dominated by the executive; a bicameral Parliament, in which the House of Commons has greater powers than the second chamber; a virtually two-party system enforced by a plurality electoral system; a centralised, unitary state organisation; an uncodified, flexible constitution without any provision for formal constitutional review.

At the same time the British political system retains elements from former, pre-democratic times, which have survived by adapting to the processes of mass democratisation and party politicisation. These include the Crown and the upper house, essentially based on a mix of the hereditary and appointive principles. While the House of Lords has been on the constitutional-reform agenda for a century, serious debate on Britain's monarchical head of state is of recent origin and is more or less confined to academic circles. Both institutions, House of Lords and monarchy, point back to a political world which served as the basis for Montesquieu's idea of the 'identity of the division of powers and the mixed constitution'.[2] Institutional and social structures complemented each other within a political order shaped by ideas of balance, moderation and constitutional authority. Whereas John Stuart Mill still held to this view in the 1860s, Walter Bagehot decisively turned away from this 'paper description' and characterised political reality in a way which even today provides the terms for analysis of parliamentary democracies.[3] The House of Lords and the monarchy – and with them the social groups they represented – had lost their direct political influence. They had come to be 'dignified parts' of the constitution.

I have highlighted two conceptions of democracy, variations of which shape the current constitutional-reform debate: on the one hand, the idea of majoritarian democracy, in which electoral victory is interpreted as a mandate for a manifesto to be effectively transformed into policy outputs; on the other, the view that democracy is only compatible with liberty when understood as a moderate, institutionally and socially balanced political order. This is the intellectual context in which I discuss the following questions relating to reform of the House of Lords and the monarchical head of state: what proposals have been put forward since the 1960s, by whom and with what intentions, and why have most of them failed?

I will argue that failure to fundamentally alter the composition and the powers of the second chamber, as well as the enduring acceptance of a non-elected head of state, can be explained by institutional conservatism. Political actors rationally calculate the costs and benefits of changing institutional arrangements. Reform will only be brought about if the political costs of maintaining a current institutional arrangement are higher than the expected transaction costs of an alternative.[4] I will deal with the House of Lords more extensively than with the monarchy. This is because the debate on the monarchy as an institution is quite recent and has not really developed at party-political level. For the time being the parties toe the ironic line coined by *The Economist*: 'Don't mention the royals!'[5]

HOUSE OF LORDS REFORM AND THE INTERPARTY CONFERENCES OF 1948 AND 1968

Let me begin with a short sketch of the historical background of the debate on reform of the House of Lords. Although this issue had emerged from time to time in the second half of the nineteenth century, events between the landslide victory of a reform-minded Liberal government in 1906 and the outbreak of the First World War are the central starting-point for the subsequent evolution of the debate up until today. There had already developed a rudimentary 'referendal theory', according to which 'it could be right for the Lords to delay legislation about which the opinion of the nation was not clear'.[6] However, it was unclear what this meant regarding party manifestos and election results. After 1906 the Liberal majority in the House of Commons and the Tory majority in the House of Lords were set on a collision course. In 1909 the Lords blocked the Finance Bill, a challenge which the government had to take up. Two elections in 1910 were fought without an electoral resolution to the constitutional conflict. A constitutional conference between party leaders met for several months, eventually leading to the Parliament Act of 1911. It was passed only because Conservative Party leaders knew that otherwise the Lords would be swamped by a larger number of Liberal peers.

The Parliament Act removed the Lords' right of absolute veto, replacing it with a delaying power of two years. Bills certified by the Speaker of the House of Commons as money bills could be delayed only for one month. In this way the powers of the Lords were reformed but the main reason for the constitutional conflict – its composition which gave the Conservatives an inbuilt advantage – remained intact for the time being. However, the preamble to the Parliament Act of 1911 made clear that this compromise was intended only as an interim measure. It nourished expectations that the second chamber would soon be comprehensively reformed, if not wholly replaced by an elected upper house. Meanwhile, the constitutional crisis lingered. A new attempt to bring forward a home rule bill for Ireland was rejected repeatedly in the second chamber. The new Parliament Act procedure was used but when the bill finally reached the Statute Book, it had to be suspended because of the outbreak of war. What this makes clear is that the constitutional compromise had not finally resolved the problem of bicameralism in the context of British party government.

Since then the House of Lords has time and again been the subject of consultations and negotiations, as Janet Morgan has marvellously described:

> On summer evenings and winter afternoons, when they have nothing else to do, people discuss how to reform the House of Lords. Schemes are taken out of cupboards and drawers and dusted off, speeches are composed, pamphlets written, letters sent to the newspapers … Occasionally legislation is introduced; it generally fails. The frenzy dies away until the next time.[7]

The first major effort was the Bryce Report of 1918, which recommended a second chamber partly elected by MPs and partly chosen by a joint committee of both Houses in such a way as to ensure that a few hereditary peers remained as members, and a joint meeting of both Houses to resolve bicameral conflicts. It also set up the famous catalogue of four functions the Lords had to contribute to the political system: examination and revision of bills; initiation of non-controversial bills in order to save valuable time in the Commons; delay of legislation in order to enable public opinion to be adequately expressed upon it, especially on bills affecting constitutional issues; and full discussion of important national questions.[8] These recommendations were widely accepted. However, because the question of delay remained controversial, it led nowhere. Government proposals in 1922 and 1927 also did not make progress, because the opposition parties suspected Conservative self-interest in raising the legitimacy of the second chamber at a time when the party system was fundamentally changing.

Although the 1945 Labour government did not experience major confrontation over its nationalisation programme it was 'uncertain as to whether the House of Lords might become more obstructive on the prospect of an election'[9] coming closer. It introduced a bill to amend the Parliament Act of 1911 by further reducing the delaying power to approximately one year. During the passage of the bill all-party discussions made some progress before breaking down over the differences concerning the power the Lords should retain. The Parliament Act of 1949 therefore was passed under the provisions of the act of 1911. It took a further 20 years before a government tried again to find a broadly acceptable formula on the composition and powers of the second chamber.

Although the interparty conferences in 1948 and 1968 showed considerable consensus between the Labour government and the Conservative opposition, they were only slightly more successful than the debates on the Bryce Report after the First World War. On both occasions tactical considerations led the political actors to disagree at the last moment. In 1948 negotiations broke down over the timescale for the retention of certain powers by the Lords.[10] Some of the proposals, however, such as payment of expenses, the admission of women, the ability to disclaim hereditary peerages in order to remain eligible for Commons membership and – most significantly – the introduction of life peerages, were implemented by Conservative governments through the Life Peerages Act of 1958 and the Peerage Act of 1963.[11] The all-party talks of 1968 led to consensus over the reduction of the Lords' suspensive veto to six months. Moreover, the parties agreed on a two-tier scheme with voting and non-voting peers and on phasing out the hereditary principle. This was meant to result in a House of Lords completely based on the appointment principle, with the government of the day having a small majority over the opposition parties but, taking the non-aligned peers into account, no overall majority in the second chamber. The talks were suspended after a rebellion of Conservative peers led to an insignificant in substance but highly symbolic defeat of the government on the Southern Rhodesia Sanctions Order. Ironically, the Parliament Act of 1911 had simply neglected to abolish the House of Lords' power of absolute veto over delegated legislation. At the beginning of the twentieth century this had been a rather rare and unimportant part of legislative activity, but its importance increased in the subsequent decades.[12] Despite the breakdown of talks, the Labour government introduced a Parliament (No. 2) Bill based on these proposals. It was overwhelmingly accepted in the House of Lords but ran into considerable difficulties in the Commons. A negative coalition of left-wing Labour MPs and right-wing Tory MPs, led by Michael Foot and Enoch Powell respectively, made use of the more flexible standing orders which operated at the Committee of the Whole House to delay consideration of the bill's clauses until the government decided to withdraw it.[13] Although the two groups had very different opinions on the future of the second chamber, the Labour left being in favour of abolition and the Conservative right arguing for leaving things as they were, they agreed on preferring the status quo to adoption of the bill.

We can conclude from this episode that, despite considerable agreement between the parties on the phasing out of hereditary peerages and on a comprehensive reform of the powers and composition of the House of Lords, and despite acceptance of these measures by a huge majority of the peers themselves, a small minority in the Commons was able to increase the political costs for the government by absorbing limited parliamentary time in a way which at last brought about the downfall of the whole reform. The would-be reformer has to be aware that similar delaying and obstructive tactics are available to individual MPs. Contrary to the textbook version of British politics, MPs can use procedural rules either to win concessions from government or to block the legislative process. In other words, given the constraints of the parliamentary timetable MPs can occasionally act as veto players. As in 1968, the Parliamentary Labour Party today contains some MPs who are only willing to accept

complete abolition, not reform, of the second chamber. And recent reactions to reform proposals indicate that some Conservative MPs do
not accept any deviation from the constitutional status quo at all.[14]
Moreover, MPs today are clearly more inclined than in the 1960s to
vote against party lines on specific occasions.[15]

PARTY POLARISATION AND CONSTITUTIONAL POLITICS
SINCE THE 1970s

In the 1970s the all-party consensus on the desirability of changing
some features of the House of Lords was replaced by polarisation. In
1977 and 1980 Labour Party annual conferences overwhelmingly
voted for motions calling for 'total abolition'[16] of the House of Lords.
A National Executive Committee paper carried by the 1977 conference
stated:

> We believe that Labour's next Manifesto should contain a
> commitment to introduce legislation at an early stage in the new
> Parliament, and should include a passage along the following
> lines: 'Should we become the Government after the next General
> Election, we intend to abolish the House of Lords. No doubt
> given such an electoral mandate, the Lords would agree to this,
> but should they not, we would be prepared to use the Parliament
> Acts or advise the Queen to use her prerogative powers to ensure
> this. Unless something else were done, this would remove the
> Lords' complete veto on an extension of the life of a House of
> Commons beyond five years. To safeguard the electors' rights,
> therefore, we propose that such an extension should be subject to
> approval by a referendum or, in time of war, by a two-thirds
> majority of the House of Commons.[17]

Whereas Prime Minister James Callaghan successfully excluded this
proposal from the 1979 manifesto, it naturally formed part of the
notorious 'longest suicide note in history' of 1983.[18]

Labour's programmatic reorientation, energetically put in place by
Neil Kinnock in the second half of the 1980s, led to a moderation of
positions towards constitutional reform. The 1987 manifesto therefore
was silent on the second chamber. Currently the Labour Party has
returned to the reform option developed in the 1960s. Tony Blair
outlined a two-step approach to the issue in his much-publicised John
Smith Memorial Lecture.[19] In a first step, voting rights for hereditary

peers will be abolished. The second step, in a second term of office, will be the replacement of the House of Lords by a mainly elected second chamber, in which the nations and regions will be represented in a way later to be specified. This position is very similar to what the Liberal Democrats argue for.[20] Both Labour and the Liberal Democrats leave open the possibility that a certain number of non-elected peers should find a place in the new chamber, probably called 'Senate', to retain a measure of continuity and expertise available to the current House of Lords.

The development of policies in the Conservative Party has reflected that of the Labour Party. In the late 1970s, when Labour argued for abolition, leading Conservative spokesmen committed themselves to major reforms, in order to strengthen public support for the House of Lords. Lord Hailsham forcefully warned that the British political system was on the way towards an 'elective dictatorship'.[21] This catchphrase, used at the time against a Labour government which seemed to be increasingly controlled by its left wing, served as a reminder that constitutional reform would be necessary to reinforce institutional checks and balances against extreme majoritarian government. The peak of the reform mood was reached when Margaret Thatcher appointed a high-ranking party review committee under the chairmanship of Lord Home to consider the future of the second chamber. The committee favoured a mixed chamber, with two-thirds of its members elected by proportional representation (PR) and one-third appointed, to 'allow some historic continuity'.[22] The basic philosophy of the Home Report, published in early 1978, was the good old Tory principle: 'in order to conserve, reform is necessary'. With the election of the first Thatcher government, the diagnosis of elective dictatorship seemed forgotten overnight and desire for reform quickly faded. Although a special Cabinet committee considered the options for some time and Timothy Raison, at that time Junior Minister in the Home Office, announced in 1981 that the government was examining reform possibilities, no further initiatives have been made public. The 1983 Conservative manifesto simply declared:

> Labour want to abolish the House of Lords. We will ensure that it has a secure and effective future. A strong Second Chamber is a vital safeguard for democracy and contributes to good government.[23]

Before the 1997 general election Donald Shell speculated that 'the attitude of the Conservatives in opposition might quickly change as happened when the party was last out of office', and that 'scattered newspaper reports suggest that some Conservatives have recently begun to consider making a pre-emptive strike' and presenting proposals in the next Conservative manifesto.[24] He was wrong on the manifesto, but obviously right on the attitude in opposition. In the current constitutional-reform debate the Conservatives for a very long time committed themselves unwaveringly to the defence of the status quo. Before the 1997 election the former Conservative Party Chairman, Brian Mawhinney, announced that the party would use this issue as a central plank of its election campaign, as it did with regard to Scottish devolution in the 1992 campaign.[25] William Hague, the new party leader, however, in a major programmatic speech on constitutional reform to the Centre for Policy Studies has officially brought the status quo position to an end. Accusing the Labour government of 'constitutional vandalism' he also accepted that 'attempting to return the Constitution to its status quo ante would be a futile task … We will need to adopt our own programme of constitutional reform.'[26] With regard to reform of the House of Lords he declared that 'Conservatives are … open to suggestions about how membership of the Lords might be changed … and whether the hereditary principle is the right one to employ when choosing members for the House'. Although only 'reform in one step' would be acceptable in order to avoid 'a giant quango instead of a Second Chamber', the Conservative Party would be prepared to discuss Labour's proposal on the basis of 'six tests': the reformed chamber must be better at scrutinising and revising legislation; a substantial independent element must remain; the Prime Minister's powers of patronage must not be increased; members must be drawn from all parts of the United Kingdom; reform must be considered in the context of its effect for Parliament as a whole; and the supreme authority of the Commons must remain intact. Whilst in the 1997 election campaign one would note with a certain irony that just at the point when both major parties achieved a measure of consensus in the field of economic policy they strongly disagreed on constitutional reform, at the time of writing it seems that the British party system once again confirms the Downsian median voter theorem.[27]

FOUR STRATEGIC DILEMMAS FOR REFORMERS: AN EXPLANATORY
FRAMEWORK FOR INSTITUTIONAL CONSERVATISM

It is clear, then, that survival of a mainly unreformed, pre-democratic
second chamber cannot be explained by arguments that either
political actors are not willing to implement reforms or they have no
specific proposals to hand. On the contrary, as I have shown, political
actors have tried to introduce changes and have been at times
engaged in developing concrete alternatives to the status quo. How
can this seeming paradox be accounted for? My thesis is that political
actors find themselves in a strategic dilemma consisting of four major
elements.

First, as we saw above, institutional reform as a political issue is not
immune from the logic of party competition. Yet, even in a
majoritarian environment such as the British political system, it has
been traditionally accepted that major constitutional reforms have to
be broadly agreed upon in interparty conferences.[28] This tradition
only came to a (temporary?) end in the 1980s when the Thatcher
governments implemented local-government reforms without any
effort to achieve broad agreement, so that even the institution on
which we focus here, the House of Lords, felt inclined to oppose parts
of the government's bills in that policy area.[29]

Second, as the 1968 episode demonstrates, small minorities of MPs
have the chance to block legislation in the Commons to a degree
unacceptable to governments with an ambitious programme.
Parliamentary time is a limited and therefore valuable resource; thus
intraparty dissent may prohibitively increase the costs of the
legislative process.

Third, a willingness to reform is not synonymous with the
acceptance of a specific reform proposal. This is all the more so since
every reform proposed may be risky and may have unintended
effects. I shall consider this in more detail below.

A fourth problem, which has arisen in the 1980s, is quite a
powerful obstacle to broad consensus over the need to replace the
House of Lords by a second chamber more in tune with the
democratic mode. The working of the House of Lords itself has
changed dramatically since the late 1950s when it was considered to
be in terminal decline. Therefore, the functional argument can be
made – and it is made powerfully time and again in both the political
and the academic debate – that there is no need for fundamental
reform. The systematic logic behind these developments is that
institutions which are objects of reform desires can turn into actors

themselves, calculating that survival lies in adaptation to external reform demands. If they succeed, they consequently increase transaction costs for reform-minded political actors.

The introduction of life peerages at the end of the 1950s and the Lords' reaction to the events of 1968 breathed new life into the ancient institution. Looking at some quantitative indicators (see Table 2) of the way the House works, it is justified to talk about a revival. It is, of course, revealing in itself that the House of Lords has for the first time become a serious subject for political scientists engaged in legislative studies. A recent study edited by Donald Shell and David Beamish focused upon the 1988–89 session in considerable detail.[30] Its findings show a dramatic increase in activity. In the 1959–60 session there were 907 peers on Roll. Sixty per cent attended at least once; 31 per cent spoke at least once; and the average daily attendance was 15 per cent. In the 1988–89 session there were 1,183 peers on Roll. Sixty-seven per cent attended at least once; 45 per cent spoke at least once; and the average daily attendance was 27 per cent.

TABLE 2:
GROWTH IN ACTIVITY IN THE HOUSE OF LORDS

	1959–60	*1971–72*	*1981–82*	*1988–89*
Peers on Roll	907	1,073	1,174	1,183
Peers who attended at least once	542	698	713	816
Peers who spoke at least once	283	419	503	537
Average daily attendance	136	250	284	316
Average length of sitting	240 min.	345 min.	380 min	424 min.
Number of amendments to government bills	n/a	924	1,309	2,359
Number of divisions	16	171	146	189

Source: Donald Shell, 'The House of Lords in Context', in Donald Shell and David Beamish (eds), *The House of Lords at Work: A Study Based on the 1988–1989 Session* (Oxford: Clarendon Press, 1993), p. 10. I am grateful to Donald Shell for permission to reproduce this material.

If one categorises peers according to their attendance and voting rates it becomes clear that it is possible to distinguish a 'working House' and a 'voting House' from the amorphous group of more than 1,000 peers on Roll.[31] The average length of sitting has nearly doubled since the late 1950s, and the numbers of amendments to government bills and of divisions have multiplied. Although, until 1999, about two-thirds of the members were hereditary peers – most of them Conservatives – it is not only Labour governments who were defeated in the second chamber. There has been indeed an increasing trend for governments to face defeats in the Lords. The Heath government 1970–74 lost 26 divisions; the Wilson and Callaghan governments 1974–79, at times with precarious minority status in the Commons, lost more than 300 divisions; while the Thatcher governments 1979–90 lost 156 divisions. The Major governments lost 65 divisions between 1990 and 1994.[32] Nor do these numbers take into account the amendments which are eventually accepted by the government and the House of Commons. It must be pointed out, however, that the majority of the greatly increased number of amendments in the Lords are brought in by the government in order to modify its own carelessly drafted bills. It is no wonder, therefore, that members of the second chamber sometimes have the impression that their House is misused as a 'legislative sausage-machine'.[33] In terms of length of sitting, the House of Lords today comes second only to the Commons as the most active legislative chamber in Europe.[34] This level of activity, moreover, has to be seen in the context of the remarkably low cost of operating the House.[35]

In addition to changes in the level and intensity of activities, it has to be acknowledged that the House of Lords has reacted sensitively to its problematic position in the constitutional order. In a number of reports and parliamentary debates on the working of the House, peers have endeavoured to strengthen their public image.[36] This is most strikingly indicated by the reactions of the Lords to the 1968 disaster. Lord Aberdare, spokesman for the Heath government, later declared:

> Many of us supported the reform of the House of Lords along the lines suggested in the Parliament (No. 2) Bill in the last Parliament. But those proposals failed to gain the approval of the other place [that is the Commons] and there seems at present little prospect of any fundamental reform. But it would be a pity not to follow up some of the impetus behind those proposals in order to ensure that we function as efficiently as possible within our present constitution and in our present role.[37]

It was agreed that an advisory committee would be set up to deliberate and report from time to time on possible improvements to procedure in the House. From the beginning, however, some peers felt that most of those changes implemented – time-limited debates, for example – merely helped streamline business and favoured the front benches at the expense of back-benchers and cross-benchers – those, that is, who belong neither to the government nor to the opposition. Lord Alport complained:

> the proposals made by that Committee which have been accepted are those which tend in all probability somewhat to curtail rather than extend the responsible position of private Members in this House.[38]

Looking back after more than two decades, the two most important improvements seem to be, first, the introduction and growing use of select committees and, second, the televising of the House.

The number of select committees, partly ad hoc on special subjects, partly on a sessional basis, has greatly increased since the 1960s, although, unlike the Commons, there has been no systematic attempt at reform. The two most important are the Select Committees on the European Communities and on Science and Technology. Both deliberately fill gaps the House of Commons has left. The European Communities Committee was established in 1974 alongside one in the House of Commons. By comparison, however, the Lords Committee has much wider terms of reference, namely:

> to consider Community proposals, whether in draft or otherwise, to obtain all necessary information about them, and to make reports on those which, in the opinion of the Committee, raise important questions of policy or principle, and on other questions to which the Committee consider that the special attention of the House should be drawn.[39]

Whereas the House of Commons Committee mainly serves as a crude filter for selecting topics for plenary debates in a partisan atmosphere, the Lords Committee with its various subcommittees is able to scrutinise EU draft proposals on a much grander scale.[40] It produces about 20 to 30 reports annually, working 'on the assumption that good well-researched reports, pushing forward ideas at timely moments, echoing both their relevance and their practicality, can be influential'.[41] This role as an agenda-setter draws our attention to the possibility that the House of Lords might be more influential in specific cases of policy production than a superficial look at its formal powers suggests. The same is true of the Science and Technology Committee which was established in 1979 after a Commons committee of the same name had been abolished in the wake of the comprehensive reform of select committees. With membership drawn from the ranks of eminent academic experts serving as life peers, Nobel Prize winners and members of the Royal Society among them, it is highly regarded. Not surprisingly, commentators conclude that its recommendations are quite influential, if only indirectly: 'The reports [are] difficult for ministers to ignore.'[42] But proposals to establish public bill committees and select committees on a larger scale, and in this way to improve deliberation and scrutiny of legislation, have so far been regularly turned down, mainly on the grounds that the number of professional staff as well as peers available for this kind of activity on a full-time basis simply would not be sufficient.[43] This shows that there are clear limits to a professionalisation of the House of Lords under present conditions.

The second improvement is the televising of proceedings of the House of Lords. This was first introduced as an experiment in 1985 and accepted on a permanent basis in 1986. The decision had a lot to do with the surprising fact, for peers as well as for broadcasters, that audience ratings were much higher than expected. Another factor was competition with the Commons. Parallel efforts to enable televising the proceedings in the House of Commons were frustrated until 1990. The most important motive, however, was the hope that in this way the public image of the second chamber could be improved. As Lord Boyd-Carpenter succinctly argued, 'This public understanding and appreciation may at some time be very important indeed from the point of view of the survival of your Lordships' House.'[44] And Lord O'Neill of the Maine reported:

> Ten years ago if you hailed a taxi and said, 'House of Lords please', as likely as not you would be taken to the House of Commons. Now that very seldom happens. What is more, I find that taxi drivers are very interested in what is going on in your Lordships' House. The status and position of your Lordships' House has improved out of all recognition, and television is merely the latest example of your Lordships' enhanced situation.[45]

These internal adaptations of the House of Lords to the requirements of modern parliamentarianism amount to a fourth strategic dilemma for reform-minded political actors. As a result the second chamber has arguably been rejuvenated and shown its potential for autonomous behavioural and structural changes. Indeed, the academic debate on the House of Lords in the 1980s was clearly shaped by the opposition of this 'functional' argument on the one hand, with Nicholas Baldwin as the main protagonist, and the 'legitimacy' argument, which we find most clearly expressed by Andrew Adonis, stating that ultimately an efficient second chamber requires that its aristocratic[46] composition is replaced by democratically elected representatives.

EFFICIENCY VERSUS LEGITIMACY

Nicholas Baldwin argues:

> although the House of Lords appears essentially unchanged from that which existed 10, 20, 30, even 40 years ago, in practice fundamental changes of both form and character have taken place, to the extent that many of the commonly held beliefs that have been applied to the House of Lords have in effect been rendered incorrect

and that these changes testify to the growth of 'a new professionalism and a new independence amongst the membership'.[47]

These catchwords – new professionalism and new independence – formed the basis of the controversy. 'Professionalism' has to do with increasing levels of activity, while 'independence' refers to the significant number of defeats for Conservative governments in 1979–97, showing that the former overall majority of Conservative peers in the 'working' and the 'voting' House had vanished. In the mid-1980s with the opposition in the Commons fragmented and the greater part of it, the Labour Party, conducting an internal civil war, even sober commentators went so far as to state that the House of Lords had become the only real opposition to the Thatcher government.[48]

Andrew Adonis on the other hand built his argument, first, on the fact that 'Government defeats in the Lords are … highly exceptional, and undue concentration on them has led commentators away from any appreciation of the real political character of the modern Lords'.[49] Indeed, it could be argued that the problems the Thatcher governments faced in the second chamber had more to do with tensions between traditional and Thatcherite Tories and with an unusually weak Conservative front-bench team in the Lords than with a new independence of peers.[50] It seems to me, however, that the difficulties of the Major government – which culminated in the use for the first time since 1949 of the Parliament Act procedures in order to pass the War Crimes Act of 1991 – pointed to a terminal decline of Conservative dominance in the Lords.[51]

One particularly revealing indicator for the relevance of the House of Lords is that it has increasingly served as a focus for interest-group activity. This is for three reasons.[52] First, the more active House of Lords simply gives pressure groups an additional chance to influence legislation; second, specific interests such as those of ethnic minorities, the elderly or countryside conservationists can rely on individual peers willing to promote their cause; and, third, because the membership of the Lords is not susceptible to electoral changes, long-term campaigns are facilitated.

The second argument of Andrew Adonis, relating to the new-professionalism thesis, is that procedural changes and higher levels of activity mainly increase efficiency and serve the government of the day: 'The fact that 300 or so peers are slaves to parliamentary duty does not in itself demonstrate that the Lords is a professional second chamber.'[53] Years ago Lord Hailsham bemoaned the fact that the main effect of life peerages on the character of the second chamber was to turn it into 'a pale reflexion of the House of Commons'.[54] These lines of reasoning not only counter Baldwin's functional arguments by reinterpreting empirical results, but they more or less implicitly start from a definition of what a professional and efficient second chamber should look like: a chamber with enough constitutional powers to effectively deliberate on, scrutinise and, if needs be, object to government legislation – a chamber composed of members who legitimately represent constituencies other than themselves, to modify a well-known saying.[55] Of course, no one would deny that the current constitution of the House of Lords is anachronistic and cannot easily be reconciled with democratic logic, which certainly remains true after the removal of the bulk of the hereditary Peers in 1999. The underlying question is, therefore, whether the efficiency of the House of Lords depends on its democratic legitimacy. Those who answer 'yes' tend to overlook two facts. One is that a bicameral legislature in which the representatives of both chambers are democratically elected only makes sense in federal political systems (I shall come back to this). The second is that there are types of legitimacy other than the 'rational–legal' one which is implicitly assumed here. Modern societies are moulded, too, by residual traces of what Max

Weber termed 'traditional' legitimacy. And the ancient institutions of British society are indisputably prime examples of traditional legitimacy.[56]

This supposition is confirmed by various public-opinion poll findings. In the 1983 'British Social Attitudes' survey nearly 60 per cent of respondents asked about the House of Lords answered that no change was necessary. Of the 30 per cent who thought that change was necessary one-third opted for a different body, one-quarter for abolition and the rest answered that there should be some other unspecified kind of change.[57] In a 1991 survey for BBC Radio, 9 per cent opted for abolition, 18 per cent for an elected second chamber, 19 per cent for minor changes and 30 per cent for the status quo. Whereas 50 per cent were in favour of abolishing hereditary peerages, no less than one-third opted for keeping them.[58] True, more recent opinion polls found growing disagreement with this situation.[59] But more important than the specific distribution of individual preferences is the recognition that quite a lot of people have no opinion at all and that the salience of this issue remains low compared to social and economic issues.[60] It is true that constitutional reform has achieved a prominent place on the political agenda of intellectual and political elites in recent years; Charter 88, the major lobby in this area, enjoys an astonishingly large membership. This increasing importance of constitutional politics is confirmed by the fact that four thought-through proposals for a codified constitution have been published in the early 1990s.[61] What I do dispute, however, is that rising dissatisfaction with British democracy has much to do with specific political institutions or that it can be explained simply by pointing to the majoritarian character of Britain's political system. Comparison of Eurobarometer survey data (Figure 1) on satisfaction with the way democracy works in one's own country in the United Kingdom, France, Germany and the EC average reveals that satisfaction ratings were stable until the late 1980s and have since then declined across most EU states, with the UK broadly in line with the overall trend. While the positions of individual countries have moved closer together, the ranking remains remarkably stable. That means that explanatory factors should be sought which are relevant to all member countries. Dissatisfaction with political outputs in times of economic crisis, and disillusionment with politics when facing a new global order after the collapse of the eastern bloc, are prime candidates.[62]

Public opinion data therefore do not provide a strong incentive for British governments to venture to tackle constitutional reform questions, especially when faced with scarce parliamentary time for their legislative programme. Political actors will only be willing to push ahead with reform if they calculate that the costs of the status quo are significantly higher than the expected costs of reform. Most analyses of the contemporary House of Lords underestimate the importance of time and 'impatience' factors under

FIGURE 1:

SATISFACTION WITH DEMOCRACY IN ONE'S OWN COUNTRY

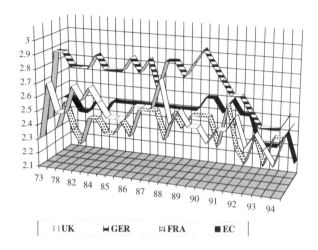

Note: This index is calculated in the following way: 'very satisfied' = 4, 'fairly satisfied' = 3, 'not very satisfied' = 2, 'not at all satisfied' = 1. Ratings higher than 2.5 indicate that a majority of respondents is satisfied with the way democracy works in their country, ratings lower than 2.5 indicate that a majority is dissatisfied. (*Source*: Eurobarometer, various surveys.)

modern conditions of parliamentarianism. Tsebelis and Rasch, investigating bicameral legislatures in western Europe, come to the conclusion that:

> there is significant evidence indicating that even those upper houses considered to be weak, like the British House of Lords ... have ... obtained concessions from powerful lower houses or even aborted legislation.[63]

Labour governments are not necessarily more likely to suffer this. Neither the Attlee nor the Wilson governments had real difficulties with the Lords. The problems of the Callaghan government in the mid-1970s were due more to the fact that it was in an uneasy minority position in the Commons than to any obstructive tactics by the Lords. In every decisive moment the so-called Addison–Salisbury 'doctrine of the mandate' has been accepted. This convention was established when Conservative peers after 1945 accepted guidance formulated by their then leader, the fifth Marquess of Salisbury, to refrain from rejecting measures which had been part of the election manifesto of the Labour government and therefore endorsed by the electorate.[64] The House of Lords knows very well that head-on confrontation with a government on an important part of the legislative programme would in all probability lead to fundamental reform because the political costs of the status quo would dramatically rise.

IMPONDERABILITIES OF REFORM

Having discussed the three strategic dilemmas of internal party dissent, the logic of party competition and the adaptability of political institutions, a fourth dilemma remains to be specified. This I have described above as stemming from the problem that a willingness to reform is not synonymous with the acceptance of a specific reform proposal. I shall outline four different reform options and discuss the difficulties they might generate.

The easiest option in conceptual terms is abolition of the second chamber. Unicameralism has at times been advocated by the Labour Party. Leaving aside for a moment the problem that constitutional lawyers disagree whether such a decision can be taken unilaterally by a House of Commons majority,[65] such a proposal would almost certainly involve considerable obstruction at the committee stage of the bill. There are additional difficulties. Abolition of the House of Lords would be a closer approach to an ideal-typical majoritarian democracy. The recent trend of constitutional-reform debates, however, is in the opposite direction, towards strengthening checks and balances. This is all the more so after the experience of strict majoritarianism in the Thatcher decade. Of course, one can point to the case of New Zealand, where the upper house was abolished in 1951, and argue that a weak second chamber is no real loss in terms of institutional dispersal of power. On the contrary, there the abolition of the Legislative Council led to a new interest in constitutional reform.[66] This eventually resulted in significant procedural and structural improvements to the now unicameral legislature; insertion of an entrenched clause in the Electoral Act of 1956, which prevents the parliamentary majority party from unilaterally changing the electoral rules of the game; and the establishment of the office of Ombudsman. The most important reform so far is the introduction in 1993 of a PR electoral system based on the German model. I do not suggest that there is some causal relationship between abolition of the second chamber in the early 1950s and renewed efforts to change the fabric of New Zealand's political system in the late 1980s and early 1990s. What is clear, however, is that political actors perceived the formal approximation to majoritarian democracy as one step too far and began to get nervous about the implied concentration of power in government.[67] In the British case these changes would be even more difficult to achieve than reform of the House of Lords. Unicameralism, to be sure, is only conceivable with the precondition of wholesale reform of the Commons. The House of Commons as it works today would simply collapse if it had additionally to take over the Lords' business.

A second option is to abolish hereditary peerages and leave other things as they are for the time being. That is what Labour has implemented as a first step. The problem here is that if the second step, replacement by a mainly elected second chamber, cannot for whatever reason be achieved, the House of Lords would consist wholly of nominated peers and resemble a 'giant Quango', a 'House of Placemen'.[68] That this would not improve the 'rational–legal' legitimacy of the House of Lords can easily be shown by the current debate on the Canadian Senate, which consists entirely of the Prime Minister's nominees.[69]

A third option, at first glance the most elegant one, is replacement by a wholly elected chamber. This, however, only makes sense if its composition differs from that of the House of Commons. The interrelationship between mode of election and powers can be systematically stated by using a typology proposed by Arend Lijphart.[70] Bicameral legislatures can be divided according to symmetry or asymmetry of powers and according to congruence or incongruence of composition. Strength and weakness of second chambers depends on the exact combination of both dimensions. The current House of Lords, for instance, clearly belongs to the group of weak second chambers. But in practice second chambers with both symmetric powers and a composition congruent with the first chamber are also rather weak. Accordingly, if one wishes to strengthen powers so as to achieve at least moderate symmetry, incongruent composition can be achieved either by different electoral systems, with a first-past-the-post system for one chamber and PR for the other, or by overrepresentation of certain territorial units. Recent proposals within the Labour Party and the Liberal Democrats as well as by the Institute for Public Policy Research[71] seem to prefer the first variant. All three are in favour of a PR system for electing the larger part of the members of the second chamber.[72] It should be noted that this could well mean that a government controls a majority in the House of Commons, but not in the second chamber. This is no small inconvenience in parliamentary democracies. Lijphart argues that 'the logical solution to the "two masters" dilemma is to form a broad coalition so that the government has sufficient support in both houses'.[73] I do not think that it is as easy as that. Strong bicameralism seems to me to be only acceptable under democratic conditions, if the different composition of the second chamber reflects a federal political structure.[74] And even then the 'two-masters' dilemma can lead to deadlock and constitutional conflicts. In 1975 the Australian Prime Minister Whitlam, whose Labor government controlled the House of Representatives, was dismissed by the Governor-General because the opposition parties used their bare majority in the Senate to defer appropriation bills for the supply of essential government services.[75] What we can learn from the Australian experience is that structural incentives lead members of a second chamber in federal political systems to behave more as representatives of political parties than of states.[76] This makes deadlock very likely where the party-political compositions of the two chambers diverge. Moreover, strong bicameralism in Westminster democracies is especially difficult to establish because political actors are unaccustomed to compromise.

What can we conclude from this? To avoid the Australian situation, the powers of an elected senate would have to remain small.[77] Those who hope that an elected second chamber will be a strong one will be disappointed. This is true at least as long as the British state is not radically federalised. Consequently it will be difficult to find enough qualified candidates for such a weak senate. In addition to the problem of compatibility of second chambers with parliamentary democracy there is the fact that the House of Commons has an institutional interest of its own and will suspiciously watch efforts to strengthen either powers or public support for a senate. The logical answer to this problem is to simultaneously reform, that is strengthen, the Commons.

A final option, and to me the most realistic at hand, is a combination of elected and appointed members. Such a solution would have three advantages. First, it would be possible to use the nominated contingent to ensure that the government of the day has at least a plurality in the second chamber. Second, this would make it clear that the Commons is the superior chamber, not only in terms of powers but also in terms of democratic legitimacy.[78] And, third, this would ensure that some of the expertise of current life peers from science, the civil service and the professions continues to be at the senate's disposal. The fact remains that mixed membership will be only a suboptimal solution to the legitimacy problem.

Each reform alternative contains inherent problems. Accordingly, there is no logical solution which reform-minded political actors simply have to agree upon. The most important difficulty is that bicameralism cannot be easily reconciled with majoritarianism as it is institutionalised at Westminster. Reforms would have side-effects which can be studied in countries like Australia, Canada or New Zealand. Hence, if there has been a comparative perspective at all in recent constitutional-reform debates, these are the countries which have been examined.[79]

PROSPECTS OF REFORM

Having pointed out major strategic dilemmas for reform, are there any factors which might make the task of reform-minded political actors easier in the near future? I think that there are two developments which might facilitate constitutional reform as a whole. The first has to do with the fact that there has been a quantitative expansion and a qualitative change in the reform movement in recent years. In the 1970s only the natural losers in the majoritarian political game – the Liberals and their academic sympathisers, as well as some Conservatives, nervously registering the rise of the Labour left – argued for electoral reform or specific consolidations of traditional institutions. The reform agenda today is much broader and much more consistently based on a democratic philosophy which on the one hand emphasises the importance of checks and balances to political power (a stronger second chamber, a Bill of Rights and a Freedom of Information Act) and on the other focuses on decentralising and participatory devices (sub-national legislatures, referendums, possibly electoral reform). It cannot be discussed here if these measures add up to a coherent concept. I doubt it. What is clear, however, is that in intellectual circles as well as in important parts of the political arena majoritarian democracy itself has become the target of criticism. This derives from experiencing a pre-eminent Conservative Party which at times used the decision-making powers of government in a majoritarian democracy to its limits. Moreover, the Thatcherite discourse of utility extended even to venerable institutions, with the paradoxical effect of diminishing their dignity. The second factor is that the Labour Party has participated with increasing energy in the constitutional-reform debate and may therefore be forced to implement something in office. In the first major programmatic speech of the new government on its constitutional agenda, Gordon Brown, the Chancellor of the Exchequer, proclaimed: 'Today the constitutional debate – once the politics of protest and on the margins of political discourse – has advanced to become essential to the politics of power at the heart of the agenda of government.'[80] By comparison with plans for regional assemblies in England or a referendum on electoral reform, a first step towards an at least symbolic reform of the House of Lords seems to me an easier task. In other words, House of Lords reform has become a second-order issue on the agenda and can be implemented much more readily than in the past.

Paradoxically, however, House of Lords reform was not part of the first Queen's Speech of the Blair government. A bill to provide for the removal of all but a rump of hereditary peers and a Royal Commission inquiry into a more permanent solution was only announced in the second session of the 1997 Parliament. In legislative terms abolition of the hereditary peers proved to be a simple matter. The Constitution Unit produced a two-page draft bill on the subject in 1996.[81] However, the Labour government has had considerable difficulty in agreeing on a concept for the second stage, reflected in the decision to hand the matter over to a Royal Commission. Labour's Joint Consultative Committee with the Liberal Democrats before the general election of 1997 had agreed upon a continuing role for a cross-bench or non-party element in the reformed second chamber a limited number of hereditary peers to become life peers and a composition of the House reflecting the proportion of votes received by the parties in the previous general election.[82] The Wakeham Comission on Reform of the House of Lords published its report in early 2000.[83] Under this proposal the new chamber would have a small number of elected members alongside appointed ones. The report was not well received in the press or by the political parties

REFORM OF THE MONARCHICAL HEAD OF STATE

Up to now discussion about the monarchical head of state has been mainly an intellectual concern. Only *The Economist* has devoted itself to the republican cause in recent years. It is true that Jack Straw, as Labour Shadow Home Secretary, in 1994 publicly reflected on proposals to redefine the Queen's role along Scandinavian lines.[84] It seems to me that this was not so much a serious attempt at opening up debate as a test of public reaction. There is currently much discussion of the crisis of the British monarchy. This has to do with a sharp decline in public confidence in the dramatis personae of the court cabals and not with the monarchy as an institution, which continues to be highly respected.[85]

Intellectual debate concentrates on the argument by some writers that monarchy is the most obvious expression and at the same time the most effective reinforcement of an aristocratic, elite-dominated and conservative society. A precondition for effective modernisation, so these authors reason, would be a republicanisation of the constitutional order. Even the most ardent proponents of the modernisation thesis consider this an illusory prospect. Tom Nairn argues that 'the successive and futile formulae of modernisation proposed by British governments since 1945 have aimed at a more "classless" and homogeneous nation-state. But were this realised, the miraculous oneness of the traditional Royal identity would be sharply diminished: there would be more, and more open, conflict, not less.' This would not be in any political actor's interest, so 'one might as well demand a lowering of the British annual rainfall as ask for "the abolition of Monarchy"'.[86] A similar conclusion is drawn by Will Hutton:

> Britain needs what might be called a republican attitude to its culture and institutions. To argue for a republican approach is not the same as calling for the abolition of the monarchy, although implanting a republican tradition and institutional structure will mean stripping away prerogative powers and the hereditary principle, which are both aspects of the continuing royal influence on the constitution.[87]

In view of these diagnoses it is important to recall that there are another seven monarchies in western Europe: Belgium, Denmark, Luxembourg, the Netherlands, Norway, Spain and Sweden. These are countries with very different political and economic trajectories to modernity. To my mind, the modernity argument cannot be maintained.

The British monarchy has not survived because it has been extremely powerful or because society has been particularly aristocratic and anti-modern. On the contrary, the first reason for its survival is that it had to accept constitutionalisation and adaptation to changing political circumstances relatively early.[88] Nor was it discredited and consequently overthrown following either of the World Wars. So historical continuity is an important factor. Second, monarchy has functional advantages. A head of state who is not elected on a party ticket and therefore not perceived as involved in party politics may be better able than a president symbolically to integrate and represent the nation as a whole. Monarchs do not know terms of office. They represent historical continuity and collective identity.

This advantage, however, could be endangered if the fragmentation of the party system which began in the early 1970s continues, making 'hung parliaments' much more likely.[89] In this case political neutrality will in the long run be retained only if the discretionary powers of the monarch over the formation of a government and the dissolution of the House of Commons are either clearly fixed or entirely removed. The Liberal Democrats in a recent policy document on reform of the House of Commons proposed the introduction of fixed four-year terms for the House of Commons and a change from votes of confidence to the German model of constructive votes of confidence,[90] which would lead to the fall of the government only if the Commons at the same time endorsed a new government. Dissolution of Parliament would under normal circumstances be fixed and the power to choose whom to invite to form a government would be transferred from the monarch to Parliament itself. *The Economist* quite rightly points out that this proposal leaves open what would happen if the sitting government is not able to command a majority but neither is a new government.[91] In other words, in the event of deadlock there has to be a clearly fixed procedure on the dissolution of Parliament. In Sweden these tasks were transferred to the Speaker of the *Riksdag* in 1974. Belgium and the Netherlands have developed a system of *informateurs* who are appointed by the monarch to negotiate with party leaders on possible coalitions.[92] Both alternatives have quite successfully protected the sovereign from political involvement.

The functional advantage of having a monarchical head of state could be reversed if Britain were to experience a series of minority governments without formal coalitions. The same would be true if PR were introduced, leading to multi-party politics without parliamentary-majority status for any party. In both cases, reform would be unavoidable. As with the general model I introduced to explain institutional conservatism in relation to House of Lords reform, only when the political neutrality of the monarch is severely disturbed will the political costs of the current institutional arrangement rise sufficiently to force political actors into serious discussions. Today this seems unlikely, but it is not beyond the realms of possibility that current monarchy/republic debates in Australia and New Zealand will have repercussions in Britain.[93]

CONCLUSION

Britain's pre-democratic institutions, the House of Lords and the monarchical head of state, are only uneasily compatible with the way majoritarian democracy works today. While they have no clear, legitimate powers to limit the will of governments, they are not completely lacking in political influence. This is the core of the reform debate. Contrary to the conventional view, however, Britain does not have unusual problems with modernising its political institutions. It is only exceptional in that it had no cause to do so in the past. It should not be forgotten that Britain served for a very long time as the model for stable democracy, able to absorb the consequences of economic and social modernisation as well as the dramatic decline of its international political influence.[94] In this context anachronistic details, such as a mainly aristocratic second chamber or the non-codification of constitutional norms, could easily be accepted. That is the first, if you like, the historical part of my answer to the question of why pre-democratic institutions survived and proposals for reform failed. The more systematic part is that Britain is simply a particularly impressive example of institutional conservatism. The reason for the normally very long life-spans of political institutions is not that political actors find them ideal solutions for collective-action problems. Institutional conservatism derives more from the fact that political actors expect every conceivable reform to cause higher transaction costs than existing institutions which may not be perfect but whose effects and defects are known.

NOTES

I am grateful to Nevil Johnson for his comments and criticisms on an earlier version of this chapter.

1.   Arend Lijphart, *Democracies: Patterns of Majoritarian and Consensus Government in Twenty-One Countries* (London: Yale University Press, 1984), pp. 1–16.
2.   Alois Riklin, 'Montesquieus freiheitliches Staatsmodell: Die Identität von Machtteilung und Mischverfassung', *Politische Vierteljahresschrift*, 30 (1989), pp. 420–42.

3. John Stuart Mill, *Considerations on Representative Government* (London: Parker, 1861). Walter Bagehot, *The English Constitution: With an Introduction by Richard Crossman* (London: Fontana Press, 1993 [1867]), p. 61.
4. The idea of transaction costs was originally developed within the framework of 'new institutional economics'. See Douglass C. North, *Institutions, Institutional Change and Economic Performance* (Cambridge: Cambridge University Press, 1990). In the last few years it has featured strongly in the 'new institutionalist' approach in political science as well. See Kenneth A. Shepsle, 'Studying Institutions: Some Lessons from the Rational Choice Approach', *Journal of Theoretical Politics*, 1 (1989), pp. 131–47. Transaction costs include costs resulting from negotiations, from enforcing new institutional rules and procedures on participants, and from adapting to them.
5. *The Economist*, 9 March 1996, p. 15.
6. Donald Shell, *The House of Lords* 2nd edn (Hemel Hempstead: Harvester Wheatsheaf, 1992), p. 10.
7. Janet P. Morgan, 'The House of Lords in the 1980s', *The Parliamentarian*, 63 (1982), p. 294.
8. Lord Bryce (Chairman), *Report of the Conference on Reform of the Second Chamber*, Cd 9038, 1918.
9. Donald Shell, *House of Lords*, p. 14.
10. Ibid.
11. Even though all-party consensus on the introduction of life peerages had been achieved in 1948, Labour voted against the Life Peerages Bill in 1958. This is a good example of what I term the dilemma of the logic of party competition.
12. Janet P. Morgan, *The House of Lords and the Labour Government 1964–1970* (Oxford: Clarendon Press, 1975), pp. 137–51. Delegated legislation is derived from statutes which contain enabling clauses that allow the minister to issue directives and regulations at a later stage, subject to the relevant parliamentary procedures (mostly the so-called 'negative procedure') for approval.
13. Morgan, *House of Lords*, pp. 208–28. Committee-stage proceedings deviate from the usual rules in that MPs are allowed to speak to a clause more than once. See Clifford J. Boulton (ed.), *Erskine May's Treatise on the Law, Privileges, Proceedings and Usage of Parliament*, 21st edn (London: Butterworths, 1989), p. 587. After 80 hours at committee stage only the preamble and five out of 20 clauses had been dealt with.
14. Most prominently John Redwood MP, the right-wing contender against John Major for the party leadership in 1995, whose 'Conservative 2000 Foundation' declares: 'Are any of Britain's long standing institutions in need of reform? This question should not be asked in this form … Our constitution is flexible and it will evolve when there are real problems that require changes. It does not need a wide ranging review and it certainly does not need a continental style reform in the name of logic.' See *A Sovereign Nation: United, Strong, Proud and Free* (London: Conservative 2000 Foundation, 1996); Andrew Lansley and Richard Wilson, *Conservatives and the Constitution* (London: Conservative 2000 Foundation, 1997), pp. 13–15.
15. On the changing voting behaviour of individual MPs since the 1960s, see the work of Philip Norton, for instance, *Dissension in the House of Commons 1974–1979* (London: Clarendon Press, 1980).
16. Frederick W. S. Craig (ed.), *Conservative and Labour Party Conference Decisions 1945–1981* (Chichester: Parliamentary Research Services, 1982), p. 129.

17. Cited in Lord Longford, *A History of the House of Lords* (London: Collins, 1988), p. 181. What the Labour Party proposes here is similar to the solution New Zealanders found after abolishing their second chamber. An entrenched clause was included in the Electoral Act 1956 as a means to prevent a parliamentary majority from extending the life of a parliament beyond the normal election date. Leaving the obvious fact aside for a moment that delegated legislation seems to have been simply overlooked in 1911, the Parliament Acts 1911 and 1949 reduced the absolute veto powers of the second chamber to the question of the extension of a House of Commons to more than five years and to private bills. The Parliament Act 1949 cut the period of delay for legislation from two years spread over three sessions to one year spread over two sessions.
18. Frederick W. S. Craig (ed.), *British General Election Manifestos 1959–1987*, 3rd edn (Aldershot: Dartmouth/Parliamentary Research Services, 1990), pp. 377–8.
19. Philip Webster, 'Notice to Quit for Hereditary Peers in Lords', *The Times*, 8 February 1996, p. 1.
20. *Here We Stand*, Federal White Paper No. 6 (London: Liberal Democrats, 1995), pp. 23–4. See also *The Great Reform Bill* (London: Liberal Democrats, 1996) and *Constitutional Declaration* (London: Liberal Democrats, 1996), both of which hesitantly accept the two-step approach.
21. Lord Hailsham, 'Elective Dictatorship', *Listener*, 21 October 1976, p. 497. See also Lord Hailsham, 'The Paradox of Oppressive yet Powerless Government', *The Times*, 16 May 1975, p. 16.
22. Lord Home, *Report of the Review Committee on the Second Chamber* (London: Conservative Political Centre, 1978), p. 23.
23. Craig, *British General Election Manifestos*, p. 338.
24. Donald Shell, 'Reform of the House of Lords', manuscript, 1996, p. 3.
25. Peter Riddell, 'Both Parties Need to Think Again on the Constitution', *The Times*, 8 February 1996, p. 11.
26. William Hague, 'Change and Tradition. Thinking Creatively about the Constitution'; speech to the Centre for Policy Studies, London, 24 February 1998 (http://www.conservative-party.org.uk/newspags/02241637.htm).
27. This theorem, simply stated, argues that in the long run and given a unidimensional distribution of voter preferences parties will compete for votes in the centre ground, thus bringing their party programmes as close together as possible.
28. Interparty conferences in British politics are a neglected phenomenon which I will explore in a forthcoming study on institutional reform in majoritarian democracies. For a historical treatment, see John D. Fair, *British Interparty Conferences: A Study of the Procedure of Conciliation in British Politics, 1867–1921* (Oxford: Clarendon Press, 1980). See also Rodney Brazier, *Constitutional Reform* (Oxford: Clarendon Press, 1991), p. 2.
29. Damien Welfare, 'An Anachronism with Relevance: The Revival of the House of Lords in the 1980s and Its Defence of Local Government', *Parliamentary Affairs*, 45 (1992), pp. 205–19.
30. Donald Shell and David Beamish (eds), *The House of Lords at Work: A Study Based on the 1988–1989 Session* (Oxford: Clarendon Press, 1993).
31. Nicholas D. J. Baldwin, 'The Membership of the House' in Shell and Beamish, *House of Lords at Work*, p. 45.
32. Donald Shell, 'The House of Lords in Context' in Shell and Beamish, *House of Lords at Work*, p. 11.

33. Gavin Drewry and Jenny Brook, 'Government Legislation: An Overview' in Shell and Beamish, *House of Lords at Work*, p. 75.
34. Shell, *House of Lords*, p. 126.
35. It has been estimated that the total cost of the House of Commons is more than four times that of the Lords. One explanatory factor is that 'the House of Lords is almost certainly the only chamber in a major national legislature whose members are not remunerated for their services'. Michael Rush and David Jones, 'Services and Facilities' in Shell and Beamish, *House of Lords at Work*, p. 323.
36. The most important introspections are the *First Report of the Select Committee of the House of Lords on Practice and Procedure*, HL 141 (1976–1977) and the *Report by the Group on the Working of the House*, HL 9 (1987). Additional material can be found in *House of Lords Debates*, 5th ser., vol. 518, cols 606–37, 25 April 1990 ('The Constitution: Powers of a Second Chamber').
37. *House of Lords Debates*, 5th ser., vol. 325, col. 908, 23 November 1971.
38. Ibid., vol. 326, col. 1280, 16 December 1971.
39. Cited in Donald Shell, 'The European Communities Committee' in Shell and Beamish, *House of Lords at Work*, p. 248.
40. Cliff Grantham and Caroline Moore Hodgson, 'Structural Changes: The Use of Committees' in Philip Norton (ed.), *Parliament in the 1980s* (Oxford: Blackwell, 1985), pp. 114–35.
41. Shell, 'European Communities Committee', p. 281.
42. Cliff Grantham, 'Select Committees' in Shell and Beamish, *House of Lords at Work*, p. 295. See also P. D. G. Hayter, 'The Parliamentary Monitoring of Science and Technology in Britain', *Government and Opposition*, 26 (1991), pp. 147–66.
43. *Report by the Group on the Working of the House*, HL 9 (1987), pp. 9–10, 19. See also *House of Lords Debates*, 5th ser., vol. 489, cols 988–1053, 4 November 1987.
44. *House of Lords Debates*, 5th ser., vol. 474, col. 965, 12 May 1986.
45 Ibid., col. 989.
46. Characterisation of the House of Lords as 'aristocratic' has to be qualified. About 30 per cent of hereditary peerages were created before 1800, 30 per cent in the nineteenth century and 40 per cent in the twentieth century: J. A. G. Griffith and Michael Ryle, *Parliament: Functions, Practice and Procedures* (London: Sweet & Maxwell, 1989), p. 458.
47. Nicholas D. J. Baldwin, 'Behavioural Changes: A New Professionalism and a More Independent House' in Norton, *Parliament in the 1980s*, p. 98; Baldwin, 'Membership of the House', pp. 33–60.
48. See, for instance, 'Up the Nobility', *The Economist*, 16 June 1984, p. 18: 'The house of lords now unquestionably out-performs the commons as a legislative review chamber.'
49. Andrew Adonis, 'The House of Lords in the 1980s', *Parliamentary Affairs*, 41 (1988), p. 385.
50. The Thatcher government's attitude to the House of Lords seems to have hardened in the 1980s. Whereas ministers before 1987 regularly accepted compromises with the Lords after defeats, they endeavoured to overturn them after 1987 whenever possible. This led even government back-benchers to complain that the Thatcher government disrespected the second chamber. Lord Beloff for instance said: 'What is the true attitude of Her Majesty's Ministers to the revising functions of this House? … It appears to some of us that in certain quarters it is thought that the House of Lords is a rather disagreeable nuisance, that it occasionally presses for measures which

Ministers have already decided are unacceptable, and that the business should be to get the Government's measures through with the maximum of celerity ... I believe that it is difficult for this House fully to exercise either its powers of questioning the Executive or its legislative powers when in most cases the individual who responds from the Front Bench is a junior Minister or even a Whip with only that status': *House of Lords Debates*, 5th ser., vol. 518, cols 610–11, 25 April 1990.

51   In the 1975–76 session on the Trade Union and Labour Relations (Amendment) Bill as well as in the 1976–77 one on the Aircraft and Shipbuilding Industries Bill, Parliament Act procedures were activated, 'but in neither case did these procedures run their full course because compromise between the House of Lords and the Labour Government was eventually attained'. See Shell, *House of Lords*, p. 132. On both occasions the Prime Minister strongly reminded the Lords of the 'doctrine of mandate'. See, for example, *House of Commons Debates*, 5th ser., vol. 919, col. 1560, 18 November 1976.

52.   Donald Shell, 'The House of Lords: Time for a Change?', *Parliamentary Affairs*, 47 (1994), p. 733. For results of empirical research see Nicholas D. J. Baldwin, 'The House of Lords' in Michael Rush (ed.), *Parliaments and Pressure Politics* (Oxford: Clarendon Press, 1990), pp. 152–77.

53.   Adonis, 'House of Lords in the 1980s', p. 389.

54.   Lord Hailsham, 'Paradox of Oppressive but Powerless Government', p. 16.

55.   'It represents nobody but itself, and therefore enjoys the full confidence of its constituents': cited in Carl J. Friedrich, *Constitutional Government and Democracy: Theory and Practice in Europe and America*, 4th edn (Waltham MA: Blaisdell, 1968), p. 316.

56.   Lansley and Wilson characteristically argue that 'the legitimacy of the Lords is grounded on values other than democracy ... [It] rests on its utility, its independence, the collective wisdom of its members and on the longevity of the institution itself', *Conservatives and the Constitution*, p. 88.

57.   Lindsay Brook *et al.*, *British Social Attitudes Cumulative Sourcebook: The First Six Surveys* (Aldershot: Gower, 1992), A–38.

58.   Donald Shell, 'Conclusion' in Shell and Beamish, *House of Lords at Work*, p. 350.

59.   The latest 'British Social Attitudes' survey records 36 per cent in favour of the status quo in 1994 and 29 per cent in 1997. See the *Guardian*, 19 November 1997.

60.   See, for instance, Patrick Dunleavy and Stuart Weir, 'Ignore the People at your Peril', *Independent*, 25 April 1991, p. 27. Dunleavy and Weir report results of a MORI 'State of the Nation' survey in which respondents were evenly divided between those in favour of replacing the House of Lords with an elected chamber and those opposed. What the authors do not point out in their analysis is that more than 30 per cent answered 'Don't know'.

61.   The Institute for Public Policy Research's *The Constitution of the United Kingdom* (1991), the Liberal Democrats' Federal Green Paper No. 13 *We the People ... Towards a Written Constitution* (1990), Tony Benn's Commonwealth of Britain Bill (HC 161, 1990–1991) and Frank Vibert's (formerly Deputy Director of the Institute of Economic Affairs) *Constitutional Reform in the United Kingdom* (1990). For particulars and discussion of these proposals as well as the work of Charter 88, see Anthony Barnett, Caroline Ellis and Paul Hirst (eds), *Debating the Constitution: New Perspectives on Constitutional Reform* (Cambridge: Polity Press, 1993).

62. For an association between the level of satisfaction and the state of the economy, see Manfred Küchler, 'The Dynamics of Mass Political Support in Western Europe: Methodological Problems and Preliminary Findings' in Karlheinz Reif and Ronald Inglehart (eds), *Eurobarometer: The Dynamics of European Public Opinion* (Basingstoke: Macmillan, 1991), pp. 275–93.

63. George Tsebelis and Bjørn Erik Rasch, 'Patterns of Bicameralism' in Herbert Döring (ed.), *Parliaments and Majority Rule in Western Europe*, (Frankfurt: Campus, 1995), p. 388.

64. Shell, *House of Lords*, p. 13.

65. See, for instance, A. W. Bradley, 'The Sovereignty of Parliament – in Perpetuity?' in Jeffrey Jowell and Dawn Oliver (eds), *The Changing Constitution* (Oxford: Clarendon Press, 1989), p. 33. The main difficulty lies in interpreting the scope of the Parliament Acts 1911 and 1949.

66. Keith Jackson, 'The Abolition of the New Zealand Upper House of Parliament' in Lawrence D. Longley and David M. Olson (eds), *Two into One: The Politics and Processes of National Legislative Cameral Change* (Boulder CO: Westview Press, 1991), pp. 43–76; Keith Jackson, 'Bicameralism and Unicameralism in Australia, Canada and New Zealand' in Malcolm Alexander and Brian Galligan (eds), *Comparative Political Studies: Australia and Canada* (Melbourne: Pitman, 1992), pp. 27–44; G. A. Wood, 'New Zealand's Single Chamber Parliament: An Argument for an Impotent Upper House?', *Parliamentary Affairs*, 36 (1983), pp. 334–47.

67. See, for instance, Geoffrey Palmer, *New Zealand's Constitution in Crisis: Reforming our Political System*, (Dunedin NZ: John McIndoe, 1992). Geoffrey Palmer, Professor in Constitutional Law and former Prime Minister, was a central figure in the implementation of constitutional changes in the late 1980s.

68. Shell, *House of Lords*, p. 2.

69. Robert A. Mackay, *The Unreformed Senate of Canada*, 2nd edn (Toronto: McClelland & Stewart, 1963); C. E. S. Franks, 'Not Yet Dead, but Should It Be Resurrected? The Canadian Senate' in Samuel E. Patterson and Anthony Mughan (eds), *Senates: Bicameralism in Contemporary World*, (Columbus OH: Ohio State University Press, 1999), pp. 120–69. For proposals to establish an elected senate effectively representing the federal character of Canada, see Donald Smiley, *An Elected Chamber for Canada? Clues from the Australian Experience*, Discussion Paper No. 21, Institute of Intergovernmental Relations, Queen's University, Kingston, Ontario 1985 and also Randall White, *Voice of Region: The Long Journey to Senate Reform in Canada* (Toronto: Dundurn Press, 1990). After prolonged negotiations a proposal for an elected senate based on equal representation of the provinces was finally part of the Charlottetown Accord 1992, which was turned down by referendum in the same year. See *Consensus Report on the Constitution*, Final Text, Charlottetown, 28 August 1992, pp. 4–6.

70. Arend Lijphart, 'Bicameralism: Canadian Senate Reform in Comparative Perspective' in Herman Bakvis and William M. Chandler (eds), *Federalism and the Role of the State* (Toronto: Toronto University Press, 1987), pp. 101–12.

71. Jeremy Mitchell and Anne Davies, *Reforming the Lords* (London: Institute for Public Policy Research, 1993).

72. All three proposals at the same time argue that keeping a small contingent of nominated members could have advantages. Mitchell and Davies, for instance, propose 270 elected senators and 30 senators appointed by the Prime Minister after nomination by a joint committee of both Houses. The

judicial function of the Law Lords as a court of appeal could easily be transferred to a new institution because the House of Lords effectively ceased to be involved in legal matters after the Appellate Jurisdiction Act 1876 established that legal expertise is an essential requirement for Law Lords and appointment of life peers as Lords of Appeal in Ordinary began. Mitchell and Davies, *Reforming the Lords*, pp. 32–6, 38.

73. Lijphart, 'Bicameralism', p. 111.
74. This argument is reflected in empirical findings. Bicameralism and federalism are highly correlated. Longley and Oleszek found in 1989 that 16 of 17 federal political systems have bicameral legislatures (the exception being the Comoros): Lawrence D. Longley and Walter J. Oleszek, *Bicameral Politics: Conference Committees in Congress* (New Haven CT: Yale University Press, 1989), p. 13.
75. Brian J. Galligan, 'The Kerr–Whitlam Debate and the Principles of the Australian Constitution', *Journal of Commonwealth and Comparative Politics*, 18 (1980), pp. 247–71.
76. 'The Senate … has no past, and no future, as a States House', judges Liberal Senator D. J. Hamer, 'Towards a Valuable Senate' in Michael James (ed.), *The Constitutional Challenge: Essays on the Australian Constitution, Constitutionalism and Parliamentary Practice* (St Leonards NSW: Centre for Independent Studies, 1982), p. 61.
77. Suzanne S. Schüttemeyer and Roland Sturm, 'Wozu Zweite Kammern? Zur Repräsentation und Funktionalität Zweiter Kammern in westlichen Demokratien', *Zeitschrift für Parlamentsfragen*, 23 (1992), p. 526 come to the same conclusion.
78. John Grigg, 'Making Government Responsible to Parliament', in Richard Holme and Michael Elliot (eds), *1688–1988: Time for a New Constitution* (London: Macmillan, 1988), p. 175.
79. It is commonplace, of course, that other second chambers occasionally serve as reference points in order to make clear the anachronistic nature of the House of Lords. Upper houses which are cited in this regard are the US Senate, the Irish Seanad and the German Bundesrat. Most of the relevant literature on the reform of the House of Lords, however, is without any comparative perspective. Mitchell and Davies, *Reforming the Lords*, p. 58 mention Australia. Lord Northfield, 'Reforming Procedure in the Lords' in David Butler and A. H. Halsey (eds), *Policy and Politics* (London: Macmillan, 1978), p. 31 points to select committee procedures in Australia and Canada. 'The Restoration of Parliament', *The Economist*, 4 November 1990, p. 52 refers to unicameral democracies such as New Zealand, Denmark, and Sweden. Vernon Bogdanor, 'The Problem of the Upper House' in H. W. Blom, W. P. Blockmans and H. de Schepper (eds), *Bicameralisme: Tweekamerstelsel vroeger en nu* ('s-Gravenhage: Sdu Uitgeverij Koninginnegracht, 1992), pp 411–22 is broadly comparative. See also Lord Shackleton and George Clark, 'The Role of Second Chambers: The Report of a Study Group of the Commonwealth Parliamentary Association', *The Parliamentarian*, 63 (1982), pp. 199–252 which, quite naturally, focuses on Commonwealth member states. Meg Russell, *Reforming the House of Lords: Lessons from Overseas* (Oxford: Oxford University Press, 1999) refers to Canada, Australia, Ireland, Germany, France, Italy and Spain.
80. Gordon Brown, 'Charter 88 Speech', 12 July 1997, manuscript, p. 1.
81. Robert Hazell, 'Delivering Constitutional Reform', CIPFA/Times lecture, 14 July 1997. *Reform of the House of Lords*, (London: Constitution Unit, 1996),

Appendix A: Draft Parliament Bill.

82. 'Report of the Joint Consultative Committee on Constitutional Reform', (press release), Labour Party and Liberal Democrats, London 1997, pp. 16–17.

83. Lord Wakenham (Chairman), *A House for the Future: Report by the Royal Commission on Reform of the House of Lords*, Cm 4534, 2000.

84. Colin Randall and George Jones, 'Labour in Row over Royal Role', *Daily Telegraph*, 5 December 1994, p. 1. Recently a Fabian pamphlet urged the Labour leadership to end 'Labour's last taboo' and to consider reforms to the monarchy. The leadership, however, moved swiftly to distance the Labour Party from the pamphlet: see Rebecca Smithers, 'Labour would Discuss Reform with Monarchy', *Guardian*, 13 August 1996, p. 4.

85. For empirical findings, see Richard Topf, Peter Mohler and Anthony Heath, 'Pride in One's Country: Britain and West Germany' in Roger Jowell, Sharon Witherspoon and Lindsay Brook (eds), *British Social Attitudes: Special International Report* (Aldershot: Gower, 1989), pp. 121–42.

86. Tom Nairn, *The Enchanted Glass: Britain and its Monarchy* (London: Picador, 1990), pp. 13, 62.

87. Will Hutton, *The State We're In* (London: Vintage, 1996), p. 287.

88. Peter Graf Kielmansegg, *Von Gottes Gnaden: Die europäischen Monarchien im zwanzigsten Jahrhundert*, manuscript, p. 3.

89. They have occurred five times in the twentieth century: January and December 1910, December 1923, 1929 and February 1974. See Vernon Bogdanor, *The Monarchy and the Constitution* (Oxford: Clarendon Press, 1995), pp. 145–66.

90. This procedural rule has been adopted so far in the Spanish constitution of 1978 and in the Belgian round of constitutional changes in 1993.

91. 'On yer bike', *The Economist*, 15 June 1996, p. 34.

92. Bogdanor, *Monarchy and the Constitution*, pp. 166–82.

93. Malcolm Turnbull, *The Reluctant Republic* (Port Melbourne: Heinemann, 1993). *Republic Advisory Committee: An Australian Republic: The Options. Vol. 1: The Report* (Canberra: Commonwealth of Australia, 1993). A recent People's Constitutional Convention on the republican issue nicely illustrates my third dilemma for would-be reformers. A clear majority of the partly government-appointed, partly elected delegates opted for a republican head of state. However, from the start this majority split over the question of whether the head of state should be appointed by the Prime Minister, elected by Parliament or directly elected by the people. Finally, the convention came up with a compromise which, unsurprisingly, was voted down in the constitutional referendum. Meanwhile, the Jamaican Prime Minister has announced that Jamaica will become a republic in the next five years, with a ceremonial president (See Canute James, 'Jamaica: Government Eyes Timetable for a Republic', *Financial Times*, 7 January 1998), though in the last two years little has been heard of this idea.

94. In the French case, for instance, the decolonisation process first led to turmoil in domestic politics and then, in 1958, to a complete change of the constitution. This makes clear that adaptability to external shocks is a crucial variable in explaining institutional persistence and change.

5

The Politics of Electoral Reform since 1885

PETER CATTERALL

In June 1998 the Home Secretary, Jack Straw, promised that a referendum on an alternative voting system for Westminster would be held well in advance of the next general election. This was in fulfilment of a pledge given before the 1997 election as part of a package of constitutional reform measures agreed with the Liberal Democrats. Quite what that alternative might be was already under consideration by a commission set up under the chairmanship of Lord Jenkins with an inbuilt majority for change following the 1997 Labour victory. Meanwhile, alternatives were already being brought forward for non-Westminster elections. A closed party-list system was to be introduced for elections to the European Parliament, variations on the additional-member system for Scotland, Wales and the Greater London Assembly and the supplementary vote for the new mayoralty of London. After over a century of more or less stability in terms of the nature of the electoral system the new Labour government seemed set on an orgy of experimentation.

VICTORIAN PRELUDE

Debate about and experimentation with alternative electoral systems is not, of course, new. As was acknowledged by the Royal Commission into Electoral Systems set up by Asquith in 1908, there were by then already said to be 300 different systems of proportional representation.[1] Some of these systems, such as the single transferable vote (STV) elaborated by Thomas Hare in the 1850s, were developed in Britain. STV was taken up by a short-lived group known as the Representative Reform Association, one of whom, John Stuart Mill, unsuccessfully attempted to incorporate it into the Reform Bill of 1867. One minor change was made then, however. The existing system of simple-majority voting in constituencies with one to four members was amended in a number of large constituencies by the introduction of the limited vote.[2] This did little violence to the contemporary distribution of seats, whilst ostensibly providing for the better representation of minorities.

The need to ensure the representation of minorities was a leitmotif of Victorian proposals for alternative electoral arrangements. Schemes such as the limited vote, the cumulative vote or STV were all designed to ensure the representation of minority opinion and combat the perceived risk that the simple-majority system, as used by an expanding and unsophisticated electorate, would highlight divisions and promote social conflict or indeed the tyranny of the majority that Lord Hailsham was to warn of in referring, during the 1970s, to the risks of 'elective dictatorship'.[3] Victorians were persuaded of the need to ensure this minority representation in the case of delicate issues such as education, the cumulative vote being introduced for elections to the school boards created in 1870.[4]

The representation of minorities remained a significant consideration when the extension of the franchise in 1884 reopened the issue of the electoral system. One of the fruits of this was the founding of the Proportional Representation Society (PRS). In an early publication the PRS pointed out that the existing simple-majority system was open to:

> grave objections because, while it does not in all cases obtain for majorities their due predominance in the legislature, it fails to secure for minorities that proportion of representation to which their numbers justly entitle them. The present system ... may bring about either the rule of the minority or the political extermination of the minority.[5]

This not only led to rogue results, such as the Tory majority in 1874 apparently secured on a minority of votes, a feat repeated in 1886.[6] The PRS also argued, prefiguring arguments that were to recur throughout the twentieth century and to become particularly prominent in the 1970s,[7] that it led to fluctuations in the balance of power and a resulting instability in policy. Furthermore, extension of the franchise in Ireland without reform of the voting system could mean 'that those who hold loyal and moderate opinions, although numbering more than one-third of the whole electorate, might be everywhere out-voted and reduced to silence',[8] an accurate prediction as it turned out.

Initially, however, the PRS did not favour any particular remedy. This vagueness helped it to pick up wide support, including 184 MPs more or less evenly divided between Liberals and Conservatives.[9] The fragility of this support was, however, made clear by a survey of Liberal associations in 1884. Of the 21 associations which declared support for proportional representation (PR) it turned out that for most this simply meant equal electoral districts.[10] It was widely assumed at the time that this reform alone would result in 'a general correspondence between the support in votes and the representation of the two great parties'; a view which the Royal Commission recognised was not supported by subsequent experience.[11] A new system of single-member constituencies was seen as likely to lead to a fairer result, a clearer mandate and relationship with the voters for each candidate and a more straightforward test for parties, faced as they were with the challenge of organising for a greatly expanded electorate. By the time the PRS eventually decided that it ought instead to campaign for STV it was already too late; a redistribution scheme based on single-member constituencies and supported by both party leaders by then commanded the field. Accordingly, the PRS's parliamentary support proved chimeric and it is not surprising that only 31 MPs were prepared to support Sir John Lubbock's motion against the 1885 Redistribution Bill. The case for reform, insofar as it had been made, gained little headway against an amendment of the existing arrangements which did not have STV's disadvantage of being, as Gladstone put it, 'artificial, not known to our usages or history'.[12]

Although a handful of multi-member constituencies survived until 1950, the result of the 1885 redistribution was that single-member constituencies elected by simple-majority became and have remained the norm. At a time when the idea of party programmes was beginning to be developed by Joseph Chamberlain and others, this system, for its supporters, provided for popularly elected government with a clear mandate. This objective was more important than the representation of minorities argued for by contemporary reformers, devices to secure which, such as the limited vote, were rejected or dropped in 1885.

The 1885 system, for supporters such as Lloyd George, provided for this, securing the democratic principle that the majority should rule.[13] However, the majorities secured could be grossly disproportionate as became increasingly apparent by the Edwardian period. Concern on this point in the light of the London borough elections after 1900 was to lead to the revival of the PRS after nearly

20 years of inactivity.[14] At the same time reform was also portrayed as a means of replacing the violent and exaggerated swings of the electoral pendulum, such as the elections of 1895 or 1906, with 'a coherence of method, a steady development of education, and a movement which could be relied upon – slow, perhaps, but sure – from one position to another of political advancement'.[15]

Reform was, however, seen as incompatible with decisive government, which is why groups such as the Fabians continued to oppose it in the Edwardian years. Nevertheless, other groups on the left showed more interest in such ideas. The Social Democratic Federation favoured proportional representation and the use of referendums from the 1880s. Proportional representation was also overwhelmingly endorsed at the 1913 conference of the Independent Labour Party.[16] The Trades Union Congress (TUC) meanwhile passed a resolution in favour of further investigation in 1908, which seems to have been a factor in the decision to establish the Royal Commission later that year.[17]

THE 1908–10 ROYAL COMMISSION AND ALTERNATIVE ELECTORAL SYSTEMS

By then alternative arrangements were no longer of essentially theoretical interest. Witnesses from Belgium, France, Tasmania and Western Australia testified respectively to the list system, the second ballot, STV and the alternative vote (AV) in operation. Passing reference was made to other ideas, but these were considered to be the main alternatives to the existing electoral system in Britain, and remained so up to the 1970s.

List systems were not then seen as much of an alternative. The judgement in an internal Conservative document in 1950, 'List systems of proportional representation are quite alien to our constitution and have probably no advocates in this country',[18] could stand for any party at any time up to the 1970s. So much was this the case that they were at times completely ignored in discussions of proportional representation,[19] whilst the PRS changed its name in 1959 to the Electoral Reform Society (ERS) in order to avoid being linked to continental list systems.[20] Not only were lists seen as detrimental to the constituency system (the personal touch element of which was always a potent factor in the arguments against electoral reform), they were also seen as emphasising 'party divisions in a way which is incompatible with the more elastic ideas of English politics'[21] or, in a colonial setting, as likely to encourage communalism.[22] Furthermore, lists seemed only likely to aggravate 'the tyranny of the party caucus'[23] that was already one of the principal indictments of the 1885 system.

That is a major reason why STV, until the 1970s, was effectively the only system of proportional representation considered in English-speaking countries. Its superiority was described by the ERS as follows:

> The prime purpose of a list system is merely to ensure proportional representation of political parties. The prime purpose of the single transferable vote is to ensure the equal representation of electors by *candidates* of their choice. In a political election, STV therefore ensures proportional representation of political opinion.[24]

Accordingly it has been claimed that it would improve the representation of women, or of ethnic minorities.[25] Its multi-member constituencies would also ensure that substantial minorities, such as the Labour voters of Surrey or the Tory voters of Wales, would no longer risk going unrepresented, and there would be no need for the tactical voting which, it was estimated, affected 10 per cent of the votes cast in May 1997.[26] The size of these constituencies do, however, have the perceived drawback that they would undermine the tradition of the local accountability of the MP to his or her constituents. AV, on the other hand, was seen as another way of encouraging voting for candidates without this disadvantage – for instance, the bill introduced by the Tory MP for St Albans in 1954 to allow constituencies to introduce AV was intended to protect 'the independently-minded candidate'[27] – whilst strengthening local representativeness because it required the winner to secure over 50 per cent of the vote.[28]

The second ballot and AV are in fact similar. However, whilst the second ballot only runs off the top two candidates, AV redistributes voter preferences amongst all the candidates without the expense of a second ballot. These systems would have done least violence to the post-1885 arrangements, AV being seen, not least by the Royal Commission, as 'the best method of remedying the most serious defect which a single-member system can possess – the return of minority candidates'.[29] For this reason, the Royal Commission recommended AV if the single-member system was retained, a recommendation which was overtaken by the constitutional crisis of 1910–11 and was to have no effect.

Both AV and the second ballot are primarily designed to secure the return of candidates with majority support in their constituencies. As such they are in no sense proportional over the electorate as a whole. Instead AV would have, if anything, exaggerated the swing in 1924 as the Conservatives would have picked up many of the Liberals' second preferences. The PRS study of the 1929 election, which Labour won despite garnering fewer votes than the Tories, also suggested that under AV Labour would have done even better whilst the Liberals would have won fewer seats than under first past the post.[30] Similarly, recent studies have shown that the grossly disproportionate result of 1997 would have been even more distorted if AV had been in operation.[31] This tendency was already clearly apparent from elections held under AV in Australia or Canada by the interwar period. As a result the PRS generally regarded AV as worse than the existing system. Whilst their preferred system, STV, was designed to prevent the under-representation of minorities, AV instead sought to prevent the under-representation of majorities.[32] These majorities had to be won by picking up second preferences, and in notorious Australian examples were actually won by these second preferences.[33] In effect this was a form of second ballot, without knowing who the candidates would be on the decisive second round. Not surprisingly, AV's detractors regarded this as something of a lottery; throwaway second choices which were, according to Churchill, 'the most worthless votes given for the most worthless candidates'.[34] The second ballot variant, which would have avoided this detrimental feature of AV, was meanwhile generally regarded, certainly by the Royal Commission, as too expensive.

The second ballot had been advocated in the 1880s and 1890s by leading Fabians, on the grounds that it would maximise the anti-Conservative vote.[35] Neither this nor AV, however, commanded general support on the left before the First World War. In 1914, when Ramsay MacDonald led the decisive defeat of STV at the Labour Party conference on the grounds of the need for strong government able to carry out its programme, AV was no less heavily rejected. The Party Secretary, Arthur Henderson, said that he 'could think of nothing more to the disadvantage of the party' than AV.[36] As Labour was the third party at the time, still dependent on the Progressive Alliance with the Liberals, this was a very reasonable view. In the changed political circumstances of the war, however, with Labour more likely to gain than to lose from AV, Henderson was in favour by 1918.[37]

By then, as a result of the discussions of electoral change necessitated by the wartime decay of the voting registers, reform of the electoral system was again on the agenda. This had not seemed likely since immediately before the war. Concern to protect the interests of minorities in a home-rule Ireland, not least to contain the more extreme forms of nationalism, had led to the founding of a Parliamentary Committee for Proportional Representation (PCPR) in 1912, which had helped to extract from a reluctant Liberal government, election by STV to the proposed Irish Senate and to a number of multi-member constituencies in the Irish Commons. In 1914, however, the PCPR fell into abeyance, and did not revive until after the Speaker's Conference reported early in 1917.

REFORM DEFEATED, 1917–18

The Speaker's Conference, an all-party gathering drawn from both Houses (the first of its kind), as well as recommending universal manhood suffrage and votes for women over 30 qualified on the local government franchise by owning or occupying land or premises of an annual value of £5, unanimously recommended the introduction of STV for boroughs with more than three members and London and (by a majority) AV for the remaining single-member seats.

This sudden enthusiasm for STV, albeit a limited dose of 211 seats, was curious.[38] STV had been recognised by the Royal Commission as the only system of proportional representation likely to command public support, a view reaffirmed by the Ullswater Conference in 1930. This was because it retained constituencies and election of candidates rather than party. The Royal Commission, however, felt it had a number of drawbacks. It argued: 'The greatest evil that can befall a country is a weak executive; and if a strong one can only be obtained at the cost of mathematical accuracy of representation, the price should be willingly paid.' The difficulty of minority government in 1892–95 was 'not an experience which those who underwent it are anxious to repeat'.

Second, unlike in the case of AV, it was difficult to provide for by-elections in the multi-member constituencies STV required.[39] However, the limited experiment proposed by the Speaker's Conference would have minimised these drawbacks. At the same time the scheme also tried to ensure that multi-member constituencies would only be introduced in large urban areas where the natural communities were frequently already much larger than the 1885 constituencies. It could thus be seen as a partial reversion to an attempt to represent towns and cities, as before 1885, rather than constituencies. Meanwhile the proposal that AV, which is simply the expression of STV-style preferences in a single-member constituency, be used for the remaining seats would have ensured that a common preferential system would have been used across the country.

STV was widely supported by Unionist peers, conscious of the disproportionate result of 1906 and its consequences, not least for their own House. However, it had little appeal for the MPs from those areas most likely to be affected. London members were especially hostile, forming the Anti-Proportional Representation Committee (APRC) in 1917. Buoyed by the prospects of a khaki election after the war, in contrast to their colleagues in the Lords, Conservative MPs consistently voted in the main against STV in 1917–18. Liberal and Labour MPs were marginally in favour. It was only in the changed electoral circumstances of the 1920s that Liberals were to come round to the merits of STV. By then, however, it was too late. In 1917–18 Liberals and Labour instead saw party advantage more in AV. This had only been adopted in the Speaker's Conference on a party vote, and voting on this issue during the passage of the bill continued to be on party lines. Whilst STV was defeated in the Commons, AV was thus narrowly supported, only to be repeatedly struck down by the Conservative majority in the Lords. STV was instead reinstated by the peers, who on 29 January 1918 passed a complete scheme for STV in Britain, except in sparsely populated areas, which went far beyond the recommendations of the Speaker's Conference.

Variations based on this scheme were to become Liberal Party orthodoxy from the 1920s, and continued to be enshrined, for instance, in the Liberal/SDP Alliance scheme of 'community PR' for both Westminster and local elections put forward in 1982. The 143 multi-member constituencies suggested here were supposed to represent 'natural communities'.[40] The communities proposed for rural areas, however, were distinctly smaller than those for urban Britain, an arrangement which was seen by opponents as likely to discriminate against the Labour Party.[41]

Liberal votes in the Commons, however, helped to defeat the scheme in 1918. Finally a compromise arrangement of an experimental 100 seats to be elected by STV was put forward in February 1918, but when this scheme was presented on 13 May this too was rejected by the Commons, principally on the votes of Conservative opponents.[42] One, Sir George Cave, later complained that the advocates of STV had been far too successful in the novel atmosphere of the Speaker's Conference.[43] The limited experiment proposed had been the price agreed in order to allay the anxieties engendered by a massive extension of the franchise; indeed Lord Parmoor later pointed out that 'some members of the Conference … agreed to the alterations to the franchise only on the condition that they were accompanied by a system of PR'.[44] For them, as elsewhere in Europe where its advocates were more successful, PR was a safeguard once a democratic suffrage had been installed. Outside the committee room, however, it was a different matter. Once the key issue of franchise reform had been agreed by the conference and accepted by the government, attention focused instead on this question of the electoral system. The fact that the government clearly regarded this as an optional (and, as far as Lloyd George was concerned, an unwelcome) extra, allowing free votes on all divisions concerning the electoral system, only reinforced the distinction between this issue and the rest of the bill. This decoupling not only explains the disproportionate attention paid to STV and AV in the parliamentary debates on the bill, but also the contrast between the line taken in the Speaker's Conference and in the chamber. In the end STV was retained only for the university seats that were to be abolished in 1950.

THE INTERWAR YEARS

It was a defeat Lloyd George would have cause to regret. The cause of electoral reform nevertheless made some progress in the immediate aftermath of the First World War. In 1918 STV replaced the cumulative vote for the purpose of elections to Scottish school boards, continuing until these were abolished in 1928. STV was also introduced for elections to the House of Laity of the new Church Assembly in 1919, and extended to the House of Clergy in 1921. And in 1920 the Government of Ireland Act provided for parliaments elected by STV in both Dublin and Belfast.

By 1924, however, prospects for reform were receding. Despite the rogue general election results of 1922–29, there was little public interest at any time during the interwar years in electoral reform. Meanwhile, parliamentary attitudes were hardening. Despite the fact that the stock objections to proportional representation do not apply as far as local government is concerned,[45] repeated efforts to introduce STV for local elections culminated in the narrow defeat of Harold Morris' private bill in 1923. Attempts to introduce STV for Westminster also met with failure. Private members' bills in 1921 and 1924 essentially based on the Lords' scheme of January 1918 were both defeated by majorities of about 100. Although a number of leading advocates of STV, such as Lord Robert Cecil, the chairman of the PCPR, were Tories, his party was increasingly opposed. This was already clear in a canvass for the PCPR in 1921, which also showed that the Asquithian Liberals were equally in favour. At the general election the following year the latter was indeed to become the first political party formally to adopt STV as a manifesto commitment, even if many of their Coalitionist brethren were to remain unconvinced until after the evidence of third-party squeeze became palpable in the 1924 election.[46] This politicisation of the issue might help to account for the demise of the PCPR, which ceased to meet in 1921.

The same canvass showed Labour as largely in favour of reform.[47] In the immediate aftermath of the war the party's National Executive Committee also favoured STV as part of its reconstruction proposals.[48] By 1924, however, its parliamentary ranks were greatly increased and the party was in government. The revitalised APRC contained in its ranks Labour figures such as the recently elected Herbert Morrison. As well as the familiar objections, such as the problems of maintaining the personal touch and by-elections, the complexity of the system and the allowing of cranks into Parliament, it highlighted a concern designed to appeal to Labour – the creation of large constituencies would favour the richest party.[49] Morrison, who made one of the most effective speeches against the Morris Bill of 1924, added the prospects of unsavoury bargaining and unstable government, but the main reason for the switch around in Labour to opposing STV in the 1924 vote seems to have been the inept parliamentary tactics of the Liberals, which prompted the Parliamentary Labour Party (PLP), despite considerable Cabinet support for the bill,[50] to decide by a large majority to oppose it.[51] Two years later STV was to be similarly opposed by the party conference.

By then STV was also being dismantled in Northern Ireland. Both the introduction of STV for local elections in Ireland in 1919 and the 1920 act were opposed by Ulster Unionists; the Marquess of Dufferin and Ava stating, 'We in the north who are a majority do not like proportional representation.' A major problem was that, as Lord Craigavon, the Northern Ireland Prime Minister, recognised in 1928, unlike in the South, that majority was too narrow for comfort. There was therefore 'no room for a third party in Ulster politics'; Unionist support had to be maximised by making it as far as possible a straight fight between them and the Nationalists. This meant a reversion to the simple-majority system, carried out for local elections in 1922 and for elections to the Northern Ireland Parliament in 1929. STV was only retained for the university seats and the indirectly elected Senate.[52] By 1933, as a consequence, some 70 per cent of members were returned unopposed.[53]

Nevertheless, the interwar period was also to see the first time in the twentieth century that a government brought forward legislation to change the electoral system. The legislation introduced in January 1931 did not, however, reflect enthusiasm on the part of the Labour government. MacDonald, the Prime Minister, had never abandoned his radical belief in the doctrine of the mandate. He did nevertheless mention the electoral system amongst the issues for consideration by the all-party Ullswater Conference on elections set up in 1929, amongst old Labour chestnuts such as the plural vote and the use of cars.[54] Of the party submissions to the conference, however, only the Liberals mentioned the electoral system.[55] The hung Parliament resulting from the 1929 election did, however, give them some leverage and this issue was exhaustively considered, but along party lines. STV may have been unanimously recommended for India by the Simon Commission at the end of the 1920s, as it had been for Ireland and Malta at the start of the decade, as a means of ensuring the representation of minorities in divided communities. Britain, however, was a different matter. In the Ullswater Conference, therefore, whilst STV was carried by the votes of the Conservatives and Liberals against the Labour delegates, the Tories only supported it if some change was indeed deemed necessary. From their point of view it was certainly better than AV, which in contrast was rejected by 13 to five in the conference by a combination of the Tories and some Labour delegates against Liberals supporting what they regarded as the next-best option. Reflecting that 'the main purpose of the Conference – viz. some general agreement as to the amendment of our electoral laws – had failed', Ullswater asked to be relieved of the task.[56]

He did, however, note that whilst the Tories were opposed in all circumstances to AV, fearing a combination of the other parties against them, Labour might support it as part of a package of reforms and the Liberals as at least an improvement on the current system. Conservative lack of enthusiasm for STV and personal antipathy to Lloyd George then ruled out tentative moves towards an understanding between the Tories and Liberals to remove Labour from office. The Labour leadership meanwhile recognised that its parliamentary party was no more enthusiastic about STV, but might be prepared to swallow AV as the price of continuing Liberal support for the Labour government. AV was also widely and erroneously seen as a means of preventing a repetition of the Tory landslide of 1924.[57]

However, with neither party optimistic about its prospects in an election held in the midst of economic crisis the prolongation of the government was clearly the key factor in reaching this understanding.

It was in such inauspicious circumstances that a government bill was introduced in January 1931. For Labour supporters its main features were the abolition of the business vote and restrictions on the use of cars. For the Liberals, unlike occasional private bills, including most recently Lord Beauchamp's bill in 1923, it did not even offer AV. The initial scheme was a supplementary vote arrangement, in which only two preferences were allowed; effectively a compromise between AV and the second ballot. Full AV was only added as a result of an amendment by a Labour member, C. H. Wilson, now the chairman of the PRS executive committee, at the report stage. Arguing that there was no mandate for AV, peers then proceeded to emasculate the bill, restricting its operation to the 174 seats in boroughs with a population of more than 200,000. This would have kept AV out of the Tory heartlands in the shires, and excluded virtually all the constituencies where AV might benefit the Liberals. Despite the lack of enthusiasm of some members of the government for the measure, it therefore seems likely that they would have pressed to overturn the Lords' amendments. In the event, however, the Labour administration fell in August and MacDonald, as Prime Minister of the new National government, showed no interest in continuing with the bill.

During the rest of the 1930s there were occasional suggestions from Conservatives that STV be used for a reformed House of Lords. The PRS and some Conservatives also showed interest in STV as a means of tackling electoral anomalies and one-party rule in local government.[58] However, the collapse of democracy in Europe, and especially in Germany, cast a pall over the campaign for proportional representation. This condemned it for many; even though the PRS showed that the triumph of Nazism owed little to PR. During the Second World War, for instance, Labour was to argue in *The Old World and the New Society* that 'both Continental and Dominion experience remains decisive against proportional representation'.[59] Morrison, now Home Secretary, even wished to exclude the electoral system from the terms of reference of the Speaker's Conference set up to consider various technical changes to electoral law in 1944.[60] Though eventually included, such was the general hostility in the major parties that the votes in the conference were foregone conclusions; STV being rejected by 25 votes to four and AV by 20 votes to five.[61]

TWO-PARTY DOMINANCE, 1950–70

Even three successive defeats in the 1950s, including losing in 1951 despite receiving more votes than the Conservatives, did not revive Labour interest in electoral reform. The prevalence of straight fights until the 1970s meant that for most in both of the major parties the election results reflected the decisive choice of electors in a given area. Private members' bills in favour of some kind of reform nevertheless continued to appear. And Churchill, who returned to power in 1951, also had a history of sympathy with the issue. In the 1930s he had advocated some variant on the 1918 Lords scheme involving STV for the larger cities.[62] This would not have involved any boundary problems, whilst promising both to revive the corporate identity of cities and to tackle the long-term Tory concern at their lack of representation in urban areas. Nevertheless, electoral reform in the 1950s, Churchill recognised, was 'not practical politics at this juncture'.[63]

With their return to power, electoral reform seemed to have little to offer most of his parliamentary followers. A Liberal deputation in 1953 calling for a select committee inquiry therefore received a dusty answer. Chancellor of the Exchequer R. A. Butler, pointed out:

> The one factor that would probably not emerge from a factual enquiry is really the dominant one, namely that an exact mathematical representation in the House of voting strength in the country would have the paradoxical effect of giving the Liberals an influence totally disproportionate to their support. This would not be in the interests of good government, nor would it be democratic.[64]

Calls in 1954–55 for a Royal Commission on electoral systems made little headway on similar grounds. Both major parties were interested in a number of procedural reforms, eventually leading to the establishment of another Speaker's Conference in 1965. At this stage, however, they had little interest in reform of the electoral system. In the Speaker's Conference, STV was rejected by 19 votes to one, the one dissentient being its Liberal member, Eric Lubbock, the grandson of the founder of the PRS. Alternative voting does not seem to have been even considered. When Lubbock subsequently tried to raise STV in debate he was rebuffed by Labour ministers using much the same arguments as Butler in the 1950s. The object of the electoral system according to Home Secretary James Callaghan, was to elect a government, not to be fair to the Liberal Party.[65]

The existence of a minority party with very limited support and clearly self-interested reasons for supporting electoral reform very much helped to undermine the case for it as far as the major parties were concerned. At the same time, proportional representation also continued to be damned by – often entirely erroneous – associations. For instance, Churchill's attitude towards reform had hardened by 1954; 'Logically, there is a lot to be said for it, but it had brought to a standstill almost every parliament which had tried it.'[66] The proliferation of parties to which he referred had, however, pre-dated proportional representation in Europe, whilst Tasmania, which introduced STV in 1907, retained a two-party system. France, which he particularly instanced, did not have proportional representation. However inappropriate as an example, the Fourth Republic was nevertheless a perfect illustration of the weak and unstable government which opponents claimed would be ushered in by electoral reform. Indeed, one Conservative document in 1955 argued that PR would not only hamstring government but completely stifle political debate.[67]

THE REVIVAL OF THE CAMPAIGN FOR PR IN THE 1970s

The post-1885 system did not always produce the decisive government which was frequently claimed as one of its principal virtues. The ERS in 1965 pointed out that six out of 16 elections since 1900 had failed to return a clear result.[68] Then, in 1974, this happened again in two elections in the same year. There was renewed interest in electoral reform as some began to argue that the simple-majority system neither produced strong government nor parliaments which reflected the popular suffrage.[69] Even though Labour secured a precarious majority of three at the second attempt in October, that was soon whittled away by by-election defeats, so that the government lost its majority in 1976. What majority it had had, in any case, rested upon a relatively narrow electoral base. From a 47.9 per cent share of the vote when it secured a 100-seat majority in 1966, Labour now had 39.2 per cent. The two-party system which had characterised 1945–70 seemed suddenly to have started to fall apart. One of the reasons given for the subsequent establishment of the Hansard Society's Commission on Electoral Reform in 1975, was the dramatic fall in support for the two major parties combined to below 80 per cent.[70] This reflected growing support for Nationalists and a revival of the Liberals. The fact that their revival was, however, hardly rewarded in terms of seats won made the case for considering electoral reform rather more eloquently than in their days of minimal support in the 1950s.

The Liberal revival came in the context of the 'Who Governs?' election of February 1974, called by the Conservatives against the background of a miners' strike. In a sense their strength in the elections of 1974, and the fall in both the Labour and Tory vote, was a vote of no confidence in the major parties. Not only was there widespread disillusionment about the ability of either party effectively to tackle the economic problems and industrial unrest of the period; party government was portrayed as one of the culprits. The view that the simple-majority system facilitates violent and counter-productive switches in policy had long been a staple of reformers, but it was particularly resonant when enunciated against a background of relative economic decline. Electoral reform was seen as a way to end the damage that adversarial politics was felt to be doing,[71] not least in terms of interventions in microeconomic policy, notably the waves of nationalisations by successive Labour governments, which continued in 1974–79 despite the lack, for much of the time, of either a clear mandate or a parliamentary majority. The doctrine of the mandate, one Tory pamphlet proclaimed, seemed to have become the 'divine right of minority governments to ignore everyone else'.[72] In business circles, as a result, the existing electoral system began to be seen both as destabilising and as facilitating Bennite extremism. One of the principal progenitors of the Hansard Commission, the editor of *The Times* William Rees-Mogg, argued that it was a gamble that could lead to government by the hard left.[73] Electoral reform was seen as a way of securing both a more stable and a less class-based political climate. Accordingly, there was much support from industry for the new bodies campaigning for electoral reform which appeared in these years.

One of the first was Conservative Action for Electoral Reform,[74] set up in the wake of the party's February 1974 defeat, in which it won more votes but fewer seats than Labour. Prominent members, such as Miles Hudson, were impressed by the apparent contrast between the economic difficulties of Britain and the success of West Germany, where the additional-member system (AMS) seemed to have contributed to a virtuous combination of strong and stable government and a responsible left-wing party.[75] This view was also to be championed by the prominent Liberal, Richard Holme, in his *A Democracy Which Works* in 1977.[76]

As recently as 1972 the ERS had still been able to describe STV as

'what "PR" means in the English-speaking world'.[77] STV indeed
enjoyed a revival in fortunes at the start of the 1970s. Despite initial
Unionist reluctance it was reintroduced – after direct rule had been
reimposed in 1972 – for local government in Northern Ireland in 1973
as a way of ensuring the representation of minorities and a means of
encouraging cross-community power sharing rather than one-party
rule, and has since been used for all elections, except to Westminster,
in the province. It was also retained by the Church of England when
the General Synod was created in 1970. However, its very applicability
in the troubled situation of Northern Ireland may have, if anything,
undermined its apparent validity elsewhere. In Northern Ireland,
as in the Empire during the interwar period, STV was to be used
to tackle communalism. The problem in the rest of the UK, not least
in the aftermath of the elections of 1974, was seen to be rather
different.

The Kilbrandon Commission, which reported in 1973, for instance,
only gave qualified support for STV. Set up in response to rising
nationalist support in Scotland and Wales in the late 1960s, it
supported the use of STV to elect the regional assemblies it
recommended as a means of ensuring the representation of
minorities. STV was all very well for such bodies with limited powers.
When it came to electing a government, however, it concluded that
'the relative majority system is likely to be the most effective', and
therefore did not suggest any change to Westminster elections.[78]

The failings of the existing system in 1974 were, however, to
prompt consideration of other alternatives. Whereas the only other
options Kilbrandon had looked at were AV or STV, in the aftermath of
1974 admiration for the apparent superiority of the Rhineland model
of economic management meant that for the first time STV acquired a
serious rival as a possible proportional system for Britain,[79] indeed one
which, whatever the merits of STV in the peculiar setting of Northern
Ireland, seemed to many of the most prominent reformers of the
decade better suited to the requirement of furnishing a stable and
acceptable government for Britain as a whole. This development was
underlined when the Hansard Commission reported in 1976.

The champions of STV, the ERS, had initially been invited to
sponsor the commission but refused, on the grounds that they did not
wish to be accused of prejudicing the outcome, so it was offered to the
Hansard Society instead. Whether this actually affected the result is
open to doubt. What is certain is that all but one of the Hansard
Commission's members instead preferred a variant of the German
model, consisting of 480 single-member constituencies topped up by

160 additional members who would be selected from the best losers (rather than a party list as in Germany). This, it was argued, would retain the long-cherished constituency link, facilitate by-elections which the Hansard Commission, no less than the earlier Royal Commission,[80] continued to see as useful barometers of opinion, and provide for a greater degree of proportionality amongst the parties,[81] although the weighting for single-member constituencies would still make it entirely possible to achieve a majority on a minority vote.

Enthusiasts for AMS such as Holme, Hudson and the Tory peer Lord Harlech, who in September 1974 penned the foreword to the European Movement's submission calling for the introduction of AMS for direct elections to the European Parliament,[82] were prominent in the leadership of the National Committee for Electoral Reform (NCER) which was set up in the wake of the Hansard Commission report in 1976. The NCER, however, was officially neutral between systems, being designed to try and mobilise a broad coalition for change with all-party support.

There is evidence of considerable sympathy in Conservative ranks at the time. Even just before the 1983 election an informal survey found 123 Tory MPs favourably disposed towards reform.[83] And, as in the 1930s, Tory peers, including Lord Blake, the chairman of the 1970s Hansard Commission, in the 1980s advocated STV for local elections as a means of improving accountability.[84] However, the disappearance of the threat from the left by the 1990s also gradually removed the urgency for Conservatives.[85] Nevertheless, of 23 motions from constituency associations to the 1975 party conference, 18 were in favour. The party leadership, however, not least the newly elected leader, Margaret Thatcher, were hostile to a change which would deprive them of the opportunity of winning outright and which might also harm them much more than their Labour opponents.[86]

Despite the view of reformers that the geographical spread of the Labour vote would give them an advantage under a proportional system,[87] and the founding of a Labour Campaign for Electoral Reform in March 1976, there was even less support in the then governing party. STV, Barbara Castle recorded in her diary, had been recommended by Kilbrandon as 'the only way of eliminating the perpetual Labour majorities in Scotland and Wales which devolution would produce'. The implication was clear: 'If we were not careful we could see the end of any possibility of a Labour Government.'[88] The belief that general elections were about forming majoritarian governments, to which both Kilbrandon and Thatcher subscribed, was if anything held more strongly in Labour, whatever a minority of

Labour MPs thought about the merits of proportional representation for either devolved assemblies or the European Parliament.[89]

Indeed, the Labour government showed no inclination to follow Kilbrandon's recommendation of STV for the devolved assemblies it proposed to create. Despite the grossly disproportionate results in Scotland in 1974, and the risk of a small swing delivering a Scottish Nationalist Party (SNP) majority for independence on a minority of the vote, the simple-majority system was preferred for both Scotland and Wales. Attempts by the Lords to substitute STV were overturned and the Labour MP, J. P. Mackintosh, the chairman of the Hansard Society, was ridiculed when he rose to advocate the Hansard Commission's scheme. Although this owed something to the perceived flaws of the Hansard scheme rather than of AMS *per se* – Neil Kinnock for instance pouring scorn on its idea that a defeated MP could remain in the House as one of the best losers – it also seemed to reflect an ingrained dislike in the Scottish ranks of the Labour Party.[90]

Although direct elections to the European Parliament, like those to devolved assemblies, did not involve the election of a national government, and were therefore not susceptible to one of the most widely-held objections to proportional systems, Labour initially showed no more interest in using anything other than the simple-majority system in this instance either.[91] The then Prime Minister, James Callaghan, later commented in his memoirs: 'the Party was against [PR] and so was I'. However, the Lib–Lab Pact forged in March 1977 to ward off a Tory vote of no confidence changed all that. Under the agreement between the two parties the government, in its final recommendation on the form of direct elections to the European Parliament was to 'take full account of the Liberal Party's commitment'.[92]

Earlier that month Liberal peers had introduced a bill providing for STV for European elections. The government's White Paper, however, offered only a choice between the status quo, STV or a list system. A list system, long anathema as far as electoral reformers in Britain were concerned, seems to have had the virtue of not being associated with any particular party, as was the case with STV. Some members of the Cabinet also felt it would be easier to implement. In these circumstances the scheme put forward by the Liberal political scientist, Michael Steed, in his pamphlet *Fair Elections or Fiasco?* seemed to offer a workable compromise. He suggested an open-list system based on the Finnish voting model, which allowed votes for candidates as well as parties. Although the votes in this system are cast for candidates, the seats are allocated proportionately to each party; accordingly, unlike in STV, a popular candidate could fail to get elected if a different party, overall, received more votes.[93] The primacy thus accorded to party was, the ERS argued, particularly inappropriate in a situation 'where the national parties will be less relevant than opinion on European questions which cut right across the party lines'.[94] However, this ignores the obvious point that it was the need to avoid an exacerbation of existing internal Labour divisions on Europe which underpinned the relative attraction of list PR for the government. Steed's proposal was incorporated in the November 1977 bill, which thus became only the second occasion in the twentieth century when a government measure had put forward an alternative electoral system for a national poll.

Although a few members of the Cabinet had long favoured proportional representation, the fact that 16 of them voted for the government's proposal probably reflects more the tactical exigencies of the Lib–Lab Pact. Callaghan, meanwhile, despite his personal doubts, seems to have worked hard to try and persuade his party to vote for the measure.[95] However, with a majority of his back-benchers joining the bulk of the Tories in opposing the scheme, it was defeated by 319 to 222 votes. With a number of private members' motions in favour of STV, AMS and AV being even more heavily defeated, the bill then defaulted to the simple-majority system in England, Wales and Scotland, and STV in Northern Ireland.[96] The one consolation for electoral reformers was that a Unionist motion to overturn this last provision was defeated by 241 votes to 150.

ELECTORAL REFORM IN THE 1990s

Despite the three successive election defeats that followed, a motion favouring electoral reform was comfortably defeated at the 1989 Labour conference. And the May 1990 policy paper, *Looking to the Future*, explicitly stated, 'Labour is opposed to changing the electoral system for the Commons.'[97]

It was, however, already starting to show greater willingness than in the 1970s to contemplate alternatives for other types of elections. In March 1990, for instance, the Scottish Labour conference voted against using a simple-majority system for a future Scottish parliament. The background to this was Labour's awareness of the political capital the SNP could make out of the unpopularity of policies pursued north of the border by a Tory government which lacked a mandate – having won less than one-quarter of the Scottish vote in 1987 – pointed up by the SNP by-election triumph in Govan in 1988. The Labour-dominated Scottish Constitutional Convention (SCC) was set up the following year as a means of building a broad coalition of support for devolution to outflank the SNP's policy of independence in Europe.[98] This included agreement with the Liberal Democrats and others on the SCC on a voting system which would meet some of their objectives and allay concern that a future Scottish parliament would be dominated by Labour machine politicians from the one-party local councils of central Scotland.[99] Therefore, in contrast to the devolution bill prepared in opposition in 1987, some alternative voting system was envisaged.

STV, however, was rejected as an option. If it had to be a proportional system in order to achieve the widest possible consensus for devolution, Labour's preference by the early 1990s was increasingly AMS. Even those prepared to advocate STV for local government preferred a variant of AMS.[100] This had the perceived virtue of retaining single-member constituencies and a strong party system, as well as providing a means whereby Labour and the Liberal Democrats could co-operate to defeat the hegemony the Tories had seemingly established under first past the post. The scheme that was eventually adopted and enshrined in the 1997 White Paper, by ensuring that a majority of the members of the future Scottish Parliament are elected in existing UK single-member constituencies, may also perpetuate the pro-Labour and anti-SNP bias of the simple-majority system as observable in Scotland over the period since the 1960s. Indeed, the small number of additional members Labour initially proposed would have helped to ensure this. In the end the SCC compromised on the number of additional members – just as the adoption of a variant of AMS was itself a compromise – halving the difference between the numbers proposed by Labour and by the Liberal Democrats.[101]

AMS was also to be advocated for use at Westminster elections by the left-wing think tank, the Institute for Public Policy Research in 1991.[102] Even the Liberal Democrats seemed increasingly prepared to regard AMS as an acceptable alternative; their draft Reform Bill of 1997, for instance, simply providing for a referendum to decide between it, STV and the simple-majority system.[103] However, AMS was still far from entirely capturing the Labour Party, as was to be apparent from the history of the Plant Commission.

This was set up in 1990 to look at voting systems appropriate for devolved legislatures and the proposed elected second chamber to replace the House of Lords, and only belatedly – at the 1990 party conference and against the wishes of the party leadership – was it invited to look at Westminster elections as well.[104] It did not examine local government, which was then being reorganised by the government commission under Sir John Banham.

In discharging its task the commission did not receive any steer from the party leadership, which did not help to resolve the tensions between the various views held by its membership. Some members of the commission, including its chairman Raymond Plant, favoured AMS. Others, notably Margaret Beckett, who was to become the Deputy Leader of the Labour Party in 1992, strongly supported the retention of the simple-majority system. The result was a dual compromise. Early in its deliberations, following the distinction made by Kilbrandon, the commission distinguished between 'legislative' and 'deliberative' bodies. For the latter, felt to include the European Parliament and an elected upper house, the commission was able to agree on open-list PR, which was endorsed by the 1993 Labour Party conference. This was a relatively uncontentious matter, although AMS had initially been favoured for both.[105]

Far more controversial was the question of the appropriate system for Westminster elections. On this matter the desire of many members to retain single member constituencies and single party government clashed with an equally widespread feeling that the existing system needed reform. The result they came up with was described by Plant as 'a fair compromise between First Past the Post and a stricter form of proportional representation'. More pungently, one disgruntled member of the commission called it an example of 'classic decision making by committee'. The supplementary vote (SV) which emerged from this process as the recommendation was, as in 1931 when it had last been advocated, a compromise which would involve minimal change rather than an idea with widespread support. Conscious, no doubt, of the circumstances of the recommendation, John Smith, a supporter of the existing system who had replaced the more pro-reform Kinnock as party leader by the time the commission reported in 1993, was therefore only prepared to offer a referendum on electoral reform for Westminster, rather than adopting SV as Labour Party policy.[106]

SV has, however, been put forward by the government of Smith's successor, Tony Blair, as the means for electing the proposed London mayor. Plant had suggested that different electoral systems are appropriate for different institutions, though he might have added that they are, as in Scotland, also a means of binding in other parties to minimise opposition.[107] In the case of an executive mayor, where a single office-holder is being elected, a majoritarian system clearly has its merits as a means of maximising the victor's legitimacy, though it is unclear whether a limited majoritarian system was preferred over AV simply for reasons of likely party advantage. The Labour Party, so far, has not, however, advocated SV for any other type of elections.

Nor, except in the case of Scotland where it was committed by the conclusions of the SCC to introduce it, Wales, and for the new London Assembly, has Labour so far proposed AMS. AMS may have become the most popular proportional system amongst Labour reformers by the 1990s, but the experience of New Zealand with a version of it in 1996 hardly suggested it would be easy to sell in the UK for Westminster elections. Not only was the outcome after protracted power-broking a coalition no one had voted for – it was exactly the negation of democracy which opponents readily associate with proportional systems.[108] AMS also continued to be attacked by Labour opponents on the grounds that it 'would mean two classes of MP: some constituency-based, the others constitutional free-loaders … without any constituency responsibilities'.[109] This was quite apart from the objection to which German experience laid it open, that it gave too much influence to minor parties. This was no doubt in Blair's mind when, in January 1997, he expressed his doubts about proportional representation on very traditional grounds; 'you must have a system where you have a strong link between MP and constituency and where you don't have disproportionate power in the hands of small parties'.[110]

As with Plant, these objections did not seem to apply with European elections. Instead the introduction of list PR (except for Northern Ireland, which will retain STV) effected by Blair could simply be portrayed as ending Britain's anomalous position as far as elections to the European Parliament are concerned. However, as John Curtice has pointed out,[111] the effect of the legislation is just to replace one anomaly with another. Britain is the only EU state with a closed-list system *and* small constituencies. Whilst the latter reduces the proportionality of the outcome, the former limits voter choice to between parties rather than candidates, which prompted Tories in the debates to suggest MEPs would be more accountable to their party bosses than the electors. The adoption of closed lists breaks with Plant's recommendations, which favoured both open selection policies and open lists.[112] Those on the Labour left were also inclined to see the scheme as being as much an exercise in party management, a means of excluding the left-wing Labour MEPs who gave Blair a hard time over the revision of Clause IV in 1995, as of electoral reform.[113]

The closed-list scheme certainly would not pass the criteria against which the Jenkins Commission, set up in December 1997, were to judge alternative electoral systems. These were: 'broad proportionality', the need for stable government, an extension of voter choice and the maintenance of links between representatives and geographical constituencies. A Home Office official had warned in 1953: 'it would be a mistake to attempt to construct the perfect system without first deciding what you want to achieve'.[114] The Jenkins terms of reference did at least go some way towards deciding that. However, not all of these criteria are clearly compatible with each other; there is no rank order; and they are also susceptible to different interpretations. SV, for instance, could be seen as an extension of voter choice, but if the result is to ensure that the candidate with the most first preferences is defeated, it could also be seen as the denial of choice in favour of compromise – the election of the least disliked rather than the most favoured candidate.

A further objection to the Jenkins terms of reference is that they left out the criterion which has been the most important in shaping attitudes towards electoral systems in twentieth-century Britain, certainly at least until the 1970s. This is that general elections are, as the Royal Commission put it, 'considered by a large proportion of the electorate of this country as practically a referendum on the question which of two Governments shall be returned to power'.[115] In other words, the key exercise of voter choice under the system bequeathed by the Victorians – a system the merits of which the Jenkins Commission was explicitly excluded from considering – was not the election of a broadly representative parliament but the formation of a government. Even the famous MORI opinion poll in April 1991 which was widely touted as showing a popular conversion to PR also recorded the much less bruited fact that only 35 per cent of those polled preferred coalitions to single-party rule.[116]

Governmental stability – despite its inclusion in the Jenkins conditions – apart perhaps from a brief period in the 1970s, has never been as important historically as this ability to choose or reject governments. Stability, meanwhile, might come at the expense of voter choice. AMS, for instance, has delivered great stability to the German political system, but it is also a salutary thought that no government from the creation of the Bundesrepublik in 1949 until Gerhard Schröder's victory in 1998 had been rejected at the polls.[117] In contrast, in Britain general elections have made or broken governments regularly during the twentieth century. This, for its defenders, was the prime merit of the simple-majority system; 'it provided the means for removing a government from office'.[118] Although they had just suffered ignominiously exactly this kind of rejection, the Tories continued to recommend this as the key criterion by which an electoral system should be judged in their submission to the Jenkins Commission. In contrast, it is alleged that Blair is determined to avoid Major's fate by devising 'an electoral system which has the best chance of delivering a centre-Left coalition to keep the Conservatives out of power for the foreseeable future'.[119]

CONCLUSIONS

In practice, of course, to win under the simple-majority system already generally requires the forging of some kind of coalition, but it is a coalition within parties, rather than between them. The electoral system has structured parties into leviathan coalitions of interest that compete with each other for the ultimate prize of office. The protection of minorities – the objective of Victorian reformers – was always a distraction from this end. Significantly, it never animated more than a fraction of the Liberals themselves, until they woke up to the fact that, by the 1920s, they were one of those minorities. Meanwhile, the anxiety to guard against the post-1867 possibilities of the tyranny of the majority also faded. Regardless of the value of STV on the imperial periphery or in Ireland, in Britain the smoothness of the transition to universal suffrage undermined the case for protecting minorities through the electoral system.

From the 1970s the debate has been qualitatively different. The marginalisation of STV as an alternative and the rise of AMS and list systems not only reflected the impact of entry into Europe in 1973 and the economic anxieties of the time. It also marked a shift in objectives amongst would-be reformers – from maximising voter choice between candidates to ensuring 'broad proportionality' between parties. Instead of the supposed evils of adversary rule, more consensual government was to be pursued, not by increasing accountability to voters, but by the institutionalisation of coalitionism. With the long years of Tory rule which began in 1979 the attraction of this idea grew, founded on the myth that there was a natural centre-left alignment which would be permanently in, rather than seemingly permanently out of power if only the electoral system was restructured to put the relative majority of Conservatives that then obtained into a lasting minority. It is a myth which does not bear close examination – *vide* the electoral history of the interwar years or the

1950s – but it has nevertheless proved powerful. Its influence has contributed to the growing support for AMS, seen in the 1970s as a Tory system, and list PR, in Labour ranks. It has also revived Labour interest in SV and AV. And it undoubtedly was one factor in the idea, yet to be tried anywhere, of AV plus – a system of AV together with 82 additional members to try to achieve some kind of proportionality – which the Jenkins Report advocated in October 1998. This may be touted as 'fair votes', whilst preserving the cherished constituency link. However, its principal effect if introduced might still be to create party-dominated majorities or coalitions,[120] rather than the representation of minorities which the Victorian reformers sought.

NOTES

I am grateful to Tim Lamport and Paul Wilder for their comments on earlier drafts of this chapter.

1 . *Report of the Royal Commission Appointed to Enquire into Electoral Systems*, Cd 5163, 1910, p. 13.
2. Ibid., p. 12. There had been an unsuccessful attempt to introduce the limited vote as early as 1832. The limited vote gave fewer votes than there were seats to be filled.
3. Lord Hailsham, *Elective Dictatorship* (London: BBC, 1976).
4. *Royal Commission*, p. 12. It had also been proposed for large constituencies in 1867 but defeated by 173 to 34. The cumulative vote enabled the electorate to give multiple votes to a particular candidate or candidates if they so chose.
5. McDougall Trust, Lakeman Library, London (henceforward McD): PRS early documents; untitled memorandum *c.*1885.
6. According to PRS, *Report for the Year 1906*, p. 7, although the number of unopposed returns makes it difficult to be categorical about such matters for nineteenth-century elections.
7. See especially S. E. Finer (ed.), *Adversary Politics and Electoral Reform* (London: Wigram, 1975).
8. *Proportional Representation Society First Annual Report 1885*, p. 5.
9. Jenifer Hart, *Proportional Representation: Critics of the British Electoral System 1820–1945* (Oxford: Clarendon Press, 1992), p. 102.
10. *Pall Mall Gazette*, 30 January 1884.
11. *Royal Commission*, p. 8.
12. Quoted in Hart, *Proportional Representation*, p. 114.
13. Ibid., p. 184. He was to change his mind in the face of electoral adversity in the 1920s.
14. Ibid., p. 145.
15. McD: Memoranda on Electoral Reform 1916–52; Lord Courtney of Penwith quoted in 'The Case for Proportional Representation as presented in the House of Lords', p. 4.
16. Logie Barrow and Ian Bullock, *Democratic Ideas and the British Labour Movement 1880–1914* (Cambridge: Cambridge University Press, 1996), pp. 17, 166–7, 277.

17. *Electoral Reform Society 1884–1984: The Best System: An Account of Its First Hundred Years* (London: McDougall Fund, 1984), p. 9; Hart, *Proportional Representation*, pp. 155, 166.
18. Public Record Office, London (henceforward PRO): PREM 11/865, 'Aspects of policy to which reconsideration might be given on the following lines in the light of the need to attract the Liberal vote', 12 April 1950, p. 1.
19. See, for example, Hansard Society, *Parliamentary Reform* (London: Cassell, 1961).
20. *The Best System*, p. 19.
21. *Royal Commission*, p. 19.
22. 'Problems of Parliamentary Government in Colonies', *Parliamentary Affairs*, 6 (1952–53), p. 71.
23. See especially *The Globe*, 31 March 1917.
24. *Representation*, 15, 60 (July 1975), p. 35.
25. See *Electoral Reform: First Report of the Joint Liberal/SDP Alliance Commission on Constitutional Reform*, July 1982, p. 15.
26. *Representation*, 35, 1, (1998), p. 82.
27. *House of Commons Debates*, 5th ser., vol. 525, cols 1599–602, 26 March 1954.
28. See, for instance, Peter Hain MP, 'The Case for the Alternative Vote', *Representation*, 34, 2 (1997), p. 125.
29. *Royal Commission*, p. 8.
30. McD: Memoranda on the Operation of AV; 'General Election 1924', 28 January 1929; 'The Effect of Proportional Representation and of the AV Vote', 8 February 1930.
31. P. Dunleavy *et al.*, *Making Votes Count: Replaying the 1990s General Elections under Alternative Electoral Systems* (Colchester: Democratic Audit of the UK, University of Essex, 1997).
32. See PRO: PREM 1/81, Lord Craigmyle to MacDonald, 19 July 1930. See also F. A. Newsam to E. M. Watson, 15 July 1929.
33. The most glaring example was in Victoria in 1967, when the Liberals won three times as many seats as Labor on fewer first preferences: Robert A. Newland, *Only Half a Democracy*, 2nd edn (London: ERS, 1975), p. 10.
34. *House of Commons Debates*, 5th ser., vol. 253, col. 106, 2 June 1931.
35. This was not borne out by experience in New Zealand, where it was briefly tried at the turn of the century.
36. *Daily Citizen*, 30 January 1914.
37. Hart, *Proportional Representation*, p. 189; see also *Labour Party Conference Report*, 26 June 1918, p. 21.
38. McD: Memoranda on Electoral Reform, 'Memorandum on a Redistribution of Seats and Equitable Representation', 13 June 1916. This begins, 'Until recently it did not seem that anything in the nature of electoral reform or of a redistribution of parliamentary seats during the continuance of the war was conceivable.'
39. *Royal Commission*, pp. 28, 36. After prolonged debate the PCPR decided on 26 February 1914 to favour a system of allowing members to choose subdivisions of the constituency based on their order in the poll, where by-elections could take place on an AV basis if necessary (McD: Minutes of the PCPR). The 1973 Kilbrandon Commission, in contrast, recommended a by-election in the whole constituency on an AV basis.
40. *Liberal/SDP Commission*, p. 9.
41. Hain, 'The Case for the Alternative Vote', p. 122.
42. See Martin Pugh, *Electoral Reform in Peace and War 1906–18* (London:

Routledge & Kegan Paul, 1978), pp. 154ff; Hart, *Proportional Representation*, pp. 178ff; McD: Memoranda on Electoral Reform 1916–52, *passim*. Indeed, the Conservative whip was applied against the scheme, see papers of the 2nd Earl of Selborne, Department of Western Manuscripts, Bodleian Library, Oxford: MS Selborne 87, Selborne to Younger, 11 June 1918.

43. McD: Minutes of the PCPR, 6 June 1917.
44. Ibid., 27 March 1917.
45. See McD: Memoranda on the Operation of AV; Enid Lakeman to Donald Johnson MP, 12 May 1964, 'few people worry about strong government at the Town Hall'.
46. David E. Butler, *The Electoral System in Britain 1918–1951* (Oxford: Clarendon Press, 1953), pp. 46–7.
47. McD: Minutes of the PCPR, 6 April 1921.
48. *Parliament and Electoral Reform*, PR Pamphlet 70, May 1930, p. 6.
49. McD: Memoranda on Electoral Reform 1916–52, circular *c.*1924 by APRC.
50. And Cabinet members such as Lord Parmoor, J. R. Clynes and Philip Snowden were Vice Presidents of the PRS.
51. Butler, *Electoral System in Britain*, pp. 44–5; Hart, *Proportional Representation*, p. 221.
52. Hart, *Proportional Representation*, pp. 172–4, 200–11.
53. *Fair Representation and Government*, PR Pamphlet 81, May 1937, p. 18.
54. PRO: PREM 1/81, MacDonald to Ullswater, 16 July 1929. Ullswater, as J. W. Lowther, had chaired the 1916–17 Speaker's Conference.
55. Ibid.: Ullswater to MacDonald, 21 November 1929; McD: Memoranda on Operation of AV, 'The Electoral Reform Bill', *c.*1931, p. 5.
56. *Conference on Electoral Reform*, Cmd 3636, July 1930, p. 6.
57. Hart, *Proportional Representation*, pp. 238–9; Butler, *Electoral System in Britain*, pp. 63–8.
58. See Conservative Research Department papers, Bodleian Library, Oxford (henceforward CRD): 1/72/1, Henry Brooke, 'Proportional Representation', 17 December 1935, p. 9.
59. Quoted in *A New Speaker's Conference on Electoral Reform*, PR Pamphlet 87, June 1942, p. 11.
60. PRO: PREM 4/81/5 Part II, memorandum on electoral reform, WP(43)440, 5 October 1943.
61. *Conference on Electoral Reform and Redistribution of Seats*, Cmd 6534, May 1944, p. 8.
62. *Daily Mail*, 29 May 1935.
63. PRO: PREM 11/865, Churchill to Clement Davies MP (the then leader of the Liberal Party), 27 August 1952.
64. Ibid., Butler to Churchill, 20 February 1953.
65. *Conference on Electoral Law*, Cmnd 3202, February 1967, p. 5; Hart, *Proportional Representation*, pp. 278–9.
66. *House of Commons Debates*, 5th ser., vol. 531, col. 234, 27 July 1954.
67. CRD: 2/53/17, 'Proportional Representation', revised November 1955, p. 10.
68. *Memorandum to the 1965 Speaker's Conference*, p. 8.
69. Joe Rogaly, *Parliament for the People: A Handbook of Electoral Reform* (London: Temple Smith, 1976), pp. 9–10.
70. Lord Blake (Chairman), *The Report of the Hansard Commission on Electoral Reform*, June 1976, p. 16.
71. Particularly influential was Finer's book, *Adversary Politics*.
72. Tom Benyon *et al.*, *Easy as ABC – Electoral Reform*, Bow Group, January 1976.

73. Hart, *Proportional Representation*, pp. 284–5. See also Gareth Smyth (ed.), *Refreshing the Parts: Electoral Reform and British Politics* (London: Lawrence & Wishart, 1992), p. 11.

74. Although this was preceded by a Tory body called Taper. I am grateful to Paul Wilder for this information.

75. Miles Hudson, *Electoral Reform: A Conservative View* (London: CAER, *c*.1982), p. 15.

76. Richard Holme, *A Democracy Which Works* (London: Parliamentary Democracy Trust, 1977).

77. *Representation*, 46 (January 1972), p. 7. It was still regarded as 'the best bet now' in *The Economist*, 2 August 1975.

78. Lord Kilbrandon (Chairman), *Royal Commission on the Constitution 1969–1973, Volume I, Report*, Cmnd 5460, 1973, p. 240.

79. There was also some interest in the single non-transferable vote, an idea put forward in Benyon *et al.*, *Easy as ABC*.

80. *Royal Commission*, p. 23. There is no provision for by-elections under AMS as operated in Germany.

81. *Hansard Society Commission*, pp. 37ff. See also the motion introduced by the Conservative peer, Lord Alport, on 23 April 1975.

82. *Representation*, 15, 59 (April 1975), p. 23.

83. Smyth, *Refreshing the Parts*, p. 11.

84. Hart, *Proportional Representation*, p. 285.

85. Interview with Lord Caldecote, 12 July 1996.

86. Vernon Bogdanor, *The People and the Party System: The Referendum and Electoral Reform in British Politics* (Cambridge: Cambridge University Press, 1981), pp. 157–8; Norman Lamont, *Electoral Reform, No Reform*, Bow Group, 1975, p. 5.

87. See Constitutional Reform Centre papers, British Library of Political and Economic Science, London (henceforward BLPES): CRC3/3, 'Electoral Reform: Advantages for the Labour Party', n.d.

88. Barbara Castle, *The Castle Diaries 1964–1976* (London: Papermac, 1990), p. 445.

89. Bogdanor, *People and the Party System*, p. 155; BLPES: CRC3/3, David Owen MP to Goldenberg, 7 June 1979.

90. Bogdanor, *People and the Party System*, p. 171. *Representation*, 17, 67 (April 1977), p. 14.

91. Some on the left were totally opposed even to the idea of direct elections; see Tony Benn, *Conflicts of Interest, Diaries 1977–80* (London: Hutchinson, 1990).

92. James Callaghan, *Time and Chance* (London: Collins, 1987), pp. 455–7.

93. Bogdanor, *People and the Party System*, pp. 165–6, 229–32; interview with Edmund Dell, 22 September 1998.

94. *Representation*, 18, 7 (January 1978), p. 1.

95. Alistair Michie and Simon Hoggart, *The Pact: The Inside Story of the Lib–Lab Government 1977–8* (London: Quartet, 1978), pp. 155–6.

96. The latter was the result of a last-minute approach by Labour electoral reformers to protect their allied Northern Irish party, the SDLP.

97. Quoted in Smyth, *Refreshing the Parts*, p. 16.

98. The SNP withdrew from the SCC early on.

99. Smyth, pp. 16, 70–2; James Mitchell, 'Conceptual Lenses and Territorial Government in Britain' in U. Jordan and W. Kaiser (eds), *Political Reform in Britain 1886–1996: Themes, Ideas, Policies* (Bochum: Dr. N. Brockmeyer, 1997), pp. 212–14.

100. Andrew Adonis and Stephen Twigg, *The Cross We Bear – Electoral Reform for*

Local Government (London: Fabian Society, 1997).
101. Labour originally proposed a parliament of 112 members (73 elected in single-member constituencies) and the Liberal Democrats one of 145 members. They compromised on 129 members. See Peter Lynch, 'The Scottish Constitutional Convention 1992–5', *Scottish Affairs*, 15 (1996), pp. 1–16. The proposed reduction of Scottish constituencies to 57 for both Westminster and the Scottish Parliament by 2005 should, if implemented, ensure a more proportional system.
102. Institute of Public Policy Research, *A Written Constitution for the United Kingdom* (London: Mansell, 1993).
103. *The Reform Bill 1997*, Liberal Democrats, 25 September 1996, p. 3.
104. Tim Lamport, 'The Plant Report 2 Years On – Some Reflections', *Representation*, 33, 2 (1995), p. 17.
105. Raymond Plant, 'The Plant Report: A Retrospective', *Representation*, 33, 2 (1995), p. 14.
106. Joanne Robertson, 'Labour and Proportional Representation', *Scottish Affairs*, 4 (1993), pp. 33–9.
107. Smyth, *Refreshing the Parts*, p. 17; Lynch, 'The Scottish Constitutional Convention', p. 3.
108. Philip Norton, 'The Case for First-Past-The-Post', *Representation*, 34, 2 (1997), p. 86.
109. Peter Hain, 'The Alternative Vote' in Smyth, *Refreshing the Parts*, p. 47.
110. Quoted in Peter Kellner, 'Blair's Modest Proposal on Reform', *Representation*, 34, 2 (1997), p. 111.
111. John Curtice and Martin Range, 'A Flawed Revolution? Britain's New European Parliament Electoral System', *Representation*, 35, 1 (1998), pp. 7–15.
112. Lamport, 'Plant Report 2 Years On', p. 20.
113. See Michael White, 'D'Hondted House of British PR', *Guardian*, 24 September 1998.
114. PRO: PREM 11/865, R. J. Whittick to P. G. Oates, 2 February 1953.
115. *Royal Commission*, pp. 33–4.
116. *Scottish Affairs*, 4 (1993), p. 25.
117. Though the Christian Democrats have also enjoyed a relative majority at every election except 1972 and 1998.
118. Norton, 'Case for First-Past-the Post', p. 84.
119. Michael Ancram, 'Do You Want Blair to be PM for Life?', *Sunday Telegraph*, 10 May 1998. See also Tessa Keswick, 'Stay Off the Bland Wagon', *Daily Telegraph*, 16 March 1998.
120. And for a detailed critique, see Michael Dyer, '*Caveat Emptor*: Reflections on the Report of the Independent Commission on the Voting System', *Representation*, 36, 2, (1999), pp. 156–66.

6

Transforming Relations of Gender: The Feminist Project of Societal Reform in Turn-of-the-Century Britain

ULRIKE WALTON-JORDAN AND JUTTA SCHWARZKOPF

The late Victorian age was a pivotal period for reform politics in terms of both short-term effectiveness and long-term implications. In a number of ways, this second phase of industrialisation brought to a head many of the long-standing issues which contemporaries had been grappling with since the opening decades of the nineteenth century. One of the most complex and intricate of these was the condition of women, because, on account of the pervasive influence of gender, women's position in society could not be dealt with in isolation, inextricably bound up as it was with virtually all the social and political questions of the day. In this chapter, we will concentrate on the reasons for, and the specific manner of, women's contribution to late Victorian and Edwardian reform politics.

Our analysis is premised upon the assumption that the supreme goal of feminism was fundamentally to transform social structures.[1] The bestowal on women of the status of legal subjects was one important element of a deep-reaching change in gender relations. This objective of feminism was referred to by Queen Victoria, one of the most vociferous and doubtless the most prominent opponent of the women's movement, as 'this mad, wicked folly of "Women's Rights"'.[2] In the aims of Victorian feminism, long-term social change meshed with highly focused, single-issue reforms. The time frame we have chosen mirrors this interplay: while we propose to look at the movement from the 1860s to the 1920s, the emphasis will be on the concluding decades of the Victorian and the early Edwardian age, because it was in this period that the interconnection of reform, gender relations and women's social role crystallised.

Nineteenth-century feminism has received, and continues to attract, the interest of researchers on a large scale.[3] While detailed case studies are crucial for deepening our understanding of the social texture of the movement and identifying points of conflict – often at a regional or local level – the need for a comprehensive perspective remains. Any consideration of the British feminist movement before the First World War must not restrict itself to the struggle for the suffrage, despite the claim to prominence that this issue may rightfully lay. Rather, as will be explored below, the suffrage campaign should be considered in the wider context of women striving to forge for themselves an identity which encompassed both the private – proclaimed to be women's rightful domain – and the public – to which feminists also laid claim. Thus we move away from the notion of 'separate spheres'. While acknowledging the power of this idea in the formulation of Victorian middle-class precepts of the masculine and the feminine, which marked the ideological framework of women's social existence, we dispute the notion's accuracy as a description of the ways in which gender identities were lived. Bringing down the boundaries between what was considered the properly feminine realm and what was forbidden territory for women was one of the most ambitious objectives of the feminist movement, with the profound change in conditions and mentalities this entailed.[4] It was precisely this subversion of domesticity which incited the opponents of female suffrage to organise themselves in order to avert what they saw as the most pernicious consequence of the feminist project.

Striving for an improvement of women's condition need not automatically include the suffrage, and certainly not voting rights for those believed to be unfit to exercise them. A case in point is the Women's Imperial League which sought contact with leading intellectual and political circles and personalities like Lionel Curtis, who was secretary to Sir Alfred Milner, British High Commissioner in South Africa and founder, in 1910, of the 'think tank' Round Table for the propagation of liberal imperialist thought. More generally, these imperialist leanings confirm that social elitism was integral to at least one particular strand of the feminist movement and the wider circle in which some of these women moved.[5]

Taken in its entirety, the feminist movement contributed to both the concept and the pushing through of reform in a variety of ways. Any consideration of women's issues in isolation therefore precludes a new typology of nineteenth-century reform movements. Bearing this in mind, we will deal, first, with the objectives of legal reform before, secondly, looking at the social implications of the various reform campaigns associated with the Victorian women's movement. Special attention will be paid throughout to the methods of reform campaigning that characterised the period up to the First World War. We conceive of feminism as both a coherent analysis of society as pervaded by interrelated gendered subordinations and a vision of non-hierarchical gender relations,[6] evolved in historically specific contexts and hence liable to variation. Rejecting any normative understanding of 'feminism', we will use the terms 'women's' and 'feminist' movement interchangeably.

OBJECTIVES OF LEGAL REFORM

The dynamics of political and legal change that unfolded between the first meetings, in 1865, of the Kensington Committee, formed to campaign for the election to Parliament of John Stuart Mill, who championed women's suffrage, and the achievement of the franchise on fully equal terms with men in 1928 provides only one, albeit an important one, of the long-term issues of reform to which feminists were committed.[7] Rather, the full picture mirrors in many ways a vision of the 'citizen in society'. Education was regarded as the crucial first step towards well-informed and self-confident participation in the public sphere, at both the local and national level. Another key area in need of legal reform and change of attitudes was paid employment in general, and the professions in particular. Bearing upon these with the potential of reinforcing as well as undermining any gains made was sexual morality. The fight against the double moral standard was an item of prime importance on the feminist agenda.

The reforms which nineteenth-century feminists strove for were clearly circumscribed by the Victorian key concepts of citizenship, property and morality, which were identifiable in civil institutions like marriage and the vote and reinforced by the powerful religious institutions of the Church of England and nonconformity alike. Of paramount importance was the relatively inclusive character and the mutual reflection of all these reform issues upon each other, which, seen retrospectively, appear to have been informed by a vision of middle-class female citizenship, mirroring women's desire to fluctuate between the private and the public spheres in new, refreshing and imaginative ways. In the last third of the nineteenth century, divisions within the movement did occur – over the inclusion of married women in the demand for the vote, over supporting the campaign for the repeal of the Contagious Diseases Acts, over home rule for Ireland, and over state intervention in areas of personal morality – but the founding of the National Union of Women's Suffrage Societies (NUWSS) in 1897 revealed the marked degree of ideological homogeneity among committed suffragists. Their shared understanding of women of a similar background as a social group apart due to their lack of voting rights united them across their various party-political outlooks. This unity was sustained until the outbreak of the First World War, during a period in which, spurred by the gains made in other areas, feminists concentrated their efforts on storming Parliament, the last political bastion of exclusively male power.

Both co-operation, in the shape of networking, and the underlying concept of citizenship propagated by feminists had the potential of serving as a model not only to women, but to society as a whole. In contradistinction to its German counterpart, the women's movement in Britain was never riven between a bourgeois and a socialist strand.[8] Millicent Garrett Fawcett, who lived from 1847 to 1929 and was the long-time leader of the movement for women's suffrage in Britain, typifies in many ways the attitudes held by British feminists. She was the seventh of ten children of Newson Garrett, a radical corn and coal merchant, who ardently supported the persistent efforts of his eldest daughter, Elizabeth, to gain access to the medical profession. At the age of 20, Millicent married Henry Fawcett. Their marriage was characterised by an uncommon degree of interdependence. Forced by his blindness to rely on the support services of his wife in the pursuit of his political career, Henry Fawcett thereby enabled Millicent to build up contacts, knowledge and experience she was to put to good use in the suffrage campaign later on. In 1869, Millicent Garrett Fawcett gave her first speech on women's suffrage. Afterwards, she and her co-speaker, Mentia Taylor, were referred to in the House of Commons as 'two ladies, wives of members of this house, who have disgraced themselves by speaking in public'. Yet, from the first, the movement also boasted distinguished male supporters, among whom counted John Stuart Mill, Charles Kingsley, John Morley and Sir Charles Dilke. In fact, the philosophical and political case for female citizenship had been made most effectively by John Stuart Mill, who advocated a fundamental change in gender relations by arguing:

> the principle which regulates the existing social relations between the two sexes – the legal subordination of one sex to the other – is

wrong in itself, and now one of the chief hindrances to human improvement ... it ought to be replaced by a principle of perfect equality, admitting no power or privilege on the one side, nor disability on the other.[9]

The 60-year campaign for women's suffrage placed a great many strains on Millicent Fawcett and her co-campaigners. Every year the struggle dragged on, bringing in its wake a steadily growing volume of meetings, petitions and press campaigns. Yet, undeterred, the women plodded on. In 1907, Millicent Fawcett was elected president of the NUWSS. When suffragette militancy, instigated by the Women's Social and Political Union (WSPU), escalated, she made sure that the severely critical attitude of some NUWSS members was never made public so as not to jar the impression of unity of all groups fighting for female enfranchisement.[10]

Despite her fight for a fundamental change in women's condition, Millicent Fawcett's activities were by no means incompatible with deeply ingrained middle-class attitudes like patriotism. Indeed, she was always intensely patriotic, if not imperialistic, and, during the South African War, was sent by the government to investigate the concentration camps set up for Boer women and children. The report she produced, despite numerous recommendations for improvements, vindicated – or whitewashed, as her opponents alleged – the setting up of those camps. The severest blow she had to sustain during her political career was dealt by the outbreak of the First World War. Immediately, she brought the NUWSS into line behind the government to join the efforts for 'sustaining the vital forces of the nation', which led to the secession from the organisation of suffragist pacifists, who, in their turn, joined forces with like-minded women of other countries, laying the foundations for an international women's peace movement.[11] What marked these women off from those that remained in the NUWSS was not only their anti-militarist stand, but also their groping for a synthesis of feminism, pacifism and socialism, leading Catherine Marshall, for one, to make connections between different forms of social oppression, including that of subject nations.[12] In January 1918, as a result of the political compromise eventually reached on reform, for which Millicent Fawcett's patient work had helped pave the way, the Representation of the People Act was passed, enfranchising about 6,000,000 women. Significantly, by tying female suffrage to age, the act aimed to enfranchise wives, deemed to be a stable element in a changing world and unlikely to press radical, feminist issues.[13] A year later, the NUWSS having become the National Union of Societies for Equal Citizenship, Millicent Fawcett resigned from its leadership. She was created Dame of the British Empire in 1925, and died in London on August 5, 1929.[14]

As Millicent Fawcett was aware during the long years of her intense commitment to women's issues, all the key areas of reform in which Victorian women's rights campaigners were involved had one important objective in common: the reform of the legal framework affirming women's inequality with men. There were, however, considerable differences of degree and kind in the obstacles to be overcome. Let us now take a closer look at some of these.

With regard to education, the years between 1869 and 1880 constituted a period of highly effective organisational change, with female educationalists injecting their concern with women's particular needs into the contemporary debate about educational reform. The concept of a curriculum not segregated by gender was only one aspect of the criticism voiced by women like Emily Davies, Frances Buss and Frances Martin, who also attacked the principles upon which the entire education system was based. The reform of female education, it is true, was mainly confined to the middle classes, and, by the turn of the century, the new feminist-inspired schools for girls were beginning to 'feed' the recently established women's colleges in Cambridge and Oxford. Many of their graduates became recruits to the women's movement. The campaign for female education may be regarded as a classic example of successful and sustained institutional reform with a hard-to-measure, yet undeniable long-term effect on mentalities in general. Furthermore, this campaign underlines the quality, prevalent in the women's movement, of viewing reform issues as closely interrelated. This inclusive and flexible vision, which was quite advanced for the period,[15] carried a great deal of potential for social transformation, which was to bear fruit in political ideas of the future. The Fabian Women's Group – comprising, among others, Alice Clark, Barbara Drake, Barbara Hutchins, Maud Pember Reeves and Beatrice Webb – provides one example of the highly specific ways in which this insight was adapted. Members of the group clearly perceived women's economic exploitation and their lack of political rights as interconnected. However, due to the precedence they gave to class over gender in their analysis of women's condition, their concept of exploitation was confined to the economic sphere, and the feminist critique of the manifold ways in which women were the subordinate gender was reduced to their economic dependence on men.[16]

The public sphere, more narrowly understood as the political realm, formed another main area of activity. Women's active role in legal reform preceded by several years the beginnings of the suffrage campaign, which was subsequently to take centre stage. The need for an improvement of the legal position of women, both married and divorced, had been pressed upon Parliament since the 1850s. Reform efforts centred on the rights of wives to property and child custody, the wrenching of which from the hands of men touched simultaneously on the legal and material aspects of the family as well as on its role of socialising agency. The reforms were highly controversial not least because they went right against the grain of the Victorian ideal of family life, in which there was no room for the abuse of power by the male head. Gaining the right to both child custody and the control of their own property was indispensable to enabling women to set up on their own after the breakdown of marriage. The passage of the Infant Custody Acts of 1839 and 1873 and of the various Married Women's Property Acts between 1870 and 1882 owed a great deal to the involvement of women's supporters in Parliament, such as Russell Gurney. He was MP for Southampton and instrumental in steering the Married Women's Property Act of 1870 through the House. The preservation of women's property rights in marriage was intimately connected with the feminist fight against the double moral standard in that the economic independence of wives was a necessary safeguard against sexual exploitation and, ultimately, a precondition of female self-determination.[17]

This was also true of political participation which began at the local level:[18] the Municipal Franchise Act of 1869 – the first of many measures to follow over the course of 30 years – entitled unmarried women ratepayers to vote for councillors and other local officers. The school boards became accessible to women in 1870 with the passage of the Elementary Education Act. Another area of local responsibility, the Poor Law guardianships, were also opened up to women in the course of the 1870s. In 1894, the Local Government Act extended these voting rights to married women. Involvement at the local level had brought together both feminists and female philanthropists who did not necessarily see eye to eye with regard to women's political participation at the national level.[19]

Self-confidence and self-assertion, produced by solidarity and tangible success in social and political participation at local level, played an equally crucial role in the more prominent field of national politics. Between 1870 and 1913, almost every year a women's suffrage bill was introduced into the House of Commons, only to be blocked or defeated. Yet persistence paved the way for final success in 1928. Opposition to feminist causes, in both attitude and organisation, remained powerful throughout the period under consideration and should be contrasted with the women's often unideological and imaginative 'networking'. The resistance feminists met with should not obscure the considerable gains made in both tangible legal, and hard-to-measure psychological terms as well as the increase in female self-confidence which occurred between the 1850s and the early 1900s. While a fundamental challenge to widespread myths about the condition of Victorian women is necessary and is being posed by many historians,[20] the variations in regional conditions – for instance Lancashire and London as against the rest of England – and areas of activity – for instance working conditions, political participation as well as work for the Empire – merit closer inspection. These variations hold the key, too, for the assessment of structural change in gender relations and social conditions, and suggest a challenge to the widely held view that the late Victorian age was characterised by quiescence.

The whole array of legal and political reforms pursued by feminists was geared towards one overriding objective, which consisted in a fundamental change of gender relations through the attainment of female autonomy. This is why the ideology of separate spheres formed one of the prime areas of attack in feminist campaigns and propaganda. Activists consistently pointed out how the conception of women as inherently domestic beings, presiding as guardian angels over home and hearth, concealed women's lack of rights, thereby laying them open to all manner of abuse. By contrast, feminists strove to establish women as legal and political agents in their own right, ultimately regardless of marital status. These demands went right to the centre of male hegemony, aiming as they did at enabling women to lead lives free of supervision by, and dependence on, men.

SOCIAL IMPLICATIONS OF REFORM CAMPAIGNS

The enormity of the changes envisaged was clearly perceived by those opposing them, who were fearful of what they saw as a 'revolution' in gender relations. The majority of legislators persistently resisted any attempt at a fundamental transformation of gender relations by legislative means and diluted feminist demands in those legal measures eventually enacted.[21] Granting women limited rights as a way of enhancing their protection – such as the right to seek a separation order with maintenance from an abusive husband –

could moreover be seen by Members of Parliament as part of their chivalrous duty towards women, while leaving the distribution of power in gender relations intact. Indeed, male dominance was being affirmed by such a transfer of power from individual men to the male legislature. Despite their frustration with legislators' reluctance fundamentally to restructure the legal regulation of gender relations, the majority of feminists were sufficiently pragmatic to suffer the dilution of their demands in order to safeguard what improvement for women these watered-down versions entailed.

Yet the stand taken on female suffrage was not determined by gender. Thus, in 1908, certainly not least in response to the publicity for the female franchise achieved by the WSPU, the Women's National Anti-Suffrage League was formed, followed in 1910 by the founding of the Men's League for Opposing Women's Suffrage.[22] Conversely, between 1890 and 1920, there existed a range of exclusively or predominantly male pro-suffrage societies. The scope for variation of gender relations, to which these associations bear witness and which had opened up by the concluding decades of the nineteenth century, testifies to the impact of the women's movement. While playing an important part in shaping alternative ways for men and women to relate to each other, male support for women's suffrage still operated within a society based on gender inequality. This is also true for those couples, like the Pethick-Lawrences, who worked for the cause as both a private and a political partnership.[23]

By pointing to the manifold ways in which women's disenfranchisement and their subordination, if not degradation, in private were interconnected, feminists effectively demonstrated how untenable, and pernicious in its consequences, was the belief that a particular section of society should remain barred from citizenship and thereby be deprived of the opportunity to participate in determining the political and legal conditions in which they lived. Feminists thus challenged one of the fundamental tenets of liberalism, which held that the private, centred on the family, should be exempt from state interference. Indeed they were able to show how this exemption operated to the detriment of women by leaving unchecked men's ability to tyrannise over them. The staunch opposition to feminist demands put up by the majority in the House of Commons owed a great deal to the interconnection between the public and the private, around which feminist discourse revolved. Feminists consistently argued that women's lack of rights in both the public sphere – their disenfranchisement – and the private realm – their legal submergence in their husbands and the virtual impossibility of an existence independent of men – were predicated upon, and reinforced, one another.

In their methods of campaigning, too, feminists were both innovative and challenging of the division between the public and the private. Kinship and friendship circles had played a key role in the evolution of a feminist stance since the early nineteenth century.[24] Thus the women's movement grew out of small, close-knit groups of friends who shared a belief in the need for a fundamental improvement in women's condition as well as the strength and enthusiasm required to work towards such change. The London-based Langham Place Group was a classic and early example of such small bands of friends who knew that they could trust and rely upon each other,[25] as were most of the other local associations formed to promote women's rights. Indeed, the feminist movement can be seen as a series of social networks, often linked by personal friendships. Those involved, moreover, tended to be active in more than one campaign, either simultaneously or successively.[26] The NUWSS only formalised in organisational terms and on a national scale the networks of like-minded women and their supporters which existed locally. Feminists infused their social networks of relatives and friends, both male and female, with a political purpose. In view of women's disenfranchisement, the attempts by feminists to exert influence in Parliament had to rely exclusively on their ability to mobilise male members of their networks to take action on their behalf. This gender division of political labour reversed the customary allocation of tasks, according to which women provided emotional and practical support for men active in the public realm of politics. In the context of the feminist movement, men acted at the instigation of women, providing the male front of what was essentially a female project.

In their campaigns, feminists developed an idiom of women's rights that drew on liberal natural-rights ideology as well as identifying wrongs and grievances specific and common to all women. The abstract individualism of liberal theory[27] provided them with a basis from which effectively to challenge the increasingly prevalent view of women as 'the sex', as beings defined by their sexuality.[28] While stressing women's difference from, feminists simultaneously emphasised women's claim to equal rights with, men. This particular blend of notions of equality and difference in feminist discourse produced tensions that manifested themselves among women activists themselves as well as in their dealings with other social groups and which crystallised around the issues of gender, class

and ethnicity. Within the movement, friction occurred between those
identifying most strongly with the particular political perspective of
women and those subscribing to a liberal model of political action,
which emphasised an identity of interests between men and women
of the middle class.[29] Yet the priority given to gender over class
allegiance by the former was in itself class-bound, leading them to
assume a position of dominance over lower-class women. This well-
worn attitude had long been characteristic of middle-class
philanthropists' contacts with the lower-class objects of their charity.
Furthermore, suffragists based their demand for the vote not on the
claims of the independent, propertied individual alone, but also on the
wish to develop the feminine character, buttressing their claim for the
franchise by placing themselves in the discourse of the progress of
civilisation and modernity.[30] By contrasting Britain with her colonies,
British feminists saw their country – and this view in part accounts for
the more or less pronounced imperialist leanings to be found among
them – as the pinnacle of civilisation, affording the best opportunities
for improving the position of women.[31] The concept of citizenship
proposed by feminists, while transcending the limits of gender
enshrined in the successive Reform Acts of the nineteenth century,
chimed with the dominant conception of the nation as defined by
'race' and level of civilisation.[32] By and large, feminist discourse thus
failed to overstep ethnic boundaries in search of female solidarity.
Rather, its concept of female political subjectivity derived from holding
the public and the national to be synonymous. In turn, pro-suffrage
men in Britain would often justify the imperial presence in India by a
salvationist and civilising impetus for reform. In this view, British
women had a special part to play in the enlightened imperialism that
was advocated: in taking care of Indian women, both British women's
roles and British rule were expected to change in the long term.
Opponents of the suffrage, by contrast, conjured up fears of colonial
insurgence and upheaval in the wake of female enfranchisement.[33]

   At particular historical junctures, however, gender solidarity could
override that of class. The ability of at least some feminists to accept
women from a different social background came to the fore for the
first time, and most dramatically, in the campaign for the repeal of the
Contagious Diseases Acts. In their fight for the civil rights of
prostitutes, Josephine Butler and many of the members of the Ladies
National Association (LNA) did not stoop to these women in an effort
to reform their character, but portrayed them as epitomes of the
condition of contemporary womanhood, highlighting in the extreme
the lack of rights and the degradation all women had to endure. In so

doing, the middle-class ladies of the LNA managed to bridge the deepest gulf existing between women in contemporary perception, which rigidly classified females as either Marys or Eves, as either saintly virgins or depraved sluts. By exposing the double standard involved in the persecution of prostitutes, while leaving their male clients unmolested, middle-class ladies for the first time aired their views on sexuality, equally taboo to respectable women in language and in practice by the standards of the Victorian age.

Josephine Butler, the charismatic leader of the repeal campaign, typifies Victorian feminists in a number of ways. Prior to the movement against the Contagious Diseases Acts, she had been involved in philanthropy. In an effort to come to terms with the tragic death of her daughter, she had sought out help for those who were more miserable and downcast than herself, turning to rescue work for prostitutes. In her philanthropic endeavours, she was sustained by her strong religious belief, feeling that she had received a calling to improve the lot of social outcasts.[34] It is this kind of fervour, whether fuelled by religion or convictions of a more secular kind, that accounts for feminists' perseverance in their long-drawn-out struggle for women's rights. Moreover, Josephine Butler received the unwavering support of her clergyman husband, who stood by her despite the set-backs to his career he had to suffer on account of her activities. Many feminists were able to rely on the unconditional support of their husbands, or came from families who had fostered in their daughters a keen sense of the injustice of women's position in society.[35]

The members of the LNA did not confine themselves to campaigning for the civil rights of alleged prostitutes, but tried to help the victims of the Contagious Diseases Acts to find ways of earning a living other than by prostitution. Unlike most contemporaries, who regarded the moral depravity of these women as lying at the root of their way of life, Josephine Butler and her co-campaigners viewed prostitution as the well-nigh inevitable result of starvation wages and restricted employment opportunities for women. What was being battled out in the campaign against the Contagious Diseases Acts was the conflict between two modes of social reform: one, male-dominated and pushed mainly by the medical profession eager to establish a reputation for advancing effective measures to contain pollution of any kind, the other, female-dominated and acted out by the large number of women philanthropists. Their approach was informed by a belief in the reforming power of personal influence and centred on the individual. This belief underlay the very close interaction between reformer and reformee.[36]

Thus, the LNA approach shared the contradictions apparent in the vast array of female philanthropic ventures. The LNA's defence of motherhood, while vesting the control over their daughters' sexuality in mothers rather than fathers, at the same time legitimised a hierarchical relationship between older, middle-class and young, working-class women.[37] In their dealings with women of their own class, middle-class women's celebration of motherhood led them to cherish the nurturing and empowering, the accepting and forgiving side of mother-love. In contacts with the poor, by contrast, the protective and punitive aspects of motherhood appeared, linked by their tendency to infantilise fully-grown people, especially the adult poor.[38] While Josephine Butler predominantly used the language of victimisation, portraying prostitutes as oppressed by employers paying starvation wages, by the state, the police, the medical profession and male lust, other members of the LNA adopted a more punitive approach which sat uneasily with the LNA's advocacy of women's civil rights. It was from among those repealers that the Social Purity Campaign, aiming to cleanse the public sphere from all manifestations of vice, drew its recruits.

The divergence of the LNA and the Social Purity Campaign, then, can be traced back to opposing views of the state in relation to women. The LNA was, by definition, anti-statist, having been formed with the express aim to fend off state encroachment on civil liberties. With this attitude, it cast itself firmly as an organisation of libertarian individualists, subscribing to the goal of achieving uncoerced self-control for women. The Social Purity Campaign, by contrast, demanded, and achieved, state protection of women by means of laws intended to regulate sexual behaviour. While some feminists, such as Josephine Butler, turned in horror from the state repression called for by purity campaigners, others were alerted to the possibility of harnessing the state to some degree to women's ends. What became obvious in the closing decades of the nineteenth century were the shortcomings of the abstract individualism of liberal theory when applied to a society deeply imbued with inequalities of power and resources.[39]

The potential ability of feminism to forge an identity of all women which was based on gender and transcended divisions of class and morality counts among its greatest achievements. It had come to full fruition by 1903 when, with the formation of the Lancashire and Cheshire Textile and Other Workers' Representation Committee, the middle-class exclusiveness of the feminist movement was visibly overcome, and female cotton workers became involved in the suffrage campaign in large numbers. Lancashire cotton workers, though forming the largest working-class contingent among the suffragists, were by no means alone. What marked them off from other working-class women joining the campaign was the sustained and massive character of their involvement. Support among them for the suffrage had begun to grow noticeably in the late 1890s and did not flag until 1914. In 1901, cotton workers presented to Parliament a petition bearing the signatures of 29,359 female Lancashire mill operatives. In 1902, this was followed by a petition, signatures for which had been collected among the women woollen workers of Yorkshire and the female cotton and silk workers of north Cheshire.[40]

The idea of tapping the pool of potential support represented by the female cotton workers was conceived by Esther Roper and Eva Gore-Booth who were deeply committed to both women's suffrage and women's trade unionism. Esther Roper, who came from a middle-class family, was one of the women in her generation to profit from reforms in female education and held a university degree. Her close friend, Eva Gore-Booth, hailed from the Irish aristocracy and, apart from her political commitments, wrote poetry.[41] The links both women managed to forge between the suffrage movement and women's trade unionism were not a case of middle and upper-class leaders shepherding their working-class flock in whatever direction they saw fit. The women working in the Lancashire cotton factories, and in weaving in particular, looked back upon several generations of female employment away from home and boasted the longest tradition as well as the highest degree of unionisation among women workers in Britain. Especially in weaving, it was women's labour-process-based equality with men which rendered them particularly sensitive to their lack of a political voice with which to make their grievances heard. Many working-class suffragists came from a trade-union background, but had found their unions less than helpful when it came to pressing gender-specific demands. In the very masculine world of the labour movement, weaving union officials were at pains to prove that the predominantly female rank and file of their organisations did not detract from their manliness. Disappointed by their unions, yet strengthened by their successes in fighting for their industrial rights, many female cotton workers had turned to the far more responsive Women's Co-operative Guild for support and encouragement. It was thus with a considerable degree of self-confidence that these working-class women joined the ranks of middle-class suffragism. They perceived, and favourably responded to, feminism's language of women being unified across class lines by their exclusion from rights on the basis of gender, a perception buttressed by their experience of gender discrimination within the ranks of the labour movement.

The loyalty of these women was sorely tested by the latter's less than lukewarm attitude to female suffrage. It took them some time to realise that the maximalist demand for adult – that is universal – suffrage endorsed by the TUC was but a tactic covering up the movement's unwillingness to take any action for female suffrage at all. The distance that working-class suffragists kept to the labour movement over the franchise issue, though achieved at great personal costs, was in keeping with the refusal by the entire women's movement to align itself with any particular party, a refusal doubtless aided by most parties' equivocal, if not openly hostile, stand on female franchise.

Although most of the feminist campaigns had their headquarters in London in a sensible move to be as close as possible to the centre of political power, Manchester can actually be seen as the cradle of the movement. It was here that both the Slavery Abolition Movement and the Anti-Corn Law League, the two chief Radical campaigns of the first half of the nineteenth century, had had a stronghold. In both movements, women had been involved on a large scale, if often behind the scenes.[42] The success of both campaigns, and the significant part they had taken in securing it, had boosted middle-class women's self-confidence sufficiently to induce them to devote their energy and abilities to abolishing grievances of their own. Furthermore, they drew on anti-slavery rhetoric in their indictment of women's contemporary condition – a rhetoric deployed to particularly good effect by John Stuart Mill and Harriet Taylor in their *The Subjection of Women*.

Both the first national women's suffrage society, founded in 1867, and the WSPU, formed in 1903, originated in Manchester. In the latter year, the suffrage campaign was boosted by the large-scale support of female Lancashire cotton operatives. By involving themselves in the suffrage movement, they not only widened its social base, but also helped pave the way for the political realignment of the campaign that was to take effect in 1912 with an alliance being formed between the NUWSS and the Labour Party. This alliance marked the departure by the NUWSS from reliance on private members' bills or an amendment to the Reform Bill of a hostile government to attain the vote. Female suffrage required the backing of a party in order to pass through Parliament, and only the Labour Party, though insufficiently represented to be able to implement the policy, could be won over to the women's cause.[43] In this alliance, the union of all women regardless of class – one of the cornerstones of feminist beliefs – was successfully translated into practice in the smooth co-operation of middle-class ladies, many of them volunteers, and working-class female organisers paid for their services to the cause, to which they brought their contacts in, and experience of, trade unionism and thus the ability to speak as equals to working-class audiences.

CONCLUSIONS

By the eve of the First World War, several decades of campaigning on behalf of women had left their mark on British society, although full admission to the political realm had not yet been gained. Public awareness of the specific grievances of women from all social backgrounds had been significantly heightened, and certain areas, particularly in education and the professions, had ceased to be exclusively male domains. More and more women attained prominence in positions of influence, thus demonstrating women's abilities for a whole range of occupations. This was to a large part the result of the access women had gained to universities.

The early phase of WSPU militancy, lasting roughly from 1905 to 1909, had been a skilfully orchestrated publicity campaign hammering home women's demand for the vote to a public that was anything but unequivocally friendly. It was not least the NUWSS which profited from this publicity in organisational terms. Its membership, which counted 13,000 in 1909, rose to over 30,000 by 1911, reaching over 42,000 by 1912, and was distributed over more than 400 local societies. By 1915, membership exceeded 50,000.[44]

Feminists were most likely to be at least partially successful in pressing their demands in those areas where reform was being pursued by other social groups. Thus feminists' wish to see married women's property laws revised chimed with the designs of the Law Amendment Society intent on doing away with the iniquities arising out of the existence of two different legal systems in Britain – common law and the law of equity. Conversely, failure was almost certain where the meeting of feminist demands would have jeopardised other political concerns. Thus the political alignments arising out of the home rule issue effectively prevented the granting of the franchise to women in the years leading up to the First World War.

Regarding access to education and training as well as employment, women's demands were effectively underscored by the striking demographic imbalance between men and women. As each successive census drove home, there was a large number of women – dubbed 'superfluous' or 'redundant' – who could not expect to secure their livelihood by marriage and who, without any means to support themselves, were proving an increasing burden on their families, less and less willing and able to support single female relatives without an income of their own. Due to the obvious shortage of men, there was no way in which this growing number of single women was able to attain the position of wives and mothers. Hence their quest for finding self-fulfilment and making a useful contribution to society outside the family circle became increasingly difficult to invalidate.

The change in feminists' stand towards the state, coupled with a claim to citizenship which was based on the specific qualities that women would bring to the running of state affairs appears to have been crucial in securing victory. It was when women claimed to be a corporate interest group, vital as mothers to the future prospects of 'the race' and qualified by 'nature' to play a key role in the running of a 'nurturing' as opposed to an order-enforcing state, that they were able to present a claim to political and social recognition that was eventually acknowledged.[45]

That shift in the relative weight given to equality and difference in feminist discourse, which was to shape the policies of the women's movement in the interwar years, was precipitated by the First World War. Under the impact of the horrors of the war, British society craved for order, peace and well-regulated societal relations. Given the pivotal role of gender relations in signifying the state of social order, it appeared that this could be achieved best by reasserting gendered spheres of public and private, after the first instalment of female suffrage had been granted in order to placate women and avoid a sex war that was seen as lurking in the wings. By accepting the terms of the larger culture and advocating a politics of sexual difference, feminism lost much of its critical edge,[46] and many of the demands put forward by the feminists of the interwar years could be fulfilled by social policies which, precisely by meeting what new feminists of the Eleanor Rathbone type portrayed as women's specific requirements, failed to advance women's quest for equality by one iota. For decades, feminists had of necessity focused their attention on Parliament as the one institution alone able to meet their demand for the franchise. By continuing to formulate demands addressed to this institution, interwar feminists blinded themselves to the root causes of women's oppression in society. Women, who had once advanced a concept of citizenship so expansive and transformed as to enable them to address the problem of gender relations, had turned into voters, whose interests were submerged in the programmes of the established parties. In the process of being adopted so as to be palatable to a wider constituency, feminist demands were disfigured beyond recognition.[47] Thus, the spate of laws concerning women passed up to 1929 all addressed them in their capacity as wives and mothers.

Yet an assessment of the more than 50 years of campaigning which measures the women's success solely in terms of the number and quality of the reforms gained fails to do justice to what may be regarded as the movement's greatest achievement: awakening female awareness of the need, and their own capacity, for fundamentally changing the social condition common to all women. Ultimately, the principal difference from other reform movements, be they institutional or constitutional, lay in the necessity to effect a thorough-going change of self-perception on the part of the reform instigators. The persistent topicality of women's issues is therefore not bound up with the historically specific content of reforms, but is sustained by the vision of women being able freely to fluctuate between the public and the private. The granting of the suffrage has made clear that formal political equality does not suffice to eradicate the inequalities of gender. This is why feminism to this day is grappling with the difficulty of striking a balance between equality and difference that is not detrimental to women. The shortcomings of both 1918 and 1928 at the same time point out the limitations of the political reform the British state was able to effect in that the abstract equality of men and women as citizens failed to be supported by a fundamental change in gender relations which would have abolished male structural hegemony in all spheres of life. It was to take the women's movement until the 1960s for this objective to be placed again at the top of its political agenda.

NOTES

1.   This assumption takes its cue, apart from women's own testimonies, from the wider social changes that occurred in Britain in the late Victorian period. Following the 'economic miracle' of the 1850s, the financial crises of 1857 and 1866 led to an adjustment of the precepts of middle-class femininity. On many levels, the psychological and political consequences of such changes were discussed in the late Victorian and Edwardian periods, with the debate turning increasingly public after the end of the Boer War in 1902. See, especially, Anna Clark, 'Gender, Class and the Constitution: Franchise Reform in England 1832–1928' in James Vernon (ed.), *Re-reading the Constitution: New Narratives in the Political History of England's Long Nineteenth Century* (Cambridge: Cambridge University Press, 1996), pp. 239–53; Leonore Davidoff, *Worlds Between: Historical Perspectives on Gender and Class*

(Oxford: Polity Press, 1995); T. R. Gourvish and Alan O'Day (eds), *Later Victorian Britain 1867–1900* (Basingstoke: Macmillan Education, 1988); Philippa Levine, *Victorian Feminism 1850–1900* (London: Hutchison, 1987); June Purvis, 'Women's History in Britain: An Overview', *European Journal of Women's Studies*, 2 (1995), pp. 7–19.

2. Queen Victoria to Theodore Martin, quoted in Margaret Cole, *Women of Today* (London: Nelson & Sons, 1946), pp. 150–1.

3. A selection from the ever-growing body of literature might include, for instance, Barbara Caine, *English Feminism 1780–1980* (Oxford: Oxford University Press, 1997); Lee Holcombe, *Wives and Property* (Oxford: Martin Robertson, 1983); Sandra Stanley Holton, *Feminism and Democracy: Women's Suffrage and Reform Politics in Britain* (Cambridge: Cambridge University Press, 1986); Susan Kingsley Kent, *Sex and Suffrage in Britain 1860–1914* (Princeton NJ: Princeton University Press, 1987); Jill Liddington and Jill Norris, *One Hand Tied Behind Us: The Rise of the Women's Suffrage Movement* (London: Virago, 1978); June Purvis and Sandra Holton (eds), *Votes for Women* (London: Routledge, 2000); G. R. Rubin and David Sugarman, *Law, Economy and Society: Essays in the History of English Law 1750–1914* (Abingdon: Professional Books, 1984); Leila J. Rupp, *Worlds of Women: The Making of an International Women's Movement* (Princeton NJ: Princeton University Press, 1998); Mary Lyndon Stanley, *Feminism, Marriage and the Law in Victorian England 1850–1895* (Princeton NJ: Princeton University Press, 1989); Martha J. Vicinus (ed.), *A Widening Sphere: Changing Roles of Victorian Women* (London: Indiana University Press, 1977).

4. See, for instance, Patricia Thompson, *The Victorian Heroine: A Changing Ideal* (London: Oxford University Press, 1956).

5. For detailed illustration of these attitudes see, for instance, the periodical *Imperial Colonist* 1901–27, and also the records of the South African Colonisation Society (1903–19) and its predecessor and successor organisations (all held at the Fawcett Library, London Guildhall University). See also Antoinette Burton, *Burden of History: British Feminists, Indian Women and Imperial Culture 1865–1955* (Chapel Hill NC: University of North Carolina Press, 1994); Deborah Gaitskell, 'Housewives, Maids or Mothers: Some Contradictions of Domesticity for Christian Women in Johannesburg 1903–39', *Journal of African History*, 24 (1983), pp. 241–56; Rana Kabbani, *Imperial Fictions: Europe's Myths of the Orient* (London: Pandora Press, 1994).

6. See Philippa Levine, *Feminist Lives in Victorian England: Private Roles and Public Commitment* (Oxford: Blackwell, 1990), p. 1.

7. See Constance Rover, *Women's Suffrage and Party Politics in Britain 1866–1914* (London: Routledge, 1967).

8. See Richard J. Evans, *Comrades and Sisters: Feminism, Socialism and Pacifism in Europe* (Brighton: Wheatsheaf Books, 1987).

9. John Stuart Mill, *The Subjection of Women* (1869), reprinted in *idem*, *Three Essays* (Oxford: Oxford University Press, 1975), p. 428. It should be noted that although commonly attributed to Mill alone, *The Subjection* was the result of his close collaboration with Harriet Taylor.

10. See, for instance, the reason for Helena Swanwick's resignation from the editorship of *Common Cause* in Jo Vellacott, 'Feminist Consciousness and the First World War', *History Workshop*, 23 (1987), pp. 84–5.

11. See Gertrude Bussey and Margaret Tims, *Pioneers for Peace: Women's International League for Peace and Freedom 1915–1965* (London: Allen & Unwin, 1965); Catherine Foster, *Women for All Seasons: The Story of the Women's*

International League for Peace and Freedom (London: University of Georgia Press, 1989); Anne Wiltsher, *Most Dangerous Women: Feminist Peace Campaigners of the Great War* (London: Pandora Press, 1985).

12.   See Vellacott, 'Feminist Consciousness', pp. 82, 86.

13.   See Martin Pugh, *Women and the Women's Movement in Britain 1914–1959* (Basingstoke: Macmillan, 1992), pp. 35ff.

14.   See her autobiography, Millicent Garrett Fawcett, *What I Remember* (London: T. Fisher Unwin, 1924); Levine, *Feminist Lives*, pp. 58–69; David Rubinstein, *A Different World for Women: The Life of Millicent Garrett Fawcett* (Hemel Hempstead: Harvester Wheatsheaf, 1991).

15.   Josephine Butler's comments in *Woman's Work and Woman's Culture* (1869) illustrate this view poignantly:

> There is a necessary, a very significant connection, among all the claims at present advanced. Growth may be imperfect if one part is pushed on and another intimately related to it, is held back. The simultaneousness of the demand for industrial freedom and for higher education is based on a necessity. The education which most women need is one which will fit them for business in professions and industry. With this latter is closely connected the degree of political freedom and responsibility which we seek in asking for the parliamentary vote.

This is quoted in Patricia Hollis, *Women in Public 1850–1900: Documents of the Victorian Women's Movement* (London: Allen & Unwin, 1979), p. 315. See also June Purvis, *Hard Lessons: The Lives and Education of Working Class Women in Nineteenth Century England* (Cambridge: Polity Press, 1989), pp. 223–34; Sheila Fletcher, *Feminists and Bureaucrats: A Study in the Development of Girls' Education in the Nineteenth Century* (Cambridge: Cambridge University Press, 1980).

16.   For the historical background to, and an edition of relevant, if controversial, Fabian tracts, see Sally Alexander (ed.), *Women's Fabian Tracts* (London: Routledge, 1988).

17.   See Pat Jalland, *Women, Marriage and Politics 1860–1914* (Oxford: Clarendon Press, 1986), pp. 45–72.

18.   See Patricia Hollis, *Ladies Elect: Women in English Local Government 1865–1914*, (Oxford: Oxford University Press, 1987).

19.   See Jane Lewis, *Women and Social Action in Victorian and Edwardian England* (Aldershot: Edward Elgar, 1991).

20.   See, for instance, Leonore Davidoff and Catherine Hall, *Family Fortunes: Men and Women of the English Middle Class 1780–1850* (London: Hutchison, 1987); Jose Harris, *Private Lives, Public Spirit: A Social History of Britain 1870–1914* (Oxford: Oxford University Press, 1993).

21.   See Holcombe, *Wives and Property*, and Shanley, *Feminism, Marriage and the Law*.

22.   See Rover, *Women's Suffrage*; Brian Harrison, *Separate Spheres: The Opposition to Women's Suffrage in Britain* (London: Croom Helm, 1978).

23.   See Angela V. John and Claire Eustance (eds), *The Men's Share? Masculinities, Male Support and Women's Suffrage in Britain 1890–1920* (London: Routledge, 1997), pp. 209–10. The essays collected in this volume provide a stimulating introduction to new research trends on feminism and masculinities in the Victorian and Edwardian eras. See also Michael Roper and John Tosh (eds), *Manful Assertions: Masculinities in Britain since 1800* (London: Routledge, 1991).

24.   See Kathryn Gleadle, *The Early Feminists: Radical Unitarians and the Emergence*

of the Women's Rights Movement 1831–51 (Basingstoke: Macmillan, 1995); Sandra Stanley Holton, 'Women and the Vote' in June Purvis (ed.), *Women's History: Britain 1850–1945* (London: UCL Press, 1995), pp. 278–9.

25. Jane Rendall, '"A Moral Engine"? Feminism, Liberalism and the English Woman's Journal', in *idem*, (ed.), *Equal or Different: Women's Politics 1800–1914* (Oxford: Blackwell, 1987), p. 137.

26. See Olive Banks, *Becoming a Feminist: The Social Origins of 'First Wave' Feminism* (Brighton: Wheatsheaf, 1986), p. 160.

27. See Richard Bellamy, *Victorian Liberalism: Nineteenth Century Political Thought and Practice* (London: Routledge, 1990).

28. See Stanley, *Feminism, Marriage and the Law*, p. 102.

29. See Rendall, '"A Moral Engine"?', p. 138.

30. This line of argument is typified by Mill's *The Subjection of Women*.

31. See Mrs Fawcett, 'Women's Suffrage', speech delivered in the Town Hall, Birmingham, 6 December 1872, quoted in Catherine Hall, 'Rethinking Imperial Histories', *New Left Review*, 208 (1994), p. 26.

32. See Hall, 'Rethinking Imperial Histories', p. 29.

33. See Inderpal Grewal, *Home and Harem: Nation, Gender, Empire and the Culture of Travel* (London: Leicester University Press, 1996); Carolyn Spring, 'The Political Platform and the language of support for Women's Suffrage 1890–1920' in John and Eustance, *The Men's Share?*, pp. 158–81.

34. See Nancy Boyd, *Josephine Butler, Octavia Hill, Florence Nightingale: Three Victorian Women who Changed their World* (Basingstoke: Macmillan, 1982), pp. 35f.

35. See Banks, *Becoming a Feminist*.

36. See Frank Mort, *Dangerous Sexualities: Medico-Moral Politics in England since 1830*, (London: Routledge, 1987), pp. 63–150.

37. See Judith R. Walkowitz, *Prostitution and Victorian Society: Women, Class and the State* (Cambridge: Cambridge University Press, 1980).

38. See Eileen Janes Yeo, 'Social Motherhood and the Sexual Communion of Labour', *Women's History Review*, 1, 1 (1992), pp. 77ff.

39. See M. J. D. Roberts, 'Feminism and the State in Later Victorian England', *Historical Journal*, 38, 1 (1995), p. 109.

40. See Liddington and Norris, *One Hand Tied Behind Us*, pp. 143, 148, 149ff.

41. See Gifford Lewis, *Eva Gore-Booth and Esther Roper: A Biography* (London: Pandora Press, 1988).

42. See Claire Midgeley, *Women Against Slavery: The British Campaigns 1780–1870* (London: Routledge, 1992), pp. 18–19; Alex Tyrell, '"Woman's Mission" and Pressure Group Politics in Britain 1825–1860', *Bulletin of the John Rylands Library*, 63, 1 (1980), pp. 194–230.

43. See Vellacott, 'Feminist Consciousness', p. 85.

44. See Leslie Parker Hume, *The National Union of Women's Suffrage Societies 1897–1914* (New York: Garland, 1982), pp. 229–30.

45. See Roberts, 'Feminism and the State', p. 110.

46. See Susan Kingsley Kent, 'The Politics of Sexual Difference: World War I and the Demise of British Feminism', *Journal of British Studies*, 27 (1988), p. 253.

47. See Martin Durham, 'Suffrage and After: Feminism in the Early Twentieth Century' in Mary Langan and Bill Schwarz (eds), *Crises in the British State 1880–1930* (London: Hutchison, 1985), p. 188; Susan Kingsley Kent, *Making Peace: The Reconstruction of Gender in Interwar Britain* (Princeton NJ: Princeton University Press, 1993).

7

The Concept of Citizenship in Twentieth-Century Britain: Analysing Contexts of Development

EUGENIA LOW

'Citizenship' has been something of a political buzzword recently. It has, as Tony Wright put it, 'established a ubiquitous presence in the language of British politics'.[1] Yet, far from reflecting the emergence of a single ideological framework for British politics, the 'ubiquitous presence' of the idea of citizenship in political language has revealed merely the extent to which citizenship is a contested concept. As Anthony Rees has suggested, the idea of citizenship 'has something for every shade of opinion', and 'appears to be promiscuous in the company it keeps'.[2]

The way in which the concept of citizenship has been used in the context of British politics in the 1990s would seem to provide clear evidence of this. Citizenship discourse in twentieth-century Britain has tended to be associated with the problem of social inclusion and, more specifically, especially after the Second World War, with the nature of state welfare.[3] It is not surprising, therefore, to find that concerns about deteriorating social conditions and the costs of social welfare lie at the heart of at least part of the recent revival of interest in the concept of citizenship. The debates over the future of the welfare state in the late 1980s and 1990s, however, hit a contradictory note over the idea of citizenship. On the one hand, elements of the right seized upon citizenship as the basis for championing a personal and social responsibility on the part of citizens, to overcome what they denounced as a morally debilitating, passive reliance on the provisions of the welfare state.[4] At the same time, on the other hand, the left and centre continued to insist upon the idea that the modern welfare state should be seen as the embodiment and the very basis of the rights and entitlements of citizenship, with welfare 'rights' being seen as 'integral to the contemporary sense of citizenship' and 'a core element of citizenship in Western society'.[5] The concept of citizenship was central to the debate, but it did not provide a means by which the ideologically contested ground could be transcended. In this sense, citizenship itself became little more than an ideological tool.

To some extent, this apparent impasse in the development of a coherent notion of citizenship in the social sphere was exacerbated by the fact that there is very little meaning to a legal definition of citizenship in Britain. Historically, the British conception of the relationship between the individual and the state has borne the influence of the concept of subjecthood. Indeed, it was only with the enactment of the British Nationality Act of 1948 that the concept of a 'citizenship of the United Kingdom and Colonies' was introduced as a sub-category within the status of a 'British subject'.[6] The citizenship created by this act, however, was not attached to any positive body of citizen rights. The 'definition' of the content of British citizenship was limited to 'immunity from the various disabilities which attach to alien status', and there has been no real change to a constitutional settlement based upon the supremacy of the Crown in Parliament.[7] The key axiom of the constitution rests on the sovereignty of the Parliament, and citizens of the United Kingdom owe allegiance to the Crown in the form of the sovereign. The continuance of the notion that the British citizen stands in a subject–sovereign relationship to the state has imposed an essentially personal and reciprocal character to the legal understanding of the relationship. The rights of the British citizen are not 'entrenched': they have not been codified into statements of general principle; nor are they guaranteed any greater legal sanctity than that accorded to routine acts of Parliament.[8] Citizenship rights are protected by the ordinary law of the land, but these are enacted by Parliament, and there are no legal limits as to what it can do.[9]

In recent years, this has come to be seen as a problem by those frustrated by the operation of the so-called Thatcherite 'elective dictatorship'. In reaction to 11 years in which the exercise of a parliamentary will was seen in practice to be 'the will of a Prime Minister presiding over a cowed Cabinet and protected by an impregnable parliamentary majority' – one based, moreover, on the support of little more than one-third of the electorate – calls have been made for a reform of the hitherto 'unwritten' British constitution.[10] At the heart of the envisioned reform was to be a clear and legally defined status of citizenship which was seen as the means by which

Britain's status as a democratic polity could be restored. As Lord Scarman put it, 'The less internal control Parliament is prepared to accept, the greater the need for a constitutional settlement protecting entrenched provisions in the field of fundamental human rights.'[11] In 1992, he concluded that 'today our constitution is not "unwritten" but hidden and difficult to find', and regretted the fact that the British citizen lacked 'a constitution which he can read and understand and which enables him, if need be, to claim a right which he can enforce'.[12]

Thus, at about the same time that the notion of citizenship came to be contested ideologically in the social arena, it was made the foundation for the rebuilding of what was seen to be a derelict constitutional edifice. In the hands of groups such as Charter 88, the 'citizenship of entitlement' that had been the basis for social citizenship became part of a different agenda, and what was meant by citizenship took on yet another interpretation. In the context of threats to social cohesion and questions over the legitimacy of the political order, therefore, citizenship – a concept that had not too long ago been seen as having 'gone out of fashion among political thinkers'[13] and widely regarded 'as a litmus test of corny moralism, false consciousness and intellectual confusion'[14] – seems to have re-emerged in the 1990s in Britain as a somewhat fragmented concept, with its definition constructed in response to particular ideological agendas or political aspirations. This begs the question of the extent to which citizenship can be appealed to as an abstract ideal that somehow transcends the specific boundaries of the contexts in which it is applied, and raises the wider issue of the way in which citizenship occurs as a concept.

CONTEXT AND THE CONCEPT OF CITIZENSHIP

'The nature of citizenship,' Aristotle maintained, '... is a question which is often disputed: there is no general agreement on a single definition'.[15] Essentially, citizenship represents a conception of the relationship between the individual and the state. However, as Aristotle recognised, this relationship would differ according to different conceptions of the state.[16] Indeed, it may be added that different notions of the individual would also affect the way in which citizenship may be conceived. Citizenship, moreover, tends to occur as a cluster of ideas, rather than a monolithic concept.[17] Inasmuch as the relationship between the individual and the state is multi-faceted, this is reflected in the conception of citizenship. These considerations may appear to suggest that it is in a sense impossible for the idea of citizenship to exist as a coherent and transcendent notion. Yet, it may be argued that a multi-faceted relationship does not *have* to imply a fragmented concept; nor should the fact that conceptions of citizenship are affected by other notions render the concept meaningless except as an ideological tool.

Michael Freeden has suggested that the specificity of political concepts derives from the combination of 'the presence of an ineliminable component' – a minimum core understanding, without which the concept would be bereft of any stable meaning, but which alone cannot define the concept – and 'a non-random, even if widely variable, collection of additional components that are secured to that vacuous "*de facto*" core in a limited number of recognizable patterns'.[18] A multi-faceted concept may consist of a greater number of 'additional components', but as long as these may be located within the regular system of interrelated structural categories by which it is defined, the concept does not disintegrate. In addition, it is the structural categories that are seen to be indispensable to the definition of the concept, while their particular instances are contingent.[19] Insofar as the varying conceptions of the individual and the state are merely occupiers of a structural category, it may be argued that their effects do not threaten the integrity and validity of citizenship as a political concept. Indeed, as Charles Taylor has noted, 'things only have meanings in a field, that is, in relation to the meanings of other things … there is no such thing as a single, unrelated meaningful element'.[20] Citizenship thus occurs as a concept in much the same way as any other political concept. What needs to be recognised is that political concepts derive a major part of their meaning from what may be seen as a holistic political and intellectual setting, and it is within this context that the various aspects of the concept of citizenship are related.

What is problematic about the concept of citizenship, however, is the fact that we have inherited a dualistic ideal of citizenship, based on a classical frame of reference. On the one hand, there is the notion of 'active citizenship', based on the doctrines of Greek and Roman republicanism; on the other, there is 'passive citizenship', drawn from the juristic notions of the Roman Empire. The context for active citizenship assumes 'a closely knit body of citizens, its members committed to one another',[21] and presupposes a communal consensus of values, resulting in a positive conception of an objective common good. It involves the identification of the private, individual will with the public, social world. Indeed, there is little recognition of a realm apart from this social world: the public and the private are one.

Citizenship is tied up with the moral, cultural and personal good of each citizen, because it is through citizenship and social life that the individual is seen to realise his humanity. Passive citizenship, on the other hand, is usually premised on the very idea of a distinction between the public and private realms. In the context of a 'diverse and loosely connected body, its members (mostly) committed elsewhere', citizenship forms the outer frame of one's life: law making and administration are seen as 'someone else's business; the citizen's business is private'.[22] Such citizenship may be seen as constituting the formal legal and moral framework of a classical liberal society, and a prerequisite for the adequate functioning of an amoral and impersonal commercial market society.[23] The vision of human nature expressed is one of self-interest and competitiveness, fulfilled in intense individualism.

Two different understandings of what it means to be a citizen are thus represented: in the first, citizenship is primarily a political concept, based on the idea of personal involvement and participation; in the second, it is a legal concept, based on an external framework of procedural rights to protect the private individual's person, property and liberty from being interfered with. There are, thus, two fundamentally different senses in which an individual can exist as a citizen, with no obvious way of objectively establishing the primacy of one sense over the other. The form of citizenship that becomes the dominant understanding within a particular setting is largely determined by the intellectual and political context in which the concept is articulated. Thus, it may be argued that it is only through an understanding of the holistic setting that a consistent meaning may be achieved, and intellectual confusion averted.

In the light of this, the disintegration of the concept of citizenship in the context of the recent debates over the meaning of citizenship in Britain may be seen as a lack of recognition of the holistic framework within which citizenship works as a concept. The way in which the Conservatives have laid claim to a notion of 'active citizenship', for example, seems to involve an attempt to derive the active citizen from the possessive market individual. When, in April 1988, Home Secretary Douglas Hurd called for 'a new definition of "good citizenship"', what he had in mind was the idea that 'strong and able people' would discover a responsibility to 'the weak and less fortunate in their community'.[24] The 'active citizen', it would appear, is the successful market individual, whose positive moral duties to the community emerge from the financial gains made through productive activity.

The idea of active citizenship is thus imposed upon a context in which the single-minded pursuit of a commercial-market ethos is seen as the solution to all social and economic problems.[25] The market, however, as A. H. Halsey has commented, 'promotes neither solidarity nor equality'.[26] The notion of 'active citizenship' proposed by the Conservatives does not tap into any sense of the communal aspect of human nature. Citizens are not expected to act collectively, and the value of mutual obligation is seen to derive from a self-interest in maintaining the social order. The nature of this obligation, moreover, is characteristically non-political. Indeed, the Conservatives have seemed 'anxious to eliminate political activity from many aspects of community life'.[27]

In nearly all respects, therefore, the context for the Conservative notion of 'active citizenship' may be seen as a negation of the republican setting for a political conception of citizenship. The idea that citizenship consists of obligations and duties has been abstracted from the activist context of political participation and human fruition through involvement, and attached instead to conceptions of the individual and the state which are more attuned to a passive conception. Such a concept of citizenship no longer operates within any recognised or meaningful framework. This, in turn, affects the construction of alternatives to the Conservative conception. The grounds for citizenship have been rearranged in such a way that further paradoxical relationships have become, to some extent, inevitable. Thus, for example, the appeal of constitutional reformers for a clearer legal framework of citizenship rights, which may be seen as tending towards an idea of citizenship as a legal status, is made on the grounds of encouraging greater political participation, and has taken the mantle of an activist notion. Similarly, the idea of social citizenship advocated by the left, insofar as it appears to represent a more communal understanding of society, may have been more conducive to the active tradition. Without recourse to the idea of mutual obligation, however, it has become 'tied to the passive, if more extensive, entitlement theory of citizenship'.[28]

To make sense of these recent developments in the notions of active and passive citizenship, it is necessary to consider the way in which the idea of citizenship has emerged historically in Britain, through interactions with particular social, political and intellectual contexts. Forms of the active and passive conceptions of the citizen have been reflected in earlier articulations of the idea of citizenship, and, by analysing the contexts in which they developed, a sense of the holistic settings within which the concept of citizenship operated may be recovered. Interest in the idea of citizenship in Britain has tended to be subject to the vagaries of intellectual fashion and the political preoccupations of particular historical periods. In the twentieth century, two distinct periods in British political history may be identified as being significant occasions for the development of conceptions of citizenship: the late nineteenth century through to the 1910s, and the 1940s through to the 1960s. In the next two sections, the way in which citizenship formed a part of holistic understandings of society in each of these periods, and how the notion developed in relation to its context, will be examined.

THE IDEALIST CONCEPTION OF CITIZENSHIP

In the period lasting from the late nineteenth century to the years immediately after the First World War, the idea of citizenship was being articulated in Britain within the context of a society that was perhaps the most urbanised, industrialised and class-stratified in the world at the time.[29] This society could no longer be seen in terms of 'petty rural or urban units, each leading its own secluded life, speaking its own dialect, cherishing its own particular customs, meeting its own peculiar wants', but had become 'one tumultuous whole'.[30] The social fabric, moreover, was being threatened by the periodic depressions which hit the economy, the decline of British agriculture, and the pressures of the growing ranks of casual and poorly-paid unskilled labour in large urban centres. Poverty and unemployment emerged as national problems, and heightened anxieties about the degeneration of the body politic.[31]

In the midst of all this, however, British society was also beginning to open itself up to popular democracy. Given the structure of the constitution, the extension of the franchise in this period, although by no means complete, indicated that some degree of popular control of the state would result.[32] Within this context, worries about the breakdown of community and the sacrifice of social harmony resulting from the enlargement of society took on a political significance. In connection with the preoccupation of many late nineteenth-century writers with the search for a basis for the ideal of a cohesive community, citizenship was seen as the means by which the idea of community could be given a political meaning, and the extension of suffrage associated with 'a spiritual advance imposing new duties as well as new rights'.[33]

Such formulations were particularly associated with the idealist movement which, by the turn of the century, had established a certain prominence in British intellectual life through the activities of such men as T. H. Green, Edward Caird and Bernard Bosanquet. Working from a belief in 'the conjunction between philosophy and public life',[34] idealists in this period drew upon ideas from Plato and Aristotle, mediated through the influence of Hegelian thought, to articulate a conception of citizenship through which isolated individuals could recover a sense of their roles within a larger social organism. The idealist conviction was of the existence, in the world, of a fundamental metaphysical unity to be realised through a process of developing self-consciousness, and there was to be no distinction between the metaphysics and the practice of citizenship.[35] This shaped a particular conception of the state and the constitution of a body politic, and placed the understanding of the relationship between the individual and the state within a specific moral framework.

The following analysis will consider the way in which these conceptions interacted with ideas about rights and duties, and political participation, within the context of the idealist conception of citizenship. It will proceed by concentrating mainly on the articulations of one particular idealist philosopher, Henry Jones (1852–1922), in whose thought citizenship has been described as being 'the key motif'.[36] Although, as an idealist, Jones does not have the authoritative stature of Green or Bosanquet, his practical involvement in the Liberal politics of the time meant that his ideas were presented at the crucial interface between theory and practical politics, and directed at an audience that reflected the whole nation. Jones often articulated his conception of citizenship directly to the general public, pitching his ideas at the level of public consciousness. It is on these grounds that his ideas are taken to be representative of the idealist discourse on citizenship in the public arena, and of the way in which these ideas engaged with political reality.

At a fundamental level, Jones' conception of citizenship assumed the existence of a transcendent moral universe within which both the state and the individual found their being. Outside of this relation, Jones argued, the actions of men and states had little value.[37] The welfare of the state and the well-being of its citizens thus depended upon moral conditions, and it was within a moral framework that the unity of the body politic was to be realised. According to Jones, the state could not reject morality, nor stand above its obligations. As a moral agent, it was bound 'to aim at a moral good, and to base its sovereignty on its obedience to it'.[38] However, the moral 'personality' of the state was complex. Its 'individuality' was not focused upon a distinct 'ego', because the state could be seen to be, as Jones put it, 'nothing apart from its citizens, except an empty name'. The relations by which it was constituted were 'the relations of will to will, or of man to man', and, in this sense, the state was 'nothing more than an institution and a mere product of men's activities'.[39] Yet, although it was impossible to deny that the state was in this respect nothing more than an instrument for the well-being of its citizens, Jones argued that there was equally a sense in which 'legislators, judges, soldiers, nay every common citizen at his station and amidst his duties' served as instruments of the state when they acted in their country's interest. In such actions, citizens often appeared to be expressing the will of 'a more or less harmonious unity and individuality', rather than a mere aggregate of individuals.[40] The state, as such, was a moral entity possessed of its own moral purposes. Its citizens were as much the means for the fulfilment of these purposes, as the state was the means of their well-being.

Within the metaphysical unity of the transcendent moral universe, Jones held that the state could not claim authority over its citizens, except by being itself in the service of a higher moral authority, which was 'rooted in righteousness'. Provided that the state's authority *was* rooted in righteousness, however, Jones believed that service to the state was the citizens' 'one way to self-respect'.[41] Thus, the state and its citizens stood in moral relation to each other, and were mutually implicated – with 'the unity and intensity of a single life', as Jones saw it – in their respective pursuits of moral ends.[42] The state could not seek to achieve moral perfection independently of its citizens. Insofar as it was a moral personality, Jones maintained, it depended 'entirely for its being and character upon the character of its citizens'.[43] The moral personality of the individual citizen, however, derived its substance and significance, according to Jones, through a process of assimilating the traditions of society represented by the state. The individual, in Jones' conception, developed in the context of the universal.[44]

The relationship between the individual and the state thus involved a process by which the moral purposes of the individual came to be identified with those of the state. For the idealist, 'virtuous people and good citizens rather than well-contrived policies', as Jose Harris put it, 'were the indispensable prerequisites of a well-ordered state'.[45] Although economic and constitutional arrangements were recognised to be important, in the idealist conception of the state the justice and well-being of the body politic depended, ultimately, upon the ethical disposition of its citizens. In the light of this, the focus for the idealist conception of citizenship fell upon the individual. The nature of the individual was seen to be 'social, rational, and developing in ethical awareness'.[46] The citizen, as such, was not a static entity, and citizenship could not be conceived simply as a political or a legal category. It was, rather, a state of mind and being, within a process of moral growth and development.[47] The idealist conception of citizenship, it may be suggested, sought to address the internalisation of subjective experience within the individual mind. As the basis for social integration, citizenship was seen to depend upon the internal realisation by the individual of the moral unity that existed between himself and the state. The internal development of the individual was seen as the key to the development of a citizenship that was defined in terms of spiritual and personal identification, operating within a transcendent moral framework.

In such a setting, rights, according to Jones, were 'rooted in the conception of a good which is absolute both for States and individuals'. The value of this good depended on nothing beyond itself, was complete and not to be made better in quality, or added to and made more comprehensive.[48] For Jones, there were no rights or duties that were not moral. However, as morality only occurred through being willed by the state and its citizens, according to Jones,[49] rights could only occur as an expression of the moral consciousness of the society. Thus, although Jones accepted that the rights of a human being were innate, inalienable and grounded 'in the man himself', he maintained that it was only as a 'social being' that the individual enjoyed them.[50] The 'purely individual or isolated will', in Jones' view, could not constitute a right.[51] The individual's rights, therefore, were 'not individual in the isolating sense, but social'.[52] Rights, according to Jones, belonged to the individual 'in virtue of the recognition of a common good by the community in which he lives a more or less rational life'.[53]

The extension of such rights by the state to its citizens developed their citizenship insofar as it 'widen[ed] the compass of their private effective wills and enlarg[ed] the significance of their personality, thus encouraging a closer moral identification with the purposes of the state'.[54] Rights, however, were not external to the condition of citizenship. Neither the state nor the citizen could assert rights which did not derive their legitimacy from a shared recognition of the moral framework. In this sense, it may be suggested that the articulation of rights represented the expression of a moral unity, rather than a basis from which unity would be established. In the context of this moral unity, Jones held that rights and duties not only implied one another, but were the same facts looked at from opposite points of view.[55] Thus, just as the rights of the individual depended upon the recognition of the community, duties were binding only to individuals who discovered and imposed them upon themselves.[56] The balance of rights and duties was predicated upon the individual internalisation of the collective moral consciousness.

Political participation was also conceived in these terms, insofar as it involved the identification of the individual will with the purposes of the state. In the idealist setting, participation in the body politic was the means by which the individual realised his social being, as well as the key to the moral well-being of the state. In this sense, however, what was seen as 'political' participation did not refer merely to the narrowly defined sphere of electoral politics. For Jones, the private station and duties of each individual had a 'political significance'. 'The good citizen', he argued, 'goes forth to his labour in the morning and returns at eve, and he knows not that by fulfilling the duties of his station he has been strengthening the structure of his State, and serving purposes which far outspan his own.'[57] Political participation, as such, merely required a conscious identification of the private sphere of activity with the wider purposes of the state, which did not have to involve the individual directly in the processes of democratic politics. What this identification did imply, however, was a developed moral consciousness from which an active social conscience could evolve. To improve society, Jones maintained, citizens needed to learn 'to mass together the will for good', and 'to set free the latent moral forces and direct them towards social ends'.[58] Although he accepted without doubt that many laws and institutions did need to be changed, he believed that 'if the social conscience were more generally active, and civic duties were more unconditionally imperative, reforms, wise in their conception and far-reaching in their beneficent effects, would follow almost of themselves'.[59] What was required was a 'community whose morals are genuinely socialized' and legislative enactments that did not 'lag behind the moral convictions and purposes of the times'.[60] Politics, according to Jones, had to be moralised,[61] and the means by which this would be done was by educating the citizen to a moral consciousness of his social identity, which would be expressed through his participation in the body politic.

With its emphasis on individual moral development within the context of an objective common good, and its idea of the interpenetration between the private and the public spheres, the idealist notion of citizenship may be characterised as a form of 'active citizenship'. The particular way in which the concept was formulated, however, reflected the effects of an engagement with specific political realities. The idealists' 'active citizenship' was articulated as an attempt to recover the idea of social unity in the face of an enlarged social entity and threats of social disintegration. The closely-knit republican community, it may be suggested, was seen as an ideal to be gained through the conceptualisation of an active citizenship, rather than the foundation of the conception. The aim of the idealist conception of citizenship was the creation of a morally motivated community, through which social inclusion and unity would be achieved. The moralisation of social relations, it was believed, was the means by which a sense of civic solidarity would emerge. These ideas, it has been argued, depended upon a conception of the moral and material order that was effectively destroyed by the First World War. It belonged, as Gilbert Murray put it, to a time when people 'were actuated by hope rather than fear ... believed that men were as a rule influenced by reason, [and] that justice was the great healer of social troubles and the natural aim of wise statesmanship'.[62] In the aftermath of the war, however, these no longer seemed to hold true.

Yet, the idealist enterprise did not simply disappear. Jones' articulations of citizenship during and immediately after the First World War, for example, engaged with the new political realities. Arguments about the morality of nations, and a realised experience of sacrifice and national duty, were used to emphasise the importance of conceiving the state as a moral personality, and the possibility of a spiritual identification of the individual will with its purposes. Similarly, concerns raised by the development of popular democracy and the extension of the sphere of state intervention were addressed by appealing to ideas of moral development and the mutual implication of state and citizen. Ultimately, the idealist conception involved a notion of citizenship as the expression of social unity through an internalised moral consciousness. As such, it depended on internal and moral, rather than external and material, conditions. Citizenship could not be 'enacted' by legislation, and it was only by educating the individual mind, within a framework of moral relationships, that a citizen identity would be discovered as the basis for a morally motivated community.

THE POSTWAR CONCEPTION OF CITIZENSHIP

By way of contrast, the conception of citizenship that emerged in the context of the Second World War and its aftermath was premised on almost entirely different grounds. 'In virtually no other period of British history', Jose Harris has suggested, 'were the powers and functions of government so radically extended and redefined, and in no other period were the roles of state, citizen, economy, society and private voluntary associations more drastically remoulded.'[63] These changes, however, occurred almost purely as the result of practical legislation, and no attempt was made to analyse or justify them with regard to a philosophical foundation. The exigencies of war, it has been suggested, had given 'reality and legitimate purpose to the collective interests of society and the corporate role of the state'.[64] On the assumption that wartime standards of national solidarity and devotion to a common cause would endure, there was a sense of 'the democratic redundancy of political theorising',[65] and little sense of any need to address the individual consciousness in the attempt to create a better society.

The agenda for the creation of this better society had itself been shaped by the 'people's war'. In the spirit of collective endeavour and radicalism generated by the Second World War – encouraged by a wartime rhetoric that stressed liberty, equality and democracy as cherished institutions of British life against the fascism and intolerance of Hitler's Reich – support for a future that would be socially just and based on citizenship became 'identified with patriotic sentiment and the justification for war'.[66] The process by which such a future was to be realised, however, was conceived in relation to the possibilities of social and economic planning, rather than in terms of political or ideological change. The wartime experience of the benefits that could be achieved through the reorganisation of the economy, industry and social services along systematic and planned lines had led to a consensus that social and economic problems were to be viewed comprehensively, and tackled through an application of the principles of scientific management. The planning that had been an 'indispensable condition of victory' in the war, came to be seen as 'the key to a fair and efficient society when the war was won'.[67] Thus, effective, rational legislation – neutral, mechanical and non-moral in its impact – was to be the means by which the state, assuming a corporate responsibility for the welfare of its citizens, would produce a better society.

Such, indeed, was the legislation that established the Beveridgian postwar welfare state, which is seen as having defined the terms for a new civic bargain between the citizen and the state. This new relationship was based on a system of universal social insurance in which, by virtue of his contribution to a common fund, the citizen could, as a matter of right, expect to be protected against illness, old age and unemployment.[68] The rhetoric emphasised the virtues of universal and 'impersonal' entitlement, as opposed to the discretionary and 'moralistic' treatment that had gone on before.[69] Social welfare was no longer seen as a means of addressing the finite needs of specific individuals, with a view to helping them regain their citizenship function. It was concerned, instead, with promoting the kind of social structures in which it was believed autonomous and self-reliant individuals could multiply and flourish. Although Beveridge saw it as 'a medium for the promotion of personal independence, enlarged citizenship, enforcement of duties, and common civic culture',[70] the welfare state was associated with a concept of citizenship that did not seem to depend on the internal development of the individual. Through the operation of the system of universal contributory insurance, the relationship between the individual and the state had taken the form of a material, contractual arrangement by which the external conditions for citizenship were guaranteed, but individual attitudes and beliefs were seen as being, for the most part, irrelevant.

It was within this context that the sociologist T. H. Marshall (1893–1981) conceptualised a model of citizenship, which has since come to be seen as the definitive articulation of the idea of 'social citizenship' in Britain. Marshall's significance in the discourse on citizenship may have been inflated by the fact that recent writers on the subject have almost invariably used his ideas as their starting point.[71] In the following analysis, however, Marshall's conception of citizenship will be considered with regard to the way in which it engaged with its institutional context, and reflected prevailing notions about the role of the state and its relationship with the individual citizen within the body politic. Marshall, it should be noted, did not formulate his ideas through a process of abstract political theorising from an autonomous philosophical standpoint, but saw them as being derived from the workings of an institutional reality. As Marshall himself saw it, the institution of the welfare state 'implie[d] … a new conception of citizenship'.[72] The importance of the political reality of the postwar welfare state in providing a context for his ideas cannot, therefore, be overlooked.

Within this context, Marshall defined citizenship as 'a status *bestowed* on those who are full members of a political community'.[73] To some extent, this statement may be seen as tautological: those who were 'full members of a political community', it may be suggested, would already possess a sense of citizenship and would not need it to be 'bestowed'. For Marshall, however, citizenship involved more than a sense of belonging. Citizenship as 'status', in Marshall's conception, entailed 'distinctive rights or duties, capacities or incapacities, determined and upheld by public law'.[74] In this light, Marshall saw citizenship as 'the single uniform status' which would provide a 'foundation of equality' for social relationships: all who possessed the status of citizenship would be 'equal with respect to the rights and duties with which the status is endowed'.[75] Citizenship, as such, was not seen in terms of a personal identification with the political community, nor, it may be argued, was it something that could be individually earned or acquired. Insofar as it depended upon conditions that were to be 'upheld by public law', it would appear that Marshall's conception of citizenship could only be established through legislation by the state. The ideal of citizenship did not need to be internalised by the individual, but was an external political reality created by a state concerned with the mechanical planning of social relationships. In this way, Marshall's conception was distanced from the notion of personal, moral responsibility as an element of citizenship. Instead, citizenship was to be regarded as the product of an institutional framework, maintained and protected by the operations of existing social institutions.

This had important implications for Marshall's understanding of the rights and duties of citizenship. For Marshall, citizenship was to be understood in terms of rights, and the institutional context through which rights were expressed. Moreover, as J. M. Barbalet has noted, his approach seemed to indicate that rights were meaningful only in particular institutional contexts, and realisable only under specified material conditions.[76] It was on this basis that Marshall portrayed citizenship rights as being divided into three parts – the civil, the political and the social – and established under the aegis of different institutions, at different times.

According to Marshall, the development of the civil element of citizenship, consisting of 'the rights necessary for individual freedom – liberty of the person, freedom of speech, thought and faith, the right to own property and to conclude valid contracts, and the right to justice', was to be associated with the establishment of the rule of law in the eighteenth century.[77] The political element – represented by 'the right to participate in the exercise of political power, as a member of a body invested with political authority or as an elector of the members of such a body' – was seen to belong to a process of franchise reform which began in the nineteenth century, but only became fully established with the institution of universal adult suffrage in the twentieth century.[78] Finally, Marshall saw the social element of citizenship – which, for him, involved 'the whole range [of rights] from the right to a modicum of economic welfare and security to the right to share to the full in the social heritage and to live the life of a civilised being according to the standards prevailing in the society' – as only becoming 'woven into the fabric of citizenship' in the twentieth century, with the development of the welfare state.[79] Although he accepted that social rights could be seen as having existed previously in the form of the Poor Law, and that a tentative move towards the concept of social security had been attempted at the end of the eighteenth century, Marshall maintained that, by the act of 1834, social rights had come to be detached from the status of citizenship. Under the new Poor Law, the claims of the poor were met on the grounds that, as paupers, they forfeited in practice the civil right of personal liberty and, by law, any political rights that they might possess.[80] Within the context of the welfare state, on the other hand, the status of citizenship was 'the basis of claims to society and economic welfare which must be met as of right and not by acts of charity'.[81]

The institutional framework within which these claims were seen as rights, however, was a system of national social insurance in which 'all who pay the premiums are entitled to receive the benefits'.[82] The basis for the rights, therefore, was 'a fiscal arrangement devised by the citizens of a particular society to adjust the distribution of the income of that society in a manner considered most conducive to the welfare of all'. The rights it conferred were 'not rights rooted in the nature of man as a human being, but rights *created* by the community itself and *attached* to the status of its citizenship'.[83] As such, these rights were, according to Marshall, 'precise' with each individual knowing 'just what he is entitled to claim'. Following from this, the duties which were 'most obviously and immediately necessary' for the fulfilment of these rights – such as the duty to pay taxes and insurance contributions – were 'compulsory', such that 'no act of will is involved, and no keen sentiment of loyalty'. Other duties were, as Marshall put it, 'vague' and 'included in the general obligation to live the life of a good citizen, giving such service as one can to promote the welfare of the community'. 'But,' he continued, 'the community is so large that the obligation appears remote and unreal.'[84] Thus, the balance of social rights and duties in Marshall's conception of citizenship was determined by a contractual understanding based on material, rather than moral, grounds.

The idea of a material framework, it may be argued, was central to

Marshall's understanding of citizenship in relation to political participation. As he saw it, the setting for the progress of citizenship had been profoundly altered by the social and economic changes that had occurred in the twentieth century. As the 'components for a civilised and cultured life' were brought within the reach of many, the basis for social integration, according to Marshall, had 'spread from the sphere of sentiment and patriotism into that of material enjoyment'.[85] In such a setting, social rights appeared to refer to individuals, as Marshall put it, 'as consumers, not as actors':[86] they did not, in themselves, constitute a means by which citizenship could be expressed by the individual. Given the contractual basis for the expression of rights and duties, participation by the citizen seemed to be limited to a 'citizenship-by-consumption'.[87] To some extent, this dovetailed with the effects of postwar planning on the role of the individual citizen. With the operations of society becoming increasingly dominated by large-scale organisations, there was a sense on the part of the individual that the centralised authorities which controlled his or her life were increasingly remote.[88] There appeared, therefore, to be no compelling moral need for the citizen to participate; and, although a significant amount of time and intellectual effort was given to the consideration of the problem, no solution was ultimately sufficient to address it, given the strength of the public's preference for consumption, affluence and, above all, privacy.[89]

Thus, the dominant sense of citizenship in the postwar period came to be identified as a series of rights, entitlements and benefits, with no real opportunities for active political participation. The idea that the postwar conception of citizenship represents a notion of 'passive citizenship' has tended to stem from this identification. There are, however, other ways in which postwar citizenship may be seen as more closely approximating the passive notion. The idea that it was essentially the responsibility of the state to produce a better society through planning represented a clear distinction between the private sphere of consumption and the public sphere of legislation. Moreover, it led to a tendency to focus on the external conditions of citizenship rather than the internal development of the individual, implying a conception of citizenship that was based on a material, rather than a moral, framework. Yet, like the idealist conception, the postwar conception of citizenship was concerned with developing social cohesion. The difference was that the social unity envisioned had a strong material basis, depended upon a guarantee of equality that was bestowed by legislation, and was to be realised by the individual as a passive consumer, rather than as an actor. These developments had occurred as a result of changes in political, social and economic realities, and the dominance of a different intellectual framework for the understanding of the relationship between the individual and the state.

CONCLUSION

To a large extent, the fact that a more active conception of citizenship was proposed in the first period, and a more passive one in the second, may be seen to reflect the effects of applying two different intellectual approaches to the conceptualisation of citizenship, rather than a strictly ideological difference. The transition was from a conception of citizenship as a form of social virtue, to a conception of citizenship as an instrument of equality. In the idealist approach, the real world was seen as being structured by thought; it followed, therefore, that citizenship was to be predicated on the processes of the individual mind and individual moral action. In the more 'positivistic' postwar approach, the concern seems to have been with the (often mechanical) solving of particular and specific problems; citizenship was seen as an organising principle of mass democracy, with the material framework as the medium for its realisation. Both approaches, however, were concerned with citizenship as the means by which a sense of social unity would be achieved. What had changed was the basis on which this was seen to occur: whereas the idealist approach emphasised a moral basis for social identity, the postwar understanding of social relations was more materially based. Perhaps because of the lack of a legal tradition of constitutional citizenship, discourse on the concept of citizenship in Britain has tended to occur as an aspect of social thought, defined in social terms and concerned with 'the nature of social membership within modern political collectivities'.[90] Civic solidarity, as such, tended to be sought through social conceptions. It was in these terms that both the idealist and the postwar conceptions of citizenship were conceived; except that, within the moral framework adhered to by the idealists, the focus for these social conceptions was the moral individual, whereas, in the material framework of the postwar period, state planning was seen as the key.

If the present situation with regard to citizenship is considered in this light, however, it may be suggested that there is a less than clear conception of the framework within which citizenship should occur.

In the last three decades, the material conditions upon which the postwar conception of citizenship depended have been eroded, and the idea that it was within the power of the state to control the operations of the economy and society has waned in the face of the rise of the global economy. The material framework that buttressed the 'social citizenship' of the postwar years has thus been weakened. The reaction to this has involved a return to a conception of the individual as the central concern in social and economic thought. However, the individual is seen as a rational, self-interested economic actor, rather than a repository for social traditions within a moral unity. The Conservative attempt to promote a conception of active citizenship within this context may have involved making moralistic demands on the individual, but the basis for these demands was not a conception of a unified moral framework within which both state and citizen found their being. There was no sense of the need for an active, morally motivated community and state as the foundation for the idea of citizenship, and civic solidarity remained, for the most part, undeveloped. In the face of this apparent current inadequacy of the social frameworks that had hitherto been seen to form the bases for civic solidarity in Britain, it may be argued that a different framework for citizenship has come to be sought. The constitutional reformers' call for a clear legal definition of citizenship may be understood, in this regard, as an attempt to establish a legal framework within which an expression of the unity of the democratic polity could occur. It remains to be seen, however, if this direct relationship between citizenship and constitutional reform will provide a successful context for the development of citizenship in present-day Britain.

NOTES

The author wishes to thank Jose Harris, Marc Stears and Paul Martin for continued intellectual and moral support, Brian Harrison and Cecile Laborde for help and useful comments, and to acknowledge the financial support received from the Overseas Research Students Awards Scheme.

1. Tony Wright, *Citizens and Subjects: An Essay on British Politics* (London: Routledge, 1994), p. 126.
2. A. M. Rees, 'The Other T. H. Marshall', *Journal of Social Policy*, 24, 3 (1995), p. 342.
3. A. M. Rees, 'The Promise of Social Citizenship', *Policy and Politics*, 23, 4 (1995), p. 313.
4. Derek Heater, 'Citizenship: A Remarkable Case of Sudden Interest', *Parliamentary Affairs*, 44, 2 (1991), p. 141. It should be noted that such ideas

have, more recently, also been adopted by elements of the 'New Labour' left, whose citizenship agenda may be seen as an endorsement of a similar approach.

5.   Desmond King and Jeremy Waldron, 'Citizenship, Social Citizenship and the Defence of Welfare Provision', *British Journal of Political Science*, 18, 4 (1988), p. 417.
6.   Clive Parry, *British Nationality, Including Citizenship of the United Kingdom and Colonies and the Status of Aliens* (London: Stevens, 1951), p. 8.
7.   J. P. Gardner, 'What Lawyers Mean by Citizenship', Appendix D in *Encouraging Citizenship: Report of the Commission on Citizenship* (London: HMSO, 1990), pp. 65, 66.
8.   S. E. Finer, Vernon Bogdanor and Bernard Rudden, *Comparing Constitutions* (Oxford: Clarendon, 1995), p. 98.
9.   Gardner, 'What Lawyers Mean', p. 67. It may be argued, however, that the development of a European dimension for its operations has introduced the possibility of a check on the British Parliament's exercise of complete sovereignty.
10. Heater, 'Citizenship', p. 147.
11. Leslie Scarman, *English Law: The New Dimension* (London: Stevens, 1974), p. 75.
12. Lord Scarman, 'Why Britain Needs a Written Constitution', quoted in Brian Harrison, *The Transformation of British Politics, 1860–1995* (Oxford: Oxford University Press, 1996), pp.155–6.
13. Herman van Gunsteren, 'Notes Towards a Theory of Citizenship' in Fred Dallmayr (ed.), *From Contract to Community* (New York: Marcel Decker, 1978), p. 9.
14. Jose Harris, 'Political Thought and the State' in S. J. D. Green and R. C. Whiting (eds), *The Boundaries of the State* (Cambridge: Cambridge University Press, 1996), p. 16.
15. Quoted in Dawn Oliver, 'What is Happening to Relationships Between the Individual and the State?' in Jeffrey L. Jowell and Dawn Oliver (eds), *The Changing Constitution* (Oxford: Clarendon, 1994), p. 442.
16. See Aristotle, *Politics*, Bk. III, Ch. 1, 1275^b 4–5.
17. Oliver, 'Individual and the State', p. 442.
18. Michael Freeden, *Ideologies and Political Theory: A Conceptual Approach* (Oxford: Oxford University Press, 1996), pp. 64–5.
19. Ibid., p. 66.
20. Quoted in Freeden, *Ideologies*, p. 67.
21. Michael Walzer, 'Citizenship' in Terence Ball, James Farr and Russell L. Hanson (eds), *Political Innovation and Conceptual Change* (Cambridge: Cambridge University Press, 1989), p. 216.
22. Ibid., p. 216.
23. Andrew Vincent, 'Citizenship', *Contemporary Record*, 4 (September 1990), p. 16.
24. Katherine Fierlbeck, 'Redefining Responsibility: The Politics of Citizenship in the United Kingdom', *Canadian Journal of Political Science*, 24, 3 (1991), p. 585.
25. Vincent, 'Citizenship', pp. 17, 18.
26. A. H. Halsey, *Change in British Society: From 1900 to the Present Day*, 4th edn (Oxford: Oxford University Press, 1995), p. 221.
27. Dawn Oliver, 'Active Citizenship in the 1990s', *Parliamentary Affairs*, 44, 2 (1991), p. 165.
28. Vincent, 'Citizenship', p. 18.

29. Jose Harris, 'Political Thought and the Welfare State 1870–1940: An Intellectual Framework for British Social Policy', *Past and Present*, 135 (1992), p. 140.
30. Henry Jones, 'The Working Faith of the Social Reformer' in *The Working Faith of the Social Reformer and Other Essays* (London: Macmillan, 1910), p. 22.
31. Sandra den Otter, *British Idealism and Social Explanation: A Study in Late Victorian Thought* (Oxford: Oxford University Press, 1996), pp. 4–5.
32. Harris, 'Political Thought and the Welfare State', p. 140.
33. Melvin Richter, *The Politics of Conscience: T. H. Green and his Age* (London: Weidenfeld & Nicholson, 1964), p. 344.
34. Den Otter, *British Idealism*, p. 1.
35. David Boucher and Andrew Vincent, *A Radical Hegelian: The Political and Social Philosophy of Henry Jones* (Cardiff: University of Wales Press, 1993), p. 93.
36. Ibid., p. 21.
37. Henry Jones, *The Principles of Citizenship* (London: Macmillan, 1919), p. 70.
38. Ibid., p. 46.
39. Ibid., p. 51.
40. Ibid., p. 53.
41. Henry Jones, 'The Education of the Citizen' in *Essays on Literature and Education* (London: Hodder & Stoughton, 1924), pp. 257–8.
42. Jones, *Principles*, p. 90.
43. Henry Jones, 'The Corruption of the Citizenship of the Working Man', *Hibbert Journal*, 10, 1 (1911), p. 155.
44. Boucher and Vincent, *Radical Hegelian*, p. 93.
45. Jose Harris, 'The Webbs, the Charity Organisation Society and the Ratan Tata Foundation: Social Policy from the Perspective of 1912' in Martin Bulmer, Jane Lewis and David Piachaud (eds), *The Goals of Social Policy* (London: Unwin Hyman, 1989), p. 55.
46. Boucher and Vincent, *Radical Hegelian*, p. 98.
47. Ibid., p. 95.
48. Jones, *Principles*, p. 142.
49. Ibid., p. 71.
50. Ibid., p. 148.
51. Jones, 'Working Faith', p. 97.
52. Ibid., p. 98.
53. Jones, *Principles*, p. 148.
54. Henry Jones, 'The Obligations and Privileges of Citizenship', *Rice Institute Pamphlet*, 6, 3 (1919), p. 172.
55. Jones, *Principles*, p. 138.
56. Henry Jones, 'Social Responsibilities' in *Working Faith of the Social Reformer*, p. 297.
57. Henry Jones, 'The Moral Aspect of the Fiscal Question' in *Working Faith of the Social Reformer*, p. 133.
58. Jones, 'Social Responsibilities', p. 262.
59. Ibid., p. 260.
60. Ibid., pp. 260, 270.
61. Henry Jones, 'Ethics and Politics', *Friends' Quarterly Examiner*, 44, 175 (1910), p. 408.
62. Quoted in Richter, *Politics of Conscience*, p. 375.
63. Harris, 'Political Thought and the State', p. 15.
64. David Morgan and Mary Evans, *The Battle for Britain: Citizenship and Ideology*

in the Second World War (London: Routledge, 1993), p. 113.

65. Harris, 'Political Thought and the State', p. 23.
66. Morgan and Evans, *Battle for Britain*, pp. 1, 127.
67. Ibid., p. 8.
68. Michael Ignatieff, 'The Myth of Citizenship' in Ronald Beiner (ed.), *Theorizing Citizenship* (New York: State University of New York Press, 1995), p. 67.
69. Jose Harris, '"Contract" and "Citizenship"' in David Marquand and Anthony Seldon (eds), *The Ideas that Shaped Post-War Britain* (London: Fontana, 1996), p. 122.
70. Jose Harris, *William Beveridge: A Biography* (Oxford: Oxford University Press, 1997), p. 496.
71. Anthony M. Rees, 'T. H. Marshall and the Progress of Citizenship' in Martin Bulmer and Anthony M. Rees (eds), *Citizenship Today: The Contemporary Relevance of T. H. Marshall* (London: UCL Press, 1996), p. 3.
72. Papers of T. H. Marshall, British Library of Political and Economic Science, London (henceforward MS Marshall): File 4/2, 'Social Change in Britain: A Sociological Perspective', f. 15.
73. T. H. Marshall, 'Citizenship and Social Class' in T. H. Marshall and Tom Bottomore, *Citizenship and Social Class* (London: Pluto, 1996), p. 18. Emphasis added.
74. T. H. Marshall, 'Changes in Social Stratification in the Twentieth Century' in *Sociology at the Crossroads and Other Essays* (London: Heinemann, 1963), p. 134.
75. Marshall, 'Citizenship', pp. 21, 18.
76. J. M. Barbalet, *Citizenship: Rights, Struggle and Class Inequality* (Milton Keynes: Open University Press, 1988), p. 6.
77. Marshall, 'Citizenship', pp. 8, 10.
78. Ibid., pp. 8, 13.
79. Ibid., pp. 8, 27.
80. Ibid., pp. 14–15.
81. MS Marshall: 'Social Change', f. 14.
82. MS Marshall: File 2/17, 'The Welfare State – The Next Phase', f. 6.
83. T. H. Marshall, 'The Right to Welfare' in *The Right to Welfare and Other Essays* (London: Heinemann, 1981), p. 88. Emphasis added.
84. Marshall, 'Citizenship', p. 45.
85. Ibid., p. 28.
86. T. H. Marshall, 'Reflections on Power' in *Right to Welfare*, p. 141.
87. James E. Cronin, 'Class, Citizenship and Party Allegiance: The Labour Party and Class Formation in Twentieth Century Britain', *Studies in Political Economy*, 21 (1986), p. 129.
88. Abigail Beach, 'Forging a "Nation of Participants": Political and Economic Planning in Labour's Britain' in Richard Weight and Abigail Beach (eds), *The Right to Belong: Citizenship and National Identity in Britain, 1930–1960* (London: I. B. Tauris, 1998), p. 94.
89. Ibid., p. 108.
90. Bryan S. Turner, 'Contemporary Problems in the Theory of Citizenship' in Bryan S. Turner (ed.), *Citizenship and Social Theory* (London: Sage, 1993), p. 3.

8

'Home Rule All Round': Experiments in Regionalising Great Britain, 1886–1914

ELFIE REMBOLD

Edward I by the Statute of Rhuddlan endeavoured, with a statesmanship of which no other contemporary ruler was capable, to effect a settlement of the conquered principality. He turned the patrimony of the Welsh Princes – Anglesey, Carnarvon, and Merioneth in the north, Cardigan and Carmarthen in the south – into shire-ground. He did not interfere with the use of the Welsh language. He appointed a commission to inquire into the Welsh laws and customs, and some of them he allowed to remain in force. But he adhered rigidly to one inflexible rule. No Welshman was allowed to govern the country, to administer the law, or to represent the sovereign authority. The Government could be carried on by the King and his officers alone.
(Llewelyn Williams, *The Making of Modern Wales*, 1919)

Ever since the Union of the two Crowns, it has been the work of factious turbulent spirits, to foment Jealousies, and to promote differences betwixt the Two Nations.
(Fletcher of Saltoun, *State of Controversy betwixt United and Separate Parliaments*, 1706)

What is really the meaning of this high-sounding phrase about the representation of nationalities? What is a nationality if the people of these islands do not form one?
(*The Times*, 5 August 1910)

Territorial reform became a matter of increasing political interest in Britain when Irish home rule became central to parliamentary politics. Despite industrial modernisation and increasing administrative standardisation great cultural differences remained in the 'celtic' regions which could be mobilised for political ends at the beginning of mass democracy. The first elections under the extended franchise in 1885 brought the Irish question to centre stage; and the ensuing Gladstonian endeavour to introduce Irish home rule in 1886, whilst stimulating a Unionist reaction, nevertheless also acted as a catalyst for the growth of home rule movements in Scotland and Wales, seeking devolution within the United Kingdom.

It will be shown here, first, that the split of the Liberal Party in 1886 and the consequent home rule politics of the Gladstonian party supported by regional movements in Scotland and Wales was a modern way to continue the old style of territorial management of benign neglect of local affairs whilst entrusting local elites with their control. Second, the different concepts of 'home rule all round' and their relation to specific Scottish conditions will be analysed. Finally, some reasons will be put forward as to why the Liberal government did not embark on a fundamental territorial reform in the prewar years. In a short conclusion it will be pointed out that, in the wake of the First World War, further democratisation and social and economic problems shifted the focus of political reform to social reconstruction. Consequently, the idea of home rule all round lost attraction and all the more so after Southern Ireland left the Union and became a dominion in 1921. Ironically, the only people who actually received home rule were those who most vehemently opposed home rule throughout the period under review, the Unionists of what became Northern Ireland.

THE IRISH QUESTION AND THE SPLIT IN THE LIBERAL PARTY

The consequences of the Reform Act of 1884 on the parliamentary arithmetic of late Victorian Britain meant that the Irish question could no longer be ignored. As Gladstone later put it, he had no evidence that Isaac Butt's party was popular, but the result of the 1885 election in Ireland confirmed that Parnell's party was. 'That settled the question. When the people express their determination in this decisive way you must give them what they want.'[1]

However, of the three leading politicians of the Liberal factions[2] only Joseph Chamberlain, the leader of the Radicals, openly declared himself on the Irish problem during the election campaign of 1885.[3] By propagating his idea of home rule all round he responded to the Irish demand for land reform and home rule. For him this was an expedient means of containing the centrifugal effects of Irish home rule on both Britain and the Empire; home rule all round offered a way of meeting the Irish demands whilst maintaining a superior imperial Parliament at Westminster.[4] The Radical leader employed this idea in the sense of local governments with extended powers,[5] and as a remedy to the Irish question that would finally end the continuous resort to coercion. Against this background the concept of home rule all round can be considered as an alternative to a measure of political reform purely restricted to Ireland. However, this highly controversial question also served his political ambitions to dish the Whigs and challenge Gladstone's position as party leader.[6] Chamberlain's programme of radicalisation of Liberal politics in the Age of New Democracy aimed at secularisation and free education, the establishment of popular local governments and sweeping land reform which taxed the propertied classes and thus underpinned financially these democratic reforms.[7] In terms of administration this concept inevitably implied a centralisation of politics, equating a strong central government with efficient politics. However, far from wiping out the Whigs, the Liberal representatives of the landed interest, in its failure it turned out to make them the new allies of the Radicals.

Gladstone responded to Chamberlain's electoral offensive in that he agreed that 'on local government for Ireland they [the Radicals] hold a winning position', but he pointed out that he differed from his rival in taking the problem seriously rather than seeking a tactical advantage: 'I have never looked much in Irish matters at negotiation or the conciliation of leaders. I look at the question in itself.'[8] Both, Liberals and Radicals, after all conceived the Irish problem as an unavoidable political issue that had to be solved during the next session.

These first semi-democratic elections in 1885[9] saw an Irish home rule contingent of 86, strengthened by the effects of the franchise reform, exactly holding the parliamentary balance between 335 Liberals and 249 Conservatives. After several weeks of public silence yet busy bargaining behind the scenes[10] the parliamentary stalemate was finally lifted when Herbert Gladstone gave an interview to the press that hinted at his father's commitment to Irish home rule.[11] The consequences of this decision are well known: the split of the Liberal Party. Significantly, this split was as much about the future of Liberal politics and the style of Liberal leadership as it was about the immediate question of Irish home rule.

REGIONALISING LIBERALISM

Shortly after Chamberlain resigned from the Local Government Board in dissension with Gladstone's proposals for Irish home rule in March 1886 on grounds of 'increased taxation (with which Great Britain should burden itself), not in order to secure the closer and more effective union of the Three Kingdoms, but as a currency to purchase the repeal of the Union and the practical separation of Ireland from England and Scotland',[12] Charles Waddie founded in Edinburgh the Scottish Home Rule Association (SHRA) on 20 May.[13] In their appeal to the Scottish people, 'both at home and abroad', the founders pointed to the 'national aspirations' and 'national rights' of the Scottish people and underlined their demand for Scottish home rule with reference to 'a glorious past' and 'yet a greater future' that will be achieved 'by securing to her the legitimate control of her own affairs'. Surprisingly enough, the first object of their programme was 'to protect the integrity of the Empire'. Only in second place did they claim 'to promote the establishment of a legislature sitting in Scotland with full control over all purely Scottish questions, and with an Executive Government responsible to it and the Crown'. A few weeks later the young Thomas Edward Ellis addressed the Merioneth Liberals' selection conference with a clear statement for Welsh home rule which embraced the Welsh problems as expressed by the nonconformists of Wales.[14] Although no formal Welsh home rule association was founded before 1887 when the first *Cymru Fydd* societies were set up in Liverpool and London, in April ideas were in circulation to establish 'some sort of Welsh organisation'.[15] These were realised in the winter of 1886–7 when the North and South Wales Liberal Federations were founded.

In their origin these regional movements doubtless were an offspring of Gladstone's new definition of Liberalism. As political measures in a union state will usually be applied to all its constituent parts, granting home rule to Ireland, as an integral part of the United Kingdom, might also imply home rule for Scotland and Wales.[16] In contrast, instead of regionalising Liberalism Chamberlain's radicalisation of politics pointed in the completely opposite direction – to a centralisation of British politics. Arguably, this differentiation of Liberalism in one or the other way met at least in one point: the exclusion of socialism and the integration of the working-classes, matters of growing concern in the 1880s, were two sides of the same coin. The Gladstonian espousal of Irish home rule appealed to working-class Radicals, such as Keir Hardie, happy to view the need for liberation from the oppression of landlordism and alien rule in the same light as they viewed the need for the urban working classes to be liberated from the tyranny of unemployment and the uncertainties of industrial capitalism. Ironically, what made Gladstonian Liberalism attractive to middle-class voters, however, was its provision for continuous self-government according to the old tradition of territorial management.

FROM WELSH LIBERALISM TO WELSH RADICALISM: THE CYMRU FYDD MOVEMENT

As Derek W. Urwin argues: 'the style of British politics did not change very much before the 1880s. The persistence of the traditional constitution determined that electoral politics would essentially be local politics.'[17] Change came with the electoral reforms in the 1880s when mass party mobilisation 'emanating from the centre' was confronted with local initiative. Thus, these political reforms 'helped to generate a new debate upon the territorial constitution' of the United Kingdom.[18] 'Local initiative' in the 1880s differed from local management hitherto in that it actually tackled the problems and grievances of the people rather than being concerned with the matters of the landed and propertied classes. Consequently, the new regional elites were not only locally closer to the people but were themselves partly of humble descent, for instance, the Welsh national leader Tom Ellis who was the son of a tenant farmer,[19] or David Lloyd George who was brought up by his uncle, a shoemaker in rural Caernarvonshire.[20]

When in 1885 Wales returned only four Conservatives out of 34 candidates[21] this merely confirmed the trend established earlier in the 1880 elections and which was to last until after the First World War. The Whigs representing the Anglican, English-speaking, landowning class had to give way to nonconformist industrialists and manufacturers or to men of the legal professions.[22] 'Characteristic', as Philip Jenkins puts it 'of the new type of Member were men like Alfred Thomas, an industrialist who was also president of the Welsh Baptist Union; David A. Thomas, the nonconformist coal magnate or the Methodist solicitor David Rendell.'[23]

There was one striking deviation from this rule when Stuart Rendel, an English landowner, won Montgomeryshire for the first time in 1880, thereby defeating the High Tory Sir Watkins Williams-Wynn. He was to play a leading role in forming the Welsh Party at

Westminster and in giving a voice to distinctively Welsh grievances. His political abilities were twofold: on the one hand, he could make himself acceptable to many sections of Welsh political opinion,[24] and, on the other, he was on good terms with the Liberal leadership, being friendly with Mr Gladstone himself,[25] which allowed for a transformation of exclusively Welsh issues into British politics and the achievement of political reform in Wales.

Unifying the Welsh members into a politically effective Welsh Parliamentary Party and helping to join local Liberal associations into the North Wales Liberal Federation were certainly his greatest achievements. Welsh nonconformity and its growing demand for disestablishment meanwhile provided a rallying cry for a more coherent Welsh Liberalism. But despite all this Rendel still adhered to a rather moderate apprehension of the goals of Welsh Liberalism. Although he conceded to Welsh Liberals the right to take decisive steps 'to secure full consideration of special needs of the principality'[26] he disapproved of measures like William Rathbone's proposal of a Welsh Grand Committee in 1886 or Alfred Thomas's National Institutions of Wales Bill of 1891[27] as he was anxious not to ask for too much of the Liberal leadership that might cause disruption of the Liberal Party.

Opposition to his able but temperate approach to the central Liberal leadership came from among young radical members like Tom Ellis (Merionethshire), David Lloyd George (Caernarfon), Samuel Evans (Mid-Glamorgan), Frank Edwards (Radnorshire) and D. A. Thomas (Merthyr Tydfil). They were founders and prominent representatives of the Welsh national movement *Cymru Fydd* (Young Wales). In its magazines, *Young Wales* and *Wales*, as well as in several local newspapers, Welsh literati propagated ideas of Welsh nationality while its political agents exerted pressure on the Liberal Party to achieve its ultimate goal of Welsh home rule. Men like Tom Ellis and Samuel Evans were educated in their native country, at Aberystwyth College where they studied together with Ellis J. Ellis-Griffith, educationalist and MP for Angelsey (1895–1918), T. F. Roberts, later the second principal of University College, Aberystwyth, and O. M. Edwards, later editor of *Wales* and professor of history.[28] In cultural terms they sought a Welsh national identity by laying emphasis on the vernacular as well as on the history of the *Cymru* (the Welsh people). For these intellectuals a potential career as a London barrister or lecturer in Oxford was less attractive than the challenge to 'make' Wales.

Significantly, they perceived politics in terms of Welsh nationalism rather than British Liberalism. For Tom Ellis and the young David

Lloyd George as the leading figures of Welsh radicalism, albeit with
rather different concepts of nationalism, the organisation and aims of
the Irish Nationalist Party served as a model for Wales though never
to quite the same degree. Whereas Ellis conceived of 'national self-
government' as the highest expression of nationality and a
precondition for uniting north and south Wales Lloyd George stood
for a brand of Welsh nationalism that was an ideology 'wholly and
narrowly political' and as such very different to Tom Ellis's 'gentle
visions … shot through with cultural and literary values'. Lloyd
George 'represented the spirit of equality just as Ellis reflected that of
liberty'.[29]

INDUSTRIAL SOUTH WALES REFUSES WELSH NORTH WALES

Apart from the fact that *Cymru Fydd* societies were first formed within
Welsh communities outside Wales – in traditional centres of Welsh
settlement in England such as Liverpool and London – it was
nevertheless in north Wales where radicalism developed into
nationalism and from there proliferated into the south. Indeed the
bipartite division of Wales into a rural and Welsh-speaking north and
an industrial and anglicised south seduced sceptics and open
opponents of Welsh nationalism to speak of Wales as merely a
'geographical expression'.[30] This geographical split also reflected the
dissension amongst Welsh members regarding unified political action.

The first distinctively Welsh piece of legislation was the Sunday
Closing Act of 1881. This, however, was followed by the University of
Wales Act and the appointment of a Royal Commission on Welsh land
in 1893. Gladstone expressed his sympathy with recognition of the
Welsh language at the national eisteddfod in Wrexham in 1888, and
throughout this period he was generally favourable to Welsh
demands. Gladstone 'did infinitely more than any other major political
figure … to advance Welsh causes'.[31] This degree of sympathy from the
national party leader might have meant that further enactments were
possible. And there was general agreement amongst Welsh members
about certain measures, like disestablishment and education.
However, on a sweeping measure for home rule, Liberals from south
Wales held different views from their compatriots of the north.

In 1891 and again in 1892 the MP for Mid-Glamorgan, Alfred
Thomas, a prominent businessman from Cardiff and president of the
Welsh Baptist Union, introduced his National Institutions (Wales)
Bills. These would have provided for a Minister of Wales[32] similar to

the Scottish Secretaryship introduced in 1885. Despite its being supported by Ellis, Lloyd George and six other MPs, when presented under a Liberal government in 1892 it was bound to founder since the arguments against it were all too obvious. First, Welsh, unlike Scottish, Nationalists could hardly conjure a constitutional tradition of a Welsh Secretary – a fact the Conservatives dwelt upon when defending the administrative uniformity between England and Wales. Second, reform of local government in 1888 had had two important effects. It greatly reduced the influence of old Whig and Tory elites in the management of local affairs and passed it on to the representatives of the Welsh people. As a matter of fact, however, this satisfied nonconformist interest in self-government to a great extent. And last, but not least, the bill roused the suspicions of the Liberals from south Wales that they might fall under the sway of north Wales. Certainly this seemed a risk if the proposed Welsh National Council were to be composed on the basis of the amendment to the local government reforms put forward by Ellis in 1888.[33]

This reservation and distrust of Nationalists amongst Liberals from the south and their wariness against a north Wales preponderance in any national institution was also partly responsible for the failure of a proposed amalgamation of the two Liberal Federations in 1895. Whereas the *Cymru Fydd* movement had merged into the North Wales Liberal Federation the South Wales branch decided to remain independent.[34] However, resistance had broader motives. When the industrialist D. A. Thomas convinced his followers from the south to retain their own Liberal association this entailed a decision against further democratisation of the constituencies rather than a repudiation of the Welsh national programme committed to home rule and the Welsh language. This was as much about seeking to deny the south Wales miners and tinplate workers adequate political representation within the Liberal Party. But, in addition, the demand to foster the Welsh language was less powerful in the south than in the north. After a series of conferences in 1895 showed no sign of a successful unification of the two Welsh Liberal Federations, Llewelyn W. Williams – an ardent patriot, son of a tenant farmer from Llansadwrn, and later MP for Carmarthen – disappointedly wrote:

> But now the Nationalism that has withstood centuries of armed oppression, of silent neglect, of contemptuous scorn, is withering before the blighting influence of Industrialism. Walk through the Vale, and within sight of 'Cromlech' and 'golwch', beneath the shadows of the dismantled castle of Penmark, a monument of

Glydwr's might and the strength of an awakened nation, on the banks of the Carvan, where Gildas and Caradoc walked, and on the very site of 'Cor Tewdws', you will find not only the old language disappearing, but, what is worse, a new race springing up which has no sympathy with the past, and which knows nothing and cares nothing for that 'old and haughty nation' which aroused the admiration of Milton and won the misdirected pity of Wordsworth. This is but an instance of what is slowly taking place throughout the country. The enemy which Young Wales will be called upon to fight in the future is the industrial and commercial Philistinism of Englishmen and Welshmen. Let the issue be made clear! Young Wales fights for culture, for true national development, for the only way in which it is possible in Wales to rear a nation of noble men and women, by teaching a lesson of national self-respect – men who, while not despising or undervaluing worldly success or prosperity, recognise that man's duty on earth consists of something higher and nobler than simple 'to get on'.[35]

This quotation makes it abundantly clear that by 1895 Welsh radicalism has turned into cultural nationalism of a conservative blend that was content in alliance with Gladstonian Liberalism, for it suited both factions of Welsh Liberalism: the south Wales business interest in the British economy and the north Wales intellectuals in making a Welsh nation by the establishment of a genuine Welsh educational system.

Despite the problems the nationalist movement encountered in Wales, it is clear that Gladstone's Irish home rule policy evoked regional movements that claimed self-government also for their country in the form of home rule all round. In constitutional terms this involved a reorganisation of the relationship of centre and periphery. Hitherto, the centre benevolently neglected local affairs which were to be managed by the local elite. Throughout Wales the advance of democracy expelled the old anglicised gentry class from office and entrusted a new middle-class elite of professionals and industrialists with the control of regional affairs.

However, nationalism in Wales was intrinsicly bound up with the call for disestablishment of the Anglican church in Wales. In this context another opportunity for a devolution measure seemed to arise when the Liberal government embarked on the reform of Balfour's Education Act. When the Unionist government introduced its controversial bill to reform the educational system in England and

Wales in 1902, providing for local subsidies for voluntary schools, Welsh nonconformists rose in arms with the battle cry 'the Church on the rates' and refused to pay these extra rates. During the election campaign of 1906 Welsh Liberals pledged themselves to change this detested bill and despite all difficulties Lloyd George, now a member of the Cabinet, tried to find a way which could satisfy Welsh radical demands. According to his preference for unconventional solutions he suggested the creation of a National Council of Education, which implied a Minister for Wales who should have been created by an Order in Council.

This additional clause in the Education Bill incensed the opposition and among others Sir Edward Carson denounced it as 'a clause of devolution'. Although a Liberal majority accepted this clause at committee stage, it was soon dropped after the intervention of King Edward VII. Adopting the arguments of the Unionists he considered it 'most unconstitutional' and ordered his secretary to 'inquire in my name what is the cause of this most strange and I may say unheard of proceeding'. This can be seen as the last effort to achieve devolution solely for Wales, for six years later, in 1912, E. T. John aimed at the broader solution of home rule all round.

The Scottish national movement was different to the Welsh in that it perceived home rule in legal rather than cultural terms. This view was deeply rooted in history and the way union with the more powerful neighbour, England, came about in each case. While under the Welsh Act of Union of 1536 the legal and administrative system of England was merely extended to Welsh territory, the Act of Union in 1707 with the Kingdom of Scotland united two separate parliaments yet provided for the continuation of a different legal, ecclesiastical and educational structure in each country. Social change and political reform during the nineteenth century, however, changed the character of a highly decentralised state operating on a basis of 'clientelism'[36] into an interventionist and increasingly centralised one. This had different consequences in Wales and Scotland. In Wales it entailed the reawakening of a distinctive cultural identity, and consequently Welsh home rule was about achieving an institutional expression of this newly discovered Welshness. In Scotland, however, it brought about a defence of existing Scottish institutions and traditions.

REGIONAL MOVEMENTS AND SCOTTISH AUTONOMY

Scottish nationalism in the nineteenth and early twentieth centuries never rejected the Union. The commonwealth with England not only enabled many enterprising Scots to build and benefit from an empire abroad,[37] but also to develop unimpaired from the political centre a civil society at home. Scottish interest in the Union as a means of maintaining and strengthening the Empire was shared by both Unionists and Liberals. The former also showed their willingness to countenance a measure of 'administrative devolution' as opposed to 'legislative devolution' to Scotland which was advocated by mainly Liberal-dominated home rule movements.

'Administrative devolution'[38] as it was called later in 1928, helped to preserve this Scottish autonomy, symbolised in the re-establishment of the Scottish Office in 1885. Neither Tories nor Liberals denied a Scottish national interest in managing their own affairs; what was actually disputed was how to defend this autonomy. It was a Scottish Tory, the Earl of Eglington and Winton, who founded the National Association for the Vindication of Scottish Rights in 1853[39] on the grounds that Scottish affairs were inadequately handled in Westminster. This complaint could be satisfied by expanding local boards. Just over 30 years later, in 1884, the Convention of Royal Burghs persuaded the Liberal government that Scotland wanted administrative change[40] which resulted in the re-establishing of the Scottish Office enacted by the Conservative caretaker ministry in 1885.

When in the following year (April 1886) Gladstone introduced his first Irish Home Rule Bill, Scottish Liberals founded in May the Scottish Home Rule Association (SHRA) based on precisely the same line of argument of 'vindicating her [Scotland's] rights'. In contrast to its predecessors it went well beyond the claim of 'securing her legitimate affairs' – i.e. mere administrative autonomy – and demanded 'the establishment of a legislature sitting in Scotland with full control over all purely Scottish questions, and with an Executive Government responsible to it and the Crown'.[41] Ever since, regional movements in Scotland have never considered anything but the creation of a separate parliament the adequate 'expression of their national aspirations'.[42] However, none of these more radical movements ever intended to repeal the Act of Union. Thus, the Young Scots Society, a Liberal pressure group founded during the Boer War in 1900, expressly declared:

Modern Scottish Home Rulers do not propose the repeal of the

Treaty of Union, not even of Article III under which the ancient sovereign Parliament of Scotland was abolished.

What they wanted was simply to 'extend the Treaty by creating subordinate Parliaments'.[43] Similarily, the second SHRA set up in 1918[44] emphasised the same ideal of self-government within the context of the Empire. Its sensitivity to potential criticism is revealed by the lengths it went to proclaim:

> We are not a separatist party. We merely wish for Scottish self-government, leaving the Imperial Parliament to deal with the higher questions of Imperial policy.[45]

CONCEPTS OF HOME RULE ALL ROUND

As mentioned above, it was Gladstone's Irish home rule policy which provoked a regional home rule movement in Scotland in 1886. When Gladstone introduced his first Home Rule Bill for Ireland the most controversial clause was that about the exclusion of Irish representation from Westminster. After all, this representation was a symbol of the constitutional differences between Ireland and the colonies, as the latter was neither represented directly in the United Kingdom Parliament, nor shared in its financial obligations. In other words, the exclusion of Irish members was contrary to the venerable principle of 'no taxation without representation'.[46] Chamberlain considered the 'difficulties of any plan ... almost insurmountable', and believed that 'the worst of all plans would be one which kept the Irishmen at Westminster while they had their own Parliament in Dublin'.[47] Both ways were tried and both ways failed. The first bill in 1886 excluding Irish members was defeated in the Commons with Chamberlain strongly opposing this proposal, while the second attempt in 1893 providing for Irish representation in the imperial Parliament was rejected by the Lords.

Apparently Chamberlain's prime objective in 1885 aimed at more democracy in the localities when he propagated his national council scheme, wrapped up as 'home rule all round'. But this also implied the need for greater efficiency at the centre and, as Jay rightly states, 'Chamberlain's Radicalism at least demanded a strong imperial parliament',[48] able to implement his policies. Consequently, after he parted company with the Gladstonians he also dropped any plans for extending local government and concentrated on the consolidation of the Empire. The home rule commitment of Gladstonian Liberalism, on the other hand, encouraged regionalism in the United Kingdom.

Gladstone's interest in national self-determination, demonstrated earlier in his attitude towards the Italian *Risorgimento* or in his Midlothian campaign on the Eastern question in 1876–77, favoured his conversion to Irish home rule. Though he was also sympathetic to Scottish aspirations for more self-government he, however, never pursued this matter. Ireland came first, and there was a clear electoral imperative for tackling this problem, indicated by the popular support for the Home Rule Party. His main objective was to do justice to Ireland, whatever the costs of political and constitutional rupture. In contrast with this somewhat destructive approach to home rule, Scottish regional movements, however, put forward alternative concepts of how regional self-government might be organised.

Three such concepts were predominantly circulated in political discussion: 'home rule all round', 'devolution' and 'federalism' which basically all contained the same idea of creating regional sub-parliaments whilst recognising the overall supremacy of Westminster. These concepts were often elided, confused or misused in the political discourse of the day; which concept was chosen at a particular time depended on the political opportunity a certain perspective on regional self-government might present. Evidently 'home rule all round' was meant to apply the idea of home rule to the different countries within a union state and thus to avoid obvious injustice as well as illogical legislation. William Mitchell, one of the founders of the SHRA, described himself and his colleagues as 'Home Rulers on principle, not only for Ireland but for their own country'.[49] Therefore they opposed Gladstone's Irish home rule policy, whilst generally supporting Gladstonian Liberalism. The favourite argument of the Young Scots, recurring in their writings, underlined that home rule for Ireland cannot be granted 'without introducing many anomalies at Westminster'.[50] According to their principles of New Liberalism they argued on rational rather than nationalist lines and pointed out that any home rule legislation also demanded equal treatment of all parts of the Union. Since the efforts of the Young Scots Society to influence a Liberal government arose only after the election triumph of 1906, the debate on home rule was closely related to the contemporary reconstruction of the Empire and society at home in the light of the Boer War, and proposed measures were generally embedded in a more comprehensive plan of Empire federation.

CONGESTION AND DEVOLUTION

Much earlier, when the Irish policy of obstruction heavily impeded parliamentary business, Liberal Party leaders came up with suggestions for parliamentary devolution in speeches and memorandums. In 1880 Gladstone aired ideas on how to economise on parliamentary time by devolving parts of its business to Grand Committees.[51] In the 1890s these considerations constituted the starting point for Scottish regionalists to justify Scottish home rule in terms of devolution and on grounds of parliamentary congestion. Thus, whilst arguments for Scottish home rule had hitherto been focused on complaints about the neglect of Scottish affairs, they now shifted into a wider context affecting the whole Kingdom.

The principle of devolution was derived from the problem of legislative congestion in the imperial Parliament which was aptly diagnosed by Sir Henry Dalziel, a Scottish Home Ruler, in 1894: 'We are agreed that the disease from which the patient is suffering is congestion.'[52] To base the political demand for home rule on the parliamentary congestion argument was enormously convenient as it could appease Unionists and other opponents[53] of Irish home rule – which, on the contrary, was defended on nationalist grounds. Devolution, in this light, was more a standard measure of parliamentary reform comparable with the extension of the franchise or the more controversial reform of the Lords. Moreover, it was logical in itself: it treated the four countries equally should Parliament decide to devolve upon each constituent country of the Union 'the control of all those affairs which concerns its own well being'[54] and to grant them their own legislatures. Even more important, devolution did not involve any constitutional disruption and was therefore acceptable to a wide range of political opinion. It could have been enacted as a cross-party measure and, as stated by Dalziel, there was a consensus on both sides of the House that Scottish business must be dealt with separately:

> Yesterday and to-day two proposals have been made for Committees – one by the government, and the other by an influential Member of the Tory Party. The proposals differ in character and in detail, but they are alike in this – that they proceed upon the assumption that the state of business in the House has arrived at a point when, if the Parliamentary machine is to discharge all the functions that are properly expected of it, some new and bold departure will have to be undertaken.[55]

The devolution scheme was indeed to a broad extent truely Scottish. Local autonomy in Scotland worked on a system of private bill legislation which enhanced the powers of various local bodies such as 'governing councils of cities, towns, universities'.[56] Granting Scotland its own legislature would have formally consolidated the hitherto informal system of a virtually decentralised state. Despite the fact that this moderate scheme for constitutional change was not pursued any further it, however, influenced conciliatory Irish Unionists for whom it served as a model to settle the political implications of the Irish question.[57] But even if the Conservatives had agreed on Scottish devolution they would never have conceded its application to Ireland since staunch Irish Unionists had vehemently refused it.

EMPIRE AND FEDERALISM

Scottish Nationalists claimed that Scotland had always 'desired … a federal, and not an incorporating union'.[58] To prove this they conjured up history. For, as John Morrison Davidson pointed out in 1890, it was Fletcher of Saltoun who fought for a federal union, and Davidson proudly described him as 'one of the few genuine patriots'[59] who did not betray the Scottish nation when others sold Scotland to England in 1707. Whilst A. V. Dicey in his famous anti-home rule book of 1885 proclaimed the Americans as being 'the original inventors of the best federal system in the world',[60] Morrison Davidson claimed this merit for the Scots:

> In a word, the 'country' or patriotic party were extreme federalists at the time when not one of the framers of the justly vaunted Federal constitution of America was yet born. And that Fletcher, Lord Belhaven, and their followers were entirely right there can be no earthly doubt. A federal union would have secured to both countries the advantages which have flowed from the existing incorporating union, without any of the serious drawbacks which it will be easy to show have accrued more particularly to the less powerful nationality.

Besides this complaint common amongst Scottish Nationalists that the 'incorporating union' discriminated against Scotland, Davidson also praised the sought-for federal union as a constitutional model that would have helped to avoid the present home rule trouble:

Had a federal compact been struck between England and Scotland in 1707, it is not too much to say that the example would have been followed by the legislatures of England and Ireland in 1800 or earlier, and there would be no interminable home rule agitation to-day.

Davidson's nationalist polemics not only flattered Scottish self-consciousness but also anticipated future political propaganda. At the time when the reform of the House of Lords was pending and the unity of the Empire was at stake federalism appeared a panacea in the political trafficking of Nationalists and Unionists alike. As mentioned above, the different terms expressing ideas of regional self-government were never clearly distinguished and this again accounts for the equivalent use of words such as 'federalism', 'federal home rule' and 'federal devolution'.

In 1909 a group of Unionists – among them the Lords Robert Cecil, Selborne and Wolmer and publicists like Frederick Scott Oliver (who wrote under the pseudonym 'Pacificus' in *The Times*), Lionel Curtis and Leo Amery – formed the Round Table Movement which ultimately aimed at the federation of the Empire.[61] Before this goal could be achieved they concluded that the federalisation in the United Kingdom had to come first, which they justified by reference to the congestion of business in the imperial Parliament. So while this Imperialist movement tried to influence the Unionist Party, they assisted Scottish and Welsh home rulers in their pursuit for regional self-government insofar as they linked the debate on home rule to concerns about the British Empire.

Adopting the arguments of 'Pacificus' the Scottish Liberal J. A. Murray Macdonald, for example, defended federal home rule as an ideal solution for the contemporary controversy over the Lords and the Irish question since it 'would pass [large powers] from the immediate control of the Imperial Parliament to the subordinate Legislatures in England, Scotland, Ireland and Wales'.[62] Yet in contrast to Davidson, though in accordance with his chief interest in the maintenance of the Empire, he went even so far as to contend that federal home rule was consistent with the existing Union:

Each of these countries [excluding Wales] has now its own law and its own administrative system regulating and controlling its own domestic interests; and to each of them might be given independent powers of dealing with these interests without any radical departure from the spirit of our present practice.[63]

This, in fact, was a rather simple understanding of federal home rule. However, a more thoughtful exposition of the subject highlighted its genuine complexity if it was to include the dominions, as was indeed the intention of the Round Table Movement. In a confidential memorandum, the Liberal Unionist Lord Selborne outlined the connotations of a 'federal constitution' that opens the vista to 'a federal or semi-federal system of the United Kingdom [if a Home Rule Act was passed for Ireland]':

> We cannot refuse to Ireland a voice on imperial affairs, or on the common affairs of the United Kingdom. Therefore the consequence of the establishment of home rule in Ireland will be the establishment of home rule in England and in Scotland. This means a federal constitution … it will mean subordinate Parliaments for England, Scotland, Ireland and possibly Wales; and a Parliament for the management of the common affairs of the Empire … Four Parliaments, an English, a Scottish, an Irish, a Welsh concerned only with the local affairs of those parts of the United Kingdom. A fifth Parliament for the United Kingdom concerned only with affairs common to all parts of the United Kingdom, but which are not imperial affairs. And a sixth Parliament concerned only with imperial affairs common to all parts of the Empire.[64]

THE FEDERAL IDEA AND POLITICAL REALITY

The most favourable conditions for home rule all round prevailed in the period from 1910, when the constitutional conference over the House of Lords crisis took place, until the introduction of an Irish Home Rule Bill by the Asquith government in April 1912. Scottish MPs seized the opportunity, and for the first time acted in co-ordination when they founded the Scottish National Committee[65] to put pressure on government. Neither was this chance lost on Welsh Home Rulers who were represented by the restless though somewhat naive E. T. John. He was the member for Anglesey where the Liberal Association had carried 'a resolution supporting federal devolution' which urged 'similarity and spontaneity' of treatment of Scotland and Wales with Ireland.[66] Additionally, he also presided over the Welsh Nationalist League which shortly after its formation in Criccieth in January 1911 issued a manifesto demanding 'a definite pledge from the Cabinet that home rule on federal lines will be introduced this Parliament'.[67]

Public meetings, manifestos, contact between Scottish and Welsh Home Rulers[68] and concerted parliamentary action[69] on the one side and the propaganda of the Unionist federalists on the other signify that this was a period of great home rule agitation. Considering also Lloyd George and Winston Churchill's thrusts in Cabinet in favour of grand devolution measures it is all the more surprising that nothing in fact happened. These two were the only Cabinet members actually presenting plans for an extended Home Rule Bill. Churchill's memorandum dealt with the English situation in which home rule all round was to be realised and concluded that the solution was to break up England into seven regions. It was rejected, not least because of its similarity to the ancient Anglo-Saxon heptarchy.

Lloyd George approached the problem in the spirit of the Welsh Nationalist League in that he suggested that the government should introduce the Irish bill first but simultaneously promise to proceed next to introduce similar legislation for England, Scotland and Wales. In the meantime regional affairs should be delegated to Grand Committees for Scotland and Wales.[70]

With such powerful advocates in the Cabinet and with public support from some influential Unionists why after all did home rule all round not come to pass? Four points should be advanced here.

First, the Unionist Round Table Movement was primarily interested in the federation of the Empire and promoted home rule all round within the United Kingdom only as a logical and plausible means to achieve this goal. Traditional Tories, like the Marquess of Salisbury, however, distrusted ardent home-rule-all-round advocates like J. L. Garvin; their opinions instead tended to vary according to the political opportunities available. This in fact limited their chances to capture party opinion.[71] The case of the Round Table or Tariff Reform Movement was only as strong as the dominions' desire for a closer economic and defence union. All they accepted was the connection to the mother country through the imperial conferences. But, with the Liberals back in power since 1906, any aspirations of the dominions for preferences were destroyed. Plans for imperial federation meanwhile coincided with the increasing economic and political independence of Canada, Australia and South Africa. Canada 'was showing more interest in reciprocity with the United States and with Botha's support Laurier [the Canadian Prime Minister] opposed Dominion interference in British self-government',[72] which would have been a corollary of the creation of an imperial parliament. Already during the Colonial Conference in 1902 it became clear that the outlook in the larger colonies, in Canada and Australia, was very different to plans of imperial federation at home which were only supported by the smaller colonies. Julian Amery concluded:

> the same factors which had revived their Imperial sentiment had also strengthened their local nationalism ... The immense disparity in population, wealth and experience, which separated them from the United Kingdom, robbed Imperial Federation of its attractions.[73]

Second, the British constitution was and is based on the principle of the 'sovereignty of Parliament'. Yet, in the words of a distinguished Unionist, 'Home Rule however curtailed, means the surrender of Parliamentary authority'.[74] A. V. Dicey, intellectually, crossed the floor and turned into a convinced Unionist,[75] who can be quoted as the champion of the status quo. In numerous articles and in his famous book *England's Case Against Home Rule* he vigorously defended the Union against any proposals for a federal scheme. For him:

> the principle ... which gives its form to our system is (to use a foreign but convenient expression) 'unitarianism', or the habitual exercise of supreme legislative authority by one central power, which in this particular case is the British Parliament.[76]

Contrary to a unitary system, he explains, the federal system is based upon the supremacy of the constitution. According to him, the flaws in this were threefold:

(I)   a federal system requires a written constitution; but laws reduced to writing are open to misintepretation.
(II) a written constitution is 'rigid' or 'inexpansive'. The American constitution, for example can be changed only when proposed amendments are ratified by three quarters of all the states.
(III) the division of powers is carried beyond reasonable limits.

Basically his argument can be reduced to the political prejudice that federal government means weak government.

Third, a decisive factor against home rule all round was the position of the Irish Parliamentary Party. Although the Irish members were not given a part in the negotiations of the Cabinet Committee on home rule they nevertheless exerted influence through leading Cabinet ministers. Augustine Birrell, the Chief Secretary for Ireland, played a pivotal role in advocating Irish interests and helped to remove from the second draft of the bill Lloyd George's devolution clause which provided for temporary Scottish and Welsh Grand Committees. These trajectories to federalism could have caused prolonged debates in the House 'and the possible killing of the Bill, with the inevitable consequence that home rule for Ireland will again be postponed indefinitely'. Accordingly, the Irish leaders definitely rejected any suggestion of home rule all round.[77] In this they were actively supported by Birrell, Morley and indirectly by other Cabinet members including the Prime Minister, who preferred to deal with the Irish problem than tackle some more grandiose scheme.

Finally, there existed no Home-Rule-All-Round Party. However, home rule for Ireland was voiced in Parliament by a monolithic party and was based on a nationalist movement in the country. Regionalism was to a great extent the Scottish and Welsh offspring of Liberalism facing the onset of mass democracy and consequently falling apart. Geographically, Scotland and Wales were, like Ireland, divided into one mainly agrarian and another predominantly industrial part. In both countries, these industrial areas produced a strong middle class which was not only traditionally bound to the Liberal Party but also beneficially pursued its economic and career interests within the United Kingdom and the Empire. These interests ruled out sectional and national particularism in Scotland and Wales, unlike in Ireland, and united their respective countries under the Liberal banner tinged with the St Andrew's cross and the Red Dragon. As regionalism also appealed to the working classes and their leaders in the nascent Labour Party, the death of the Liberal Party after the First World War did not wipe out the idea of home rule.

Home-rule agitations continued after the war almost on the same lines as before. In Wales conferences were held at the well-known places of the 1890s and the Scottish Home Rule Association was re-established towards the end of the war, in September 1918. The pursuance of 'war socialism'[78] had fundamentally changed economic and social conditions[79] and thus augmented the traditional Liberal approach to regional home rule with more radical movements. As the Liberal Party was in a process of rapid decline and the Labour Party on the other had entered upon centralist politics, the various regional home rule movements concentrated forces and founded for the first time independent nationalist parties: the Welsh *Plaid Cymru* in 1925 and the National Party of Scotland in 1928. Moreover, the excision of Southern Ireland from the United Kingdom by 1922 made it abundantly clear that any opportunity for a sweeping constitutional reform had now been postponed to an indefinite future. Home rule all round had indeed not been implemented; institutional recognition of a separate nationality, however, had taken place. But it is open to discussion whether, for example, the remodelling of the post of the Scottish Secretary into a Secretary of State in 1926 or the opening of St Andrew's House in 1939 – which moved the centre of Scottish administration from Whitehall to Edinburgh – can be counted as genuine administrative devolution or as merely symbolical acts to satisfy Scottish national aspirations.

NOTES

1. Quoted in the *Young Scots Handbook 1911–1912* (Glasgow: Young Scots Society, 1912), pp. 60–61.
2. Apart from Chamberlain there was Lord Hartington, the leader of the Whigs, and W. E. Gladstone as the main party leader.
3. C. H. D. Howard, 'Joseph Chamberlain and the "Unauthorized Programme"', *English Historical Review*, 65 (1950), pp. 477–91.
4. In the 'Unauthorized Programme' Chamberlain demanded 'Home Rule all round, on equal terms for the different nationalities of the United Kingdom, leaving the Imperial Parliament in composition and authority as the supreme legislature of a common realm', J. Garvin, *The Life of Joseph Chamberlain*, ii, p. 75–6, quoted in C. D. H. Howard, 'Joseph Chamberlain', p. 478.
5. Joseph Chamberlain, 'Local Government and Ireland', *Fortnightly Review* (July 1885), p. 4.
6. Richard Jay, *Joseph Chamberlain: A Political Study* (Oxford: Clarendon Press, 1981), p. 126.
7. Ibid., p. 12.
8. Gladstone to Lord Hartington, 30 May 1885, quoted in John Morley, *The Life Of Gladstone: Volume II* (London: Edward Lloyd, 1908), p. 328.
9. See Neil Blewett, 'The Franchise in the United Kingdom, 1885–1918', *Past and Present*, 32 (1965), pp. 27–56.
10. A. B. Cooke and J. Vincent, *The Governing Passion: Cabinet Government and Party Politics in Great Britain, 1885–86* (Bristol: Harvester Press, 1974).
11. This incident is know to historians as the 'Hawarden Kite', named after Gladstone's manor in Hawarden, North Wales; see D. A. Hamer, *Liberal Politics in the Age of Gladstone and Rosebery. A Study in Leadership and Policy* (Oxford: Clarendon Press, 1972), p. 113.
12. Chamberlain to Gladstone, 15 March 1886. Although Gladstone persuaded him to stay (16 March) he finally accepted his resignation on 23 March 1886. Gladstone Papers, vol. XLI, Correspondence with J. Chamberlain 1884–93. (British Library, London: MS Add. 44126).
13. Pamphlet, Scottish Home Rule Association, 20 May 1886, Glasgow Scrapbooks, No. 23, p. 165.
14. Emyr W. Williams, 'Liberalism in Wales and the Politics of Welsh Home Rule, 1886–1910', *Bulletin of the Board of Celtic Studies*, 37 (1990), p. 195.
15. The Liberal agent Tilston of Wrexham proposed a national organisation in Wales. See Graham V. Nelmes, 'Stuart Rendel and the Welsh Liberal Political

Organisation in the Late Nineteenth Century', *Welsh History Review*, 9, 4 (1979), p. 470.

16. The Young Scots later argued that devolution for Ireland made no sense without self-government for Scotland. See *Young Scots Handbook 1911–12*, p. 8.

17. D. W. Urwin, 'Towards the Nationalisation of British Politics?: The Party System, 1885–1940' in Otto Büsch (ed.), *Wählerbewegung in der europäischen Geschichte* (Berlin: Colloquium Verlag, 1980), pp. 225–57.

18. Ibid., p. 235.

19. His uncle was one of the victims in 1859 when farmers were evicted for not voting for the local Anglo-Catholic landlord (in Merioneth); see K. O. Morgan, *Wales in British Politics 1868–1922* (Cardiff: University of Wales Press, 1980), p. 20. See also *Dictionary of Welsh Biography* (Oxford: Blackwell, 1959), p. 214.

20. K. O. Morgan, *Lloyd George* (London: Weidenfeld & Nicholson, 1974), p. 10.

21. Hon. G. T. Kenyon (Denbigh Boroughs), P. Pryce-Jones (Montgomery Boroughs), Hon. F. C. Morgan (Monmouthshire, South) and Hon. A. H. J. Walsh (Radnorshire).

22. Among the elected Liberal members of 1880 were 'nine ... industrialists or manufacturerers, and a further eleven were barristers or solicitors'. K. O. Morgan, *Wales in British Politics*, p. 40.

23. Philip Jenkins, *A History of Modern Wales 1536–1990* (London: Longman, 1992), p. 332.

24. Nelmes, *Stuart Rendel*, p. 469.

25. Morley, *Gladstone, Vol. II*, p. 580.

26. Humphreys-Owen to Rendel, 21 December 1891; quoted in ibid., p. 481.

27. J. Graham Jones, 'Alfred Thomas' National Institution (Wales) Bills of 1891–92', *Welsh History Review*, 15, 26 (1990), pp. 218–39.

28. See Obituary of The Right Hon. Sir Ellis J. Ellis Griffith in *Transactions of the Honourable Society of Cymmrodorion* (1927), p. 184.

29. K. O. Morgan, *Rebirth of a Nation: Wales 1880–1980* (Oxford: Oxford University Press, 1981), p. 35.

30. Bishop Basil Tickell Jones, quoted in Morgan, *Rebirth of a Nation*, p. 3.

31. K. O. Morgan, 'Gladstone and Wales', *Welsh Historical Review*, 1, 1 (1960), p. 66.

32. Jones, 'National Institutions Bills', p. 225.

33. Tom Ellis, 'Wales and the Local Government Act, 1894' in Annie J. Ellis (ed.), *Speeches and Addresses by the late Tom Ellis, M.P.* (Wrexham: Hughes & Son, 1912), pp. 165ff.

34. See the excellent study by Emyr W. Williams, 'Liberalism in Wales and the Politics of Welsh Home Rule 1886–1910', *Bulletin of the Board of Celtic Studies*, 37 (1990), p. 202.

35. *Young Wales*, Vol. I, 1895, p. 21.

36. J. Graham Jones, 'E.T. John and Welsh Home Rule 1910–14', *Welsh Historical Review*, 13, 4 (1987), p. 456, Urwin considers 'it ... not ... unfair to apply the term clientelism as a blanket description of traditional British politics' in 'Towards the Nationalisation', p. 231.

37. R. A. Cage (ed.), *The Scots Abroad: Labour, Capital, Enterprise, 1750–1914* (London: Croom Helm, 1985).

38. James Mitchell, 'Conservatism in Twentieth Century Scotland: Society, Ideology and the Union' in Michael Lynch (ed.), *Scotland, 1850–1979: Society, Politics and the Union* (London: Historical Association, 1993), p. 28.

39. R. J. Morris and Graeme Morton, 'The Re-making of Scotland: A Nation within a Nation, 1850–1920', in ibid., p. 16.
40. Lindsay Paterson, *The Autonomy of Modern Scotland* (Edinburgh: Edinburgh University Press, 1994), p. 62
41. Scottish Home Rule Association, Edinburgh, 20 May 1886.
42. Ibid., John Stuart Blackie, the romantic nationalist, circumscribed Scottish national rights as follows: 'As an independent Kingdom, inheriting its own traditions, using its own laws, boasting its own Church, and marked by a distinctive type of character and culture, Scotland had a right to demand that her public business shall be conducted seriously on Scottish grounds, in a Scottish atmosphere, and under Scottish influence'; *Young Scots Handbook 1911–12*, p. 21.
43. Ibid., p. 59.
44. The prewar SHRA fell into decay in the mid-1890s and finally 'collapsed after the outbreak of hositilities', R. Finlay, *Independent and Free: Scottish Politics and the Origins of the Scottish National Party 1918–1945* (Edinburgh: John Donald, 1994); see also R. Drost-Hüttl, *Die schottische Nationalbewegung zwischen 1886 und 1934. Nationalistische Ziele und Strategien im Wandel*, (Bochum: Universitätsverlag Dr. N. Bockmeyer, 1995), pp. 70–71.
45. Quoted in Finlay, *Independent and Free*, p. 4.
46. Lord Loreburn, 'Form of Home Rule', *Contemporary Review*, 99, 1 (1911), pp. 261–2.
47. Jay, *Joseph Chamberlain*, p. 124.
48. Ibid., p. 125.
49. William Mitchell, *Is Scotland to be Sold Again? Home Rule for Scotland* (Edinburgh: Scottish Home Rule Association, 1892), p. 7.
50. *Young Scots Handbook 1911–12*, p. 13.
51. Gladstone outlined his thoughts in a confidential memorandum on 'Obstruction and Devolution' destined for the Cabinet. It is reprinted in J. L. Hammond, *Gladstone and the Irish Nation* (London: Longman, 1938), pp. 198–204.
52. *House of Commons Debates*, 4th ser., vol. 22, col. 1287, 3 April 1894.
53. A typical representative of this kind of Liberal who declined home rule for Ireland was the somewhat eccentric John Stuart Blackie, Professor of Greek at Edinburgh University and member of the SHRA. At the third annual conference of the association he proclaimed 'that he belonged to the Association for Scottish Home Rule, and he had nothing to do with Ireland. He knew Scotland, and he knew Scotsman.' *The Times*, 25 September 1890, p. 7.
54. G. B. Clark, member for Caithness and President of the SHRA, in his motion for Scottish home rule, *House of Commons Debates*, 3rd ser., vol. 341, col. 684, 19 February 1890.
55. *House of Commons Debates*, 4th ser., vol. 22, col. 1287, 3 April 1894.
56. Paterson, *Autonomy of Scotland*, pp. 49 and 54.
57. Immediately after its constitution in August 1904 the Irish Reform Association with Lord Dunraven as its president issued a preliminary report on 31 August which pronounced 'that such [political] union is compatible with the devolution to Ireland of a larger measure of local government than she now possesses' and continued about how the association perceived it possible 'to extend to Ireland the system of private bill legislation which has been so successfully worked in Scotland'; quoted in F. S. L. Lyons, 'The Irish Unionist Party and the Devolution Crisis of 1904–5', *Irish Historical Studies*, 6,

21 (March 1948), p. 2.

58. 'A Scottish Home Rule Manifesto', *The Times*, 18 February 1888, p. 15.

59. *Scotia Rediviva: Home Rule for Scotland: With Lives of Sir William Wallace, George Buchanan, Fletcher of Saltoun and Thomas Spence* (London: William Reeves, 1890), p. 7. The following quotations are also derived from this source.

60. A. V. Dicey, *England's Case Against Home Rule* (Richmond: Richmond Publishing, 1885), p. 160.

61. See J. E. Kendle, 'The Round Table Movement and "Home Rule All Round"', *Historical Journal*, 11, 2 (1968), pp. 332–53.

62. J. A. Murray Macdonald, 'The Constitutional Controversy and Federal Home Rule', *Nineteenth Century*, 70, 1 (July 1911), p. 34.

63. Ibid., p. 41.

64. Lord Selborne to Austen Chamberlain, 4 September 1911, quoted in D. George Boyce (ed.), *The Crisis of British Unionism: The Domestic Political Papers of the Second Earl of Selborne, 1855–1922* (London: Historians' Press, 1987), pp. 70–71.

65. *The Times*, 30 June 1910, p. 12; 'forty-four Scottish MPs under the general leadership of W. H. Cowan (East Aberdeen)' were associated with the Scottish National Committee; see K. O. Morgan, *Wales in British Politics*, p. 256.

66. Graham Jones, 'E. T. John and Welsh Home Rule, 1910–14', p. 456.

67. Quoted in ibid., p. 459. For the Welsh Nationalist League a major point in favour of a regional parliament was its ability to disestablish the Anglican Church in Wales.

68. See Morgan, *Wales in British Politics*, p. 256.

69. Asquith could not turn a cold shoulder to the Scottish National Committee and invited its members for an interview before the second reading of the Irish Home Rule Bill as Mr Pirie declared in the Commons in 1912: 'Had it not been for the interview which the Scottish Members had with the Prime Minister yesterday, my vote would have been absolutely against the Second Reading.' *House of Commons Debates*, 5th ser., vol. 38, col. 337, 7 May 1912.

70. For a treatment of this problem on Cabinet level see Particia Jalland, 'United Kingdom Devolution 1910–14: Political Panacea or Tactical Diversion', *English Historical Review*, 94 (1979), pp. 765–7.

71. See Boyce, *Crisis of British Unionism*, p. 74.

72. *The Cambridge History of the British Empire, Vol. III: The Empire–Commonwealth, 1870–1919*, (Cambridge: Cambridge University Press, 1959), p. 403.

73. Julian Amery, *The Life of Joseph Chamberlain, Volume IV* (London: Macmillan, 1969), p. 415.

74. Dicey, *England's Case Against Home Rule*, p. 24.

75. It is worthwhile mentioning that 'academic opinion on the whole tended towards unionism'. See Christopher Harvie, 'Ideology and Home Rule: James Bryce, A. V. Dicey and Ireland, 1880–1887', *English Historical Review*, 91 (1976), p. 298.

76. A. V. Dicey, *Introduction into the Study of the Law of the Constitution* (London: Macmillan, 1961 [1886]), pp. 138–68.

77. Redmond's and Dillon's critique expressed in a memorandum laid before the Cabinet on 25 January 1912, quoted in Jalland, 'UK Devolution', p. 768.

78. Morgan, *Rebirth of a Nation*, p. 169.

79. See for the Scottish case Christopher Harvie, *No Gods and Precious Few Heroes: Scotland 1914–1980* (London: Edward Arnold, 1981), pp. 1–34.

9

Territorial Politics and Change in Britain

JAMES MITCHELL

Spectacles magnify one set of factors rather than another and thus not only lead analysts to produce different explanations of problems that appear, in their summary questions, to be the same, but also influence the character of the analyst's puzzle, the evidence he assumes to be relevant, the concepts he uses in examining the evidence, and what he takes to be an explanation … But in offering his explanation, each analyst attempts to emphasize what is relevant and important, and different conceptual lenses lead analysts to different judgements about what is relevant and important.[1]

The importance of 'conceptual lenses' in determining what is seen as relevant and important in politics is as true of debates on territorial politics and constitutional change in Britain as anything else.[2] The way we look at and understand the United Kingdom[2] will, in large measure, determine those matters which are important, and what impediments exist in the way of constitutional change, indeed whether change is possible or desirable. Drawing on the literature on state formation, it is here argued that there are two distinct views of Britain: those of unitary state and union state. Each carries with it implications for understanding and assessing the prospects for and implications of constitutional change. It is further argued that one of the central weaknesses in analysing the case for regional government has been that the debate has taken place within an understanding of Britain as a unitary rather than a union state. This chapter will argue that an understanding of Britain as a dynamic or organic union state makes constitutional reform more viable and desirable.

Numerous schemes of reform have been hatched over the course of the last century. This chapter does not consider these. None has been successful in bringing about a regional tier of government. The focus of this chapter is on the existing arrangements of territorial governance of Britain, how they evolved and, crucially, the parameters within which change is deemed possible. It is contended that by understanding what has evolved, rather than focusing on various failed schemes, a better understanding of the nature of territorial governance is provided.

STATE BUILDING AND NATION BUILDING IN BRITAIN: THE UNITARY STATE, UNION STATE AND DYNAMIC UNION STATE

Any attempt to understand the territorial politics of constitutional reform in Britain must include an understanding of different conceptions of the state. How one views Britain will, in large measure, determine the extent to which and manner in which one believes that it should be reformed. Most textbooks refer to the United Kingdom as a unitary state, even books on Scottish politics.[3] This conception of Britain as a unitary state is important in debates on constitutional reform. Though rarely defined in texts using the term, the meaning of unitary state is important. According Rokkan and Urwin, who offer an interesting typology of state building:

> The unitary system, built up around one unambiguous political centre enjoys economic dominance and pursues a more or less undeviating policy of administrative standardization. All areas of the state are treated alike, and all institutions are directly under the control of the centre.[4]

This clearly was not the case at the time of the creation of Britain as a new state. There is, however, an alternative conception which helps to clarify the nature of Britain. Rokkan and Urwin identified three other state forms: mechanical federalism, organic federalism and union state. Nobody would seriously argue that Britain is a federal state, whether mechanical or organic.[5] There are, however, features of the formation of Britain which conform with the union-state type:

> The union state, [is] not the result of straightforward dynastic conquest. Incorporation of at least parts of its territory has been achieved through personal dynastic union, for example by treaty, marriage or inheritance. Integration is less than perfect.

While administrative standardization prevails over most of the territory, the consequences of personal union entail the survival in some areas of pre-union rights and institutional infrastructures which preserve some degree of regional autonomy and serve as agencies of indigenous elite recruitment.

The origins of the state are important for understanding debates in the twentieth century on British territorial politics. The twentieth-century inheritance from the period when the state was formed is important less because of the institutions which were involved in the settlement and more because of the thinking which informed the settlement. In other words, the Church of Scotland, the education system, the local administrative and governmental structure and Scots law were important because they were artefacts of a union settlement which allowed for the retention of Scottish distinctiveness.

Keating has argued that the United Kingdom (UK) 'stands apart [from other European states] for its lack of an official nationalist ideology'.[6] The ambiguous nature of the state was further noted by Richard Rose:

> Trying to name the nation associated with the government of the United Kingdom displays the confusion about national identity. One thing is certain: No one speaks of the 'UKes' as a nation.[7]

The absence of an official nationalism or a collective noun does not mean the absence of a collective national identity. An alternative view is that a pervasive but banal nationalism, in the sense meant by Michael Billig, operates in Britain. Billig has noted that nationalism is often daily 'reproduced in a banally mundane way'.[8] Perceived challenges to the integrity of state such as European integration, periods of tension and international crisis such as the South Atlantic conflict in 1982 and the rise or assertion of Scottish, Welsh and Irish nationalism may, however, lead to the manifestation of a more virulent UK/British nationalism. The nature of state and official nationalism[9] tells us something about the nature of the state itself. There is no evidence that the state is jealous in its demand for loyalty. Being both British and Scottish has traditionally not been seen as impossible or even undesirable.

A key issue is whether changes in society and the role of government affect the territorial balance, whether they undermine or renew or leave unaffected the essentially pluralist nature of the settlement. Creating the British state occurred first and was followed by creating a British nation.[10] The former had implications for the latter. The essentially pluralist settlement which inspired the creation of the state was reflected in the pluralist nature of the nation. The notion of a union state needs to take account of change. Whatever forces may bring about change, these will have territorial implications.

BRITAIN AS A UNITARY STATE

Parliament is central to the unitary-state view of Britain. The notion of parliamentary sovereignty, as propounded by Blackstone in the late eighteenth century and by Dicey in the late nineteenth century, has had a considerable impact on constitutional debate. Debates on membership of the European Community/Union and on devolution have been influenced by how Britain is viewed. European integration and devolving government within Britain are seen by some as diminishing Parliament's position. Parliamentary sovereignty does not preclude regional government being established but it does impose limitations. Dicey was primarily concerned with Ireland when he developed his views on parliamentary sovereignty but he did write about the union between Scotland and England. His book with Robert Rait offers an outline of his thinking on the nature of the union settlement. The Act of Union was:

> [the] most conservative of revolutionary measures. To put the matter shortly, it repealed every law or custom of England or of Scotland inconsistent with the political unity of the new State, but it did not make or attempt any change or reform which was not necessary for the creation of the new United Kingdom.[11]

For Dicey there was no incompatibility between seeing Britain as a unitary state and satisfying the aspirations for distinctiveness of its component nations.[12] However, the position of Britain's constituent nations was circumscribed from Dicey's perspective. Parliamentary sovereignty was crucial to this view.

The unitary-state view of Britain plays a crucial part in explaining certain aspects of UK territorial politics. In particular, this conceptual lens helps to illuminate the relationship which has emerged between central government and local government. The position of regions, according to a unitary-state perspective, is viewed as the same, at least in legal terms, as local government. Local government in Britain is subject to the doctrine of *ultra vires*: that is that local authorities cannot act beyond their powers as provided by Parliament, they can only do what they are statutorily permitted to. British local government has no power of general competence as is to be found in some other European countries.

There have been calls for regional government in England. This has largely represented a 'top-down' form of regionalism rather than a demand emanating from below. The need for a regional level of administration, at the very least, followed from the increased number of activities, particularly economic and land-use planning, of central government in the postwar period. Regional economic planning councils and boards were established in England in 1964 with responsibility for drawing up and overseeing the implementation of regional plans to carry out the National Plan of central government. The failure of the latter effectively killed off this experiment. Regional tiers of administration have always existed. These have existed on an ad hoc basis and the boundaries for one function have not corresponded with those for another. The formerly nationalised utilities – water, gas, electricity – were governed by regional tiers of administration as indeed is the health service. As Hogwood has pointed out, this form of regional government still exists and has indeed grown since 1979. Regional economic planning councils and regional health authorities were abolished but 'bureaucratic mechanisms at regional level have remained'.[13] New 'integrated regional offices' were established in 1994 bringing together the existing regional offices of the Department of Trade and Industry, the Training, Education and Enterprise Division of the Department of Employment and the Departments of the Environment and Transport. These new offices administer a single integrated budget. However, this is not quite an embryonic structure for regional government. Many aspects of government work are not covered and the regions do not correspond with the territorial organisation. But, as Hogwood notes:

> Though far from all-embracing in its coverage of government departments and the regional bodies they sponsor, it would, if fully implemented, represent a greater degree of practical co-ordination of activities and alignment of regional boundaries than was actually achieved under the substantially more ambitious economic planning emphasis of the 1960s.[14]

BRITAIN AS A UNION STATE

While conceptualisation of Britain as a unitary state helps to explain the development of central–local relations from partnership to principal–agent, it fails to explain the relationship which has developed between Britain and the historic nations of which it is comprised. The development of Britain can, however, be usefully viewed through an alternative 'conceptual lens' – that of Britain as a union state.[15] If it has any validity, this conceptualisation applies only to the historic nations which constitute the UK. The union-state view stresses the asymmetrical nature of the state. There is much that is common to Britain but there are many features which make its components unique. A unitary state is relatively straightforward in terms of territorial politics. Notions of territorial equity still exist of course but this is less complicated than in a union state and will not involve opening up old debates and potentially reviving or creating territorial animosities and jealousies.

At the start of this century, the main means through which Scottish distinctiveness was catered for was the Scottish Office. Set up in 1885 its functions and responsibilities have grown over the course of the twentieth century. New functions have been added to the Scottish Office's remit while existing responsibilities have also grown. Education and local government were the Scottish Office's main responsibilities at its establishment in 1885 but law and order were added two years later. When a ministry for agriculture in Whitehall was being considered in the first decade of the twentieth century, the Scottish Office argued that Scottish agriculture should be treated as distinct and in 1912 a Scottish Board of Agriculture under the responsibility of the Secretary for Scotland was set up. Similarly, in 1919, a Scottish Board of Health, mainly responsible for housing, was established. Perhaps more significant than these new fields of responsibility was the state's growing responsibilities in areas such as education. Major pieces of legislation were passed in the field of Scottish education in 1906 and 1918 which had an impact on the work of the Scottish Office.

During the interwar period, the Scottish Office consolidated its position in British central government. The first was a symbolic change. The 1885 act set up the office of Secretary for Scotland, though campaigners in Scotland had argued for a Secretary of State for Scotland. In effect, this made little difference. Even symbolically it was marginal. That most significant statement of the worth of a government minister – the salary which went with the office –

remained unchanged until 1937 and the Secretary of State for Scotland, as he would be called from 1926, was paid less than other Cabinet ministers. Even the matter of Cabinet membership had already been resolved. With the exception of war cabinets, Scottish Secretaries had been members of the Cabinet continuously from 1892.

The process of devolving responsibility to the Scottish Office continued after 1945. There was, however, a trend in government which challenged this process. State intervention after 1945 took on a more direct and centralist form giving credence to a unitary-state conception of Britain. While the Scottish Office gained responsibilities and lost very few during this period,[16] the state at the centre did so also and at a faster rate. The balance in the relationship was altered. This also had implications for nation building. Britain gained legitimacy through the provision of its welfare state and intervention in the economy amongst those Scots who viewed these as desirable.

Amongst those Scots who opposed nationalisation, on the other hand, British legitimacy was called into question, at least in a limited sense. Scottish Tories argued that nationalisation 'denationalised' Scotland by taking control of industries affected out of Scotland. Playing the Scottish card may merely have been a means of embarrassing the Attlee Labour government, but it did tap into real fears and concerns. In 1949, the Scottish Unionist Party[17] issued a policy paper, 'Scottish Control of Scottish Affairs', which recommended an extension of Scottish Office functions, a Royal Commission on Scottish Affairs, a new Scottish Office Minister and Scottish boards for the newly nationalised industries. The language in which it was couched was probably as significant as its contents. During the 1950 general election Winston Churchill told a meeting in Edinburgh that he 'should never adopt the view that Scotland should be forced into the serfdom of socialism as the result of a vote in the House of Commons'.[18] Scottish Tories around this time took to attacking the Labour Party for ignoring the Scottish dimension. This caused the Attlee government some difficulties and it was forced to make some concessions, however minor and symbolic, in parliamentary procedures and the administration of the nationalised industries.

In 1948 the Attlee government issued a White Paper on Scottish Affairs. It proposed the extension of special parliamentary procedures dealing with Scottish affairs, a consultative Scottish Economic Conference, meeting under the chairmanship of the Secretary of State, and that the machinery of government and administration of the nationalised industries would be kept under review continuously with a view to finding opportunities for developing administrative devolution.[19] Piecemeal and defensive, it nonetheless contributed to a sense that Scotland was politically and economically distinct.

However, the central role of economic management from the centre meant that a Scottish parliament was seen as at best unnecessary and at worst as potentially damaging for much of the period from 1945 to 1975. In 1957, the executive of the Labour Party in Scotland came out against home rule on 'compelling economic grounds'.[20] The Scottish dimension was at its lowest ebb this century during the 1950s but there were still some developments. The Conservatives, when in opposition, had promised a Royal Commission on Scottish Affairs which reported in 1954.[21] It recommended that a few additional responsibilities be handed over to the Scottish Office from other Whitehall departments.[22] An official history of the Scottish Office written by its Permanent Secretary, Sir David Milne, in 1957 noted:

> the river may have flowed erratically, but its main course has been clear. There has been a definite and increasing tendency to assign to a Scottish minister matters in which there is a distinctive Scottish tradition or body of law or where Scottish conditions are notably different from those in England and Wales. The present administrative structure is not the result of design, but of constant change and adjustment over a period of 250 years. It is unlikely that it is complete but no one can say what the future changes will be. Time finds its own solutions.[23]

The Scottish Office reached its apogee under Labour in the 1960s. Willie Ross was Scottish Secretary throughout Harold Wilson's time as Prime Minister. Ross dominated Scottish politics during this period and fought hard in Cabinet for Scottish interests. This resulted in higher levels of public expenditure for Scotland. It was a paternalistic form of government. But as the country struggled to manage economic difficulties, the strains on the union state were manifested in rising support for the Scottish National Party (SNP). The perceived failure of Britain to tackle rising levels of unemployment undermined support for the state while the Scottish Office did relatively well in the carve-up of public expenditure. The union state had provided a political base for the mobilisation of a movement demanding more for Scotland. What that 'more' constituted may not always have been clear, but Scottish grievances focused on the existing arrangements.

The case of Wales highlights the difference between the actual position of Wales in British politics and how Wales is conceived in British politics. A unitary-state conception has dominated to a greater extent than in the case of Scotland yet there is evidence of features of a union state in the Welsh situation. What made Wales different were matters such as religion and language rather than the apparatus of the state.

Wales followed a similar path though the base differed from that in Scotland. The initial union of England and Wales conformed more to the unitary state than union-state form of state formation discussed above. Wales has had 'no continuous history of a distinctly Welsh dimension in British political institutions since union with England'.[24] This distinguished Wales from the situation in Scotland and Ireland.[25] Indeed, an act passed in 1746 which remained in force until 1967 provided that legislative references to England should be taken to refer also to Wales. As with Scotland, however, the position of Wales altered, most notably from the end of the nineteenth century. In 1889 a Welsh Intermediate Education Act was passed which acknowledged the distinctive Welsh nature of secondary education. In 1907, under the Liberals, a Welsh Department within the Department of Education in London was set up. Randall has argued:

> [this] formally began a process of departmental decentralisation which eventually led, over half a century later, to the establishment of a Secretary of State for Wales with direct responsibility for a range of Welsh affairs.[26]

The Welsh Department was strenuously opposed by the Conservatives. Sir William Anson, a former Parliamentary Secretary at the Board of Education, adopted a classic unitary-state view of Britain. He was concerned that there would be insufficient parliamentary accountability of the department and that a separate Welsh Education Department would result. This contrasts starkly with the situation which had existed in Scotland over 20 years before when Conservatives had joined with Liberals in supporting the establishment of the Scottish Office.[27]

But the position of Wales remained behind that of Scotland and both were circumscribed in the eyes of the postwar Labour government. Attlee opposed a Welsh Office and the Prime Minister refuted the comparison drawn with Scotland:

> Scotland, unlike Wales, had codes of civil and criminal law and a system of administration which are different in important respects from those of England. Moreover all who have the welfare of Wales at heart are particularly concerned with

differences in the economic sphere, and it is in just this sphere that there is no separate Scottish administration. Economic matters for Britain as a whole have been handled, as they must be, by departments covering the whole country.[28]

There had been pressure for a Welsh Office. As in Scotland in the 1880s, the local authorities urged the establishment of a Secretary of State.[29] The Attlee government established an Advisory Council for Wales and Monmouthshire in 1948 after pressure from the Welsh Labour Party. The Welsh newspaper, the *Western Mail* criticised the government when it issued its White Paper on Scottish Affairs in 1948:

> at the very moment when the Government are unresponsive to, and even silent on, Welsh demands for administrative devolution and a Minister responsible for Welsh affairs, Scotland is given a vast new measure of self-control. It exceeds the most sanguine demands of the Scottish members and startled Parliament by its character.[30]

This was not how it was seen in Scotland but that did not matter. The wounded dignities[31] of the Welsh needed redressing and the Advisory Council was set up.

The Advisory Council, consisting of representatives from local government, the trade unions, industry and the arts, which was set up in 1948 reported on a wide range of matters.[32] Its third memorandum in 1957 was 'Government Administration in Wales'. This was, according to Gowan, the 'most remarkable contribution the Council made'.[33] The report supported the creation of a Secretary of State for Wales. As Randall put it, 'From this date onwards an irresistible demand for a Secretary of State was set in motion which, in the end, was impossible to deny.'[34]

Lack of co-ordination in Welsh administration was identified as the key weakness in the existing arrangements. The perception that there was a need for co-ordination was in itself significant. But the Conservatives under Harold Macmillan were unconvinced. Once more, an unfavourable comparison was made with Scotland. Scotland had a different system of law and local government which made necessary a separate system of administration headed by a Secretary of State. Labour, in opposition, was now playing the Welsh card. Labour promised to establish a Welsh Office headed by a Secretary of State with a seat in the Cabinet. A ratchet effect had set in. Wales was conforming less and less with the unitary-state conception of Britain. The Conservatives accepted the office and made it clear that they had no intention of abolishing it on returning to power.

The process of institution building had gained a dynamic in Wales, as was also happening in Scotland, which had more to do with electoral politics than administrative considerations. This process had been multi-faceted in both Scotland and Wales. The dynamic was provided for by changes in the actions of the state but also by political manoeuvring and attempts to play to the Scottish and Welsh galleries. What made the components making up Britain distinct at one time proved inappropriate in another. In particular, as the state's functions changed, so too did the means of catering for its constituent nations. Whether established as a union state, as in the case of Scotland's union with England, or a unitary state, as in the case of Wales, Britain has had to take account of the territorial implications of changes in society, the economy and the functions of government; this has given rise to a dynamic union state. This was to have important implications for the future of territorial politics in Britain.

LABOUR'S RELUCTANT ADOPTION OF DEVOLUTION

So far, the discussion has focused on different conceptions of the territorial dimension of British government as it has evolved this century. These conceptions have implications for debate on constitutional change and territorial politics. The conception of Britain as a unitary state gives rise to considerable, perhaps impossible, difficulties for anything other than very limited forms of devolution. The central role of Parliament inevitably places a huge impediment in the way of a meaningful tier of regional government. The need for symmetry implicit in a unitary state must also be an impediment and makes the prospect of regional government in only one part of the state impossible. The undeviating policy of administrative standardisation could not be achieved. The powers which could be devolved would have to be circumscribed and could not be allowed to challenge the economic dominance of London.

Indeed, the debates on federalism, regional government and devolution have all struggled with these issues. Opponents have stressed the need for symmetry, the sovereignty of Parliament and desirability of strong economic powers at the centre. From the unitary-state perspective it is difficult to envisage devolution even in its most modest form. Tam Dalyell, a leading opponent of home rule, made a telling point in Parliament in 1977:

> Would it not be more honest to admit that it is impossible to have an Assembly [for Scotland or Wales] – especially any kind of subordinate Parliament – that is part, though only part, of a unitary state?[35]

The point has validity but only if the premise on which the question is asked is accepted. Contributions of others, notably Enoch Powell, were along the same lines. These contributions particularly laid stress on parliamentary sovereignty. They very much followed the line set down a century before by Dicey.[36] Dalyell's own book published in 1977 is a more vulgar version of Dicey's argument.[37]

Others have argued against devolution from a unitary perspective whilst focusing on other aspects. The Labour Party was officially opposed to Scottish home rule from the late 1950s to the mid-1970s. Its main opposition was based on a conception of the state requiring strong central powers in order to pursue egalitarian policies; and strong macroeconomic powers to manage the economy from the centre. In 1957, Labour's Scottish executive came out against devolution on 'compelling economic grounds'. Less concerned with the position of Parliament than Conservative opponents (though some Labour members have revered parliamentary sovereignty sufficiently to worry about the implications of devolution for this), Labour anti-devolutionists adopted a unitary-state perspective no less than many Tories which led them to oppose any form of regional government. Labour changed its policy on Scottish and Welsh devolution in the 1970s as a consequence of the electoral threat posed by the SNP rather than through conviction. Indeed, the Scottish Labour Party had the policy of devolution imposed upon it by the London leadership with the assistance of the trade unions. Without abandoning a unitary-state conception of Britain, the party sounded unconvinced and was deeply divided over the issue in the late 1970s. The agenda on which it campaigned was one on which it was bound to have difficulties.

The Labour Scottish Secretary during Harold Wilson's terms as Prime Minister was Willie Ross. Ross was hostile to devolution but his opposition to devolution was paternalistic and undemocratic rather than informed by a unitary-state conception of Britain. As Scottish Secretary, he insisted in Cabinet that Scotland was different but the Scottish Office, with him at its head, should be the institution through which this distinctiveness should be manifested. As fellow Cabinet member Richard Crossman noted in his diaries, Ross would play the Scottish card to prevent English Cabinet colleagues from interfering in Scottish affairs.[38] Labour in Scotland was different from the party south of the border and insisted on being treated differently when it suited it; but ultimately the notion of a unified British working class, a unified labour market and the need for central economic management influenced Labour's thinking. Macroeconomic policy making was central to Labour's thinking. Though regional policy was permitted this was centrally directed and controlled.

When change came it was reactive and imposed. The SNP's victory in the 1967 Hamilton by-election and advances in local government in the late 1960s were thought to be based on protest votes.[39] Labour was caught off guard when the Nationalists won seven seats with 21.9 per cent in February 1974. The London leadership insisted on a change of policy and a special conference of the Labour Party in Scotland was convened in August at which the trade union block votes were used to impose a policy of Scottish devolution on a reluctant Scottish Labour Party. This did not immediately stem the Nationalist tide. A second election that year, in October, saw the SNP increase its vote to 30.4 per cent, winning 11 seats. Worryingly for Labour, the SNP stood in second place in many Labour seats and polls continued to show that it was a major threat to Labour for the next two years.

Devolution was not well thought out, nor was it seen as part of a larger programme of reforming the state. Many senior Labour politicians were privately critical and many more MPs and ordinary members were publicly hostile. Labour soon lost its slender overall majority in the Commons and relied on smaller parties, including the Welsh and Scottish Nationalists, for its survival. Devolution became tied up with the survival of the government. Initially, the government presented a bill covering both Scotland and Wales. The committee stage of the bill, when its details would be debated, was scheduled to be taken by the Commons as a whole rather than sent off to a standing committee. This required strict timetabling to prevent filibustering but this failed when the guillotine motion limiting time to be spent on each section of the bill was defeated. The SNP's support rose sharply in the polls, and for a period it looked as if Labour would lose a vote of confidence in the Commons and be forced to go to the country. Had that occurred, the likeliest result, on the basis of the opinion polls, was that the Conservatives with their new leader Margaret Thatcher would be returned with a much larger contingent of SNP MPs.

The Labour government was saved by the small group of Liberal MPs led by David Steel. If Labour was keen to avoid an election, then the Liberals were desperate to avoid one. Jeremy Thorpe, the former Liberal leader had been forced to resign after accusations about his private life and with a charge of conspiracy to murder hanging over him. The Liberals had performed better in the 1974 elections than in previous postwar contests but faced annihilation if another election were to be called at this time. The Lib–Lab pact was designed to save the Labour and Liberal parties from electoral defeat. There were no major policy aspects to the agreement. It did mean that there would be a second attempt at devolution. On this occasion, bills were presented separately for Scotland and Wales.

A great deal of parliamentary time was spent on these measures. A referendum was conceded by the government after pressure from anti-devolution Labour MPs. Without this concession the legislation would not have passed through the Commons. In addition, a back-bench amendment was passed stating that unless 40 per cent of the eligible electorate (as distinct from those who actually voted) voted in favour of devolution, the government would move an order to repeal devolution. With a turnout of just over 60 per cent, this meant that devolutionists would have to get over 60 per cent of those voting to vote 'Yes'. In the event, this did not happen.

The legislation was confused and poorly drafted. A range of functions were to be given to the Scottish and Welsh assemblies but the decision on which responsibilities should be given to the Parliament was piecemeal and subject to incoherent parliamentary debates. Those who drafted the legislation had no overall conception of what the Parliament should do but instead considered each function in turn just as MPs considered each clause in turn without any obvious coherence. To some extent the responsibilities which were devolved were those of the Scottish Office, but this was not quite the case.

The referendums on Scottish and Welsh devolution were held on 1 March 1979, St David's Day. The 'winter of discontent', a period of industrial unrest, was part of the background. Opponents were far better funded and better organised. Supporters of devolution in Scotland were divided. The result in Scotland was a narrow majority in favour of devolution but far short of the required 40 per cent. In Wales, the vote against devolution far outweighed the vote in favour. See Table 3.

TABLE 3:
DEVOLUTION REFERENDUM RESULTS IN SCOTLAND AND WALES, 1979

	Scotland		Wales	
	Yes (%)	No (%)	Yes (%)	No (%)
Actual vote	52	48	20	80
Eligible electorate	33	31	12	47

The failure of devolution in the 1970s was largely due to the lack of political will. Labour voters, in particular, failed to turn out to vote in favour of a measure proposed by their own party. This was hardly surprising given that the most active Labour Party participants in the debate and in the referendum campaign were anti-devolutionists. The government was obliged to move an order in Parliament repealing the devolution legislation but it was not obliged to vote for the repeal itself. Prime Minister Jim Callaghan was in a quandary. His chief whip in the Commons warned him that he faced a massive rebellion amongst Labour MPs if he forced a vote and attempted to get Labour MPs to vote against the repeal of the legislation.[40] The SNP tried to force the government's hand and called for a vote on the repeal but Labour refused to budge. This forced the 11-strong group of SNP MPs to join with other opposition forces, including the Liberals, in a vote of no confidence in the Callaghan government. The government lost by one vote, precipitating a general election which brought Margaret Thatcher to power. The SNP lost nine of its 11 seats and Labour was in opposition.

Labour had adopted rather than embraced the policy of Scottish and Welsh devolution. Apart from a small band of Home Rulers, the motive was negative. Labour wanted to halt the advance of the SNP. Devolution was not seen in positive terms. The party had long viewed Britain as a unitary state. It was part of Labour ethos. The centralised state was seen as the vehicle through which socialism or social democracy would be achieved. Thinking within the civil service equally had unitary-state predilections. It was, therefore, hardly surprising that the party and government often seemed unconvinced when it argued for devolution. Not only was there an absence of will but what many Labour politicians were being asked to argue for was something which they could not reconcile with their understanding of British politics.

Opponents of devolution, both within the Labour Party and in the Conservative Party and beyond, displayed more confidence in the late 1970s than might have been imagined given the apparent level of support for devolution, at least in Scotland. However, they probably knew that many of those arguing for devolution shared their misgivings about devolution. Anti-devolutionists were able to exploit the contradictions and divisions in the pro-devolution camp. If the 1970s proved anything, it was that debating constitutional change within a unitary-state conception of Britain was bound to be a major impediment for those supporting constitutional change.

THE RISE OF THE UNION STATE AND RE-EMERGENCE OF HOME RULE

A union-state perspective, however, offers opportunities for reform unavailable in a unitary state. The central role of Parliament still exists but uniformity is not required and there is acknowledgement of the historic distinctiveness of the component nations of Britain. Problems still arise but these can at least be viewed in a different way. The asymmetrical nature of the state already exists so further asymmetry would cause less alarm from this perspective than a unitary-state viewpoint. Conservatives might be expected to be most willing to accept this perspective, especially those within the tradition associated with Burke.[41] At least in pre-Thatcher days, they would have been less concerned than their Labour counterparts with the need for strong, central, economic controls and indeed Conservatives celebrated diversity within Britain. The notion of the constitution as organic would also fit with this perspective. It is little surprise therefore to find Conservatives such as Quintin Hogg (Lord Hailsham) supporting devolution in the 1970s.[42]

Margaret Thatcher was, however, no respecter of traditional Conservatism and her understanding of the nature of the UK was quite different from previous Tory leaders. Thatcher had limited experience of the territorially diverse nature of the state she came to govern. Experience as Prime Minister seemed to make her less tolerant of the diversity which she came to know. In her memoirs, she made clear her view of the Scottish Office:

> The pride of the Scottish Office – whose very structure added a layer of bureaucracy, standing in the way of the reforms which were paying such dividends in England – was that public expenditure per head in Scotland was far higher than in England.[43]

Previous Conservative leaders had accepted the apparatus of the union state even if they adopted a unitary-state perspective when it came to legislative devolution. Margaret Thatcher never attempted to get rid of the Scottish Office but her sympathies were evident and explicit in her memoirs. She represented a fairly novel strain in British political thinking as far as territorial politics was concerned: Thatcher was assimilationist in thinking. This proved important in the development of debates of constitutional change in Scotland.

Scotland's constitutional status had re-emerged as an issue by the mid-1980s for a number of reasons. The defeat of Labour at the 1983 general election while the party won a majority of seats in Scotland highlighted the Scottish dimension. Devolutionists argued that Scotland would have been protected from some of the policies pursued by the Thatcher government had a Scottish assembly existed. A cross-party pressure group, the Campaign for a Scottish Assembly (CSA) was set up in 1980 with the initial aim of keeping the issue of devolution alive and, in time, hoping to find some means of bringing about a Scottish assembly. One idea was that a constitutional convention should be set up consisting of all parties and which would agree a scheme of home rule. This would then be presented to Parliament which, it was hoped, would pass the measure. Convincing the political parties to participate would be the first step which only became possible after devolution was firmly on the political agenda again.

Ironically, the Thatcher government also highlighted the diversity of the UK. In adopting an assimilationist stance, Margaret Thatcher reminded Scots that the Union was never meant to be a unitary state. With each successive Tory victory in Britain as a whole, the strength of support for Scottish home rule seemed to grow within the Labour Party. Labour was coming to support constitutional change for reasons other than as a means of undermining the SNP.

The major spur came following the 1987 election. In 1985, the government had altered the system of local taxation in Scotland. Domestic rates, a form of property tax, were used to fund local government expenditure. Changes in property values meant that periodic changes were required in the valuation which local authorities used to determine how much each ratepayer should pay; this could be a hazardous and unpopular procedure. Though some ratepayers would benefit, each revaluation resulted in many ratepayers having to pay more in local tax. In England, governments had simply avoided revaluation which had resulted in often unfair systems of local taxation and, the longer revaluation was put off, the greater the need for one grew and the greater the upheaval there would be. In Scotland, the 1985 revaluation was the third over a period when there had been no revaluation in England. It proved extremely unpopular at a very difficult time for the Conservatives. Industrial action by schoolteachers and the closure of parts of the steel industry allied with rates revaluation to make the Scottish Conservatives very unpopular.

Against this background, the Conservatives decided to introduce an alternative to domestic rates. The 'community charge' soon became known as the 'poll tax'. It was a flat-rate tax imposed on all adults, with a few exceptional categories. It was extremely unpopular. It meant that many people who had never previously had a rates bill (although they may have paid rates indirectly as part of their rent or as part of a family unit paying rates) received a poll-tax bill. Its flat-rate nature made it a regressive form of taxation, violating principles of social justice. At the time of the 1987 election, legislation had been passed, but was awaiting implementation, for Scotland only; the government promised to introduce legislation for England in the new Parliament.

The poll tax encapsulated the Scottish predicament. It was felt that a left-leaning nation was having a socially unjust measure imposed upon it, by a party with minority support; Scotland appeared to be a test-bed before a similar measure was introduced in England. Local government finance would have been the prerogative of a Scottish assembly. The Tories won in 1987 in Britain but saw their Scottish vote fall from its 1983 level of 28.4 to 24 per cent – its worst performance since universal enfranchisement – and its number of seats collapse from 21 to ten. Labour won 50 of Scotland's 72 seats, its highest ever, with 42.2 per cent of the vote – its highest share since the advent of the SNP as a serious political force. The poll tax dominated the next few years and became embroiled in debates on the constitution. The 1987 result appeared to be good news for Labour but the result contained a sting in its tail. It highlighted the impotence of Scottish Labour. The SNP dubbed Labour's new intake the 'feeble fifty', and attacked Labour with as much fervour for failing to defend Scotland as the Tories for imposing its policies against the wishes of the Scottish people.

The setbacks suffered by the SNP in 1979 had resulted in a period of internal warfare. The fundamentalist–pragmatist tension, evident since the party's inception,[44] came to the fore as an explanation for what had gone wrong was sought and a future strategy found. Fundamentalists opposed devolution as they saw it as dissipating the party's energies and as either a blind alley or even a ploy to prevent independence. Pragmatists were inclined to see devolution as a step in the right direction and believed that the party should tailor its strategy according to circumstances. In addition, a group of mainly young party members emerged who argued that the party needed to adopt a more radical image. Calling itself the '79 Group, its members were less concerned to change party policy, which was already left wing on most issues and generally to the left of the Labour Party, but to match the policies with its public image.

The 1983 election saw the SNP vote fall from 17.3 per cent to 11.7 per cent, though it held its two seats. The result forced the party to realise that internal battles were electorally costly. A new realism emerged so that by 1987 the party was more united and, though it lost both seats, it gained three others and won 14 per cent of the vote. More importantly, the SNP was in a better position to exploit political circumstances.

The party's policy on Europe was evolving. In the 1975 referendum on Britain's membership of the European Community, the SNP had argued against continued membership, but by the late 1980s it was adopting a more positive attitude. At its 1988 annual conference, the SNP officially launched its policy in favour of 'independence in Europe'. The SNP also decided to highlight the poll tax and campaigned vigorously against its implementation, including organising a mass campaign of non-payment. On Europe and the poll tax, the SNP was setting the pace in Scottish politics.

In Autumn 1987, Labour's Shadow Scottish Secretary presented a devolution bill in Parliament. There had been a series of back-bench devolution bills presented earlier in the 1980s but this was the first official opposition measure. It failed but it signalled that Labour was taking the constitution more seriously as an issue. The bill was modelled on its devolution legislation in the late 1970s. A few more responsibilities were added, such as universities, and the Scottish Parliament was to have some limited tax-raising powers.

Bruce Millan, the former Labour Secretary of State for Scotland who had worked on the devolution legislation in the 1970s, was appointed one of Britain's European Community Commissioners in 1988, causing a by-election in his Glasgow Govan constituency. The seat had been won in a previous by-election by the SNP in 1973, but Millan's 19,509 majority was thought to be impregnable. The SNP adopted Jim Sillars as its candidate. Sillars had been a Labour MP, winning a by-election in South Ayrshire in 1970 which had been a setback for the SNP, but had left Labour in 1975 to set up a new party – the Scottish Labour Party – disillusioned with Labour's weak commitment to devolution. He proved a formidable campaigner and overturned the Labour majority, taking the SNP from fourth to first place in Govan.

Labour's commitment to home rule had been developing in the 1980s but the threat posed by the SNP after Govan ensured that devolution was back on its agenda. The Campaign for a Scottish Assembly was able to gain support for its proposal to establish a constitutional convention. The problem was that in order to get

Labour to participate it would have to convince the party that it would not be outvoted in the convention, which would put others, particularly the SNP, off joining. Govan proved an important stage in this process. Labour was already committed to joining a convention and, after Govan, the convention looked appealing as the proposed structure meant that it would dominate proceedings. The convention would also give Labour a breathing space. However, the cost of Labour involvement was SNP non-involvement. The SNP feared that the convention would be used by Labour to buy time, if not as a platform to attack independence in Europe. It remained aloof though the Liberal Democrats, Greens, local authorities, trade unions and churches participated. This was not the first attempt to reach a cross-party consensus through a constitutional convention, but where it differed was that the Labour Party was officially involved.[45]

The idea of 'popular sovereignty' is part of the ethos of the national movement. Home Rulers have argued that a key aspect of Scottish distinctiveness is that government legitimacy in Scotland lies in the support of the Scottish people and not Parliament. In the 1970s, few beyond the SNP argued that this was the case. The first clause of the devolution legislation initially presented to Parliament in 1978 stated:

> The following provisions of this Act make changes in the government of Scotland as part of the UK. They do not affect the unity of the UK or the supreme authority of Parliament to make laws for the UK or any part of it.

The clause was struck out of the legislation by Parliament. Nationalist MPs combined with opponents of devolution against the government and supporters of devolution to defeat the measure. It was not a statement of popular sovereignty but, SNP and *Plaid Cymru* MPs aside, an attempt to undermine the legislation. Devolution was conceived in the 1970s as wholly within the traditions of parliamentary sovereignty. John Smith, as Devolution Minister, insisted that sovereignty was not being devolved and that Parliament at Westminster would remain the only sovereign Parliament.[46]

Perhaps the most significant change in the 1980s and 1990s, compared with the 1970s, was the assertion that Scottish home rule was demanded in the name of Scottish popular sovereignty. The cross-party Campaign for a Scottish Assembly had set up a committee to consider establishing a constitutional convention which had reported in 1988. Its report, 'A Claim of Right for Scotland', was critical of the 'English' constitutional principle of the Crown in Parliament.[47] More importantly, the statement signed by participants at the foundation meeting of the Constitutional Convention on 30 March 1989 stated:

> We, gathered as the Scottish Constitutional Convention, do hereby acknowledge the sovereign right of the Scottish people to determine the form of Government best suited to their needs, and do hereby declare and pledge that in all our actions and deliberations their interests shall be paramount. We further declare and pledge that our actions and deliberations shall be directed to the following ends:
> To agree a scheme for an Assembly or Parliament for Scotland;
> To mobilise Scottish opinion and ensure the approval of the Scottish people for that scheme; and
> To assert the right of the Scottish people to secure the implementation of that scheme.[48]

The distinction between parliamentary and popular sovereignty can seem abstruse but is significant symbolically. Basing the case for change in terms of popular sovereignty involves a different conception of the UK and limits the involvement of non-Scottish involvement in determining Scotland's constitutional status. Popular sovereignty is essentially a Scottish Nationalist conception, as used in debates on home rule, and goes well beyond even a union-state interpretation of the foundation of Britain.

Though Labour MPs signed the document asserting Scotland's right to decide its own future, this may have had more to do with reacting to the electoral pressure of the SNP, as in the 1970s, rather than a new found radicalism. John Smith, former Devolution Minister and party leader 1992–94, was one of the signatories and must have known what he was signing up to, but it is unlikely that English Labour MPs, including Tony Blair, Smith's successor as Labour leader, paid much heed. Since becoming leader, Blair has behaved as if the 'Claim of Right' did not exist and the declaration had not been signed by his party; he has even appeared in interviews to be unaware of the whole notion of Scottish popular sovereignty.

Nonetheless, the convention agreed a scheme of devolution which largely followed one presented to Parliament by the Labour Party in 1987. The key difference was with respect to the electoral system to be used in elections to the proposed Scottish Parliament. Though expressed in vague terms, as was much contained in the convention's proposals, the decision that a system other than first-past-the-post would be used was to be the convention's most significant achievement. In addition, the issue of gender equality was forced onto the convention's agenda. While no mechanism was devised to achieve the goal of '50–50' representation of men and women, this became a goal against which the parties would be judged. In time, after the 1992 election, more concrete proposals emerged for an alternative electoral system. An additional member system was agreed which would produce a greater of degree of proportional representation.

The 1992 election, however, saw the return of the Conservatives and, consequently, the postponement of devolution. The SNP had talked of 'Scotland free by '93' and Labour had promised that devolution would be 'along in a tick'. The media had speculated that the Tories would be wiped out in Scotland. The Tories held all the seats they had won in 1992 and gained another with a marginal increase in their vote. Instead of acknowledging that this had given them a final chance to listen to the Scottish public, the Tories carried on as if winning 11 out of 72 MPs with 24 per cent of the vote amounted to a major vote of confidence. With extremely weak leadership from Ian Lang as Secretary of State for Scotland, the Tories 'took stock' of their position as Prime Minister John Major had promised during the election campaign. However, this proved superficial and unconvincing. A much trumpeted 'breakfast with Major' took place in Edinburgh at which a handful of Scots, chosen for obscure reasons, met with the Prime Minister and talked over Scotland's predicament. Some of those in attendance may have naively believed that it was a genuine consultation exercise; others were probably seduced by their own sense of self-importance. The outcome was a government White Paper extolling the virtues of the Union, *Scotland in the Union: A Partnership for Good*. It was a partisan document which had little new to offer the Scots. The Tories appeared to be sleepwalking into electoral oblivion.

THE 1997 ELECTION AND REFERENDUM

In 1995, Lang was replaced by Michael Forsyth, a far more formidable politician. Forsyth had no intention of abandoning the Conservatives' opposition to devolution but tried instead to make uncompromising Unionism popular. There were two strands to this strategy. First, he attacked the tax-raising powers of the convention proposals, the weakest part of the proposals. Second, he engaged in symbolic politics in an attempt to highlight the 'Scottishness' of the Tories. The 'tartan tax' became part of the political vocabulary and, for the first time since 1979, the Tories were on the offensive on the constitution. The Stone of Destiny, a symbol of Scottish sovereignty on which kings and queens were crowned, was returned to Scotland in a fanfare of publicity.

In June 1996, Labour's leadership responded to Forsyth's 'tartan tax' offensive. Tony Blair overturned the work of the Constitutional Convention when he decided that a two-question referendum would be held. The first question would ask Scots whether they wanted home rule, and the second whether they wanted tax-raising powers. Labour's response had differed from their Liberal Democrat partners in the convention. The latter had argued that tax-raising powers would be used if necessary whereas Labour ruled this out. Blair himself maintained that a Labour-controlled Scottish parliament would not use the power. This was a change of policy based entirely on the need to counter any possibility that Labour might be thought to still harbour 'tax-and-spend' thinking anywhere in Britain.

In part, the problems with tax-raising powers were of Labour's own making. The convention had failed to work out a coherent package for financing devolution. The tax-raising powers were extremely limited and would yield little financial autonomy, but politically they were proving costly. Added to this, Labour was saying something quite different from its partners in the convention. The two-question referendum was designed to get Labour out of this difficulty, but it backfired. Blair's decision to have a two-question referendum was made without consulting John McAllion, Labour's constitutional affairs spokesman in Scotland. Such centralised decision-making made a mockery of the party's commitment to devolution. The decision to ask a question on taxation, one of the details of the scheme, suggested that the convention package was beginning to unravel and undermined any notion that popular sovereignty underpinned the work of the convention. By late 1996, the unitary-state viewpoint was reasserting itself within a highly centralised Labour Party.

But the experience of Conservative government since 1979 ran deeper than the experience of 'New Labour' and, while Blair may have preferred to dump the devolution commitment, this would have had seriously damaging consequences. The referendum proposal bought time for Labour. Forsyth's 'tartan tax' jibes were spiked and Labour sailed through the 1997 election relatively unscathed. The

Liberal Democrats had been furious when the referendum announcement had been made, but were powerless to do much. The SNP unsuccessfully attempted to exploit the situation but the electorate's desire for change precluded any risks of Labour voters switching to the SNP. Nonetheless, the SNP threat remained present as Labour's own research leaked to the press revealed.

The rejection of the Tories in Scotland and Wales in 1997 was absolute. Commentators were wary of predicting a Tory wipe-out in Scotland after the experience of 1992. The scale of defeat had implications for the referendums which were held in Scotland and Wales in September 1997. White Papers setting out Labour's proposals were produced in the summer. In the event, the details played little part in the actual outcome of the referendums. Eighteen years of Conservative rule had produced a considerable change in public attitudes in Scotland and Wales. Though the margin of victory in Wales was exceptionally narrow, it was a massive change from that recorded in 1979. In Scotland, an overwhelming majority was recorded in favour of devolution and a considerable majority for tax-raising powers. In both Scotland and Wales, the proponents of devolution worked together to a greater extent than in 1979.

Labour and the SNP suspended their war for the duration of the referendum. Few Scottish Labour politicians spoke out against devolution. Tam Dalyell was an isolated figure whose credibility had been seriously damaged by his failure to speak out against devolution before. His election address at the general election five months before had contained a commitment to a Scottish parliament. Unlike in the 1970s, he could not claim that this was a new issue about which he had not given sufficient consideration. With no MPs, the Conservatives had neither the leadership nor the will for another fight, especially one they knew they would lose. A few Tories led 'Think Twice', the anti-devolution campaign, but, in comparison with the pro-devolution campaign, it was ill-prepared and had the support of only the Tories. The death of Diana, Princess of Wales towards the end of the campaign had no impact on the outcome. Her ambiguous status – part of the establishment and anti-establishment simultaneously – ensured that no side was able to gain from the wave of public sympathy following her death. The suspension of activities meant that there was an intense period of campaigning in the last 100 hours leading up to polling day.

In Wales, the result was never the foregone conclusion that it had been in Scotland. Labour was not united in favour. Dissident Labour MPs, notably Llew Smith, spoke out strongly against the government's more modest proposals for Wales. The geography of the vote in Wales was predictable with Welsh-speaking areas more inclined to vote in favour. The turnout was low at 50.1 per cent. Nonetheless, the scale of the swing from 1979 was immense.

TABLE 4:
1997 REFERENDUM IN SCOTLAND

	%
'I agree that there should be a Scottish Parliament'	74.3
'I do not agree that there should be a Scottish Parliament'	25.7
'I agree that a Scottish Parliament should have tax-varying powers'	63.5
'I do not agree that a Scottish Parliament should have tax-varying powers'	36.5
Turnout	60.4

TABLE 5:
1997 REFERENDUM IN WALES

'I agree that there should be a Welsh Assembly'	50.3
'I do not agree that there should be a Welsh Assemby'	49.7
Turnout	50.12

All of this had implications for the English regions. With London promised an elected mayor and a new elected authority, and the possibility of a Northern Ireland assembly, the prospects for English regional government increased. Campaigners in the north of England insisted that developments elsewhere made the case for a northern assembly irresistible. Devolution altered not only the constitutional arrangements of Scotland and Wales but had implications elsewhere.

CONCLUSION

The unitary-state conception of Britain especially, has applied to the territorial politics of England, to a lesser extent, as the century developed to Wales, and to a much less extent, to Scotland. The importance of the conceptual lenses arises in understanding the position of each of the constituent nations of Britain. They have had fundamentally different roots and different trajectories of development. Central–local relations in any part of the state are best understood in terms of a unitary-state view of Britain, whether these are seen as a partnership or delegated powers in a principal–agent relationship. The historic nations, however, can best be understood in terms of a dynamic or organic state model in which history, powers and traditions have played a crucial part. The failure of federal schemes to win support in Britain should not surprise us given how dominant the unitary-state perspective is.[49]

The changing conception of the state also helps explain the growing importance attached to the issue of constitutional change and the gradual acceptance within Scotland and Wales of its acceptability and appeal. The great impediment would appear to be the pervasive nature of the unitary state conception of Britain and, most notably, the importance of Parliament. This is particularly important given that, before legislative devolution can come about, it must win parliamentary approval.

The context in which the development of territorial governance has taken place has been influenced by two antagonistic conceptions of Britain. But what is clear is that the evolving nature of the state has been paralleled by an evolving conception of territorial governance. What might have been considered impossible or unacceptable at one time becomes acceptable and even attractive later. Scotland's distinct status has always been accepted, but that of Wales is a relatively recent development. The position of the English regions remains problematic. The uneven territorial development of Britain is, ultimately, the main impediment at the close of the twentieth century to prospects for reform. Even if Scotland's status is accepted as requiring special institutions, it remains part of Britain and a Scottish legislature will have implications elsewhere. As we have seen, Wales followed Scotland, and the example of territorial government in Scotland was cited as a model for Wales.

The so-called 'West Lothian question' – Scots MPs after devolution having a vote on English domestic affairs in the Commons when similar Scottish domestic affairs will have been devolved to a Scottish parliament – highlights the messy nature of asymmetry. The existing arrangements are, of course, messy but devolution will add a new dimension which remains unacceptable to all who adopt a unitary-state perspective and probably to some with a union-state perspective. The Labour government intends that there will be a reduction in the number of MPs at Westminster. This does not remove the problem, though it slightly reduces the likelihood of a Labour government wholly dependent on Scottish and Welsh MPs being returned to Parliament.

Just as aspects of the territorial governance of Britain can now best be understood from a union-state perspective when a unitary-state perspective was more appropriate at the beginning of the century (the position for Wales in particular), so too might the UK come to be best seen in terms of an organic federation.[50] The nature of the state at its formation is clearly important in its future development, but equally it should not be seen as cast in stone. Britain today is a more complex state territorially than it was a century ago. Its dynamic or organic nature may mean that it changes slowly, but change has occurred and looks set to continue. With the advent of devolution, it will be difficult for anyone to argue that Britain is a unitary state; whether the new construction will remain a union state, become a (quasi-)federal state or break up into independent states is difficult at this juncture to predict.

NOTES

I would like to thank Laura Cram for her comments on an earlier draft.

1. The idea is derived from Graham Allison, *Essence of Decision: Explaining the Cuban Missile Crisis* (Boston MA: Little, Brown and Company, 1971), p. 251.
2. In this chapter, the term Britain is used rather than the United Kingdom to refer to that part of the UK which excludes Northern Ireland. Wherever the UK has been used, it refers to the whole of the state. Many of the points made about Britain will, of course, be relevant to Northern Ireland though some will not.
3. A. Midwinter, M. Keating and J. Mitchell, *Politics and Public Policy in Scotland* (Basingstoke: Macmillan, 1991), for example, begins 'The title of this book begs a question. Is there such a thing as Scottish politics? The United Kingdom is, after all, a unitary state with a single government and parliament.'
4. Derek Urwin and Stein Rokkan, 'Introduction: Centres and Peripheries in Western Europe' in Stein Rokkan and Derek Urwin (eds), *The Politics of Territorial Identity: Studies in European Regionalism* (London: Sage, 1982), p. 11.
5. Though see W. J. M. Mackenzie, 'Peripheries and Nation Building: The Case of Scotland' in Per Torsvik (ed.), *Mobilization, Centre-Periphery Structure and*

Nation-Building (Bergen: Universitetsforlaget, 1981): 'What makes the UK so like a federal system, in a practical sense, is that Scotland is administered by two separate and parallel systems: the UK system and the Scottish Office system.' p. 164.

6. Michael Keating, *State and Regional Nationalism* (Hemel Hempstead: Wheatsheaf, 1988), p. 56.
7. Richard Rose, *Understanding the United Kingdom* (London: Longman, 1982), p. 11.
8. Michael Billig, *Banal Nationalism* (London: Sage, 1995), p. 6. Billig's definition is similar to the classic definition offered by Ernest Renan in 1882 who suggested that nations had a sense of common past and a present will to live together. Renan maintained that the existence of a nation is a 'daily plebiscite'. E. Renan, 'What is a Nation?' in Alfred Zimmern (ed.), *Modern Political Doctrines* (London: Oxford University Press, 1939), p. 203.
9. Keating, *State and Regional Nationalism*, distinguishes between state and regional nationalism when referring to UK/British nationalism and sub-state nationalism such as Scottish, Welsh or Irish nationalisms. James Kellas, *The Politics of Nationalism and Ethnicity* (Basingstoke: Macmillan, 1991), pp. 51–2 similarly distinguished between 'official' and 'ethnic' and 'social' nationalisms.
10. Linda Colley, *Britons: Forging the Nation, 1707–1837* (London: Yale University Press, 1992).
11. A. V. Dicey and R. S. Rait, *Thoughts on the Union Between England and Scotland*, (London: Macmillan, 1920), pp. 244–5.
12. For a defence of Dicey's views as applied to debates following the report of the Royal Commission on the Constitution (Kilbrandon), 1973 see D. G. Boyce, 'Dicey, Kilbrandon and Devolution', *Political Quarterly*, 46 (1975), pp. 280–92.
13. Brian Hogwood, *Whatever Happened to Regional Government?: Developments in Regional Administration in Britain since 1979*, Strathclyde Papers on Government and Politics 97, (Glasgow: Department of Government, University of Strathclyde, 1994), p. 17.
14. Brian Hogwood, 'Regional Administration in Britain since 1979: Trends and Explanations', *Regional and Federal Studies*, 5 (1995), pp. 289–90.
15. The position of Northern Ireland is not considered here though it would apply.
16. National Insurance was removed from the Scottish Office's responsibilities with the establishment of the National Health Service, though a separate health service continued to operate north of the border.
17. The Conservatives' official designation between 1912 and 1965 was the Scottish Unionist Party. This aligned Conservatives with Unionism and the substantial 'Orange' vote and had more to do with the union with Ireland than the Anglo-Scottish Union. From 1965 the official designation of the Conservatives has been Scottish Conservative and Unionist Party. See J. Mitchell, *Conservatives and the Union* (Edinburgh: Edinburgh University Press, 1990).
18. *Scotsman*, 15 February 1950.
19. *Scottish Affairs*, Cmd 7308, 1948.
20. *Scotsman*, 20 January 1957.
21. Lord Balfour (Chairman), *Report of the Royal Commission on Scottish Affairs*, Cmd 9212, 1954.
22. The appointment of Justices of the Peace, and issues of animal health, roads,

bridges and ferries were to transfer to the Scottish Office on the recommendation of the Royal Commission in 1955. Roads and bridges had been taken from the Scottish Secretary in 1919 when the Ministry of Transport was established. Electricity and food were also transferred to the Scottish Office.

23. Sir David Milne, *The Scottish Office* (London: George Allen & Unwin, 1957), pp. 1–21.
24. Ian C. Thomas, *The Creation of the Welsh Office: Conflicting Purposes in Institutional Change*, Studies in Public Policy 91 (Glasgow: Centre for the Study of Public Policy, University of Strathclyde, 1981) p. 2.
25. P. J. Randall, 'Wales in the Structure of Central Government', *Public Administration*, 50 (1972), p. 353.
26. P. J. Randall, 'The Development of Administrative Decentralisation in Wales from the Establishment of the Welsh Department of Education in 1907 to the Creation of the Post of Secretary of State for Wales in October 1964', unpublished MSc thesis, University College Wales, Aberystwyth 1969.
27. The Secretary for Scotland Act, 1885 was unique in that it was presented in Parliament under Gladstone's Liberal government which fell and was replaced without an election by Lord Salisbury's Conservative government. The bill proceeded without change under the Conservatives and, in fact, was led through the House of Lords by the Liberal peer and future Prime Minister, Lord Rosebery even though the Conservatives were in power.
28. Quoted in Edward Leon Gibson, 'A Study of the Council for Wales and Monmouthshire, 1948–1966', unpublished LLB thesis, University College Wales, Aberystwyth 1968, p. 13.
29. The Convention of Royal Burghs had played a significant part in the campaign for a Secretary of State for Scotland in the late nineteenth century and had sponsored a rally addressed by senior Scottish politicians in 1880. The Conference of Welsh Local Authorities adopted a motion urging the appointment of a Welsh Secretary of State in June 1943.
30. *Western Mail*, 30 January 1948.
31. The phrase 'wounded dignities' was originally used by Lord Salisbury when, as Prime Minister, he urged the Duke of Richmond and Gordon to accept the office of Secretary for Scotland in 1885. As far as Salisbury was concerned the office was unnecessary and the 'whole object of the move is to redress the wounded dignities of the Scottish people – or a section of them – who think that enough is not made of Scotland'. Salisbury to Richmond and Gordon, 13 August 1885, see H. J. Hanham, 'The Creation of the Scottish Office, 1881–87', *Juridical Review* (1965), pp. 205–44.
32. Unemployment, marginal land use, depopulation in rural Wales, the south Wales ports, small sea-ports and harbours, government administration, the mid-Wales spas, the problems of Welsh national servicemen, rural transport problems, Welsh holiday industry, Welsh language, disabled persons, road development, forestry development, the arts in Wales.
33. Ivor Gowan, 'Government in Wales', inaugural lecture as Professor of Political Science, University College, Aberystwyth, Wales, 1 December 1965.
34. Randall, 'Development', p. 238.
35. *House of Commons Debates*, 5th ser., vol. 939, cols 78–9, 14 November 1979.
36. A. V. Dicey, *England's Case Against Home Rule* (Richmond: Richmond Publishing, 1973 [1886]).
37. Tam Dalyell, *Devolution: The End of Britain* (London: Jonathan Cape, 1977).
38. Richard Crossman, *The Diaries of a Cabinet Minister, Volume 2*, (London:

Hamish Hamilton & Jonathan Cape, 1976), p. 48.

39. Iain McLean, 'The Rise and Fall of the Scottish National Party', *Political Studies*, 18 (1970), pp. 357–72.
40. James Callaghan, *Time and Chance* (London: Fontana, 1988), p. 560.
41. See Mitchell, *Conservatives*, chapter 1.
42. Quintin Hogg, *The Dilemma of Democracy* (London: William Collins, 1978).
43. Margaret Thatcher, *The Downing Street Years* (London: Harper Collins, 1993), p. 627.
44. See James Mitchell, *Strategies for Self-Government* (Edinburgh: Polygon, 1996), pp. 172–254.
45. Ibid., pp. 113–35.
46. *House of Commons Debates*, 5th ser., vol. 924, col. 509, 19 January 1977; col. 1586, 26 January 1977; vol. 943, cols 403–4, 31 January 1978.
47. Owen Dudley Edwards (ed.), *A Claim of Right for Scotland* (Edinburgh: Polygon, 1989) contains the full text of the Claim, pp. 9–53, with comments from various sources.
48. Constitutional Convention statement, Edinburgh.
49. This also has relevance to Britain's problems with the EU. Many of the issues addressed in this chapter apply to Britain's membership of the EU. The notion of parliamentary sovereignty and the unitary conception of Britain has been challenged since 1973. The major impact of EU membership on domestic territorial politics, from this analysis, is that it has challenged in a very direct way a central assumption of the unitary state. Parliament is not sovereign in practice and this must have some impact on how the state is viewed.
50. 'Organic federalism, imposed from below as a result of voluntary association of several distinctive territorial structures. These retain their distinctive institutional outlines with wide discretionary powers. Control by the centre is limited, having to take cognisance of the large degree of institutional autonomy residing in the constituent parts.' Urwin and Rokkan, 'Introduction: Centres and Peripheries', p. 11.

10

The British State and Northern Ireland: Can the National Question be Reformed?

BRIAN GIRVIN

REFORM AND THE NATURE OF THE IRISH QUESTION IN BRITISH POLITICS

Edmund Burke reminded his readers in the *Reflections on the Revolution in France* that 'A state without the means of some change is without the means of its conservation.' Echoing this view during the parliamentary debates on the reform of the franchise in 1831, Macaulay promoted this change on the grounds that:

> At present ... we drive over to the side of revolution those whom we shut out of power ... Turn where we may, within, around, the voice of great events is proclaiming to us, Reform, that you may preserve!

In turn, when the Reform Bill was finally passed, Sir Robert Peel in his address to the electors of Tamworth accepted the outcome as a final settlement of a great constitutional issue. He carefully added that he would not support continuous agitation for its own sake. While the pillars of the constitution could not be challenged he accepted that:

> if the spirit of the Reform Bill implies merely a careful review of institutions, civil and ecclesiastical, undertaken in a friendly temper, combining, with the firm maintenance of established rights the correction of proved abuses and the redress of real grievances, in that case I can, for myself and for my colleagues, undertake to act in such a spirit and with such intentions.

In each of these cases, three quite different politicians were grappling with the question of political change by adopting an approach to reform.[1] Burke, for example, explicitly demanded the reform of the Irish political system on the grounds of better government and the extension of civil rights to Catholics, believing that if this did not happen revolutionary influence would increase among the oppressed.[2] Burke's reasoning was to remain central to British thinking about Ireland throughout the second half of the nineteenth century. Macaulay applied a similar view to Britain, while Peel reasoned that some changes were necessary to prevent more serious challenges to the constitutional status quo.

Each of these elements has played a role in the British reform tradition during the nineteenth and twentieth centuries.[3] The tradition itself has had a number of features. One of these is the extent to which preservation is central to the reform process and the sentiments expressed by these three writers. Even the Great Reform Act of 1832 is seen by Macaulay as preservative; and this continued to be a feature of both Conservative and Liberal thinking for most of the nineteenth century. Reform for its own sake is rarely the issue. The case must be made for change, the offence obvious to all (or most of the political elite at least), but in essence reform is a response to a threat of disruption to the state and society. Whether the question involved electoral reform, Catholic emancipation or social reform, change in response to pressure is justified on three grounds. There must be a case for reform; there is an agitation which is a political threat to the good order of society; and the action proposed by reformers will preserve the fundamentals of the constitution. One does not have to share the views of Mr Podsnap in *Our Mutual Friend* who explained to a foreign enquirer that 'We Englishmen are very proud of our constitution ... it was Bestowed Upon Us by Providence', to recognise that this approach to reform has been extremely successful in accommodating disruption and in preventing revolution in the United Kingdom.[4]

This preservative aspect of reform had placed both reformers and radicals on the defensive in their criticism of the constitution and the nature of the British state, a difficulty which continues down to the present day.[5] The preservation of the constitution through reform may be one of the 'myths' of contemporary Britain, but it continues to be a powerful one. When then is reform not revolutionary? The answer must be when the constitution has not been radically altered. But when has this not been the case: Catholic emancipation, electoral reform, the Parliament Act of 1911? In each case reformers emphasised the partial and preservative nature of the changes, but critics stressed the revolutionary aspects of them. This has something to do with party politics and the nature of a two-party system within a first-past-the-post political system. If the 'essence' of the constitution has not been changed has there been a reform? Radical criticism of the British constitution would certainly support this version of the question, but there are other ways of interpreting it.

Does reform require some form of continuity to be a reform and to distinguish it from revolution or, more ambiguously, from disruptive change which is radical in intent and consequence? Again a reform might be radical but because the elements of continuity remain strong the impression is one of continuity. However, if a reform, no matter how moderate, destabilises the political system, can this be considered a reform within this meaning? A concept of reform must not exclude change, but at the same time any one change as a consequence of reform cannot change the system entirely. At this level we are approaching revolution rather than reform. The change will be a reform if in this instance it does not transform the system but a large number of changes may do so over the longer term. In their discussion of political stability Dowding and Kimber offer the following outline of what stability might consist of:

> Continuity of some elements is needed between moments in time in order that the system may be said to survive – but as long as continuity of some elements is maintained, over a long period there is no reason why all the elements could not be replaced.

If this approach is applied to the question of reform, it allows for continuity within the system, but also provides for long-term change which can have cumulatively radical consequences. The gradual nature of change is what links reform to stability, thus eschewing in the short term at least more radical (or revolutionary) consequences. If the emphasis in reform is placed on continuity it is possible to draw a distinction between change *in* a system (reform) which preserves the system and the change *of* a system into something entirely new and perhaps unrecognisable (revolution). If change is accepted, then the process is one of reform, whereas forced change brings about the instability of the political system and usually the disruption of the system itself.[6]

The legitimacy of a political system may be said to be challenged when significant sections of a society excluded from power and influence organise to challenge that exclusion. A crisis will affect that system if the ruling groups are unable to either counter or meet the demands. One solution is the reactionary one, the effective repression of the challenge and a restoration of the status quo. This option has not been available in Britain since the 1830s. The alternative is to introduce reforms to meet the insurgents' demands, and this has been the most authoritative response on the part of British elites since the 1820s. If a legitimisation crisis can normally be met by reform, this does not always prove to be the case. In the decade before 1914 the United Kingdom entered a period of political instability and established notions of power and authority were seriously challenged. Yet not all the issues of concern at this time have equal status in terms of reform and continuity. In principle, though more difficult in practice, the demands of the suffragettes, the Labour movement and for social reform were amenable to reform and indeed as we now know were in fact resolved as a consequence of legislative reform within two decades. This is not to deny the seriousness of the challenge, but to argue that British political institutions were flexible enough to come to terms with the key elements of the insurgents' demands.[7]

The Irish question and home rule are often bracketed with other movements as part of the reform tradition. British reformers believed that the Irish question was amenable to reform and that Irish Nationalist demands were not qualitatively different from those of nonconformists, trade unions or suffragettes. If continuity is central to the reform process then is it arguable that home rule was not in principle resolvable within the existing constitution. It is a grey area, however. At the beginning of the twentieth century there were few examples of regions within states gaining home rule or indeed seceding; Hungary in 1867 is one exception as is Norwegian independence from Sweden in 1905. Home rule remained uncharted territory for British politics and for constitutional theory. What distinguishes the Irish question from British reform are the following:

- the presence among Irish Catholics of a strong sense of nationality which distinguishes this population from the rest of the United Kingdom, expressed in political terms by a well-organised and self-confident national political movement;
- the serious divisions which emerged within Ireland between Nationalists and Unionists do not respond to reform and are based on quite different senses of identity, reflecting older divisions between Catholic and Protestant.

Nevertheless, both Liberals and Conservatives believed that it was possible to reform Ireland to take account of these differences, to provide better government and to integrate Ireland more fully into the United Kingdom. The home rule movement and especially the divisions which emerged between 1905 and 1914 undermined this strategy. The evolution of the Irish crisis between 1912 and 1922 highlighted the limits of reform as a strategy when nationality is involved. While a settlement based on home rule might have been achieved at one time or another, more ominous outcomes were likely even in the absence of war in 1914. The home rule question was a surrogate for self-determination by Irish Nationalists and it is likely that any reform would fall short of what would be expected. Even before the war in 1914 the polarisation of opinion within Ireland, and in Britain, indicated that the reformist approach had been exhausted.[8]

FROM HOME RULE TO PARTITION

The various home rule bills are frequently presented as moderate reforms and the failure of the British state to concede them seen as the stimulus to more radical strategies by Irish Nationalists. What this ignores is the growth of nationality as the main source of identity among Irish Catholics during the nineteenth century and the emergence of a British political identity among Protestants. These views were increasingly polarised by 1914. By then the island of Ireland had already divided in political, social, economic and, to an extent, military terms. Home rule for Ireland came increasingly to mean home rule for Nationalist Ireland because Protestant Ireland refused to participate in devolution. The difficulty here is that successive British governments meant something different when they referred to Home Rule than was the case with Nationalists. For the British, home rule was devolution and no more, but for Nationalists it was increasingly a first step on the road to sovereignty.[9] Nationalist Ireland was prepared to take power in Ireland by 1914 and to establish a regional government which would in many ways be different to that of the United Kingdom generally. The opposition of Unionists in Ireland was based on the fear of what Irish Nationalism would do with its new power. Issues of nationality are not easily resolved, especially when there are overlapping claims between a secessionist nationality and the metropolitan state. These pressures become even stronger when there is also a minority left behind by the withdrawal of the metropolitan power.[10]

The Irish War of Independence and the establishment of the Irish

Free State tends to obscure the real shift in British government policy towards Ireland after 1918. Partition was not at first seen as an attractive option by British governments either before or after the First World War. However, the political terrain was transformed by the war. In many parts of Europe partition became the normal way to resolve boundary problems, especially when they involved ethnic conflict. In the case of Ireland it was evident to the British government that it would prove difficult to refuse some partitionist solution to the Ulster Unionists. Increasingly the question was not whether there should be partition, but what form it would take and its territorial extent. Lloyd George and his government were influenced by the presence of leading Conservatives in the Cabinet, but also by the loyalty of the Ulster Unionists to Britain during the war. In this context, it would be near impossible for a British government to force a settlement on the Unionists, but policy had also to recognise the radicalisation of Irish opinion between 1916 and 1919. Partition emerged out of this environment as a solution to the difficulty posed by incompatible loyalties.[11]

During these years policy and perception in relation to Ireland, but especially to Ulster, changed. The presuppositions underwriting British policy altered appreciably. The war contributed to this outcome, but the growing appreciation of the strength of Nationalism and its moral validity deeply affected the behaviour of politicians and the general public. The sea change is not only detectable in public documents, but in the general climate of opinion.[12] Irish public opinion at the time and subsequently was sceptical about the British claim to be fighting for small nations, yet this was an important contribution to the change in British attitudes. Imperial self-confidence was seriously weakened in the face of strong and self-reliant nationalism (whether in Ireland or in India).[13] By 1922 the intellectual terrain had shifted and all of Ireland was removed from the centre of British politics in a fashion which would have been unthinkable a decade previously. Ireland and Northern Ireland no longer divided the British political parties. A bipartisan approach was adopted which has been maintained since the 1920s, though the Labour Party has made more of its commitment to a united Ireland in the long term. Northern Ireland, though remaining part of the United Kingdom, was defined as different and apart. Northern Ireland was not only seen as not as British as Finchley, as Margaret Thatcher once famously claimed, but was also not as British as Glasgow, Newcastle or Cardiff. This is a significant shift which is apparent in the structure of Northern Ireland and in the development of policy towards Ireland from 1919.[14] This treatment of Northern Ireland as different predates by nearly half a century the decline of Unionism within Britain itself.[15]

The Government of Ireland Act of 1920 was intended as a reform to address the consequences of political instability in Ireland. In its application to both parts of Ireland the British intention was to create conditions for reconciliation within Ireland by retaining the two home rule governments within the structure of the United Kingdom. This act falls within the meaning of reform, but the Treaty Settlement which established the Irish Free State with dominion status in 1921 went beyond that meaning. This action actually broke up the United Kingdom and established a new state, admittedly one with somewhat limited sovereignty at that time.

If by 1919 government policy reluctantly accepted some form of partition, this was not a prospect which was at first welcomed. The First Report of the Cabinet Committee on the Irish question concluded that two premises operated in policy: that the government should do 'everything possible to promote Irish unity', but that it would not be imposed on the Unionists. To an extent this is the origin of the Nationalist view that the Unionists have a veto over policy, but what it actually meant is that a British government would not use force to bring about a united Ireland. Despite this the government continued to work for a united-Ireland solution. At the end of 1919 the view of the Cabinet was that Ulster would not remain part of the United Kingdom as then constituted; 'the ultimate aim of the Government's policy in Ireland was a united Ireland with a separate parliament of its own, bound by the closest ties to Great Britain'.[16] This was not a realisable policy on the part of Lloyd George or his government: there was a war in Ireland, the Conservative Party was restless, the Unionists were well organised and influential in Conservative circles. To attempt a resolution of the impasse without taking into consideration either the views of the Unionists or those of the Conservative Party would have involved breaking up the coalition government and/or war with the Unionists, with all the uncertainties which that would bring.[17]

The Government of Ireland Act of 1920 was an attempt to resolve the basic contradiction in the government's policy. It sought to make concessions to the Irish Nationalists, secure Unionist acquiescence but also provide a mechanism for the eventual unification of the island. When the second reading of the bill was moved, Ian Macpherson, the Chief Secretary for Ireland, claimed that the division of Ireland was 'distasteful to the Government, just as it is distasteful to all Irishmen'. By late 1919 this was somewhat disingenuous, for while Sir Edward

Carson opposed the bill on grounds of principle, the northern Unionists under the leadership of James Craig accepted partition for the six north-eastern counties of Ireland. Macpherson outlined the government's hopes for the bill:

> All of us hope that the division may be temporary only, and our arrangement has, therefore, been to frame the Bill in such a manner as may lead to a union between the two parts of Ireland.[18]

The bill aimed to 'provide for the better government of Ireland', a reflection of traditional reformist politics. However, the bill's objectives went well beyond the reform tradition. The intention of the legislation was to set up two parliaments in Ireland with clearly devolved power. While neither would be entirely sovereign, each would have considerable local authority. This, it was anticipated, would persuade the Republican movement in Ireland to agree to end the armed conflict and accept the act as the basis for a settlement. The long-term objective of the legislation was to create the conditions for a united Irish parliament, though one with continuing close links with the United Kingdom. The emphasis within the legislation was, therefore, on all-Ireland institutions and arrangements. Section 2 (1) provided for the establishment of a 'council of Ireland' comprising the Lord Lieutenant with equal representation from North and South. The purpose of the council was:

> the promotion of mutual intercourse and uniformity in relation to matters affecting the whole of Ireland, and to providing for the administration of services which the two parliaments mutually agree should be administered uniformly throughout the whole of Ireland, or which by virtue of this act are to be so administered.

Section 3 (1) provided further that an all-Ireland parliament could be established at some future date if both parliaments voted by a majority to replace the council of Ireland with a parliament for the whole island. The intention of British legislators was that the act would allow for the eventual reconciliation of Unionists and Nationalists in Ireland, a well-intentioned if unsuccessful objective. Northern Unionists were prepared to accept a devolved government in Northern Ireland if this was the only alternative to an all-Ireland devolved government. Both the British government and Irish Nationalists attempted to persuade the Unionists during the treaty negotiations in 1921 to accept rule from Dublin, but to no avail. One of the aims of constitutional nationalism since 1921 has been to detach Northern Ireland from the United Kingdom but retain its devolved status within a federal but united Ireland. Sections 6 and 75 of the Government of Ireland Act sustained the Unionist position by providing that the United Kingdom Parliament would remain the 'supreme authority' in the context of devolved government. The act offered attractions to Unionists and Nationalists, but Unionists gained considerably more from its protection than did Northern Irish Nationalists from its promise.

The Government of Ireland Act proved to be inoperative in the southern counties of Ireland due to its rejection by the Nationalist movement. The treaty between the British government and the Irish Nationalists led to the southern counties receiving dominion status, similar to that of Canada, Australia, New Zealand and South Africa. The Irish Free State acquired effective, though not formal, sovereignty and began its gradual journey towards establishing a Republic in 1949.[19] Henceforth, the two parts of Ireland evolved separately, though connected in mutual hostility and incomprehension. One other factor affected the future of the relationship between the two parts of Ireland. The treaty between the United Kingdom and the Irish Nationalist movement acknowledged Northern Ireland's status but contained a commitment to establish a boundary commission to adjust the border between the two jurisdictions. Many Nationalists believed that the outcome of this deliberation would lead to the effective dismemberment of Northern Ireland, therefore making the region unmanageable. These hopes were to go unrealised. The commission's report (only published in 1969) was partially leaked in 1925 and was essentially a technical document recommending minor alterations to the border as it then stood. In the context the North would have fared better than the South, leading the Irish Free State to denounce the outcome but also providing the opportunity for the three governments to negotiate a formal agreement to sustain the existing boundaries in the Ireland (Confirmation of Agreement) Act of 1925.[20]

This latter agreement has been considered to be 'a significant agreement' and in some respects it was. It appeared to stabilise the territorial situation between North and South and to offer some hope for cordial relations between the two Irish governments. Yet it also highlighted the extent to which the two parts of Ireland were developing separately and did not provide a means for developing relationships between the two. Furthermore, the leaked report radicalised Nationalist opinion in the Irish Free State, making it more difficult to co-operate with the Northern government. This was reinforced by the existence of the nationalist minority in Northern Ireland, who were seen by southern Nationalists as hostages in a state alien to their identity but seen by the Unionists as a force hostile to the very existence of that state.[21]

THE CONSEQUENCES OF PARTITION

The Government of Ireland Act had quite different consequences to those intended by the British government. By devolving power to a parliament in Northern Ireland the act locked both Unionists and Nationalists into a conflict where the status of the state remained the central political issue. Unionists had been unhappy about devolved government, considering integration within the British state to be the best security for the future. In turn, Nationalists believed that the border was an imposed and artificial entity and refused for the most part to accept the legitimacy of the northern government. The basic political framework enhanced rather than reduced tensions within Northern Ireland. Whereas in the South the treaty settlement enhanced stability, in the North instability was built into the system by the presence of a sizeable minority hostile to the existence of the state, and a government in the South which continued to challenge the legitimacy of its northern neighbour – a feature which characterised policy after 1932 in particular. Consequently, conflict remained the main features of the politics of Northern Ireland.[22]

If, in a formal sense, Northern Ireland remained not only part of the United Kingdom and subordinate to Westminster, the relationship between the two parliaments was characterised by irresponsible neglect on the part of successive British governments and abuse of power within Northern Ireland by the Unionist governments. Westminster neglected the region, consistently refusing to invoke its power over the devolved government. In effect, the Northern Ireland Parliament was given almost total autonomy over the governing of the North. This led to the paradoxical outcome that in some areas the Northern Ireland Parliament was able to function as a state, while in others it was not. Thus formal sovereignty was retained at Westminster, yet successive British governments refused to intervene in northern affairs even when there was clear evidence that the Unionist government was behaving oppressively against the Nationalist minority. At the same time Northern Ireland cannot be considered a state: it certainly had a monopoly over the means of violence, but it did not have the required autonomy to function as an independent state. The autonomy to act that it acquired was a consequence of the neglect which the British governments considered to be proper policy in that case.[23]

The attraction for the Unionists of this situation was that while they might not have wanted a devolved government, once given the power this was exercised ruthlessly when required against their perceived enemies. The dilemma for the British government was that while it might not have welcomed this behaviour, it was not prepared to act against the Unionists. For 45 years the Northern Ireland government was permitted to function as an autonomous region within the British state, utilising resources, particularly military and judicial, which would not have been acceptable elsewhere in the United Kingdom. Time and again during that period British governments were faced with the same choice:

> the imperial government could do little to supervise the conduct of government in Northern Ireland. This incapacity was partly self-induced, arising from an unwillingness to become once more directly involved in Irish affairs and from a respect for the sovereignty of parliaments. But it was also, and very largely, based upon an appreciation of political realities. The plain fact was that there was no alternative government to call upon in Northern Ireland should the unionists resign in protest against the exercise of Westminster's sovereignty.[24]

Once the British government accepted the Unionists' right to self-government within the Six Counties, their choices were limited. However, they were not as powerless as this might imply. An assertion of authority on questions relating to policing, electoral mismanagement and civil rights would have made a significant difference to political outcomes in Northern Ireland and might have enhanced the legitimacy of the British government among the Nationalist minority. In a sense, Northern Ireland only operated as a state while Westminster permitted it to do so. That it did, in the way it did, was a result of the British government's unwillingness to become directly involved in the management of ethnic conflict.[25]

The management of ethnic conflict by imperial powers is notoriously difficult, and the British experience in Northern Ireland is no different in this respect than was to be the case subsequently in India, Palestine or Cyprus. The unique feature of Northern Ireland was that a majority in that region wanted to remain in the United Kingdom.

However, the difficulty arose with the minority in Northern Ireland which not only refused to accept the legitimacy of partition and the northern government, but was supported, alternately passively and actively, by successive Irish governments. The behaviour of the northern government may have alienated northern Nationalists, but the behaviour of Irish Free State governments reinforced the Nationalists' hostility to Unionism and enhanced the fears of the Unionists.[26] At first the government of the Irish Free State did attempt to develop more cordial relations with the northern government, but after 1932 with the election of a *Fianna Fáil* government this process ended.[27] The new government blamed the British government for partition and believed it was incumbent on Britain to resolve the problem. While it was never clear what steps the *Fianna Fáil* administration thought the British could pursue to achieve Irish unity, its public statements and its increasingly nationalistic legislation further divided North and South. In these circumstances the British government, given its policy of inaction in Northern Ireland, could do little. When in 1937 the Irish government introduced a new constitution which replaced the one imposed by the British in 1922, the British authorities could complain but do very little else. For the future the 1937 constitution is of importance as it institutionalised the Nationalist claim over Northern Ireland in articles 2 and 3 of the new document:

> Article 2: The National territory consists of the whole island of Ireland, its islands and the territorial seas.
>
> Article 3: Pending the re-integration of the national territory, and without prejudice to the right of the parliament and government established by this constitution to exercise jurisdiction over the whole of that territory, the laws enacted by the parliament shall have the like area and extend to application as the laws of Saorstat Eireann and the like extra-territorial effect.[28]

The British government complained about the claim implicit in these articles, but chose to ignore the demand contained in them. In 1938 during the negotiation of the Anglo-Irish Trade Agreements, the Irish government returned to the question of partition. De Valera argued that without an agreement on partition the talks would fail. In response to this Chamberlain insisted that 'the suspicion that the United Kingdom desired the disunity of Ireland was a profound delusion', adding:

the government of the United Kingdom had no desire to prevent in any way a free and voluntary agreement between the two Irish Governments on the subject if such an agreement could be reached.

The Dominions Secretary, Malcolm MacDonald, argued with de Valera that the partition of Ireland would not be changed even if the British withdrew all subsidies from the North. Interestingly, Chamberlain suggested that a transfer of population in border areas might help, but this was not pursued by the Irish government.[29]

One of the ironies of the policy of appeasement is that it was most successful in respect of the Irish Free State in 1938. Concern over the threat of a European war prompted Chamberlain to make considerable concessions to de Valera, including returning the treaty ports to the Irish. As a consequence of these agreements, the North took on a more strategic importance than heretofore. This certainly increased the negotiating power of the northern government, but even this had limits. When Britain announced its intention to introduce conscription in 1939, the Irish government successfully pressurised it not to include Irish people in Britain and to exclude Northern Ireland. Although Northern Ireland remained part of the United Kingdom, and its government wished to play a part in the war against Nazi Germany, the British government continued to treat it as a separate entity within the state. This can be best appreciated in 1940 when the British government offered to secure a united Ireland in return for Irish participation in the war effort. While de Valera rejected the offer, and there is considerable doubt concerning the ability of the British government to enforce its offer, it is clear that the northern government was seriously concerned that a British government under pressure was prepared to reconsider its relationship with the devolved government in Belfast.[30] While the nature of this 'offer' remains open to debate, the evidence suggests that British governments at various times were considering reopening the issue of Northern Ireland's status if that was required by the interests of the state.

Irish neutrality during the Second World War alienated British opinion from the Nationalists during the postwar years. At the same time the North entered a period of uncertainty with the election of a Labour government in the United Kingdom in 1945. The Labour Party remained committed to a united Ireland and had a well-organised pro-unity lobby on the back benches. Sir Basil Brooke, the northern Prime Minister, was certainly concerned about the political changes in

Westminster, believing that a socialist regime would not have much sympathy with the pro-Conservative Unionist government in Belfast. A Dominions Office report in 1945 was critical of the 'religious persecution' in Northern Ireland, while in 1947 during the Commons debate on the Northern Ireland Bill there was considerable criticism of the Unionists' record in respect of civil rights. Yet, as Brian Barton points out, Irish issues had a fairly low priority for the Labour government: the main focus of legislation was on economic and welfare legislation, indeed the Northern Ireland Bill itself was introduced to provide for the extension of British welfare and economic legislation to the North. In addition, the active participation of the North in the war effort persuaded many, including Attlee, that the Unionists were part of the British political system and should be treated as such. This, in fact, was to be the relationship between Northern Ireland and Westminster until the mid-1960s.[31]

The one direct involvement by the British government in Northern Ireland during this period was to secure the area as a part of the United Kingdom. This was a consequence of the decision by the Dublin government to declare a Republic and to leave the Commonwealth in 1949. There were a number of responses to this. The Unionist government called an election in the face of what it considered to be a threat to its integrity and won an impressive victory on the partition issue. The British government introduced legislation to regularise the position between it and the new Republic. The Ireland Act of 1949 declared that though Eire was no longer part of the dominions neither was it 'a foreign country for the purposes of any law in force in any part of the United Kingdom or in any colony, protectorate or United Kingdom trust territory'. The act also committed the British government to maintain the link between the North and the rest of the United Kingdom on the following terms:

> 1. (2) It is hereby declared that Northern Ireland remains part of His Majesty's dominions and of the United Kingdom and it is hereby affirmed that in no event will Northern Ireland or any part thereof cease to be part of His Majesty's dominions and of the United Kingdom without the consent of the Parliament of Northern Ireland.

The preamble to the act had made it categorically clear that the intention of this clause was 'to declare and affirm the constitutional position and the territorial integrity of Northern Ireland'. This is the direct source of the complaint by Nationalists that the Unionists have a veto over the future. Although most of the act concerned the Irish Republic, and indeed conceded a considerable amount to that state, it was these two elements of the act which drew criticism from Dublin. This led to the formation of an all-party anti-partition campaign, the revival of the Irish Republican Army (IRA) and perhaps also the IRA border campaign during the 1950s. During the furious exchanges which continued throughout the late 1940s and early 1950s the British government insisted that the Dublin government had no cause to complain about the British position in Northern Ireland nor did it have any privileged role to play in the region.[32]

Little changed between 1949 and 1966, by which time the civil rights movement had emerged in Northern Ireland. Attempts at reconciliation between Dublin and Belfast during the 1960s were warmly welcomed in London in the belief that closer relations between the two parts of the island would bring about accommodation. The proposed entry to the Common Market by the Irish Republic and the United Kingdom reinforced the belief that the border and partition might in time cease to be a dividing line between the two parts of Ireland. The initiatives, however, rested on rather fragile foundations. It remained an arrangement between elites which did not have deep roots on either side of the border. Polarisation between the two communities in Northern Ireland continued to be the main experience for the vast majority of people. The year 1966 is important in that it contributed to the revival of a more fundamentalist attitude on both sides of the border. The positions taken then and during the next two years did much to negate all the positive work by the two governments and by 1969 there was an effective return to polarisation.

NATIONAL IDENTITY AND RELIGIOUS POLARISATION IN NORTHERN IRELAND

The polarisation since 1969 is not new and its presence has frequently undermined British attempts to introduce change into the region. In contrast to Scotland or Wales, Northern Ireland remains a deeply divided society along ethno-religious lines. Whereas in Scotland and Wales, a majority in favour of devolution and new institutional arrangements will be respected by the minority, no such assurances can be given in Northern Ireland. The divisions are real and deep-rooted in the historical antagonism between two peoples with distinct world views. That both groups are Christian has often caused comment and condemnation, yet the failure to reach accommodation and agreement in Northern Ireland has everything to do with religious difference. Religion in Northern Ireland has been the template of difference for 300 years and the institutionalisation of these differences within Northern Ireland after 1920 simply engrained them deeper than ever. In this sense Northern Ireland can be compared with the former Yugoslavia and the Indian sub-continent where the existence of an external force restrained the conflicting groups, but, once political power was removed from the state and majority rule became the norm for decision making, those in a minority asserted their independent and separate identity.[33] Comparisons with consociational democracies, such as the Netherlands or Austria, are mistaken in Northern Ireland; more accurate comparisons can be made with Sri Lanka or the Lebanon where such arrangements failed to secure the necessary accommodation. In one, intercommunal conflict and attempted secession became the norm; in the other it was only the imposition of Syrian state power which led to a settlement of the conflicts between the different components. This is not to claim that change is impossible in Northern Ireland, but it is to claim that when national identity is central to the conflict and especially when it is expressed in religious terms, the likelihood of a 'solution' is much more remote. National identity in the Netherlands has not been in doubt and this provided the basis for a consociational solution; this condition is simply not available in the case of Northern Ireland – indeed it remains at the heart of the problem.[34]

By the time renewed violence broke out in 1968–69, little had changed formally in Northern Ireland. At the constitutional level the British government maintained its guarantees, but retained the right to exercise ultimate sovereignty, as it was to do in 1969 and again more emphatically in 1972. Successive Irish governments maintained the view that the only solution was a united Ireland. The revival of the IRA was not just a reflection of the polarisation of the two communities after 1968, but it was also the traditional response to intercommunal violence in Northern Ireland. Irish Nationalists had been effectively excluded from political influence in Northern Ireland, partly due to their own reluctance to legitimise the Unionist state but also due to the conscious strategy of the Unionists. Although an equilibrium was achieved between 1922 and 1966, it was one which remained unstable. The two communities remained polarised throughout this period. For the most part Nationalists and Unionists found themselves on opposite sides on virtually all the major political issues during the twentieth century and this reinforced both the confrontation with one another and the degree to which each side did not communicate with the other. During the Falklands War, for example, a significant section of nationalist opinion supported Argentina, while unionists emphasised the similarities between their position and that of the islanders.[35]

Voting patterns reflect this polarisation. Despite the introduction of proportional representation, there is little evidence that Nationalists or Unionists are likely to transfer votes to the other camp. Support for all the political parties is largely based on ethno-religious identity. Only the Alliance Party receives support from both Catholics and Protestants, but its vote normally does not exceed 10 per cent. Likewise on many major political issues Unionists and Nationalists display quite different attitudes. Most Unionists favour the death penalty, whereas Nationalists oppose it. When the IRA declared the first cease-fire in 1994, 92 per cent of Protestants believed that *Sinn Féin* should not be allowed to enter into political dialogue until the IRA had handed over its weapons; the comparable figure for Catholics was 46 per cent with 37 per cent maintaining that this would not be necessary. When asked whether the Irish government should have a say in the affairs of Northern Ireland, 70 per cent of Catholics agreed with this notion while 82 per cent of Protestants disagreed.[36]

A December 1993 poll, taken after the joint declaration between the two governments, further highlighted the differences between the two communities. When asked how they would vote in a referendum on the future status of Northern Ireland the breakdown reinforces the distance between the two communities. The overwhelming majority of Protestant voters wished to remain in the United Kingdom (over 90 per cent); in contrast 52 per cent of Catholic voters supported a united Ireland, but 28 per cent wished to remain in the United Kingdom.[37] This evidence suggest that whatever changes have taken place between the two sovereign governments, there has been remarkably little change in the disposition of opinion on the constitutional issue in Northern Ireland. Some writers have objected to this pessimistic approach on the grounds that there are significant differences between the political parties and 'ordinary' public opinion. The premise of this view is that there is an untapped 'non-sectarian' sentiment available across the communities which the political parties are subverting. The evidence that we have suggests that Rose's observation that both communities are socialised into violence and polarisation still holds. In fact, recent research suggests that segregation of the two communities has accelerated since 1969, especially in urban areas. For the most part the communities do not meet socially and spend most of their time within their own 'pillar' but without the benefits of consociationalism. What may be in place in Northern Ireland is pillarisation without consociationalism.[38]

This is closely linked to the different sense of identity held by the communities, and everything rests on this. Because identity is so divided within the region, it is unlike other regions of the United Kingdom where similar tensions do not appear. The complex nature of identity in Northern Ireland is closely linked to the data presented above. In 1994 71 per cent of Protestants considered themselves to be British, 3 per cent Irish, 11 per cent Ulster and 15 per cent Northern Irish. Among Catholics 62 per cent considered themselves to be Irish, 28 per cent to be Northern Irish and 10 per cent British. The boundaries of identity remain firmly established and may have become more segmented since the late 1960s. In 1968 Protestant identity was more fluid than in 1994, with some 39 per cent considering themselves British, 20 per cent Irish and 32 per cent Ulster. However, once Unionist identity was challenged there is a reassertion of Britishness on the part of the Protestant community, an identification which has remained fairly solid ever since. On the basis of this evidence, Gallagher has argued that there are three nations in Ireland (or alternatively two nations and a part of another one). Different interpretations are possible, but nevertheless polarisation remains deep and most importantly is closely associated with different senses of identity.[39]

The rather pessimistic conclusion is that little has changed in Northern Ireland. Despite the violence, the end of devolved government, the break-up of the Unionist Party and the emergence of *Sinn Féin* as an electoral force of some importance the same cleavages take precedence and people are politically deployed within their own historic ghettos. The source of the conflict remains deep-rooted ethno-religious divisions, which the society reflects and which has remained almost impermeable to change. Why this has been so, and the ineffectiveness of reform, is discussed in the next section. This account is not affected by the exceptional changes that occurred during 1999 and 2000, though as discussed in the final section is still not unwarranted.

THE FAILURE OF NORTHERN IRELAND AND BRITISH
ATTEMPTS AT REFORM

As a deeply segmented society Northern Ireland is not a problem which British politicians have found easy to deal with. Having ignored the difficulty for 45 years the collapse of the power of the Unionist government was not welcome to the Wilson or Heath governments, which was more concerned with 'mainland' matters such as industrial relations and welfare issues. Yet the circumstances for British government re-entry into Northern Ireland were aspects of a wider breakdown of public order and a challenge to political legitimacy during the late 1960s and early 1970s. The first stage of this response was to maintain the Unionist government in place but to insist on a number of reforms which , it was believed, would undercut the unrest and allow for a return to 'normality'. The entry of British troops into Northern Ireland in 1969, the decision to disband the paramilitary B-Specials and the reorganisation of the Royal Ulster Constabulary were all parts of this process. Nor did the change of government in 1970 challenge this approach. The Heath government maintained the view that what was required was continuing reform of institutions and close co-operation with the northern government. However, this failed for a number of reasons. In the first place ethnic conflicts in deeply segmented societies are always difficult to control, especially by outsiders. In addition, the British army in the North was not seen as neutral by either side and the organisation of the Provisional IRA increased the perception of the army as partisan. The Unionist Party was in crisis and its government could not be depended upon by any British government, for it was also partisan and seen to be so by a significant portion of the Nationalist population.

The introduction of internment by the British in 1971 on the advice of the Unionist government highlighted the failure of Unionism in this context. It did not recognise that the British government was not especially sympathetic to Unionism, and the failure of internment as a policy undermined further the legitimacy of the Unionist government in the eyes of British policy makers. By 1972 radical action was required and in the Northern Ireland (Temporary Provisions) Act of 1972 devolved government ended and direct rule by the British government was introduced. The legislation may have been conceived as temporary, but despite every effort on the part of successive British governments it proved impossible, prior to 1998, to generate a set of institutions in Northern Ireland which would command enough support to justify a return to devolved government. In this context, Northern Ireland provides an interesting example of the failure of reform in the face of ethnic segmentation and political polarisation. In general terms three approaches have been attempted in respect of Northern Ireland by British governments. The first of these is the legal/administrative approach. The approach here is to create new institutions and legal frameworks with the objective of establishing a framework within which 'progress' can occur. The weakness of this approach is that 'progress' is not always clearly defined, or, if it is, agreement cannot be secured for its objectives. The second method is to seek agreement among the political parties in Northern Ireland through all-party talks and then to establish the administrative means to facilitate this. Until 1998, all-party talks and consociational arrangements have all failed because agreement has always proved elusive. The third approach is intergovernmental and this has proved the most successful in terms of establishing new frameworks, but in the absence of all-party agreement within Northern Ireland there are limits to this strategy.

It is not the purpose of this chapter to review in detail the failed attempts at reform in Northern Ireland, but it is important to illustrate some of the examples to highlight why it has proved so difficult to achieve agreement. The Sunningdale Agreement of December 1973 was based on the assumption that power sharing between the communities, a constitutional guarantee for the Unionists and a Council of Ireland for the Nationalists would provide the means to secure support for new institutions and structures. It was an unprecedented move and at first seemed likely to succeed. Yet, at its heart, the initiative was flawed. Brian Faulkner, the leader of the Unionist Party believed that a Council of Ireland would destabilise Unionist opinion and in this he was correct. By February 1974 a majority of Unionist opinion in Northern Ireland had demonstrated electorally its opposition to the power-sharing government. The Nationalist view was that this should be ignored, but the British government was also under pressure from instability in Britain and was reluctant to use force. The Ulster workers' strike in May 1974 brought down the power-sharing executive which led to an escalation of the conflict and further polarisation. Subsequent attempts to return power to Northern Ireland either through the Northern Ireland Convention of 1975 (dissolved in March 1976), or rolling devolution and the Northern Ireland Assembly in 1982 failed in their intended purpose. The various initiatives associated with Peter Brooke and Sir Patrick Mayhew during the early 1990s did not at first achieve much progress, due to the continuation of violence by the IRA. However, it is clear in retrospect that these intiatives did lay the basis for further progress during the second half the 1990s.[40]

When the British government has not had to take direct account of the political parties in Northern Ireland, its initiatives have been far more successful. Most legislation for Northern Ireland is a result of Orders in Council and, for the most part, Northern Irish legislation is not scrutinised in Westminster in the same way as British legislation is. This has allowed for considerable flexibility in respect of direct rule. There have been significant advances in the introduction of anti-discrimination legislation to Northern Ireland. The Fair Employment (Northern Ireland) Act of 1976 and its 1989 successor act provided extensive powers for the Fair Employment Agency to investigate and prosecute discrimination on the grounds of religious and political opinion. The 1989 act has been described as 'the toughest and most extensive anti-discrimination measure passed by parliament', and 'is among a number of social, economic and political initiatives directed since the mid-1980s at the roots of conflict in the province'.[41] In these and other matters direct rule has had an important impact on the socio-political environment in Northern Ireland. Yet few enough of these changes have affected the polarisation of the communities or the political parties. For example, the decision to establish a Northern Ireland Affairs Select Committee in 1993 was opposed by the Labour Party and by the Social Democratic and Labour Party (SDLP) on the grounds that it was a trade-off between the Unionists and the British government for the former's support of the Conservative Party in the Maastricht vote in 1993. Yet in 1990 and again in 1993 the all-party Procedure Committee had recommended the establishment of a select committee for Northern Ireland on the grounds that in the context of the United Kingdom its isolation in this respect was anomalous in comparison with Wales and Scotland. The select committee has the same responsibilities and powers as other committees and in that sense places Northern Ireland in the same relationship to Westminster as other regions of the United Kingdom. The real objection to the select committee is based on Nationalist opposition to any action which would integrate Northern Ireland further into the United Kingdom.[42]

The other impact of Northern Ireland on the British political system has been the continuing refusal of parties organised in Britain to extend membership to Northern Ireland. The Labour Party has consistently refused to do so. However, in a successful campaign against the leadership, grass-roots Conservatives succeeded in persuading the 1989 Conservative Party conference to support party organisation in Northern Ireland.[43]

There has also been a significant shift in British policy since the election of Margaret Thatcher in 1979. The paradox here is that a party with a strong Unionist tradition and a Prime Minister personally attracted to the integrationist position on Northern Ireland should enter into new and quite important intergovernmental arrangements with an Irish government. There are a number of factors which help to explain this. The most important was Margaret Thatcher's notion of the state. For her the focus of policy was on the state as a whole, of which Northern Ireland was but a part. While she was personally more sympathetic to the Unionist case than her Labour predecessors, or some of her colleagues, there were limits to this in policy terms. The defence of the realm was more significant by 1985 than maintaining Unionist support. This general factor was reinforced by a belief that Britain could reach an accommodation with the Irish government on security issues and on a political framework for progress. Further influences include the successful diplomatic offensive waged by the Irish government especially under the Taoiseach Garret Fitzgerald in 1984–85, concern with the electoral success of *Sinn Féin* in the aftermath of the hunger strikes and disillusionment with the actions of Unionism.[44] This recognition that intergovernmental arrangements could deliver a measure of co-operation had been absent during the 1970s, but during the 1980s the basis for widespread agreement was established. In 1981 the two governments set up the Anglo-Irish Intergovernmental Council with membership drawn from both states. This co-operation did not emerge easily or quickly however. Indeed, the decision by the Irish government to convene the New Ireland Forum as a Nationalist response to the electoral rise of *Sinn Féin* was independent of relations with Britain. Furthermore, Thatcher openly rejected the findings of the forum in 1984 on the grounds that none of them was acceptable to her notions of sovereignty. Despite this, the institutional work was already in place before this for a change in policy. This was implicit in the Northern Ireland Act of 1982 and more especially in the 1982 White Paper *Northern Ireland: A Framework for Devolution*, part of James Prior's rolling-devolution strategy. Though Prior was replaced by Douglas Hurd as Secretary of State in August 1984, the contours of policy were in place and maintained by him through to the Anglo-Irish Agreement in 1985. Prior's intention between 1982 and 1984 was to create a momentum for negotiations between the parties in Northern Ireland in the hope that co-operation would be facilitated. He recognised too that an Irish dimension was also required to make co-operation work. The failure of this approach to create the conditions for internal agreement persuaded Thatcher that an intergovernmental approach might improve the security position and isolate *Sinn Féin.*[45]

The Anglo-Irish Agreement did not deliver what Thatcher and the British government hoped it would. Meanwhile, the establishment of the Intergovernmental Conference and its secretariat (article 2 (b)) gave the Irish government a significantly enhanced role within Northern Ireland and over the British administration of direct rule.[46] For the SDLP, in particular, the agreement was a vehicle for achieving a united Ireland, a view endorsed as a 'constitutional imperative' by the Irish Supreme Court in 1990.[47] For the Unionists the agreement widened the gap between them and the British government and alienated them from the political and negotiating process until the mid-1990s. Although the British government did not achieve its aims, the agreement continued in place on the grounds that it facilitated negotiations between the two states and, perhaps, offer a bargaining chip to Unionists in the event of movement on an internal settlement. The extent of British disquiet can be appreciated in Ken Hind's attack on the Irish government for its failure to deliver on the security aspects of the agreement, pointing out that violence was at a much higher level in 1991 than in 1985.[48]

Peter Brooke's appointment as Secretary of State in July 1989 generated new momentum in the Northern Ireland process. Although the Anglo-Irish Agreement remained in place, there was an effective stalemate in the process. In introducing the 'three-strand' approach to the North, Brooke hoped to bring about movement which would allow all the parties to co-operate. While he was anxious to include the Unionists in this process, his most significant contribution was the insistence that a British government would accept Irish unity if it was consensual and that there was a place at the negotiations for the Republican movement if it eschewed violence. This was a view which had been promoted with some vigour by the leader of the SDLP, John Hume.[49] Brooke's successor, Sir Patrick Mayhew, continued this approach though the tone and substance of his politics were subtly different from Brooke's. In July 1992 he openly and contemptuously condemned the behaviour of Orange marchers – an uncharacteristic attack by a British minister on a central symbol of Unionism. More importantly, in September 1992 he tabled a paper during the talks process which advocated the need for an 'agreed Ireland', and the desirability of North/South institutions, while recommending the establishment of an Irish government office in Belfast and a Northern Ireland office in Dublin. While this paper was withdrawn under Unionist pressure, the change in emphasis in British policy and intentions was widely noted. Furthermore, in a speech in Coleraine in December 1992, Mayhew appealed to *Sinn Féin* to renounce violence and to enter the negotiations. He insisted that the government's role was of a 'facilitator' in any negotiations, implying that it was neutral as to outcome. This speech takes on greater importance in the context of a later revelation that *Sinn Féin* had a preview of its content as early as October.[50] In response to Unionist criticism of his role as Secretary of State Mayhew was at pains to insist that the government was not adopting joint rule with Dublin as an objective. In a speech in April 1993 Mayhew maintained that the status quo would be upheld by the government, while adding an interesting 'but':

> there is no prospect of an agreement precluding a politically united Ireland if, at some future date, the public's view should change. The key to the whole issue is public opinion in Northern Ireland, which would be decisive.[51]

This speech might be open to a number of interpretations, but the intention was to register the British government's commitment to open-ended negotiations on the future of the North.

SUCCESSFUL ANGLO-IRISH CO-OPERATION

This movement in British attitudes has to be placed in a wider perspective. Irish opinion had also moved considerably since the Anglo-Irish Agreement. The Irish Minister for Foreign Affairs, Dick Spring, announced Six Principles upon which his government believed progress could be made. Although general in form, their content was important as they included a commitment to accept the right of Unionists to withhold consent to a united Ireland.[52] In November 1993 it was announced that *Sinn Féin* and the British government had been in communication in an attempt to secure an end to violence. According to the British a genuine end to violence, 'whether or not that fact had been announced', would lead to dialogue. Government policy on this issue was outlined in detail in a letter dated 19 March 1993:

> the British government has no desire to inhibit or impede legitimate constitutional expression of any political opinion, or

any input to the political process, and wants to see included in this process all main parties which have sufficiently shown they genuinely do not espouse violence. It has no blueprint. It wants an agreed accommodation, not an imposed settlement, arrived at through an inclusive process in which the parties are free agents.

While the British government would not enter the negotiations with a commitment to the 'ending of partition':

Should this [a united Ireland] be the eventual outcome of a peaceful democratic process, the British government would bring forward legislation to implement the will of the people here. But unless the people of Northern Ireland come to express such a view, the British government will continue to uphold the union, seeking to ensure the good governance of Northern Ireland.[53]

The Downing Street Declaration, (formerly Joint Agreement for Peace) agreed on 15 December 1993, advanced the intergovernmental process further. The general intention of the declaration was to provide the means for the IRA to end its campaign of violence and to establish the basis for all-party discussions. The detail of the declaration has been discussed elsewhere, but the British government in paragraph 4 maintained the views outlined in the exchange with the IRA earlier in the year and:

reiterated, on behalf of the British government, that they have no selfish strategic or economic interest in Northern Ireland. Their primary interest is to see peace, stability and reconciliation established by agreement among all the people who inhabit the island, and they will work together with the Irish Government to achieve such an agreement, which will embrace the totality of relationships. The role of the British government will be to encourage, facilitate and enable the achievement of such agreement over a period through a process of dialogue and co-operation based on full respect for the rights and identities of both traditions in Ireland.[54]

One conclusion which can be drawn from these commitments is that the British government has accepted the rubric of the Irish government in presenting its case on Northern Ireland. There is a token insistence that the constitutional status of Northern Ireland will be accepted, but this is not framed in the language of Unionism which one finds in Conservative Party policy on Scotland or Wales. In this important sense Northern Ireland remains outside the Union for Conservative policy makers. It is a passive rather than an active support for the Union.[55]

The declaration was successful in achieving one of its aims. Despite the IRA's rejection of the declaration, it came under serious pressure to call a cease-fire. This was achieved on 31 August 1994, preparing the ground for further negotiations. On 22 February 1995 the two governments agreed to *A Joint Declaration*, comprising two documents. The first of these, *The New Framework for Agreement* outlined in detail the commitments of the two governments on agreed matters, especially constitutional. The second, *A Framework for Accountable Government in Northern Ireland*, presented the position of the British government on how local accountability might be returned to Northern Ireland and the conditions for achieving this. According to the British government, any new institutions would have to be based on democratic principles, but would not be simply majoritarian. This was justified on the grounds that any institution would have to provide 'an appropriate and equitable role for both sides of the community, such that the main parts of the Northern Ireland community should be able to identify with them and feel their representatives have a meaningful function to perform'. Of considerable importance is the belief that a stable and durable outcome could not be 'dependent on a particular election result or political deal. The system should, so far as possible, be self-sustaining.' Developments would have to achieve widespread agreement and polarisation would have to be avoided. The commitment to consociational arrangements is serious and deep. Institutions created under these circumstances would have to:

> provide all the constitutional parties with the opportunity to achieve a role at each level of responsibility, and to have a position proportional to their electoral strength in broad terms.

In effect, the government accepted that the Westminster model simply does not apply in deeply segmented societies and the various possible arrangements suggested reflect this reality in detail. An assembly with 90 members would be established alongside an executive with specific powers for devolved government in Northern Ireland. Elections would be on the basis of proportional representation while a separate panel of three people would also be elected to complement the working of the assembly. Assembly committees would reflect the strength of the parties in the assembly. Detailed checks and balances would be introduced, including weighted majority voting in the committees in the region of 65 to 70 per cent. While many matters would be transferred to the new assembly and executive (the government seems to have had the 1973 power-sharing model in mind), law and order and raising public expenditure would remain in the hands of the Secretary of State. The document also outlined the governments' recognition of the equality of both political traditions in Northern Ireland, recognising in particular the Nationalist right to work for a united Ireland. Annex B offered 'An Outline of a Comprehensive Settlement' drawing together the main elements of the proposals discussed above. New North/South bodies would be established and it was envisaged that the relationship at the administrative level would be denser than that of the Anglo-Irish Agreement. This would require the latter to be replaced by a new agreement between the two governments to reflect the changing circumstances.[56]

The Downing Street Declaration and the *Framework* documents provided the foundations for a renewed drive to 'solve' the Northern Ireland problem. They also established a consensus upon which the two governments agreed to work. Tony Blair and the Labour Party, which adopted a fairly consistent bipartisan approach to Ireland, have extended this consensus. As part of his campaign to modernise the Labour Party, Blair also de-emphasised the party's commitment to Irish unity, adopting the role of facilitator rather than persuader. This pragmatism alienated some sections of the party but is an indication that Labour policy on Northern Ireland did not differ appreciably from that of the Conservative government by the time of the 1997 general election.[57] While the groundwork for change had been established, it was more insecure than at first thought. Though Nationalist politicians insisted that the IRA would not return to violence, British and Unionist politicians wanted greater proof and John Major in particular maintained that an indication that the IRA would decommission arms was required. This was not forthcoming during 1995 and the situation gradually deteriorated. Despite the cease-fire, polarisation between the communities continued, especially during the Orange marching season in 1995. A proposed summit between the two Prime Ministers collapsed in September 1995, leading to a crisis in Anglo-Irish relations. The report of the Mitchell Commission on decommissioning in January 1996 did not resolve the situation. John Major's response to it was considered inadequate by Nationalists and his call for elections was at first rejected by the Nationalist parties. The IRA response to this was to resume its campaign of violence in February 1996, a decision which was widely condemned, but with different nuances.

The end of the IRA cease-fire prompted responses that were entirely predictable and based on ethnic identity. Nationalists blamed the British rather than the IRA, while Unionists believed their position had been vindicated.[58] The two governments quickly responded and after an Anglo-Irish Summit on 28 February 1996 agreed to a strict timetable to re-establish negotiations. This involved intensive consultations with the political parties, but if no agreement could be reached an election would be held prior to the beginning of all-party negotiations on 10 June 1996. However, the election to the Northern Ireland Forum and to all-party negotiations resolved few of the outstanding difficulties. *Sinn Féin* was excluded from the negotiations because of the failure of the IRA to reinstate its cease-fire. Unionists objected to the proposed appointment of former United States Senator George Mitchell as chairman of the talks process. Furthermore, the confrontations which became a feature of the Orange Order's 'marching season' in July and August led to a serious deterioration of relations between Nationalists and Unionists by September. As the negotiations opened again on 9 September, the prospects for progress were not good.[59]

The British public response to this was one of exasperation. This can be seen in the opinion polls. Around 50 per cent of the British public want troops removed from Northern Ireland, while political independence for the region is the option most favoured by them. In a 1994 Gallup poll, some 44 per cent of respondents considered events in Northern Ireland to be taking place in another country.[60] In effect, although the British public will not actually expel Northern Ireland from the United Kingdom it has little interest in retaining the region. This is why successive British governments have been able to experiment with Northern Ireland and treat it as a distinct and separate entity within the United Kingdom since 1920, but especially since 1972. As has been argued above, the problem in Northern Ireland cannot be construed in reformist terms because the essential ingredients for successful reform are missing.[61] While the institutional structure of the region has been significantly changed this has had little impact on the polarisation between the two communities. What this demonstrates in a British context is that it is possible to reform the institutional, political and legislative environment without these changes affecting the dynamics that led to the decision to introduce reforms. The reason for this is that the basis for agreement to make the reforms work within and between the communities has rarely existed at any time since 1920. Thus, it is mistaken to deal with Northern Ireland in the context of the British reform tradition; a more appropriate response is one which accepts that the conflict reflects deeply felt ethno-religious divisions which often manifest themselves in sectarian fashion. Such an approach would allow for Northern Ireland to be placed in a wider framework, but one which begins to assess the real nature of the conflict and the difficulty of dealing with polarised communities. The main difficulties encountered in seeking a resolution to the conflict in Northern Ireland have been internal. Either Nationalists or Unionists have refused to endorse agreements reached by the two governments. Recent developments indicate that the British and Irish governments have begun to appreciate the nature of the difficulties and to address this. This has entailed recognition that the management of the conflict by the two governments can establish the basis for constitutional change, but other factors are required for this to be successful.

The Downing Street Declaration and the Framework documents established a political environment within which both governments could persuade the non-governmental actors, especially the paramilitary groups, to join in realistic negotiations. The key players in this were the IRA and Sinn Féin, though the significance of the loyalist paramilitaries should not be ignored. It was recognised by all participants that without a cease-fire by the IRA, Sinn Féin would not be included in the multi-party negotiations. Little was achieved prior to the general elections in the United Kingdom in May 1997 and in the Irish Republic in June. Tony Blair made it clear in a major speech in Belfast on 16 May, just two weeks after his election, that the incoming government would pursue the same policy as the Conservatives. He stressed that he supported the Union and that he did not expect to see a united Ireland in the lifetime of the youngest person present. He also gave the IRA a five-week deadline to announce another cease-fire, promising that if this happened Sinn Féin could enter the negotiations which he believed could be concluded by May 1998. Blair's close identification with the peace process surprised many nationalists, including leading politicians in the Republic. They were sceptical that the new Prime Minister could achieve the goal that had eluded his predecessors. However, most Irish politicians (both Nationalist and Unionist) underestimated Blair's commitment to changing the Labour Party and its traditional policies, including achieving a united Ireland. Blair recognised that this was unrealistic and therefore should be abandoned, but he also appreciated that the aim was an obstacle to peace itself, as it continued to present Irish unity as a realistic prize to the IRA. The new negotiations attempted to cut across this by offering an agreement that would provide the conditions for cross community consensus on the immediate future of Northern Ireland. Under internal and external pressure the IRA did announce a cease-fire in July 1997 and as a consequence Sinn Féin was included in the negotiations shortly after. While there was some scepticism about Blair's timetable for the negotiations, as well as considerable difficulties inside and outside the process, the multi-party talks reached agreement in April 1998.[62]

The *Belfast Agreement*, 10 April 1998 (more popularly known as the Good Friday Agreement) draws on the earlier documents and sets out to provide the basis for consensus in Northern Ireland while recognising the need to secure majorities within both communities. The Agreement is a major diplomatic success for the British and Irish governments and establishes a political environment within Northern Ireland which for the first time is genuinely inclusive. In the 'Declaration of Support', the participants to the multi-party negotiations openly recognise 'the substantial differences between our continuing, and equally legitimate political aspirations', while agreeing to pursue them within a constitutional context. Moreover, all the parties accept that the future of Northern Ireland can only be determined by the will of the majority within that area and a recognition that at the time of the Agreement the majority wish to remain within the Union. The British government agreed to introduce legislation to clarify the constitutional position of Northern Ireland within the United Kingdom. These read:

> 1. (1) It is hereby declared that Northern Ireland in its entirety remains part of the United Kingdom and shall not cease to be so without the consent of a majority of the people of Northern Ireland voting in a poll held for the purposes of this section in accordance with Schedule 1.
> (2) But if the wish expressed by a majority in such a poll is that Northern Ireland should cease to be part of the United Kingdom and form part of a united Ireland, the Secretary of State shall lay before Parliament such proposals to give effect to that wish as may be agreed between Her Majesty's Government in the United Kingdom and the Government of Ireland.
> 2. The Government of Ireland Act 1920 is repealed; and this Act shall have the effect notwithstanding any other previous enactment.

The schedule provides for a referendum to determine the will of the people of Northern Ireland, but an interval of seven years must pass after one has taken place before another can be called.[63]

To complement this the Irish government agreed to hold a referendum to amend a number of articles in its constitution. In particular articles 2 and 3 would be substantially rewritten and an aspiration to unity put in place of the original irredentist claim. Despite this commitment, the Irish government still does not recognise British sovereignty in Northern Ireland. The Agreement is a lengthy one and its details will not be documented in full here.[64] There are three strands to the Agreement. The first, and probably the most innovative in the context of British constitutional history, addresses the issue of inclusive institutions in Northern Ireland. Devolved government in Northern Ireland is a marked departure from the British constitutional tradition, and quite unlike devolution in Scotland and Wales. Consensus between the two communities in consociational fashion is essential to the system. Elections to the Assembly are by a proportional representation (single transferable vote) system, while each elected member must register as a nationalist, unionist or other. It is intended that this will provide for the smooth operation of voting in the Assembly. Decisions can only be made on the basis of simultaneous majorities in each community or a weighted majority (60 per cent), but this must include 40 per cent of nationalist and unionist members present and voting. These are important changes, for they remove the possibility that one community could impose its will on the other by the use of a simple majority. The system is clearly designed to bring about consensus, though that can only be guaranteed by the continuing involvement of the various parties within the Assembly. Indeed, at every level of government, proportionality is explicitly included in the framework.

The second strand creates a *North–South Ministerial Council*, which is a long-standing demand of the Irish goverment and nationalists in Northern Ireland. This provides an all-Ireland context for discussion and agreement between ministers from Northern Ireland and the Irish Republic. Any decision taken will have to be ratified by the Northern Assembly and Dáil Eireann, though at the moment its suggested remit is confined to a number of social, economic and cultural matters considered to be of concern to both parts of the island. Specific safeguards are included in the Agreement to prevent opponents from undermining its functioning and it is made explicit that 'participation in the Council to be one of the essential responsibilities attaching to relevant posts in the two administrations.'

The third strand establishes a *British and Irish Council* that includes not only representatives of the British and Irish governments, but also representation from the devolved institutions in Northern Ireland, Britain, the Isle of Man and the Channel Islands. At the time of writing, the operations of this Council remain unclear and its role vague. In contrast to the *North–South Minsterial Council*, the *British–Irish Council* lacks focus and is much weaker, politically and institutionally. In effect, it is an optional extra, one that does not currently carry with it any of the strong imperatives contained in strand one or two. In addition to these three strands, the Agreement provides that issues such as decommissioning, policing, the justice system and prisoners will be addressed as part of the process. Furthermore, a new Intergovernmental Conference will replace the institutions established under the 1985 Anglo-Irish Agreement. This move maintains the crucial role already established by the two sovereign governments, providing further security and assurances to both sided.

The *Belfast Agreement* advanced the prospects for peace in Northern Ireland considerably. Much of what it contained had been in the public domain for some time, what was important was the broad spectrum of support that it received. It was endorsed by the simultaneous referendums that took place in Northern Ireland and the Irish Republic on 22 May 1998, and was followed by elections in Northern Ireland to the Assemby on 25 June. The Assembly elections demonstrated that, despite the endorsement gained in the referendums, a significant minority of unionists voters continued to view the peace process with suspicion. Despite this, David Trimble was elected First Minister, while Seamus Mallon was elected to be Deputy First Minister. In September, the Assembly met in 'shadow' mode prior to establishing a fully devolved government for the province. While developments were positive at first, most unionists were deeply concerned at the prospect of the pro-Agreement unonists sharing cabinet office with Sinn Féin. The spectre of Sunningdale and the Ulster Workers' Council haunted the new Executive and the Agreement itself, a reminder that in 1973–4 a consensual government was unable to maintain the support of the majority of Unionists. This in turn led to the collapse of power sharing government in Northern Ireland for 25 years. The main danger to a consociational arrangement in Northern Ireland is that a majority of unionists will shift their support to the anti-Agreement camp, a threat that David Trimble has had to take into account during the eighteen months since his election as First Minister. While time may help in consolidating Unionist support for power sharing, it would be dangerous to conclude that this can be guaranteed, as events during the first half of 2000 demonstrate.

This helps to explain his reluctance to agree to the establishment of an Executive without the clear commitment on the part of the IRA to decommission its arms. That this was not forthcoming created a major crisis during the second half of 1999. The compromise, which emerged, was a delicate one, but it did allow for the formation of the Executive with Sinn Féin participation. However, the weakness at the heart of the compromise became evident quite quickly. Trimble persuaded his party to endorse participation with Sinn Féin on the understanding that the IRA would begin to decommission its arms within a specific time, generally understood to be at the end of January 2000. Although Trimble gained a majority for his strategy, it was narrow and there was no guarantee he could maintain this. Consequently, he promised to resign if the IRA did not act in response to the unionist shift in its position. In the circumstances the Executive lasted just eight weeks, at the end of which the new Secretary of State, Peter Mandelson, suspended the Executive rather than allow Trimble to resign as threatened. The decision to suspend was based on the report of the Independent International Commission on Decommissioning (IICD) chaired by the Canadian General John de Chastelain issue on 31 January 2000. The IICD was not in a position to report progress, as 'we have received no information from the IRA as to when decommissioning will start'. Under pressure, another report was issued on 11 February, after discussions with the IRA's representative, and while different emphasis was placed on its significance it did not prevent the suspension of the Executive.[65]

Although Trimble indicated that he had reached an understanding with Sinn Féin over decommissioning prior to the formation of the Executive, this was denied by Sinn Féin who insisted that their only commitments were those contained in the Belfast Agreement. The IRA's response to the suspension including breaking off contact with the IICD and 'withdrawing all propositions put to the IICD by our representatives since November'. In an angry interview in early March Sinn Féin's chairman Mitchel McLaughlin not only maintained that no agreement had been reached with David Trimble but that the IRA could not give up its arms because the war was not over.[66] Sinn Féin continues to blame Mandelson on the grounds that his decision endorses a new unionist veto. But the Dublin government was also critical of the decision and while its position is unclear at the time of writing a certain hardening in its position is evident. Within the unionist camp, Trimble is under renewed political pressure and it will be more difficult for him to gain support for a further compromise short of decommissioning. This should not be surprising given the history of polarisation within Northern Ireland. Consociational arrangements are delicate compromises, which require considerable nuance to work. When Trimble persuaded his party to support Sinn Féin's inclusion in the Executive he anticipated a reciprocal response from Sinn Féin and the IRA. On the evidence to date it would appear that either Trimble was misled by Sinn Féin or that the pro-Agreement section of Sinn Féin could not persuade the IRA that movement on this issue should be part of the compromise. If consociational success is based on institutional arrangements plus implicit agreements then the Belfast Agreement failed its latest test. The agreement to re-establish the Executive provides a more optimistic basis for progress and confidence building, though major obstacles in the future, which could threaten the cohesion of the Executive, cannot be ruled out.

Despite this continuing setback, considerable progress has been achieved. The contribution of Tony Blair and the Secretary of State Mo Mowlam to the success of this process should not be underestimated, nor should the more recent involvement of Peter Mandelson. They have simultaneously retained bi-partisanship in Westminster, deepened co-operation with the Irish government and, most importantly, persuaded most nationalists and unionists of the legitimacy of the changes. This has been an immense achievement by any standard. A peaceful outcome is not inevitable, especially as Sinn Féin and the IRA continue to be reluctant to give up the revolutionary alternative to democratic politics, but its chances have been enhanced since 1998. Yet, for the British state there is some ambiguity in this. Blair had adopted a reform strategy for the United Kingdom, one in which constitutional changes takes priority. It is possible that the recent changes will prove satisfactory and stabilise politics around the implementation of devolved government. This is by no means certain, a majority demand for Scottish secession or Northern Ireland's integration into the Irish Republic moves the process beyond reform and in to qualitatively new political terrain. While change in Scotland is a purely internal matter, this is not the case for Northern Ireland. Here a sovereign state exercises considerable influence (if not yet joint-sovereignty) within the institutions of devolved government and a significant minority of the population is allied to the foreign power. The political demand of this (current) minority cannot be met within the reform tradition, as it will require ending the Union. It remains possible that a workable devolved and consensual government in Northern Ireland will acquire widespread legitimacy and secure the province within the United Kingdom for the forseeable future. But if it does not, it may be that a reforming government will administer the break up of the British state at the beginning of the twenty-first century.

NOTES

1. Edmund Burke, *Reflections on the Revolution in France*, ed. Conor Cruise O'Brien (Harmondsworth: Penguin, 1968), p. 106; Thomas Babinton Macaulay, 'Speech delivered in the House of Commons on the 2nd of March, 1831' in Lord Macaulay, *The Miscellaneous Writings and Speeches* (London: Longmans, Green and Co., 1891), pp. 483–92; citation can be found at pp. 485 and 492; Robert Peel, 'Address to the Electors of the Borough of Tamworth' in Philip W. Buck (ed.), *How Conservatives Think* (Harmondsworth: Penguin, 1975), pp. 56–8.
2. Conor Cruise O'Brien, *The Great Melody: A Thematic Biography of Edmund Burke* (London: Sinclair-Stevenson, 1992), pp. 468–503.
3. Brian Girvin, *The Right in the Twentieth Century: Conservatism and Democracy* (London: Pinter, 1994), pp. 40–45 for a discussion of the nineteenth-century origins of the reforming movement.
4. John Morison and Stephen Livingstone, *Reshaping Public Power: Northern Ireland and the British Constitutional Crisis* (London: Sweet & Maxwell, 1995), p. 4 for the Dickens citation.
5. See the discussion in Morison and Livingstone, *Reshaping Public Power*, pp. 35–88; Tom Nairn, *After Britain: New Labour and the Return of Scotland* (London: Granta, 2000).
6. Keith M. Dowding and Richard Kimber, 'The Meaning and Use of "Political Stability"', *European Journal of Political Research,* 11, 3 (1983), pp. 229–43.
7. Girvin, *The Right in the Twentieth Century*, pp. 49–53.
8. Vernon Bogdanor, *Devolution in the United Kingdom* (Oxford: Oxford University Press, 1999), pp. 55–81.
9. D. George Boyce and Alan O'Day (eds), *Parnell in Perspective* (London: Routledge, 1991) for a number of contributions concerning the consequences of devolution.
10. Anthony D. Smith, *National Identity* (London: Penguin, 1991)
11. T. G. Fraser, *Partition in Ireland, India and Palestine* (London: Macmillan, 1984); Thomas Hennessey, *Dividing Ireland: World War I and Partition* (London: Routledge, 1998).
12. D. George Boyce, *Englishmen and Irish Troubles: British Public Opinion and the Making of Irish Policy, 1918–1922* (London: Cape, 1972)
13. Judith M. Brown, *Modern India: The Origins of an Asian Democracy* (Oxford: Oxford University Press, 1985), pp. 187–242.
14. Arthur Aughey, 'Conservative Party Policy and Northern Ireland' in Brian Barton and Patrick J. Roche (eds), *The Northern Ireland Question: Perspectives and Policies* (Aldershot: Avebury, 1994), pp. 121–50.
15. Graham Walker, *Intimate Strangers: Political and Cultural Interaction Between Scotland and Ulster in Modern Times* (Edinburgh: John Donald, 1995) for an

evaluation of some of these themes.

16. PRO: CAB 24/92, First Report of the Cabinet Committee on the Irish Question, 4 November 1919; Cabinet Meeting PRO: CAB 23/18, 3 December 1919, cited in Fraser, *Partition in Ireland*, pp. 27–30.

17. Richard Murphy, 'Walter Long and the Making of the Government of Ireland Act, 1919–20', *Irish Historical Studies*, 25, 97 (1986), pp. 82–96.

18. Fraser, *Partition in Ireland*, p. 37.

19. David W. Harkness, *The Restless Dominion: The Irish Free State and the British Commonwealth of Nations, 1921–31* (London: Macmillan, 1969); W. K. Hancock, *Survey of British Commonwealth Affairs, Volume I, Problems of Nationality, 1918–36* (London: Oxford University Press, 1937).

20. Geoffrey Hand (ed.), *Report of the Irish Boundary Commission, 1925* (Shannon: Irish University Press, 1969).

21. David Harkness, *Ireland in the Twentieth Century: Divided Island* (Basingstoke: Macmillan, 1996), p. 46; Paul Bew, Peter Gibbon and Henry Patterson, *Northern Ireland, 1921–1994: Political Forces and Social Classes* (London: Serif, 1995 new edn).

22. Brian Follis, *A State Under Siege: The Establishment of Northern Ireland 1920–25* (Oxford: Clarendon Press, 1995); Eamon Phoenix, *Northern Nationalism: Nationalist Politics, Partition and the Catholic Minority in Northern Ireland 1890–1940* (Belfast: Ulster Historical Foundation, 1994).

23. Patrick Buckland, *The Factory of Grievances: Devolved Government in Northern Ireland 1921–39* (Dublin: Gill & Macmillan, 1979); D. W. Miller, *Queen's Rebels* (Dublin: Gill & Macmillan, 1978).

24. Buckland, *Factory of Grievances*, p. 275; Follis, *A State Under Siege.*

25. Brian Girvin, 'National Identity and Conflict in Northern Ireland' in Brian Girvin and Roland Stürm (eds), *Politics and Society in Contemporary Ireland* (Aldershot: Gower, 1986), pp. 105–34.

26. Dennis Kennedy, *The Widening Gulf: Northern Attitudes to the Independent Irish State 1919–49* (Belfast: Blackstaff Press, 1988), pp. 133–240.

27. Harkness, *Restless Dominion*; Kennedy, *Widening Gulf.*

28. *Bunreacht na hÉireann (Constitution of Ireland) 1937* (Dublin: Stationery Office, 1980).

29. National Archives Dublin, Department of the Taoiseach: S.10389, Annex: Transfer of Ports, Finance and Trade Agreements, Conference in London, minutes of meeting 17th January 1938.

30. J. J. Lee, *Ireland 1912–1985: Politics and Society* (Cambridge: Cambridge University Press, 1989), pp. 248–51; Brian Girvin, 'Politics in Wartime: Governing, Neutrality and Elections', in Brian Girvin and Geoff Roberts (eds), *Ireland and the Second World War: Politics, Society and Remembrance* (Dublin: Four Courts, 2000), pp. 24–46.

31. Brian Barton, 'Relations between Westminster and Stormont during the Atlee premiership', *Irish Political Studies* 7 (1992), pp. 1–20.

32. Dermot Keogh, *Twentieth-Century Ireland: Nation and State* (Dublin: Gill & Macmillan, 1994), pp. 185–213 for a discussion of this relationship.

33. Andrew Adonis suggested to me that Cyprus might provide a better comparison than Yugoslavia or India. The point to be emphasised in all cases is that beneath an apparent stability or cordial inter-ethnic relations, deep resentment remain.

34. Girvin, 'National Identity and Conflict in Northern Ireland'; although this is

a historical observation, its continuing relevance in early 2000, despite considerable progress in conflict resolution, reinforces the point.

35. Girvin, 'National Identity and Conflict in Northern Ireland', pp. 116–17; Richard Rose, *Governing Without Consensus* (London: Faber & Faber, 1971), p. 334. The Fianna Fáil government had reluctantly agreed to support EC sanctions against Argentina after its invasion of the Falklands islands. Once the *Belgrano* was sunk the government refused to support sanctions and one Minister condemned the British as the aggressor in the conflict.

36. For detail see 'Data Section', *Irish Political Studies*, 10 (1995).

37. 'Data Section', *Irish Political Studies*, 9 (1994), p. 225.

38. Rose, *Governing Without Consensus*; Kevin Boyle and Tom Hadden, *Northern Ireland: The Choice* (London: Penguin, 1994); Andy Pollak (ed.), *A Citizen's Inquiry: The Opsahl Report on Northern Ireland* (Dublin: Lilliput Press, 1993); Bernadette C. Hayes and Ian McAllister, 'Generations, Prejudice and Politics in Northern Ireland' in Anthony F. Heath, Richard Breen and Christopher T. Whelan (eds), *Ireland North and South: Pespectives from Social Science* (Oxford: Oxford University Press, 1999), pp. 457–92, who suggest that prejudice continues in each generation due to the polarisation of politics in Northern Ireland.

39. Karen Trew, 'National Identity' in Richard Breen, Paula Devine and Lizanne Dowds (eds), *Social Attitudes in Northern Ireland: The Fifth Report 1995–1996* (Belfast: Appletree Press, 1996), pp. 140–52; Michael Gallagher, 'How Many Nations Are There in Ireland?', *Ethnic and Racial Studies*, 18, 4, (1995) pp. 715–39.

40. I have examined some of the reasons for the move to negotiation in Brian Girvin, 'Nationalism and the Continuation of Political Conflict in Ireland' in Heath, Breen and Whelan (eds), *Ireland North and South*, pp. 369–400.

41. Richard Jay and Rick Wilford, 'An End to Discrimination? The Northern Ireland Fair Employment Act of 1989'; *Irish Political Studies*, 6 (1991), pp. 15–36; other examples of measures noted by the authors are the repeal of Flags and Emblems (Northern Ireland) Act 1953; the Education Order 1989; the establishment of the Central Community Relations Unit within the Northern Ireland Office (1987); and the Community Relations Council (1989).

42. Rick Wilford and Sydney Elliott, 'The Northern Ireland Affairs Select Committee', *Irish Political Studies*, 10 (1995), pp. 216–24.

43. Aughey, 'Conservative Party Policy and Northern Ireland', pp. 121–50.

44. Garret FitzGerald, *All in a Life* (Dublin: Gill & Macmillan, 1991); Brian Girvin, 'The Anglo-Irish Agreement 1985' in Girvin and Sturm, *Politics and Society in Contemporary Ireland*, pp. 150–65; Brendan O'Leary, 'The Anglo-Irish Agreement: Meanings, Explanations, Results and a Defence' in Paul Teague (ed.), *Beyond the Rhetoric: Politics, the Economy and Social Policy in Northern Ireland* (London: Lawrence & Wishart, 1987), pp. 11–40.

45. Compare FitzGerald, *All in a Life* with Margaret Thatcher, *The Downing Street Years* (London: HarperCollins, 1993) for the different emphases of the two leaders.

46. Brian Girvin, 'Constitutional Nationalism and Northern Ireland' in Brian Barton and J. Roche (eds), *The Northern Question: Perspectives and Policies* (Aldershot: Avebury, 1994), pp. 5–53; Brendan O'Leary and John McGarry, *The Politics of Antagonism: Understanding Northern Ireland* (London: Athlone

Press, 1993), pp. 220–76.

47. *McGimpsey* v. *Ireland*, *Irish Law Reports* (Dublin: Incorporated Council of Law Reporting for Ireland, 1990), pp. 110–25.

48. Ken Hind was the Parliamentary Private Secretary to Peter Brooke, *Irish Times*, 4 December 1991; for discussion Aughey, 'Conservative Party Policy'; John Wilson Foster (ed.), *The Idea of the Union: Statements and Critiques in Support of the Union of Great Britain and Northern Ireland* (Vancouver: Belcouver Press, 1995) for a representative sample of opinion from the Unionist perspective.

49. Paul Arthur, 'The Brooke Initiative', *Irish Political Studies*, 7 (1992), pp. 111–15.

50. Paul Arthur, 'The Mayhew Talks', *Irish Political Studies*, 8 (1993), pp. 138–43.

51. *Irish Times*, 24 April 1993.

52. *Irish Times*, 29 October 1993.

53. The documents exchanged were published in *Irish Times*, 30 November 1993; Paul Arthur, 'Dialogue Between *Sinn Féin* and the British Government', *Irish Political Studies*, 10 (1995), pp. 185–91.

54. *Joint Declaration for Peace* 15 December 1993 (London: HMSO, 1993).

55. See also the speech by Sir Patrick Mayhew to the Birmingham University Debating Society, 23 February 1994 when he cites paragraph 4, and then glosses it to illustrate Britain's neutrality in the process; for the strong Unionist case within the United Kingdom, see John Major's speech in Glasgow, 22 February 1992 which clearly included Northern Ireland as part of his Unionism, and Peter Brooke's later remarks which restricted the Unionism to Britain. Aughey, 'Conservative Party Policy', pp. 143–4.

56. *A New Framework for Agreement: A Shared Understanding Between the British and Irish Governments to Assist Discussion and Negotiation Involving the Northern Ireland Parties* (Dublin: Stationery Office, 1995); *A Framework for Accountable Government in Northern Ireland* (Dublin: Stationery Office, 1995). While this chapter has discussed in detail the latter document the reader should also be aware of the importance of the former joint document and the commitments contained therein. For a reading of the two documents together, see Brendan O'Leary, 'Afterward: What is Framed in the Framework Documents?', *Ethnic and Racial Studies*, 18, 4 (1995), pp. 862–72.

57. See interview with Tony Blair in *Irish Times*, 4 September 1995.

58. See *Guardian/Irish Times*, 28 February 1996 for results of opinion poll in Britain, Northern Ireland and the Republic of Ireland for the startling contrast in apportioning blame.

59. This can be appreciated from a number of features in *Irish Times*, 7 September 1996, which included the following headings: 'Adams describes Catholic boycott over Drumcree as legitimate tactic'; 'Alliance may quit Forum because of "play acting"'; and 'We're not there to be ordered about, says UUP head'.

60. The polls are reported in Bernadette C. Hayes and Ian McAllister, 'British and Irish Public Opinion Towards the Northern Ireland Problem', *Irish Political Studies*, 11 (1996), pp. 61–82.

61. Geoffrey Evans and Brendan O'Leary, 'Frameworked Futures: Intransigence and Flexibility in the Northern Ireland Elections of May 30 1996', *Irish Political Studies*, 12 (1997), pp. 23–47.

62. Brian Givrin, *Nationalism and the Continuation of Political Conflict in Ireland* in Anthony F. Heath, Richard Breen and Christopher T. Whelan (eds), *Ireland*

North and South: Perspectives from Social Service (Oxford: Oxford University Press, 1999), pp. 369–400. It is arguable that the IRA and Sinn Féin would have been more reluctant to enter negotiations if Fianna Fáil had not re-entered government after the June 1997 Irish general election.

63. *Belfast Agreement* 10 April 1998, can be located at http://www.Ireland.com/special/peace/agreement/agreement.htm

64. For detailed interpretation see Brendan O'Leary, 'The 1998 British–Irish Agreement: Power-Sharing Plus', *Scottish Affairs* 26 (Winter, 1999), pp. 14–15.

65. The two reports can be located at http://www.ireland.com/newspapers/special/2000/chastelain/index.htm

66. *Irish Times*, 15 February 2000 for IRA statement, 7 March 2000 for interview with McLaughlin.

Index